Contents

Preface

**Part I   Power From the East?
—Or From Beyond?**

1 What Spirits? 1
2 The Occult in the West: Australia and England 7
3 The Occult in the West: U.S.A. 15
    The above chapters include a general introduction to the subject; the reality of other forces; a personal testimony; aboriginal forces have come west; witchcraft and satanism.
4 The Influence of Hinduism 21
    The emergence of Hinduism in the west; Sri Chinmoy; Baba Ram Dass; Hare Krishna; Guru Maharaj Ji; salvation concepts comparing Hindu and Christian theology.
5 Transcendental Meditation is a Religion 33
    A critical look at TM indicating its religious nature, documented from two pivotal court cases; an analysis of TM mantras; the Hindu worldview; potential hazards—psychopathology, suicidal tendencies, and physical ailments.

6   **Transcendental Meditation is Occult, Not Christian...**   45
    TM and Christianity; an analysis of TM as an occult religion; its relation to magic, spiritism, psychic abilities, and possession.
7   **Zen Buddhism is Also With Us....................**   61
    A brief look at Zen Buddhism; its monistic worldview; its practices; a comparison with Christianity.
8   **Yoga and the Occult ....**   71
    A brief analysis, answering the question: "Is yoga dangerous?"; points out its occult nature and the difficulty of separating theory and practice.
9   **Reincarnation—Yes or No? ....**   79
    Examines the purported "relationship" between the Bible and reincarnation, noting that if one *is* true, the other *cannot be* true—a syncretism is not possible.
10 **Is There Life After Death? ....**   91
    Death research: A critical examination of clinical death research recently reported, noting its spiritistic aspects, reinterpretation of death, and necromantic implications.

Conclusion: A Tremendous Upsurge in Occult Interest....   103
    Historical perspective and social consequences.

Part II   Power From The Stars?
           —Untapped and Nonphysical Energy Sources?

11 **The False Claims of Astrology.....................**   111
12 **An Ancient Art in a Modern World ....**   121
    In Chapters 11 and 12, the ancient origin, impact, and problems of astrology are discussed.
13 **Did Astronauts Visit Earth in Ancient Times?**
    What About UFO's Today?........................   129
    Extraterrestrial life and UFO's: An analysis of extraterrestrial life theories in two of their most popular forms. The validity of von Daniken's ancient astronaut hypothesis is challenged through a summarization of his factual errors and analysis of his literary

PSYCHIC FORCES AND OCCULT SHOCK

John Weldon
Clifford Wilson, Ph.D.

GLOBAL PUBLISHERS

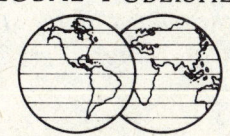

P.O. BOX 21788 • CHATTANOOGA, TN 37421

GLOBAL
Printed by Permission of
Arthur F. Whitehead, Jr., Publisher

PSYCHIC FORCES AND OCCULT SHOCK
Copyright © 1987 By Arthur F. Whitehead, Jr.

In Canada:
Purpose Products
P.O. Box 791
Aurora Ont. L4G 4J9

Library of Congress Catalog Card Number 80-81458

Cataloging in Publication Data

Wilson, Clifford A. 1923-
   Psychic Forces and Occult Shock
   1. Occult sciences. I. Weldon, John 1948-   , jt. auth.
II. Title.

ISBN 0-937931-09-08

ALL RIGHTS RESERVED

No part of this publication may be reproduced, stored in a retrieval system, or transmitted in any form or by any means—electronic, mechanical, photocopy, recording, or otherwise—without the express prior permission of the publisher, with the exception of brief excerpts in magazine articles and/or reviews.

Printed in the United States of America

style. Carrying the argument to the present, the modern fascination with anomalous aerial phenomena (UFO's) is briefly examined.

14 **Energy Forces and Holistic Health** 149
Discussion of the nature of this energy for human discernment and the occult aspect of the holistic health movement.

15 **The New Medicine**................................ 171
A look at fifteen of the "new" alternate medical practices and their spiritual and philosophic roots. Five guidelines for involvement in any new treatment modality. Topics covered include iridology, chromotherapy, witchcraft, sound therapy, applied kinesiology, acupuncture and acupressure, sonopuncture, radionics, astrologic medicine, chiropractic, orgonomy and bioenergetic therapies, biofeedback, alphagenics, and meditation, hypnotic regression, body therapies (zone therapy, functional integration, rolfing, do'in, shiatsu, etc.), and homeopathy.

16 **The "New" Energy Forces are *Very* Old** 247
An analysis of this "new" mystical energy indicating its ties to similar occult concepts throughout history. Five particular energy concepts are examined—prana, mana, animal magnetism, Od, and Higher Sense Perception.

17 **A Satanic Counterfeit to Conversion?** 265
Tying together practice and theory; common characteristics of this energy.

18 **Energy Forces and the Nature of Man** 273
A brief and tentative criticism over the question of potentially latent psychic or "soul" powers and the problems raised for Christian theology and other areas; Scriptural analysis and summary.

19 **Brainwashed by Choice . . . *for a Fee!*** 289

20 **The Dangers and Delusions of "est"** 307
Chapters 19 and 20 examine the Erhard Seminars Training (**est**), its impact, beliefs, and potential hazards. Est is representative of many new human-potential seminars and movements which attempt to

make eastern-occult philosophy palatable to western minds.

Conclusion: The Consequences and Evil Design of Nonbiblical Supernaturalism 319
The impact of occultism and semantics.

Part III Power From the Mind?
—Or a Controlled Mind?

21 **Parapsychology: The Scientific Study of Psi** 331
The scientific claims and realities.

22 **The Occult History of Parapsychology** 341
The spiritistic history of parapsychology as an indicator of its nature.

23 **The True Status of Parapsychology** 351
Further examination of the nonscientific, occult nature of parapsychology; bias against the spiritistic theory for psi events.

24 **Mediumism and the Occult in Standard Parapsychological Works** 365
Examination of some typical literary resources of parapsychology; important figures; science as magic; the "Life Force."

25 **Researchers and Psychic Laboratories: What You See is *Not* What You Get!** 377
The attempt of psi researchers to foster a credible scientific image means spiritistic involvement may be undetectable apart from extensive research; new trends; occult ties of scientific psi laboratories; a shocking story.

26 **Is There Such a Thing as "Christian" Parapsychology?** 391
A critical look at the growing idea of Christian parapsychology.

27 **The Theology of "Christian" Parapsychology** 399
An examination of how a parapsychological worldview reinterprets the Bible.

28 **The Impact of "Christian" Parapsychology** 409
Additional consequences of Christian parapsychology; two "Christian" Psychic Societies—the SFF and CFPSS—and their biblical interpretation.

29 **Discernment is Lacking About "Christian" Parapsychology** 423
A critical review of several "Christian" endeavors supporting parapsychology and mediumism; apparitions research and mediumism.

30 **Parapsychology, "Psychic Development," and Poltergeists** 441
The hazards of psychic development; a look at the phenomena of poltergeists and their methods.

Conclusion: Where Does It All Lead? 455

Appendix:

Part I—Help and Counsel About Occult Involvement ... 457

Part II—Counseling: A Brief Look at Some Means of Helping Those Involved With the Psychic World 467

Index 474

OTHER BOOKS FROM GLOBAL PUBLISHERS

ISBN Number	DESCRIPTION	UNIT PRICE
0-937931-00-4	*FAITH BROKERS* by Wally Metts. Professional Christians and their ungodly gains.	5.95p
0-937931-01-2	*THE DUAL MINISTRY* by M. Thomas Starkes.	3.95p
0-937931-02-0	*TODAY'S WORLD RELIGIONS* by M. Thomas Starkes.	7.95p 10.95c
0-937931-03-9	*THE SHINING LIGHT* by Ralph W. Neighbour, Sr.	5.95p
0-937931-04-7	*A VOICE FROM HEAVEN* by Ralph W. Neighbour, Sr.	5.95p
0-937931-05-5	*THE SEARCHING HEART* by Ralph W. Neighbour, Sr.	5.95p
0-937931-06-3	*THINE ENEMY* by Ralph W. Neighbour, Sr.	5.95p
0-937931-07-1	*THE FUTURE CHURCH* by Ralph W. Neighbour, Jr.	5.95p
0-937931-08-X	*FREEMASONRY* by Jack Harris	5.95p
0-937931-09-8	*PSYCHIC FORCES AND OCCULT SHOCK* by John Weldon and Clifford Wilson.	9.95p
0-937931-10-1	*AIDS: YOU THINK YOU'RE SAFE* by Moody Adams	7.95p
0-937931-11-X	*HOLDING THE FORT OR 50 EVENINGS WITH MOODY* by Moody	7.95p
0-937931-12-8	*JOHN JASPER* by William E. Hatcher	3.95p
0-937931-13-6	*THE REAL BILLY SUNDAY* by E.P. Brown	5.95p

(Prices subject to change)

Preface

One of the purposes of this book is to reveal the counterfeits with which Satan has inundated our world for what they *really* are . . . however, we must point out that without a *genuine* article, there cannot be a counterfeit. We believe in the supernatural power of the Almighty God, but Satan—the great deceiver—would have us believe that his power is just as great (which it is not) and also intended for the good of mankind (again, which it is not).

The penetration of the West by the East is frightening. It is not just a wind of change, but a violent cyclone. Or, to change the metaphor, a demonic explosion. Satanic powers fear that their time is fast running out and have engaged in a desperate effort to defeat all that is involved in the plan of God for man.

This is a major area of spiritual conflict. Sometimes it is subtle, with so-called "harmless" forms used, but always having the ultimate purpose of ensnaring the beginner. The "harmless" will lead to the exciting . . . and ultimately to the openly evil.

Recently in a conversation with a former warlock in Oakland, California, he stated, "I'd start with the Ouija board," he told me. "Kids thought that was fun. Then I'd encourage them in astrology." He went on to elaborate the subtle ways in which young people are trapped before they realize it. For some it is yoga, for others it is one of the forms of eastern meditation—while still others might be lured into white, then gray, and finally black magic. The methods will change and the tactics will vary—according to individuals and circumstances—but always the purpose is to oppose the Christian gospel and to lure innocent people into accepting a frightful delusion.

Is the church aware of this danger? *Not sufficiently!* Are we prepared to accept the fact of a personal devil and myriads of demons? *Again, not sufficiently!* It is true that we should not "major" on the devil, but on Christ, our Deliverer and Lord. It is also true that we need to be aware of the nature of the spiritual battle that surrounds us—and is ready even now to engulf our children.

In this book, we set out to examine—in a broad sense—the world of "secular" supernaturalism. Since the mass suicide-murders of Jonestown, much publicity has been generated on cults, the occult, and eastern religions. Still, few people are aware that in false religion the lowest common denominator is often spiritism—covert or overt—as was true in the case of Jim Jones. Occultism (or psychicism) is in its truest sense spiritistic (i.e., demonic) supernaturalism. It can come under the name of "ascended masters," "beings of light," "UFO" entities, the "higher self," psychic powers, or a hundred other guises—but the ultimate plan and purpose remain the same . . . deception and bondage under the guise of "God" and "spirituality."

In this book, we examine the occult, as well as eastern religions. These are psychospiritually and philosophically more united than most people suspect. Spiritism, astrology, poltergeists, psychic development, the gurus, Transcendental Meditation, Erhard Seminars Training **(est)**, Zen Buddhism, yoga, and reincarnation are discussed. The dangers of occult involvement are examined, as well as the means of deliverance. Newer topics of interest, such as UFO's, holistic health, life after death research, and "new" psychic energy ideas are also examined. Finally, parapsychology is given a thorough analysis. Are its claims that it is nonoccultic really valid? What are its historical origins? Can there be a "Christian" parapsychology?

Few people are aware today of the extent and power of occultism in all its forms. It can even reach to the highest level of government, e.g. MacKenzie King, a former Prime Minister of Canada, was involved in spiritism; Hitler was a possessed medium; the former Prime Minister of Grenada, Eric Gairy, was a psychic; Abraham Lincoln was involved in spiritistic activities, even holding them in the White House; Woodrow Wilson consulted psychic mediums; James Garfield often visited spiritists; "FDR" was interested in astrology; etc.[1] In the communities of certain large U.S. cities, some government officials are closet spiritists.

Wherever occultism runs rampant, it must bring with it judgment.

These pages are written in an effort to highlight the dangers. They point ultimately to the one source of deliverance, the Lord Jesus Christ Himself. His victory at Calvary was final, and its ultimate conclusion will include the destruction of all opposing evil forces. In the meantime, we look to Him, the Captain of our Salvation and claim His promise, "I am with you . . . to the end of the age."

Eastern religions continue to expand in influence in western society. Gurus, reincarnation, meditation, and yoga are gaining widespread acceptance. Unfortunately, such religions bring highly destructive teachings in their monist, pantheistic, and amoral philosophies. Ultimately, eastern religions are occultic in nature and, as such, oppose common sense spirituality and particularly Christian values. There is a price to pay for those who follow the eastern path, as many have discovered.

Not coincidentally, occultism recently has experienced a major revival in the West. Literally millions of people are directly or indirectly involved in one or more forms of the occult or psychic worlds. Far too few of them are not only unaware of the *personal* hazards, but also of the influence such activity may have on their children.

Parapsychology is a recently legitimized scientific study

of the occult, although its roots go back some 100 years. Claiming to be entirely removed from the occult, it seeks to methodologically examine the psychic abilities supposedly within us all. Born and raised within spiritistic studies, matured and aged in "science," it is currently returning to its first love.

Holistic health, life after death studies, "new" energies, astrology, UFO's, and more are all examined herein.

---

1. Gary North, *None Dare Call It Witchcraft*, (New Rochell, NY, Arlington House, 1976), p. 225; N. C. Maynard, *Was Abraham Lincoln A Spiritualist?* (London: Psychic Book Club, 1956); R. Alan Street, *In High Places: A Study of Occultism in Government,* 1977, Box 242, Finksburg, MD 21048; Dusty Skylar, *Gods and Beasts—The Nazis and the Occult* (NY, Thomas Crowell, 1977); Jean-Michel Angebert, *The Occult and the Third Reich,* (NY, McGraw Hill, 1975); Pauwels and Bergier, *The Morning of the Magicians,* (Avon, 1969) Part Two, VI, IX.

Part I

Power From The East? — Or From Beyond?

Chapter 1

What Spirits?

Is it primitive superstition—just so much nonsense—or are there really evil spirits in the world around us? In this book we say there *are* such spirits and present evidence to support our conclusion. We show some of the subtle ways in which evil spirits manifest themselves. Sometimes they even materialize . . . they can *and do* utilize psychological principles, while at other times their influence is essentially in the spiritual realm.

The fact is that *all* their activities are intrusions into the spiritual, for that is the ultimate reality. The devil and his demons know that if one method of attack fails, they will just use another. They have patience, they have skill, and they have hatred—hatred of God and hatred of man because man is God's crown of creation.

Today they have come out into the open. They have initiated an assault in ways that a generation ago would have seemed unthinkable. The fact is, the occult (the secret world of mysterious spiritual forces) can no longer be conveniently put to one side as belonging exclusively to Eastern/Oriental countries. It is now out in the open, part of the recognized culture of the West.

Until relatively recent years, most Western people gave

little serious thought to the phenomena. They just "knew" that the paraphernalia of witchdoctors, black magic, and all the rest were restricted to the Far East—where they belonged! There was no such problem for the sophisticated and enlightened West. However, all that has changed. Today it is not just the practicing Christians who believe in some sort of evil power that is taking over the minds of thousands of people in our so-called "Christian" civilization. The evidence is convincing to the unbiased observer. Clifford Wilson gives a startling personal testimony:

> I have seen men lying on beds of nails—and even of broken bottles. If I were to attempt it my skin would be pierced immediately; but these men can even have the spikes put through their flesh and no blood appears. They have given over their bodies to the power of Satan and his demonic forces, and that power can be shown through them in these "imitation" miracles.
>
> In India I have seen Hindu processions with the devotees prostrated for their gods, demon powers whom they openly acknowledge and worship .... I have watched the dance of the tiger .... I have passed nearby as milk and eggs were poured down the hole of the cobra .... I have asked about the painting of houses with red ochre, "to keep the demons away" ... listened to inhuman screechings ... and the accounts of black magic ... and in many ways I have been forced to accept the reality of powers whose evil presence could almost be felt.
>
> I have also lived in the Fiji Islands. I was in charge of the reporting of the Legislative Council debates for some time. While I was there I heard fascinating stories, many of which I did not accept—such as those of babies born with the face of a shark. Other things I had to accept, such as a man being "draunikoued"—willed to death by a priest he had offended.
>
> I have watched—and photographed—Indian

fire walkers in Fiji as they danced in procession mile after mile, chanting to their deity who would empower them to dance up and down, up and down, up and down, on those white-hot coals. They had prepared for weeks, and now the time had come. I stood near the great coal pit and had to shield my own eyes from the heat. I watched the frenzy of young men, some of whom I knew as quiet employees of the Fiji Government, now transformed into superhuman beings who engaged in nonhuman activities, fearing neither heat nor pain.

I saw long steel skewers protruding through their necks, their chests, their stomachs. They even had them through their tongues. I watched as they went from the fire to the temple where the saffron-robed priest was waiting—watched while the sacred turmeric powder was sprinkled on their bodies as the skewers were swiftly withdrawn. I had earlier watched them, as I mingled with the crowd, watched as they danced in procession for miles, with those skewers protruding right into and through their bodies. Now as they were withdrawn, there was no wound in the "patients." There was no sign of blood—and, when I closely examined two of them later, there was only the smallest of puncture holes where the skewers had been.

One man, who was not a priest, raced up and down the coal bed without being hurt. Another tried it, and his feet were shockingly burned . . . I had no "natural" explanation that really satisfied me: the answer was apparently linked to the realm of spiritual realities, of vindictive beings who would show their power in one case and spitefully withhold that power as they gleefully caused pain to another would-be-devotee. We read in John, Chapter 8, that Christ referred to Satan as being "a murderer from the beginning," and it would seem that the ultimate purpose of Satanic forces is to destroy both body and soul of human beings. As part of the strategy, temporarily there might be seeming kindness and even spiritual enlightenment, but this is trickery, utilized to gain the ultimate end.

I stood surprised at it all . . . wondering . . . doubting, yet forced to accept the evidence before my own eyes. It was nonhuman, beyond human, something that could not be gainsaid.

Suddenly there was a new intensity alongside me—an atmosphere hard to describe, yet profoundly real. It felt almost as though a whirlwind had hit us, and yet that description is not adequate. It was a nonphysical force, an oppressiveness that surrounded us, the intensity of which I had never known before.

Women screamed . . . children ran . . . but one did not escape, a woman standing just behind me.

I have often thought since this incident that probably I personally was the object of this apparent demonic attack, but that I was protected as a Christian, a follower of Jesus Christ. The woman fell toward the ground, and as I looked I was surprised at the peculiar angle at which she was lying. She appeared to be paralyzed, and her hands were held together in the typical Indian prayer gesture, as though imploring the spirit that had attacked her to leave her alone.

I could hardly believe my eyes. It was almost as though half of her body was levitated while she stayed motionless in that almost impossible angle. She remained in this unnatural position until two of the fire walkers came over and carried her along the full length of the pit of hot coals, then proceeded in the buru—a palm tree structure—which acted as a temporary temple. There an older priest sprinkled powder on her as he intoned his incantation. Then she walked back to her relatives, at least for the moment released from that oppressing spirit.

SACRIFICES: Animal and Human—Real and Imitation

In such activities, release can be obtained for one who has been so tormented, but it is by the placation of these spirits and not by their being cast out. In so-called Eastern religions, the spirits are feared, worshipped, and placated with sacrifices. More often they are animal offerings, or even vegetables over which red ochre has been splashed to resemble blood.

Such scenes from India and Fiji are no longer surprising to people of the West. Those who come from Australia know of somewhat similar practices—aborigines against whom "the bone" has been pointed by the witchdoctor. Unless a man possessed by a greater spirit—one more powerful than that of the witchdoctor—can be found, the afflicted person will "will" himself to death.

Such practices continue with "primitive" people in many lands. A report from New Guinea, published in *Missionary Tidings* of December, 1973, tells of a witchdoctor removing his laplap (clothing) so that he stood before the people stark naked, with no possibility of having anything hidden from the view of the observers. A sick person was waiting for his "cure," and the witchdoctor approached him and drew from his body a long piece of bamboo which obviously was not previously there. The witchdoctor stated that he had now freed the sick man from the arrows that spirits had shot into him in the bush. The report adds that patients so cured claim immediate, if only temporary, relief. These things can be put down to trickery, witchcraft, "mind over matter," or some form of demon possession. All are involved at times, but the stated and accepted basis is witchcraft, the involvement with demonic powers.

Witchcraft is not restricted to New Guinea and so-called "backward" countries. Demonism, Satan worship, and all sorts of occult practices have increased tremendously in the West.

This is true in the United States, Australia, and England. The evidence could be elaborated, for the revival of Satan worship has penetrated the continent of Europe and the rest of the globe. The spiritual battle is now out in the open even more, with evil forces daring to present themselves in bizarre activities around the world.

Chapter 2

The Occult in the West Australia and England

Stories about Devil worship have become common across the world. In Australia, the *Melbourne Observer* of February 17, 1974, tells the tragic story of Lorrian Faithfull who died in bizarre circumstances in her St. Kilda flat. It was some 15 days after she died of a suspected overdose of drugs that her rotting body was found, no longer beautiful, a bloated and blackened thing.

Only 10 days before her death, she had spoken to reporter Brian Blackwell and revealed how deeply troubled she was—afraid of members of the Devil cult to which she had once belonged. There were paintings and books about the Devil all over her apartment, and little bells draped around the walls were supposed to keep the spirits away. The air had been thick with incense, and she constantly drew on her marijuana joint as she told about her life as a so-called daughter of the Devil.

She admitted that she had taken part in a number of Devil orgies, and that those taking part sought Satan's help to bring harm to other people. According to Lorrian, it had worked in a number of cases. However, the time came when she felt she could not go on with these practices any longer—according to the newspaper report, the crisis came when she saw a privately-made Italian film showing an actual human sacrifice. She left the cult, but could never shake off the past, and night and day she was tormented. Though she had rejected the macabre world of the Satanic underground, she still felt its power and did not seek deliverance in the only way that could be effective spiritually. In the end this tortured and bewildered girl tried, for the tenth time, to commit suicide by an overdose of drugs. This time she succeeded.

Black Magic Sex Rituals

A recent report in *Pix-People* (Australia) tells of a young anthropologist, Greg Tillett, causing a storm in Perth, Western Australia. He exposed black magic sex rituals that were practiced in Perth, describing them in some detail. Part of his description is as follows:

> A high priest—there are only about three in West Australia—dresses up in regalia which includes a goat's headdress.
>
> A naked sacrifice, not always a woman, lies on top of the altar and the high priest has sex first, followed by as many of his followers who wish to.
>
> Other Satan worshippers take part in bestiality, sadomasochism, and bloodletting.

Another report in the Melbourne *Herald* of January 29, 1974, stated that Bishop Cecil Muschamp, formerly Bishop of Kalgoorlie in that same State of Western Australia, had received a telegram from a Devil worshipper who told him that he had only three months to live. The Bishop and other church spokesmen had issued warnings because of evidences of witchcraft that had been uncovered in Western Australia's capital, Perth.

Churchmen are right to issue such warnings. An article in the magazine *For Real* dated March, 1973, has this description of Satan worship:

> Satan worshippers usually believe that the attainment of perfection and the experience of the divine come through an ecstasy achieved in a

sensual orgy which is likely to involve sexual practices, nudity, homosexuality, and the use of drugs.

The Cross Desecrated at Satan Worship

Normally, a small group of people sit in front of a table covered with a purple velvet altar cloth, lit with candles. Over the "altar" hangs a cross upside down and a picture of the Devil, half-human, half-beast. A high priest stands by the table dressed in bishop's robes. On his person he wears an inverted cross. He throws a larger cross to the floor. *"Shemhaforash,"* he shouts. This is probably the most powerful word uttered in Satanic worship. According to the Talmud (a book of Jewish civil and religious laws and ethical lore) it was the secret mystic word spoken by God when He created the world. He then spits upon the cross, with an obscene gesture, and cries, "Hail, Satan!" Thus begins the sickening and blasphemous ritual, as the Devil worshippers repeat the Lord's prayer backwards and make mockery of the ordinances of the church. One quotation from LaVey's "The Satanic Bible" says, "Blessed are the strong, for they shall possess the earth." "If a man smite you on one cheek, smash him on the other!"

Clearly, Devil worship has become frighteningly common in Australia. The Melbourne *Observer* of January 13, 1974, has two-inch headlines, "Girls Flee Devil Cult," and it goes on to tell how frightened teenagers in Melbourne are crying out for social workers to help them break away from Devil cults. It is shown that witchcraft and black magic are fast taking over from drugs as the "in" thing for many young people. Psychiatrists and social workers are alarmed at the rapid growth of the cults in Australia, and emergency counseling has been made available to help people "get away from the grip of the Devil."

Nudity is commonly found at Satanic covens. When a witch is initiated, she is symbolically "Sacrificed" to the sun god, and this ceremony takes place while she is lying naked on the altar. The power of the witch is said to be heightened by the mysterious force that is within her own body, and when clothing is worn that power is supposedly obstructed. Their delusion is that they will gain pleasure and enjoyment in this world, especially of a sensual nature, and that in a coming age Satan will overcome the Christians' God and return to the heaven from which he was once thrown out. Satan's earthly followers, so the delusion goes, will then share fruits of eternal power with his spirit forces.

The "Queen of Britain's Witches" Converted

The same sort of happening is true in England, as well as in Australia. A recent edition of *People* magazine (Australia) runs a story about Doreen Irvine who was actually crowned as Queen of Britain's witches. She committed unspeakable acts of sacrilege, but was converted to Christ. The report states that eventually, after a tremendous struggle, the demons were exorcised from her body. She was changed from being a drug addict and a prostitute to become an active evangelist proclaiming the Gospel of Christ.

This was certainly a remarkable transformation for a person who had actually become "a child of Satan in a vile blood sacrifice ceremony" and had "helped defile churches and dig up bodies from fresh graves." In her Devil worship she had become involved with "the Chief Satanist," and in her own words:

> Soon I was using my new powers. I made an effigy of a man who owed me money. I stuck pins in its eyes, legs, and chest and cursed him.
>
> Within a week he was seriously ill in a hospital. The doctors couldn't understand what was wrong, but they knew he was dying. Then a friend told me to take the pins out because there was no point in killing him. I obliged, and to the doctor's amazement, he recovered.

Yes, such practices have been relatively common through the ages. The Egyptians had their "Execration (Cursing) Tests," and murder by substitution as shown above is known in a number of ancient cultures. Doreen Irvine's description rings true. What then do we say as to her power over other living things? She claims:

> At witches' covens around the country I showed how I could kill a bird in flight with a wave of my hand. Once I killed a parrot in a cage because its chattering got on my nerves. I made objects disappear. I levitated myself six feet. And I could make myself invisible.

Digging Up Fresh Graves . . . Walking Through Fire

The evidence of these things is widespread and convincing. It is evil in an open form. Doreen Irvine goes on to tell about digging up fresh graves, desecrating gravestones and churches, burning Bibles, and even taking human life.

She testifies that she actually walked into a great fire on Dartmoor, and she claimed that Satan himself was there and held her hand as she walked through it. Not only did she not suffer harm, but there was not even the smell of smoke on her black witch's gown.

Pix-People (Australia) also describes the activities of the "daughters of the Devil" in London. Naked girls conduct a ceremony involving symbolic death in a coffin, including the wounding of the girl in the coffin, and her descent into Hades to talk with the Devil and his demons. In various ways the teachings of the cult set out to challenge those of the Bible. It is taught that "the gates of hell are open night and day; smooth is the descent and easy is the way." When Jesus said that the way to destruction was broad and the way to heaven was narrow, He was pointing out the desirability of the narrow road, whereas these daughters of the Devil are glorifying evil, openly boasting of their desire to gain power through Satan. Hell is their goal.

Dabbling In Black Magic Is Dangerous

There are many evidences that dabbling in black magic is dangerous. Alcoholism, drug addiction, prostitution, insanity, and other abnormal conditions are all too often the fruits of such involvement. Even financial disaster can follow those who have been snared and seek to extricate themselves by their own power.

In his book *Kingdom of Darkness,* F.W. Thomas tells the story of a photo journalist and magazine photographer who set out to investigate black magic in London, in an endeavor to get material for a newspaper story. This man, Serge Kordeiv, and his wife eventually found themselves in a room where ceremonies were conducted in the name of Satan. They were told to kneel and then to swear perpetual homage to Satan, and they signed an oath written in contract form, with their own blood.

> Satan's high priest then formally welcomed this couple into the coven by abruptly placing his hands on their genitals. [Here we have a Satanic mockery of the Christian rite of the laying on of hands to impart spiritual blessing.] The strange thing about this part of the ceremony, report the Kordeivs, was the sudden inexplicable, "surge of energy" that went all through them when the obscene hands grabbed their private parts.
>
> After going through the Satanic initiation ritual, Serge Kordeiv found his whole life was dramatically changed. Everything he touched turned to money. Never had he and his wife enjoyed such financial prosperity. But after attending several more meetings, Serge and his wife decided to quit the group.

Thomas goes on to tell of some of the activities that caused them to realize how evil were the activities with which they had become associated. In one black mass a wax dummy representing a prominent businessman was "Killed" by a knife being plunged into it, whereupon red liquid gushed over a nude girl who was stretched out on the altar. The members of the coven had to drink the blood from a bird that was killed, the blood having been first drained into a chalice. At the next meeting of the group Kordeiv was shocked at being shown a newspaper report of the sudden death of the businessman they had murdered in effigy—he had collapsed and died of a heart attack on that same night.

The Kordeivs decided to withdraw at a later time when they were supposed to go through a Satanic confirmation ceremony, involving sex acts. They broke off, and in the days and weeks that followed, they went through a series of terrifying incidents and experiences—where before they had known great financial success, now the opposite was true. In various other ways, they were made to realize that they had displeased the powers of darkness. The report continues:

> Such was the experience of an unwise couple whose curiosity for black magic dragged them through untold anguish and despair. One cannot just pick up the dark bolts of magical fire and drop them at will without getting burned. There is always a price to pay for use of these forbidden powers, in this world as well as in the world to come.

The Bible says that the wages of sin is death. Satan is a hard paymaster, even in the "rewards" he gives in life. His subjects are bound, not free. They seek for pleasure, but find the cup bitter even as they consume his foul mixture.

Chapter 3

The Occult in the West: U. S. A.

Satanism is spreading like a cancer, in ways that only a generation ago would have been considered impossible. The newspaper reports in both countries are remarkably similar in their acceptance of the fact that this dreaded phenomenon in our midst is a serious problem. They recognize that the occult has come galloping into the West.

Witchcraft in California

This practice has spread to the United States. The Los Angeles *Herald-Examiner* of December 21, 1969, announced that groups of hippies all over California were holding witchcraft discussions. Dogs were being sacrificed and their blood was being drunk at Satan worshipping ceremonies, and fire-walking was carried out as part of the ritual. In initiation ceremonies, new recruits were required to eat the entrails of an animal while its heart was still beating.

The stories around San Francisco, with its neighboring cities of Berkeley and Oakland, are at times very bizarre. It is common to be told that new movements involving spiritual realities often start in this area. This is true of movements for good and evil alike—Satanism is rampant there, with an actual church of Satan established. On the other hand, the Jesus Movement had its roots in this same part of the United States.

It was not surprising to be told in San Francisco of a girl who became a Devil worshipper and had been urged by the spirits to sacrifice her baby, which she did . . . only to find that she could not live with herself, that she must seek a new environment. She renounced her allegiance to the Devil and his legions of demonic servants.

An almost casual selection of newspaper reports reveals the widespread interest in Satan worship in California.

One report tells of a former Devil worshipper bringing a "witchmobile" to church in Napa. The witchmobile is a display of objects used in Satan worship, and they are displayed by the Reverend Hershel Smith, a one-time Satan worshipper, but now a minister of the Christian gospel. The report tells how nearly 20 years ago in southeastern Missouri three lads skinned a young puppy, and they then drank its blood while it was still warm. This act was a deliberate mockery of the Christian celebration of communion and was actually part of the ritual associated with Devil worship. Smith was one of those three boys, and for years he was in bondage to Satanic forces. He tells of the lack of power he had found in Christian associations, and that he attempted to find spiritual reality in Satan worship. He became a wreck, addicted to drugs, with definite suicide intentions. He made plans to do away with himself, but instead he found himself praying to God, and a great change came over his life.

"Respectable" People Involved With Sorcery and Witchcraft

Sorcery instruments and implements can be purchased—and this makes it clear that the practices are the same as in ancient times. Magical oils, the heart of a swallow, and other black magic implements and instruments are obtainable.

That same report goes on to tell of a Los Angeles mother who claims to be a witch. She had even cast spells at the famous Hollywood Bowl and on various college campuses in the area. Her spells are supposedly in the name of love and sexual vitality, and she also has a spell which she claims will get rid of an unwanted lover.

Generally speaking, it is relatively easy to explain some of the attraction to Satanism; such worship is supposed to bring earthly and carnal delights. Physical and materialistic pleasures are especially attractive when one is not prepared to know the spiritual reality of fellowship with God. Fellowship with God by no means rules out physical pleasures, but it does place bounds and limits—bounds which are desirable for the good of society as a whole.

Young People Sacrificed to Satan

The Napa *Register* of March 30, 1973, tells of a man who was convicted for the sex slaying of a teenage girl:

"The purpose of calling [the girl] to the house was to sacrifice her to Satan," the defendant testified.

He slashed her throat, violated her sexually, and hid her body under his house. He was also found guilty of beheading a hitchhiker, of molesting him sexually, and then leaving his body near a freeway. Three prosecution psychiatrists testified that the guilty man was sane, and a jury of seven women and five men deliberated for only one hour after a two-week trial before finding him guilty of first-degree murder on both counts.

The San Francisco *Chronicle* of May 3, 1973, states that "A group of 'Satan cultists' tortured and beat a 17-year old to death, believing he was an undercover narcotics agent." He was not, but he had been lured to an apartment where members of a Satan cult had been living commune style; and he underwent a bizarre weekend of torture before he died. The report states that he was tied to a bed and beaten, then moved into a basement altar room that was decorated with a long black table on which candles had been placed in blackened bottles. In this room Satanic tridents and chains were hanging on the wall, the wall itself being painted with splotches of red that were meant to signify blood. It seems the 17-year-old youth was tied to the table, flogged with chains, and slashed with pieces of glass. When his body was eventually found in a wooded area, his head had been crushed, apparently by a pine club.

The Sharon Tate Murders

The American Opinion magazine of September, 1970, ran a special edition on Satanism, and the paper commenced as follows:

> While a battalion of tough homicide detectives puzzled over the manner in which the killers had dispatched their victims—using knives, guns, bayonets, and even a fork—the nation sickened to Press accounts of the gory "ritual" slayings. Horrifying reports of multiple stab wounds, hideous mutilations, and bloody hoods left over the heads of the victims added to growing apprehension already heightened by rumors of a practicing "witch cult" seeking victims for performance of the "Black Mass."

It is little wonder that "terrified residents of Benedict Canyon added double locks to their doors and hired private guards."

The police investigations were intense and extended over several months. What they uncovered was enough to disturb even the toughest investigator. Was this modern America, the most advanced country in the world, or a dark land of the middle ages? The report tells of drug cults and Satan worshippers, sex perversion, mutilation for pleasure, and even ritual murder. Monstrous sadists and inhuman perverts had been loosed on society. The spirits were indeed speaking and their language was totally evil.

This was the setting for the Sharon Tate murder case. The rest of the story is well known, and it is not necessary to outline the gory details of the actual murders.

A Number of Murders . . . and "Rosemary's Baby"

It is now history that a number of murders were involved and that a crude form of Devil worship was practiced by the "hippie" group responsible. Their communal practices were hardly in keeping with "civilized" society. In the bizarre incidents and murders, both victims and killers were known for their activities involving black magic and other forms of the occult. We again quote from the article on Satanism referred to previously:

> Rumors of Satanist activity continue to haunt Southern California because of the odd link between the Sharon Tate Coterie, the Manson Family, and the whole black occult bag. Found in the Tate mansion were black leather masks, whips, ropes, and chains—the "tools" of the Satanist cults. Both victims and the killers were known for their active interest in "black magic" and other aspects of the occult.

The report also connects the killers and those published reports state that Roman Polanski, husband of the slain actress, first came to Hollywood to make the controversial film "Rosemary's Baby." He has produced other films involving sexual perversion, masochism, and witchcraft.

When "Rosemary's Baby" was made, a film in which the lead actress is supposed to believe she gave birth to a child fathered by Satan, Polanski chose as his technical adviser the founder and "high priest" of San Francisco's First Church of Satan, the man who had changed his name to Anton Szandor LaVey. LaVey's reported aim is to destroy religion that believes in God and to supplant this with the worship of Satan. His view of "Satan" is not altogether that held by Christians. He claims over 7,000 members of his "church" around the world.

Esquire magazine for March, 1970, had a 26-page feature entitled "The Style of Evil" in California, and it outlined the alarming growth of Satan worship and the practice of witchcraft. Various versions of the Black Mass are practiced, and a Beverly Hills policeman is quoted as saying that it was not "safe to travel his beat alone any longer because of the heavy 'influx of Satanist dope fiends'."

The article on Satanism referred to above elaborates, telling of slaves of Satan who took part in initiation ceremonies in which participants must eat the entrails of an animal while its heart is still beating. There are also numerous reports of persons being placed under hypnotic-type spells by a head witch who slips LSD into ceremonial wine.

Much more could be written, for the California newspapers of the last ten years have reported Satanic activities that are almost incredible. There have been cult murders, children tortured, even the eating of human finger bones and the eating of a human heart—this latter confessed by a man who admitted hacking a human body to pieces. He acknowledged he was a cannibal and a member of a Satanic cult.

There is even a glorification of these things in some publications, and America and the world are reaping ugly consequences as lawlessness increases, meaningless murder is constantly reported, and even children are unsafe on the streets unless they are supervised.

Satanism and the occult are here to stay, until God eliminates them. The task is too great for men in their *own* strength, and this has been increasingly recognized. Where a generation ago the practice of Satanism and the reality of demon forces would have been ridiculed in most Western communities, today it is widely agreed that these things are real. That being the case, it stands to reason that the practice of exorcism must also be taken seriously. If these evil spirit beings are invading the areas of human personality—of human life itself, and if the power of Jesus Christ continues to be real— as He Himself said would be the case—then by His power and in His Name the exorcism of demons is a very real possibility. Jesus Christ, the Son of God, is the One in Whom "all the fullness of the godhead dwells bodily" (Colossians 2:9). We who are Christians listen to His voice and not to evil seducing spirits, the agents of Satan himself.

Chapter 4

The Influence of Hinduism

Cliford Wilson lived in India for two years. He does not claim to be an authority on Eastern religions, but he has had firsthand experience with Indian thinking.

John Weldon has done extensive work in literature, researching the occult and basic teachings of Eastern mysticism and religious cults.

Mysticism is very much a part of the Indian way of life, and in that country it has been practiced in various forms through the centuries. Lands such as India have been renowned for thousands of years for their mystic teachings, and to a great extent such teaching is basic to their whole culture. The very term "guru," which has become so intimately associated with mysticism today, is an Indian word. The guru might have been the expert in various forms of teaching, including such things as wrestling and music, but the title also had spiritual connotations that centered around the overall structure of the national religion of Hinduism.

The guru was supposed to be the living evidence that God was manifest in flesh in modern times; to follow his teachings was to make possible the acquisition of the spiritual ideals of deity. If one wanted to enter into the supreme knowledge of the gods, then one must follow the teachings of the guru, for the guru was the one who could lead to God. The earnest seeker would hear an inner voice, and that voice would lead him to a guru who was to be involved with the direction that his particular path of life would take. He could continue to lead his normal life, but the guru would prescribe his *Sadhana,* or his spiritual exercises, especially on weekends.

Some devout followers have divorced themselves from their previous routine life and have given themselves entirely to the search for the soul's merging with God.

Sri Chinmoy

One such is Sri Chinmoy. He took the step at 12 years of age and by 13 had attained *Nirvikalpa Samadhi*—this being the state whereby his soul was supposed to have merged entirely with God. At 19 years of age he went to and stayed in the *ashram* (establishment) of his guru, studying and meditating, and accepting the disciplines involved with a separated community. At 32 years of age Sri Chinmoy left Bengal and, obeying "an inner command," set off to America where there are now several thousand followers of his Sri Chinmoy Centers. He has written over 400 books and completed over 130,000 paintings and drawings, admittedly by nonhuman agency (e.g. automatic painting).

From time to time various people such as rock musicians identify themselves with his movement. He has been in the United States since 1964. In 1970 he was appointed spiritual advisor to the United Nations, and he holds biweekly sessions of meditation for about 80 delegates and staff. The goal is always the same: "to become divine, or to become God Himself" *(Life-Tree Leaves,* p. 12).

Spiritual leaders such as Sri Chinmoy are supposed to have a particular path, and his is claimed to be the path of love, devotion, and absolute surrender. As he is supposed to have become God, his disciples are expected to live in the consciousness of the guru himself, fully accepting him, and allowing him to take over their lives so that he can give them all he has—especially his capacity to enter into higher spiritual regions.

The argument is that this path is not simply devotion to him as a human, but to the divinity that lies within his human person. Intense spiritual discipline has supposedly led him to this oneness with God, and now he makes it available to the people of the West who want to accept such oneness. Receiving this involves the surrender of ourselves with all our failures, such as petty selfishness—also our other negative qualities such as frustration and worry. As we pass these over to the guru and accept what he offers, we supposedly will find peace, joy, and fulfillment in the attainment of a divine life.

This is typical of many Eastern teachings: that God can be revealed within each of us, and that to find God we must first conquer ourselves by lives of self-discipline. Individual ego is a form of bondage, and this must be overcome with true surrender. The argument is that man must forget that he himself is as important as he previously thought and reorient himself. He must forget about his vanity and self-centeredness and settle himself in God, thus dissolving his own ego. In this way man can become one with God and with everyone else: he will gain everything, because he will find a new strength when his own individuality has been recognized as nothing.

In all this, the guru is supposedly indispensable if the objective is to be realized. Only he knows the particular path, and so only he can show the path to others. The devotee must find him, meditate on him and his teachings, and adhere strictly to the course he prescribes. It is thus that the disciple can tread the path toward spiritual enlightenment.

This is the same old story of Satan as an angel of light, deceiving, if possible, the very elect. It is true that man can become "one" with God, for that is the teaching of the Lord Jesus Christ, but it is not in the Vedantic Hindu sense where we *become* God. It is true that we should meditate on a Man—but the Man is not an Eastern guru, rather the Son of God Who was born in Bethlehem. The divine path is not that which is prescribed by any man born in the

20th century, but is according to the teachings of Him Who said, "I Am the way, the Truth and the Life: no man comes to the Father but by Me"—and that includes any eastern guru of modern times.

It is true that the teachings of Jesus involved discipline, but the way to God is found at the beginning of the Christian life. We do not reach God by a series of works and disciplined activities. We *will* enter into a greater fullness with God, but the actual *finding* of God is by the way of the Cross—the bridge to Heaven that was established at Calvary nearly 2,000 years ago. God does reward those who diligently seek Him, but they find Him by personal belief in the Christ Who died on a cross to give forgiveness of sins and to make oneness with God possible.

Sri Chinmoy claims that when he accepts a disciple it is for eternity, and for this purpose he will accept the person who sincerely wants to follow the path on which he is the guide. This again is a false teaching, for only Jesus Christ can offer eternal life. Only He has power over death, power that He historically demonstrated by His resurrection. Only He can offer the sharing of eternal life to those who will follow Him (John 6). Sri Chinmoy promises each disciple that he will take him to God, but he really means he will provide you with a path of meditation that will make you think *you* are God. Satan made the same promise in Genesis 3. If the disciple is to avoid "hell," there must be a total commitment to the guru, and when that is done there is no problem in the afterlife—that disciple is now the guru's personal responsibility. Once again, this is false teaching, taking to a *man* the prerogatives of Jesus Christ Himself. Finally, an analysis of Sri Chinmoy's books indicates heavy occult involvement. Chinmoy could be classified as a spiritist. This is biblically forbidden (Deut. 18:9-12) and has consequences of which few people are aware.

Baba Ram Dass

Most of the gurus are Eastern, but there are notable exceptions—one is a man known as Baba Ram Dass who was formerly Richard Alpert. He was the son of a successful American businessman, but today he has given it all up and has become a Western guru, with thousands attending to his words. Until 1960 he was a successful Jewish American. He has his own Cessna airplane and a luxurious apartment, and the various concomitants of a life of luxury.

He himself was a social scientist who taught in such areas as human motivation, Freudian theory, and child development. He could answer other people's questions on psychology, but supposedly was himself an anxious, neurotic wreck. Despite his intellectual knowledge he was confused and ignorant. Then he met Timothy Leary, whose name has become linked with the association of spiritual trips with LSD. They became friends, and Richard Alpert followed Leary in his experiments with Psychedelics. His very first experience supposedly gave him great insight into his own inner being. However, the experience soon passed, and before long he was back to his old self with all its inhibitions and anxieties. He kept experimenting, getting high, but always coming back to the inevitable lows. In the end, he set out for the East, and in Nepal he met Bhagwan Dass, a young American who had spent five years in the East.

Bhagwan Dass was now wearing the robes that indicated he was a holy man, and he spoke fluent Hindu. Alpert believed he embodied the peace and understanding of life for which he had been searching, and he followed Bhagwan Dass into an *ashram* situated in the foothills of the Himalayas. There he met the Maharaj Neem Karoli who became Alpert's guru. Neem Karoli overawed Alpert, and to the seeking American it seemed that this guru had access to his most secret thoughts. For six months the American stayed on in silence, meditating and learning from slate chalk and even from the vibrations of his guru. Then he returned to the States, and his fame as a spiritual leader began to spread. As is typical of Eastern gurus, he also became involved in spiritism.

His book *Be Here Now* became popular, being a spiritual collection of meditations and techniques, and once again there is much that is an imitation of Christianity. He talks about pure seeking and the purity of faith. Like Sri Chinmoy, he talks about oneness with the guru. He even talks about the unattractiveness of the guru who led him into this new experience. He was despised by some of those who went to seek him, and then found he was only a little old man in a blanket. However to the initiated (such as Richard Alpert) that little old man is a personification of universal enlightenment. To him—and to his disciple, Richard Alpert (now Baba Ram Dass)—the world must listen.

The strange thing is that thousands of Americans are listening. It highlights the fact that Eastern meditation and religions are here to stay. Transcendental meditation, for example, has initiated well over a million people and continues to have a significant impact.

The Hare Krishna Movement

One of the most vocal of the groups that have invaded the West is the Hare Krishna movement.

This society is also known as ISKCON, the International Society of Krishna Consciousness. That, too, is a variation of Hinduism, and it is claimed that it came from the teachings of Krishna who appeared in India about 3,000 B.C., with a disciple named Arjuna. Krishna is supposed to have had a number of incarnations, the last being in A.D. 1486. The movement claims that there has been an unbroken chain of succession through various disciples until the present guru, Prabhupada, was initiated in 1933, supposedly with a special commission to spread Krishna consciousness in the Western world. The Movement extended to London in 1968; in 1969 he came to the United States for the same purpose. There are at least three temples in England and over 30 in the United States. Prabhupada died in 1977, but his death had little impact on the movement.

One of the distinctive features of this group is that they believe they can attain enlightenment by chanting the name of their god—and this is the reason why groups parade through various cities chanting "Hare Krishna" or

"Hare Rama," Krishna and Rama both being titles for their god. This chanting is often accompanied by trances and ecstatic devotion.

The group has very strict regulations relating to food (no meat, fish, or eggs), they ban intoxicants, and sexual relations are greatly restricted. The male disciples carry a row of 108 beads, and these are followed in rosary fashion. They wear Eastern robes—usually colored saffron, and they often paint their bodies—all this is supposed to indicate devotion to Krishna. Their magazine, *Back to Godhead,* is sold in the streets, and they claim over 66,000,000 copies of Prabhupada's books (viewed as "scripture") are in print. They recognize both the Bible and the Koran as being "divine" books, but claim that each has become distorted over the centuries. They argue that they are not trying to change people's religion, but are simply trying to make them better exponents of their particular religions by helping them to gain the experience of Krishna consciousness.

The chanting of the words "Hare Krishna" is supposed to take the individual immediately beyond the material atmosphere of illusion (the Maya), by which he is surrounded, to a higher spiritual platform. They believe that a symptom of being taken to such a platform is the accompanying urge to dance. Sometimes the symptoms of dancing and chanting mimic states of insanity.

Teachings Opposed to Christian Doctrine

ISKCON teaches that to attain salvation one must abstain from the four primary sins, chant a minimum of 1,728 times daily, and, hopefully, obey 64 different rules and duties. They teach Jesus Christ did *not* die for the world's sins; He only counteracted the disciples karma— and this had nothing to do with the cross. In fact, according to Prabhupada, Christ's "sacrifice" was "many millions of times" *inferior* to the "sacrifice" of vasudeva Datta Thakura who was a simple devotee of Krishna in his incarnation as Lord Caitanya Caritamirta (*Sri Caitanya Caritamirta,* ch. 15, text 163).

This is directly opposed to the Christian doctrine of salvation. It brings in an aspect of works and activities by which a person can attain his own salvation, whereas the Christian doctrine is that salvation is available only as a gift because of the atonement of the Lord Jesus Christ Who died to give foregiveness of sins for the entire world (1 John 2:2). Chanting a so-called holy name is not a way of salvation, and such teaching is opposed to the doctrines of the Bible. The chanting itself is a form of meditation, and this is highly relevant in the teaching and practice of the occult in various forms.

The nearest that Krishna consciousness comes to personal salvation is its teaching that the soul can be liberated from the body by this chanting of "Hare Krishna." Actually, this is not salvation, but a form of escape. This movement stresses chanting instead of drugs and self-delusion by escaping from reality into one's inner being, seeking for a state of ecstasy by repetitive chanting and dancing. Such "ecstasy" is but a passing phase and is not to be compared with the quiet peace and sense of purpose that the true disciple of Jesus Christ finds as he "looks unto Jesus, the author and finisher of his faith" (Hebrews 12:2).

Guru Maharaj Ji and the Divine Light Mission represent another Hindu religion. Maharaj Ji was initially hailed as "Lord of the Universe," "the Second Coming of Christ," etc. In 1973, however, the DLM began to tone down the "God status" of their guru, even though he was still "better than Jesus." This was a seeming reaction to his own personal troubles (e.g. familial lawsuits, etc.) and his apparent lack of omnipotence. When the grandiose claims of "Millenium 73" completely fizzled, the DLM apparently was hard pressed to retain a defense of his divinity. Recently however, after a cooling off period, the claims to deity not surprisingly have returned. The Jan.-Feb., 1979, *Divine Times,* an issue containing 24 pictures of Maharaj Ji, was titled, "The Secret and Open Pictures of God," and claims of omnipotence again surfaced. Of course, the true God has an entirely different view of such claims: "Because your heart is lifted up and you have said I am a god, I sit in the seat of God . . . yet you are a man and not God . . . because you have made your heart like the heart of God. . . you will die the death of the uncircumcised" (Ezekiel 28:2, 6, 10).

Sathya Sai Baba is a more powerful guru with a following in the millions, a man of considerable occult power. A friend of the authors, Tal Brooke, was Baba's principal U.S. disciple for nearly two years and has recently written an exhaustive expose' of Sai Baba. *The Lord of the Air* (Advent Books, New York) is based on personal experience and exposes some of the deep and dark secrets about Sai Baba heretofore unknown by the public.

The gurus continue to come to the West. One fact is clear: they bring with them teachings highly destructive of morality, common sense spirituality, and Christian values. Their open advocacy of various forms of occultism and psychicism (e.g. yoga), spiritism, and sexual immorality (e.g. tantra) has ruined thousands of lives. Whether it be the Hare Krishna attack on the sanctity of marriage, woman, and the family; Bubba Free John's ritual of god-possession and social anarchy; Meher Baba's belief that insanity is high spirituality; Ram Dass' spiritism; Muktananda's bizarre occult experiences; Paramahansa Yoganandas Hinduization of Christianity; etc., the cost of personal involvement will sooner or later be felt. A wise person, indeed, is one who avoids the "wisdom" and "spirituality" of the East altogether.

Salvation: Hindu vs. Christian

Before we conclude this chapter, it is relevant to consider the subject of salvation. What is the Hindu teaching? What do Christians believe?

Most of the gurus operating in America today are aligned to some degree with Hinduism, primarily the Vedantic School. Hence a brief comparison of the Hindu and Christian views of salvation will be useful:

Hindu	Christian
1. *Man* is God; God is everything (pantheism), or everything outwardly is maya (illusion), but its true inner essence is Brahman or God (monism).	1. *Man* is morally and in essence separate from God. Man is God's creation. The creation is distinct and separate from the Creator, forever.
2. *Evil* stems from the *idea* of true separation of God and man—because there really is no separation. (Thus Christianity is the epitomy of evil.)	2. *Evil* stems from man's sin and rebellion against God, i.e., from the *separation*.
3. *Heresy* would involve the teaching that the man is separate from God (i.e. Christianity).	3. *Heresy* involves the idea that man is *not* separated from God and does not need repentance.
4. *Salvation* is achieved by realizing the illusion (maya) of separation and accepting the unity of all life or all that is (monism).	4. *Salvation* is achieved by recognizing the *reality* of the separation and not trying to cover it up or make it an illusion. Once the separation from God is acknowledged, a person can choose to follow God by his faith in God's provision for his sin through Jesus Christ.

The above two systems are unalterably opposed to each other. They are almost exact opposites. In one system, man is blinded to his unity. In the other, man is blinded to his separation. The last thing the gurus would accept is the idea of separation from God, without which they cannot be saved. Eastern belief generally predisposes a person not to believe in Christianity. If you believe in one of these two systems, by definition you cannot believe in the other.

Notice how Eastern thought takes every Christian distinctive and either alters and/or distorts it.

Christianity	Hinduism
1. God is holy and is not tainted by sin (Isa. 5:16).	1. "God" is the author of evil. This impugns God's love, mercy, justice, character, etc.
2. God created the world a real place and pronounced it "very good" (Gen. 1:31).	2. "God" made the world an illusion—or delusion—part of a game *(lila)*.
3. God is a personal Being.	3. God is partially or fully impersonal.
4. God has spoken only in His Word, the Bible.	4. The Bible is secondary to or replaced by Eastern scripture.
5. God's Being is trinitarian—the Father, the Son, and the Holy Spirit.	5. God's being is "monist," i.e., everything That Is is a unity.
6. God is independent and distinct from creation.	6. God is the creation (pantheism) or the essence behind it (monism).
7. God sent His *only* begot-Son as a sacrifice for our sins. Christ is full deity (Col. 2:9, etc.) and unique.	7. Christ is reduced to a guru, master, or one of many avatars (incarnations). He is not unique.
8. God has full authority over His creation.	8. **"I am that"**—Man becomes God. Man has authority over "creation," demonstrated by *siddhas* (occult powers).
9. God has undertaken an infinite sacrifice to save man.	9. Salvation in the Christian sense is "blasphemy" and useless. It *prevents* spiritual growth.

10. Salvation is by Grace alone.	10. Salvation is by works through karmic law—slow evolving into the divine unity through psycho-spiritual occult advancement and/or many lifetimes.
11. Death for the non-Christian has the severest consequences and results in eternal separation from God.	11. Death is an illusion, and it unites the believer with God.
12. A unique, one-time incarnation in Christ (Heb. 9).	12. Innumerable incarnations of God throughout history.
13. Communication with God is by prayer and reading His Word.	13. Communication is by psychic-mystical meditation (destruction of the ego) and by *Sadhana* (spiritual exercises).
14. God's personal love for His creation was proven at the cross (John 3:16).	14. As an impersonal It, Brahman has no love. Brahman is beyond all duality.
15. God has a plan and purpose for His unique creation.	15. For all eternity "the creation" is no more than the eternally cyclic illusion of the universal creation, sustenance, and destruction.

Chapter 5

Transcendental Meditation Is A Religion

Transcendental Meditation is one of the more popular of the new religions. (Yes, it is a religion!) Maharishi Mahesh Yogi began his movement in 1957, after being commanded by his spiritual master (Guru Dev) to develop a simple technique that would allow the common masses of people to attain the state of Hindu God-realization. It grew to its height in 1975 when 30-50,000 people per month were being initiated in the United States. John Weldon testifies, "I was initiated in 1970 and received the mantra *'ieng,'* the word upon which I was to meditate. I soon found how deceptive the system was and shortly became a Christian, which removed my desire for TM. As a practicing Christian, I can understand better why people join TM, and yet there is really no comparison between the two. Christ gave me everything in *substance*. TM gave only in *shadow*. In fact, I'm convinced today that it is a social and spiritual evil." Most of the information we now present is drawn from his 1975 expose' which contains full documentation from Maharishi's own writings. We also refer to court records.

To date, well over one million people have become meditators, and several thousand new converts join their ranks each month. The international controlling organization, the World Plan Executive Council (WPEC), coordinates the five main branches of TM, e.g., the Spiritual Regeneration Movement, Students International Meditation Society, and others. There are TM centers in 90 countries (400 centers in the U.S.), and from 1970-75 the TM organization collected over $60 million in the U.S. alone. In spite of its Hindu nature, clergymen everywhere tout it as nonreligious and acceptable as a form of Christian meditation. It is, in fact, entirely *opposed* to Biblical meditation, and it even insulates its practitioners against the Biblical worldview.

TM, termed "The Science of Creative Intelligence" in public schools where it is taught, presents itself as a very natural method which moves one toward a "greater field of happiness." According to public statements, the method is entirely nonreligious, has a great deal of scientific verification, and can cure nearly any ailment a person might have. Allegedly, it is a simple, progressive technique which has absolutely no harmful side effects. It is said that TM can mend broken marriages, give a nation military invincibility, be an effective cure for mental illness, and can develop a variety of occult powers, as well as make one infallible.[1]

In essence, one becomes a meditator by attending three public lectures and undergoing the initiatory rite, or *puja* (a Hindu word meaning "worship"). During this time one receives his own "unique" mantra (actually despite being told one's mantra is unique to him, there are only 16 principal mantras, dispensed by age categories:[2] *eng, em, enga, ema, ieng, iem, ienga, iema, shirim, shiring, kirim, kiring, hirim, hiring, sham, shama).* The initiate predictably is told never to reveal his mantra to anyone else, but to meditate on it twice daily for 15 or 20 minutes. In essence, TM is touted as a scientifically validated method of wholesale "self-improvement." This, however, is not true. As with many other groups, to get to the real teachings and beliefs of the movement, we must disregard their public pronouncements and look at their private teachings.

The Religious Nature of TM

To begin with, the scientific "validation" for TM is hardly persuasive, despite a tremendous amount of propaganda put out by the WPEC. In fact, it is fairly shallow.[3] What TM lacks in scientific verification, it makes up for in religious matters. Despite hundreds of claims to the contrary, the true nature of TM is Vedantic Hinduism in the nondualist (advaita) tradition of Shankara. Maharishi's four principal texts are replete with thinly veiled Hinduism, particularly his *Commentary on the Bhagavad Gita* and *Meditations of Maharishi Mahesh Yogi*. The puja or initiatory rite is clearly a religious ceremony, and the mantras are related to Hindu deities.[4] For example, former TM teacher Richard D. Scott reveals in his *Transcendental Misconceptions* that his advanced mantra, *"Shree aaing namah,"* means: "O most beautiful aaing I bow down to you." He also points out that TM can lead to mental illness, suicide, and murder.[5] As evidence of the religious nature of TM, we could cite the recent New Jersey Federal Court decision banning the teaching of TM in its public schools as a violation of separation of church and state. (Malnak V. Yogi, 440 F. Supp. 1284-1977.) Despite 1,500 pages of data submitted by the TM group in defense of its "nonreligious" claims, Judge H. Curtis Meanor stated that "no inference was possible except that the teachings of SCI/TM and the puja are religious in nature; no other inference is 'permissible' or reasonable . . . ."[6] (It is interesting to note that the "Pledge to Maharishi" signed by *every* TM teacher states that he recognizes his duty to "serve the Holy Tradition and *spread the Light of God* to all those who need it." (See appendix of next chapter.) Yet every TM teacher claims in his public lecture, "TM is not a religion."

Predictably, the TM organization appealed the decision of the lower court, but on February 2, 1979, its decision was upheld. The following is a quoted verbatim press release issued by the Spiritual Counterfeits Project in Berkeley[7] on February 6, 1979:

On February 2, the United States Court of Appeals for the third circuit, sitting in Philadelphia, affirmed a lower court's ruling that had declared Transcendental Meditation (TM) to be religious in nature.

The U.S. District Court in New Jersey, Judge Meanor presiding, had delivered the original decision in the case *Malnak versus Maharishi Mahesh Yogi* on October 19, 1977. In his 80-page opinion, Judge Meanor had ruled that the teaching of TM and SCI ("Science of Creative Intelligence," TM philosophy) in the public schools violated the establishment clause of the first amendment of the U.S. Constitution. That is, the principle of "separation of church and state" had been violated, since taxpayers' money had been used to support the religious teachings and practices of the TM movement.

The defeated Maharishi and his TM movement argued that Judge Meanor did not have all the facts straight, so they proceeded to take the case to the U.S. Court of Appeals in Philadelphia.

When oral arguments were heard before the Court of Appeals on December 11, 1978, counsel for the TM movement advanced the argument that TM and SCI should be permitted entrance into the public schools as a "true science." The Court directly questioned this concept. The presiding judge quoted the following from TM's ceremony of initiation:

> Guru in the glory of Brahman, Guru in the glory of Vishnu, Guru in the glory of the personified transcendental fulness of Brahman, to Him, to Shri Guru Dev adorned with glory, I bow down.

The judge then asked, "What's scientific about that?" Instead of responding directly, Maharishi's lawyer referred to an affidavit which stated that such ceremonies were sometimes used for "secular" occasions in India. The court later remarked that the effect of that affidavit was to "take a cow and put a sign on it that says 'horse'!"

The Hindu Worldview of TM

In essence, the worldview espoused by TM involves pure Vedantic Hinduism. This is true of a good number of other guru movements, e.g., Sai Baba, Ram Dass (Richard Alpert), Muktananda, Sri Chinmoy, Bubba Free John (Franklin Jones), Meher Baba, Paramahansa Yogananda (The Self-Realization Fellowship—despite its use of Biblical texts), etc. Essentially, what is stated about TM is generally true for them as well. Most of the eastern gurus come from the Vedantic tradition. The principal belief is monism—there is One Reality and that Reality is a unity. This Reality is defined as the impersonal and ineffable Brahman. Its corollary, *maya,* is the doctrine of the illusion of the world or universe. If Reality is One, duality is nonreal. *Lila,* Brahman's "sport" or "play" is the reason for our "existence." Although both we and the world about us are "unreal," the essence behind everything is part of the divine nature, *satchitananda* (absolute being, consciousness, and bliss). The term absolute or pure consciousness actually means unthinking, inactive consciousness, i.e., unaligned with any duality. Through meditation we "progress" to a recognition of the Absolute. We perceive our self (body and personality, etc.) as unreal and recognized our true Self as Divine. Reality lies beyond all duality—good vs. evil; man vs. God, etc. Everything is One, and if we obtain this knowledge (proved to us by our experience in meditation), then—and only then—can we progress spiritually and have no need of reincarnating into another life. Remain in the world of duality, particularly Christian duality, and one will be held in bondage to *maya* and spiritual decadence.

Although many would prefer to think otherwise, the

true purpose of TM is to alter one's view of self and the world into conformity with that of Shankara's nondualist philosophy. This is done by meditating on the mantra and attaining, several times during each session, a state of "Being," or "pure creative awareness." Theoretically, by infusing more and more "Being" into the mind, the nervous system is slowly altered to the point where, in some unknown manner, one's epistemology is actually transformed. In TM there are four advanced states of consciousness—transcendental, cosmic, God, and Unity consciousness. At the start of level two, cosmic consciousness, the meditator is transformed to the point where he recognizes that *atman* (the true Self) *is Brahman*. In other words, he perceives the *maya* (illusion) of the Creation and that the true essence of everything, including himself (behind the illusory phenomenal aspect), is *satchitananda:* being, consciousness, and bliss, or Brahman, the final impersonal God of Hinduism. At this point, according to Maharishi, the meditator is following the path of Karma Yoga.[8] He detaches himself from his actions and their consequences, acts impersonally without desire, and hence absolves his karma. (We should note here that yoga is potentially a highly dangerous practice—authorities list instant death or insanity, crippling nonorganic physical ailments, blackouts, and a variety of diseases as the consequence of even slight mistakes in its practice. This is documented in our section on Yoga. Since yoga and TM are generally defined or thought of as harmless, the origin of the problem is usually sought elsewhere.) This, then, is TM and its true nature as Hindu God (Brahman) Realization. It is clearly Maharishi's plan for the world. When we examine the claims of TM by both Maharishi and his promoters, and then honestly examine the movement, we find that there are few others who can lay claim to purposeful deception of the public on such a grand scale.

The Hazards of TM

It must also be pointed out that TM is not harmless. According to former TM teachers and meditators, there is a high suicide rate among TM teachers; there are incidents of demon possession, numerous physiological problems which can result from continued use, and a number of cases of serious psychopathology, including psychosis.[9]

Several researchers and former TM enthusiasts are convinced that TM can lead directly to impaired mental functioning and can be the very definition of a bad trip. Former TM teacher Gregg Randolph had the distressing experience of helping a nearly incapacitated and very frightened fellow-meditator through the cosmic consciousness transition:

> At one time he was very concerned as to whether or not this was a state of schizophrenia. This worried him. We spent three hours one day trying to draw upon the resources that Maharishi drove into our minds in those teacher training courses . . . . The problem I had to help him with was that he had to start believing that it wasn't schizophrenia. This is the supreme state of knowledge . . . . He's just got to have faith that he's going to grow into this . . . and be able to handle it. Faith becomes a very important thing.[10]

Maharishi counsels, "In the absence of a proper interpretation of this expression of nonattachment, one might become bewildered, and this great blessing of life might become a liability."[11]

Integrating the cosmic consciousness experience into an ongoing lifestyle is the crux of the problem. Psychiatrist Arthur Janov, author of *The Primal Scream,* tells of a senior Vedanta Monk who practiced TM for some 12 years. "The final result of all this bliss was a complete breakdown and the need for therapy." Dr. Janov feels that TM leads to "a state of total unreality, a socially institutionalized psychosis, as it were."[12]

Among borderline psychotics, TM "can bring on full-blown psychosis," says researcher John White,[13] and it is generally conceded that one should be "in shape" for strenuous mental exercises, or one courts real trouble. TM requires a mental adjustment and seems to be just too much for people unprepared for such changes. Unfortunately, it is usually tired, frustrated, worn-out people who seek **just such panaceas as TM.**

John Parks, former manager of "The Beach Boys," was initiated into TM by Maharishi personally. He was thus in a position to know the inside story. He had the opportunity of seeing that TM can be exhausting and dangerous. Apparently Maharishi had not appreciated at that early date, 1969, that some Americans were just not ready for his system. Parks reports concerning a 1969 teacher training course:

> Maharishi had not put a time limit on meditating and quite a few people ended up in the mental hospital. Some are still there.[14]

There are cases of TM suicides.

Chuck Ashman of "The Ashman File," KTTV-Los Angeles, discovered a few instances in his TM inquiry, although he was not particularly looking for them.[15] He was really investigating the financial side of TM for his television talk show.

One of the statements most damaging to the TM program ever to be revealed is that of former TM instructor Kathy Filler, whose total disillusionment with the guru's program is easy to understand:

> But once we became teachers and started teaching people, I found out why the suicide rate for Transcendental Meditation teachers is way over the national average. The ones that don't kill themselves either get really weird or eventually drop back into drugs, or just fall apart—become crazy or recluses [so] that they just can't function. It's just a really sad thing. This is not something that I'm just making up. This is something that's been mentioned by Charlie Lutes (president of SRM) in the teacher's meditation courses. The last one I attended was in 1972, Thanksgiving, in Asbury Park, New Jersey, and Charlie Lutes was there. People

were asking about the suicide rate—teachers were asking why so many were killing themselves. He said, "Well, in future incarnations, Maharishi will appear to them himself, or Guru Dev, and give them their mantra . . . ."[16]

The astounding part is Lutes' casual treatment of the hard way out. People were actually taking their own lives in desperation—experienced teachers of TM—and he had no excuses or reasons, but only good wishes for some future incarnation!

Lutes' attitude perhaps serves to show the dogmatic devotion to the program inspired in the disciples by Maharishi. Even death—self-inflicted—is no cause for alarm, but holds good promise for the "future!"

Una Kroll, M.D., writing in the London *Times* the following June, mentioned the possibilities of TM-induced suicide and even murder, among the other potential dangers of the program.[17]

TM is designed to help the meditator turn inwards 180 degrees.[18] He is to go within himself to "pure awareness," "to the divine," "to brahman." Supposedly, very good things are found deeply hidden within the human being, and contact with these things will have a beneficial effect on the life led by the subject.

Biblically, one does not find God by going within one's self. One finds one's true nature, but the true nature of men and God are surely different. Jesus was very plain:

> For from within, out of the heart of men proceed the evil thoughts, and fornications, thefts, murders, adulteries, deeds of coveting, and wickedness, as well as deceit, sensuality, envy, slander, arrogance, and foolishness. All these things proceed from within and defile the man (Matt. 7:21-23).

That gives a pretty good picture of the unregenerated man within a person, at least according to God. It would be difficult for anyone to confuse that character with God Himself.

We could go on to list other maladies caused by TM, and

we could document those as we have carefully documented our evidence thus far. Suffice it to say that a brief summary will give the picture. Consider carefully these certified TM phenomena: demon possession, epileptic seizures, hallucinations, blackouts up to twenty hours, eyesight problems, extreme stomach cramps, mental confusion, sexual licentiousness, severe nightmares, anti-social behavior, the recurrence of serious psychosomatic symptoms which were previously under control, i.e. bleeding ulcer and depression requiring psychiatric care and medication.[19]

The Final Report of the Stanford Research Institute on Transcendental Meditation contains a closing statement that should be circulated very widely—at least as widely as the guru has circulated his publicity:

> Finally, the possibility of long-term deleterious effects from the practice of TM, especially in unstable individuals, should be investigated.[20]

It is likely that some of the TM casualties are related to its occult practices. Serious hazards seem to follow those involved in the occult, as surely as baby skunks follow their mother. Hence TM's recent increasing advocacy of occultism should be a warning to the wise.

References for Chapter 5

1. John Weldon, *The Transcendental Explosion* (Irvine: Harvest House) 1976, p. 23-4; appendix "TM and the Occult," p. 195-205; M.M. Yogi, *Transcendental Meditation* (NY: Signet), 1968, p. 98-100, 215, 230 with p. 56, 99, etc.
2. Weldon, *op. cit.,* appendix, "TM Mantras and Hindu Gods," p. 190-194; Scott, *Transcendental Misconceptions* (San Diego, CA, Beta Books) Ch. 7.
3. Weldon, *op. cit.,* p. 33-52.
4. Weldon, *op. cit.,* p. 52-99; 154-73; 190-214.
5. Scott, *Transcendental Misconceptions* (San Diego, Beta Books), 1978, Ch. 7, p. 91; Chs. 8-10; Interview, the *National Enquirer,* Feb. 1, 1977.
6. Spiritual Counterfeits Project, *TM In Court, The Complete Text of the Federal Court's Opinion in the Case of Malnak V. Maharishi Mahesh Yogi,* (Berkeley: Ca, SCP) 1977, p. 72. Order from SCP, Box 2418, Berkeley, CA 94702, USA $2.00.
7. Transcripts available from Box 2418, Berkeley, CA 94702.
8. M.M. Yogi *On The Bhagavad Gita,* (Penguin) 1974, p. 319-20.
9. (In chapters five and seven of John Weldon's *The Transcendental Explosion,* this is documented through research in the literature and by interviewing former teachers and practitioners.)
10. Transcript of personal interview conducted by Dave Haddon. SCP, P.O. Box 2418, Berkeley, CA, partially published in *Right On,* Nov. 1975, same address.
11. Maharishi, *On The Bhagavad Gita,* p. 434.
12. (Delta, 1970), p. 222.
13. *Everything You Wanted to Know About TM*, p. 34.
14. Personal correspondence with John Parks
15. Personal correspondence with Mr. Ashman.

16. Taped interview from SCP, P.O. Box 2418, Berkeley, CA published in *Right On,* Nov. 1975, same address. Also documented by R.D. Scott in his *Transcendental Misconceptions.*
17. *London Times,* June 30, 1973.
18. M.M. Yogi, *Meditations,* (NY: Bantam) 1973, p. 103
19. Otis, *The Psychology of Meditation: Some Psychological Changes,* p. 16-17; *The Psychobiology of Transcendental Meditation: A Literature Review,* p. 33-47, both from the Standford Research Institute, Palo Alto, CA; Marilyn Ferguson, *The Brain Revolution* (NY: Bantam) 1975, p. 70-1, 171-81 with A. Campbell, *The Seven States of Consciousness* (NY: Perrenial) 1974, p. 11 with Greg Randolph interview available from SCP, Box 4308, Berkely, CA; *Journal of Transpersonal Psychology,* #1, 1970, p. 65; Benson, *The Relaxation Response* (NY: Morrow), 1975, p. 120-1; Naranjo and Ornstein, *On The Psychology of Meditation* (NY: Viking) 1974, p. 166; Kroll, *London Times,* June 30, 1973, "The Dangers of Transcendental Meditation"; The *London Times* Education Supplement, May 17, 1974, Sri Krishna Prem, *The Yoga of the Bhagavad Gita* (Baltimore, MD: Penguin) 1973, p. 53; personal correspondence.
20. *The Psychobiology of Transcendental Meditation: A Literature Review,* p. 47, cf. note 19.

Chapter 6

Transcendental Meditation Is Occult, Not Christian

TM and Christianity

TM and other eastern movements are not simply neutral toward the Biblical revelation; they are hostile to it. Their basic premise is that all men must realize they are not separate from God; they *are* God. Thus, they represent the height of idolatry as self-worship. For the convenience of the reader, we have prepared a tabular comparison between statements made by the Bible with those made by Maharishi, whose Vedantic beliefs are paralleled by other gurus.

JESUS CHRIST

TM	Bible
"I don't think Christ ever suffered or could suffer. The suffering man from the suffering platform (i.e., the ignorant man bound to the illusion that suffering is real) sees the Bliss of Christ as suffering" (*Meditations of Maharishi Mahesh Yogi,* Bantam, 1968, p. 123).	"O foolish men and slow of heart to believe in all that the prophets have spoken. Was it not necessary for the Messiah to suffer these things and enter into His glory?" (Luke 24:25-26).

SUFFERING

TM

"No man, no Christian should ever suffer. . . .[The] Bible teaches this" (*Ibid.*, p. 63).

Bible

"To the degree you share the sufferings of Christ, keep on rejoicing. . . let those who suffer according to the will of God entrust their souls to a faithful Creator in doing what is right" (I Peter 4:13, 19).

THE OCCULT

TM

"We do something here. . .specific chanting to. . .draw the attention of those higher beings or gods living there [in the spirit world]" (*Ibid.*, p. 17-18).

Bible

"There shall not be found among you anyone. . .who uses divination. . .interprets omens or a sorcerer, or one who casts a spell, or a medium or a spiritist or one who calls up the dead. For whoever does these things is detestable to the Lord" (Deut. 18:10-12). "You shall have no other gods before me" (Exodus 20:3).

MAN'S INNER NATURE

TM

"The inner man is Divine, fully Divine, is full of bliss. . ." (*Ibid.*, p. 157).

Bible

"For from within, out of the heart of men proceed the evil thoughts, and fornications, thefts, murders, adulteries, deeds of coveting and wickedness, as well as deceit, sensuality, slander, arrogance, and foolishness. All these things proceed from within and defile the man" (Jesus, Matt. 7:21-23).

We could go on to list contrast after contrast, but the point is made: TM is anti-Christian and the one who associates himself with the name of Christ and practices TM is being doubleminded and hypocritical.

TM and the Occult

TM stems from a tradition of occultism: Hinduism. Astrology, spiritism, and a variety of occult practices are commonplace in India today. A very large section of the Indian population subscribes to at least a belief in, if not actual practice of, magic, and much of the Hindu scriptures are claimed to have been supernaturally revealed, much in the same way a medium receives messages clairvoyantly from the spirits (i.e., demons, as Gasson and others have pointed out).[1] The techniques of yoga are recognized and applied by all schools of occultism. Maharishi says TM ". . .is the technique of becoming a yogi. . . ."[2] The basis of all occultism—a desire for supernatural power and knowledge opposed to God's will—is clearly found in Hindu occultism, yoga, and TM.

Maharishi says that TM brings absolute power and occult knowledge—the basis of the occultists' dreams.[3] Few people realize that the TM initiation ceremony has many parallels to standard occult magic ritual.[4] The very goals and methods of both are similar: the contacting of "higher beings" or powers to fulfill the desire of the occultist through power received from the demon or "god." A careful reading of the secret twenty-page TM Teachers Manual *(The Holy Tradition)* as well as pp. 38-9 of *Meditations of Maharishi* and his *Bhagavad Gita* commentary (3:9-13 and 4:24-5) shows the similarities. In both cases there is a ceremonial cleansing or purification of the atmosphere. In magic ritual, this is to ban undesirable influences, i.e., evil spirits. There is the purifying of the mind and body of the participant. Having purified the inner and outer atmospheres, the Invocation begins. The gods and masters are now invoked, be they Hindu or Egyptian, with the resultant establishing of a psychic link between them and the evocator. There is the linking of the individual mind to the realm of the cosmic mind or the Absolute. According to TM's *The Holy Tradition:*

> The purpose of this invocation is to attune the active mind by directing it toward the great Masters [deities] to the essential nature of their knowledge of Absolute Being. From that level the mantra is picked up and passed on to the new initiate, thereby leading his consciousness to that same field of transcendental Being. . . .several times so that more and more of its abundance [power] is incorporated into his life.

Psychic Links for Occult Power

These psychic links are established as vehicles for transferrence of occult power *(Shaktipat),* via the TM initiatory ritual, to the teacher or initiate. Both ceremonies involve the complete surrender of the participant—be it to the possessing deity in magic ritual or to the "dead" Guru Dev in TM. Both use incense. We are not sure of its intended use in TM (although at times the presence of demons is accompanied by a particularly bad odor), but in magic ritual it has a psychological effect and is purportedly as capable of allowing demons to assume tangible form as the blood rituals used for the same purpose. Both use continuous repetition of a mantra (the *puja* is one long mantra). In the magicians' case it is to induce temporary insanity, the "sweet madness" which culminates in the loss of reason and subsequent possession by the "god-form." Possession does not apparently occur in TM initiation.

In both cases there are memorized, ritualized physical movements that accompany the ceremony, in TM done only by the teacher. In both, there is the surge of psychic force felt by the participant, generally true only for the TM teacher. In both, there is the presence of the altar of worship, the offerings placed upon it, the kneeling before it. Often in magic ritual there is something on the altar designed to psychically link the person's mind with the ancient tradition—an ancient relic, temple photograph, etc. This is designed to link the mind to the occult knowledge of the tradition being invoked, leading to occult power and knowledge.

In TM the altar picture of Guru Dev, "the yantra," is combined with the mantra to "successfully finish the job of desensitizing the mind to all alien thought systems and of transplanting the mind from one cultural system to another. . . ."[5] The function of using the yantra and mantra is to induce passive, psychically receptive mental states and is so used in a number of cults. The very term "Brahman" means "the productive power in a magical spell."[6]

In magic rituals there may be recognition of the necessity for relaxation of mind and body through singular nostril breathing (an advanced TM technique), as well as a reliance on certain types of sound rhythms (e.g., mantras) to influence the astral world.[7] In TM:

> We do something here according to Vedic rites, particular specific chanting to produce an effect in some other world, draw the attention of those higher beings or gods living there. The entire knowledge of the mantras or hymns of the Vedas is devoted to man's connection, to man's communication with the higher beings in different strata of creation.[8]

Maharishi says that contacting these gods is very beneficial, and it is even sinful not to contact them.[9] They are more than the publically-claimed impersonal powers in nature. Maharishi calls them "more evolved beings."[10]

Mental Passivity—And Mediumship

TM also places the individual in a state of physical immobility and mentally deep passivity; in an occult atmosphere these are two of the basic requirements for mediumship. The physiological immobilization in some ways may be more profound than sleep.[11] Yogananda notes that cosmic consciousness cannot be maintained initially, "except in the immobile trance state."[12] Even though Maharishi, with most gurus, warns against mediumship as a "low" spiritual path, they often replace it with other forms of spiritism, and hence a spiritistic potential cannot be ruled out for a certain percentage of meditators. Ex-medium Raphael Gasson describes how one becomes a medium:

> In any case the student is learning to relax his body and to keep his mind on one thing until he has reached a state of what could be regarded as self-hypnosis and passivity, which results in his not thinking for himself. [This is basically TM.] He becomes an automaton through which evil spirits work by taking advantage of his passivity.[13]

However, it is true that the mental state that mediums have described while in trance possession is similar to advanced TM levels: the oneness of everything, nonexistence of time concepts, etc. In fact, the states described by Maharishi are close to those described by mediums such as Mrs. Willett and Eileen Garrett.[14]

It is noteworthy also that a very gradual easing back into normal consciousness is absolutely necessary for both mediumship and TM, lest there be a mild to violent shock from too sudden a transference from the profound depths of the mind back to normalcy.[15] Sri Krishna Prem warns that "dangerous mediumistic psychisms or neurotic dissociations of personality," even insanity, can result from meditation unless certain preparatory qualifications are met, none of which are in TM.[16]

The existence of demons is quite adequately proven from Biblical and occult records. Refusing to believe in them only leaves one open to their manipulation. Even psychic researchers such as Dr. Elmer Green of the Menninger Foundation, a physicist and one of the leading neuropsychiatrists in the United States, says the evidence of thousands of years' experience is not to be taken lightly. In noting the very real dangers, he warns that psychic exploration can bring one "to the attention of indigenous beings," some of whom are "malicious, cruel, and cunning." They can obsess and even possess people by disrupting the nervous system and controlling the brain.[17] The fact that even Dr. Green is now advocating dabbling in the psychic realm (e.g. *Beyond Biofeedback)* should be a warning to all about the ease with which occult doors can be opened and not closed.

TM does have its cases of spirit contact. In Hinduism, the departed Master often reappears to the favored disciple to guide him psychically. This was often true for Yogananda, the founder of the Self Realization Fellowship, for Shankara, and we suspect it is true for Maharishi.[18] Two of Maharishi's books are said to come "as blessing from" Guru Dev. In the *Bhagavad Gita* commentary, the wisdom therein was "a gift" from Guru Dev, and he was its "inspiration and guiding light." It is relevant that Maharishi asserts that contact with the dead is beneficial because one receives their blessing and help.[19]

Mr. Lutes' statement about Guru Dev or Maharishi appearing to suicide victims in future lives shows that spirit contact is acceptable within TM beliefs. That Maharishi encourages even young children to contact the dead is highly irresponsible.[20] This is spiritism, and to encourage its use by anyone, let alone children, is deplorable. The Bible (Deuteronomy 18:10-13), as well as numerous theologians and psychotherapists, have warned of the dangers involved here.[21] Dr. Koch states: "The family histories and the end of these occult workers are, in many cases known to me, so tragic that we can no longer speak in terms of coincidence."[22]

TM and "Possession"

While actual possession from TM has not been widely publicized, there are known cases. Even occultists warn that those who seek without knowing what is sought can become prime targets for evil spirits. Meditation of the non-TM variety, still Eastern, has induced possession and near insanity.[23] Meditation, including TM, can induce automatic writing and painting which require demonization for their occurrence.[24] It is significant that the very demons[25] with which mediums communicate urge their subjects to practice meditation of the Eastern variety—even saying that it is the very key to spirit contact. This meditation is at times quite parallel to the TM variety, complete with required use of mantras.[26]

Is it a coincidence that some of the teachings of the spirits are quite parallel to those of Maharishi?[27] In TM, you are advised to sit back and let "whatever happens naturally during the practice simply happen." It is this "opening up" in a passive state which means that possession cannot be ruled out. Kent Philpott, in his *Manual of Demonology and the Occult,* lists at least one case of TM-related demon possession and says he had found numerous instances of middle class people becoming demon possessed from yoga exercises, meditation, mind awareness, or expansion groups.[28] India-born and educated Doug Shah says being taken over by an evil spirit in TM "is a very real possibility." He notes that in India, "the entire being of the worshipper" may be infused by the god worshipped during *Puja* rituals.[29]

Because TM mantras represent or worship Hindu gods, the meditator should be warned. We personally talked at length with one meditator who, via TM-induced astral projection, came in contact with extremely vicious spirits who would physically beat him up at his slightest disobedience. They literally controlled his life, and he could do nothing without their permission. They expressly warned him of the consequences of talking with a Christian. This occurred after only six months of TM. TM teacher Dave Birdsell of Connecticut stated it is not uncommon for advancing meditators to have experiences of objects and people psychically merging with them.[30]

Since Maharishi is himself psychic, it is not surprising that he urges people to develop psychic powers via TM. It is clear that Maharishi is familiar with occult terms, and he reportedly has the capacity of mind reading, telepathy, psychic perception of "auras," and probably many others.[31] It is interesting that Idries Shah, noted authority on oriental magic says:

> It is true that the Sadhus [Indian holy men] claim that their psychic power comes exclusively from spirits; that they, within themselves, pos-

sess no special abilities except that of concentration.[33]

Maharishi is no exception, although he might deny it.

TM Brain Waves—Cosmic Consciousness

Recent research has indicated, though not much is certain, that transcendental-type meditation EEG states (brain patterns) have much in common with EEG patterns observed during successful telepathy. Thus TM might produce brain waves of a frequency conducive to telepathy or other occult abilities.[34] Psychic powers are induced, either via demonic spirits, as in Indries Shah, above, or possibly by the demons opening a forbidden potential in man, which becomes controlled and manipulated by them for their purposes.

Psychic abilities are universally used in opposition to God's will, for they never honor Jesus Christ, nor do psychics and occultists ever hold to the Biblical revelation. Most psychics admit that their powers will be taken away from them if they are used outside the conditions stipulated by the spirits, conditions which keep the psychics convinced they are "doing good." In fact they are doing great harm, for they are using demonic power, not divine power.[35]

Edgar Cayce is a prime example. Against his better judgment, he developed psychic abilities which he suspected were Satanic, but he used them for the "good" they did. He ruined thousands of lives, as well as his own.[36] People today are reluctant to believe that Satan will give just about anyone power, peace, etc., to keep them side-tracked. In fact, evil spirits often masquerade as good spirits and do good things for people to deceive them about Biblical truth and salvation (II Cor. 11:13-15). Psychic powers give one the illusion of spirituality but have nothing to do with true spirituality. (For an excellent discussion of the latter, see F. Schaeffers *True Spirituality.)*

Meditation is generally acknowledged as producing the entire range of psychic abilities sooner or later, and TM-induced psychic abilities include astral projection, past-lives experiences, spirit contact, and many others.[37] In TM, at the cosmic consciousness level or sooner, occult powers are attained. Maharishi even extends an invitation to all men throughout the world "to rise and start the practice of transcendental deep meditation" to develop these powers, claiming that they are easily developed via TM.[38] He is being most irresponsible in this, since nearly all yogis and occultists warn against the dangers involved, though they themselves are often the victims.[39]

The Power Corrupts

Psychic powers are sharp traps that rip and tear the psyches of those who pull away. Occultism is littered with accounts of self-glorification, regressive mental states, possession, morbidity, ruined lives, insanity, suicide, etc. If power corrupts, then supernatural power corrupts superlatively, and only the very unwise ignore such a warning.

Finally, in Maharishi's writings, we find such concepts as the Akashic Records, a longtime mainstay of occultism and magic. Believed to be a realm of occult knowledge that one can psychically "tune into," they can easily operate as a disguise for demonic inspiration.[40] Maharishi also urges a worldwide movement into parapsychology and occultism—not too unusual since their goals and those of TM are the same—supernatural power and knowledge that oppose God's will.[41] Doing things that are opposed to God's will has never been safe and never will be (Rev. 21:8). The evidence for the truth of Christianity is there, and it should be investigated.[42]

Spiritual seeking in a blind, unreasoned way is extremely dangerous. Eric Utne, publisher and editor of *The New Age Journal,* says:

> Spiritual seeking has clearly reached the proportions of a national trend. Everyone seems to be looking for the answer. So were the people of Germany during the twenties when there was a widespread fascination with the occult and a higher rate of Indian Gurus per capita than even in the U.S. today.[43]

Books such as Angebert's *The Occult and the Third Reich,* Ravenscroft's *The Spear of Destiny,* Brennan's *The Occult Reich,* and others clearly show that Nazism was partially founded on and supported by occultism and Eastern mysticism of the TM variety. Hitler was in fact fascinated with Eastern mysticism. He was a possessed medium whose ideas of a master race were more based on personal "higher consciousness" type experiences than on Nietzsche's philosophy.⁴⁴

The lesson is clear. TM and eastern religions are potentially opening the door of occultism and a psychic elite in society. Let us keep the door shut.

A Final Note About TM:
The Pledge Every TM Teacher Must Sign

To His Holiness Maharishi Mahesh Yogi

It is my privilege, Maharishi, to promise to teach the Principles and Practice of Transcendental Meditation only as a teacher-employee of _____ which accepts me as such; that I will always hold the teaching in trust for you, dear Maharishi, and _____; that I will never use the teaching except as a teacher in _____ or other organizations founded by you for the purpose of carrying on your work of spreading Transcendental Meditation for the good of Mankind; that as a teacher in _____ I shall receive such compensation as shall be agreed between myself and _____ in writing and except as agreed in writing I expect to receive no monetary compensation but am fully compensated by the love and joy that I receive from the work, by the alleviation of suffering that I may accomplish, and by the Wisdom that I obtain, expound, and cherish. In furtherance of this pledge I acknowledge that prior to receiving the training I had no prior knowledge of such system of Teaching; that there is no other available source where the knowledge of such teaching may be obtained; that such teaching has been imparted to me in trust and confidence; that such training is secret and unique. I further recognize that as a Meditation Guide and Initiator I am a link in the chain of organizations that you have founded; and that to retain the purity of the teaching and movement, you have laid down the wise rule that, should I ever cease to teach in _____ or other organizations founded by you for the purpose of teaching Transcendental Meditation, I may be restrained by appropriate process from using this secret Teaching of Transcendental Meditation imparted to me.

It is my fortune, Guru Dev, that I have been accepted to serve the Holy Tradition and spread the Light of God to all those who need it. It is my joy to undertake the responsibility of representing the Holy Tradition in all its purity as it has been given to me by Maharishi and I promise on your altar, Guru Dev, that with all my heart and mind I will always work within the framework of the Organizations founded by Maharishi. And to you, Maharishi, I promise that as a Meditation Guide I will be faithful in all ways to the trust that you have placed in me.

Jai Guru Dev

References for Chapter 6

1. Indries Shah, *Oriental Magic*, Ch. 12, 13 (NY: Dutton) 1973; Prem, *op. cit.*, p. 204, P. Yogananda, *Autobiography of a Yogi* (Los Angeles: Self Realization Fellowship) 1973, p. 86-7; Gasson, *The Challenging Counterfeit* (Plainfield, NJ: Logos) 1969; V. Ernest, *I Talked With Spirits* (Wheaton, IL: Tyndale), 1971; M. Eliade, *Yoga, Immortality and Freedom,* (Princeton, NJ: Princeton Univ. Press) 1973, siddhi references, esp. p. 85-90.
2. M.M. Yogi, *On the Bhagavad Gita*, p. 389; Gaynor, *The Dictionary of Mysticism* (NY: Citadel), 1968, p. 206.
3. M.M. Yogi, *Transcendental Meditation*, p. 33 (The Basis), 82, 99, 216, 259, 264.
4. Conway, *Magic: An Occult Primer* (NY: Bantam) 1973, p. 30, 51, 78, 112-47: Prem. *op. cit.*, p. 99; C. Muses, A. Young, *Consciousness and Reality* (NY: Avon) 1970, p. 9-17; Naranjo and Ornstein, *op. cit.*, p. 159-60; Shah, *op. cit.*, Ch. 12-13; Doreen Valiente, *An ABC of Witchcraft* (NY: St. Martins) 1973, *Rosicrucian Digest*, Feb. 1976, p. 16, notes their use of TM principles.
5. White, ed., *What is Meditation* (Garden City, NY: Anchor) 1974, p. 201. This is a reference to White, *Everything You Always Wanted to Know About TM*, p. 74.
6. T.W. Organ, *Hinduism, Its Historical Development* (Woodbury, NY: Barron), 1974, p. 82.
7. Conway, *op. cit.*, pp. 61, 74-5.
8. M.M. Yogi, *Meditations*, pp. 17-18.
9. M.M. Yogi, *On the Bhagavad Gita,* pp. 194, 201.
10. *Ibid.*, p. 195.
11. *Journal of Transpersonal Psychology,* 1971, #1, "Meditation as Meta Therapy," pp. 12, 19: Yogi, *On the Bhagavad*

Gita, pp. 393, 45, 93; Yogi, *Transcendental Meditation,* p. 195.

12. Yogananda, Paramahansa, *Autobiography of a Yogi,* (Los Angeles, Self Realization Fellowship pubs.) 1973, p. 477n.
13. R. Gasson, *The Challenging Counterfeit,* (Logos, 1970) p. 83.
14. L. Leshan, *How to Meditate* (NY: Bantam), 1975, pp. 126-8; K. Philpott, *A Manual of Demonology and the Occult,* (Grand Rapids, MI: Zondervan) 1974, pp. 43, 138; White, ed., *The Highest State of Consciousness,* pp. 458-62.
15. Twigg, *The Woman Who Stunned the World: Eng Twigg, Medium* (Manor, 1973), p. 38; M.M. Yogi, *Transcendental Meditation,* pp. 53-5.
16. Prem, *op. cit.,* pp. 45-7.
17. *Journal of Transpersonal Psychology,* "On the Meaning of Transpersonal: Some Metaphysical Perspectives," 1971, #1, pp. 39-40.
18. M.M. Yogi, *The Holy Tradition,* p. 16 (privately published); Yogananda, *Autobiography of a Yogi.*
19. See dedications: M.M. Yogi, *On The Bhagavad Gita,* pp. 5, 16, 21, 194-5, 67, 460-61.
20. Yogi, *On The Bhagavad Gita,* p. 67 and Note 3.
21. See the appropriate writings of Drs. Kurt Koch, Merril Unger, John W. Montgomery and Walter Martin.
22. Koch, *Christian Counseling and Occultism* (Kregel, 1972), pp. 184-9.
23. M.E.P. Baker, *Meditation: A Step Beyond With Edgar Cayce* (NY Pinnacle), 1975, pp. 109-111.
24. *Ibid,* pp. 113-6; personal correspondence with meditators.
25. R. Gasson, *The Challenging Counterfeit,* V. Ernest, *I Talked with Spirits.*
26. Lehmann Hisey, *Key to Inner Space* (NY: Avon) 1975, pp. 20-21. Cooke, *The Jewel in the Lotus* (1973), pp. 17, 19-22, 83, 86-7, 91.
27. Hisey, *op. cit.,* pp. 176, 210, 231; Cook, *op. cit.,* pp. 21-22; Douglas M. Baker, *Superconscious Experience Through Meditation,* nd. no. pub.

28. Philpott, *op. cit.,* pp. 33-7, 44.
29. Shah, *The Meditators,* (Logos,1977), pp. 33-7, 44.
30. Told to the author by Tim J. Runkel of Brown University, March 1976.
31. Yogi, *On The Bhagavad Gita,* p. 26; Yogi, *Mediations,* pp. 73, 84; White, *Everything You Always Wanted to Know About TM,* p. 126; personal correspondence with meditators.
32. Merv Griffin TV special, with Maharishi, Clint Eastwood, etc., late 1975 (Nov.-Dec.).
33. Shah, *Oriental Magic,* p. 123.
34. Lyall Watson, *Supernature* (NY: Bantam) 1974), pp. 230-35.
35. See Gasson's *The Challenging Counterfeit,* Unger's *Demonology in the World Today* (Wheaton, IL: Tyndale) 1972.
36. See J. Millard, *Edgar Cayce, Mystery Man of Miracles* (Greenwich, CT: Fawcett) 1967; Swihart, *Edgar Cayce, Reincarnation and the Bible* (Downers Grove, IL: Inter Varsity) 1973; Bjornstad, *Twentieth Century Prophecy,* and the *Sorcery of America,* series, Vol. 2, by Gordon Lindsey, P.O. Box 24910, Dallas, TX 75224.
37. White, *Everything You Always Wanted to Know About TM,* p. 126-7; Hammond, *The Search for Psychic Power* (NY: Bantam) 1975, p. 222; Zaffuto, *Alphagenics* (Warner, 1975), p. 34; LeShan, *op. cit.,* p. 49; White, ed. *What is Meditation,* p. 213-7; and many others. Also, Maharishi, *On The Bhagavad Gita,* p. 194-201.
38. Yogi, *Transcendental Meditation,* p. 98-100, 215, 230, 56, 99, etc.
39. Eliade, *op. cit.,* pp. 88-90.
40. Yogi, *The Holy Tradition,* p. 13 with *Transcendental Meditation,* p. 33 (the basis).
41. Yogi, *Transcendental Meditation,* pp. 32-5, 98-100.
42. Josh McDowell, *Evidence that Demands a Verdict* (Arrowhead Springs, CA: Campus Crusade for Christ) 1975; F. Schaeffer, *He is There and He is Not Silent* (Tyndale) 1975; Montgomery, *Christianity for the Tough Minded* (Bethany) 1973; Pinnock, *Set Forth Your Case* (Chicago:

Moody) 1960; Wilbur Smith, *Therefore Stand*; H. Morris, *Many Infallible Proofs* (San Diego: ICR) 1977; Purtill, *Reason to Believe,* etc.
43. *The New Age Journal,* #8, Oct. 15, 1975, p. 2.
44. J.M. Angebert (NY: McGraw-Hill) 1975, p. xi, xiii, 163, 194-200, 278, etc.; Ravenscroft, (NY: Bantam) 1974, p. 25-33, 49, 58, 91, 95-6, 154-68, 172-3, 243-51, 288-93; Brennan, *The Occult Reich* (NY: Signet) 1974; Pauwels and Bergier, *Morning of the Magicians,* part II; D. Sklar, *Gods and Beasts* (NY: Thomas Crowell) 1977.

Chapter 7

Zen Buddhism Is Also With Us

We have considered the intrusion of Hinduism, but it is not the only eastern influence on Western culture today. Zen Buddhism is also with us, and we shall briefly consider this contradictory religious teaching.

Introduction and History

Zen, which claims to be the true Buddhism, reportedly originated in India around the 6th century A.D. From India, Zen was brought to China and then, in the twelfth and thirteenth centuries, to Japan and Korea. In the early 20th century, Zen came to the United States where today it has thousands of adherents.

There are two main schools of Zen training: The Soto and the Rinzai, the latter being the most common form practiced in the West. The goal in both schools is the same, i.e. "enlightenment" *(satori),* but the teaching methods used are different. Enlightenment is no easy path—it may literally take nine years of staring at a blank wall, as it did with Bodhedharma, the founder of Zen.

Basic Teachings

Defining Zen is somewhat difficult, because in an ultimate

sense, Zen has no required beliefs. D. T. Suzuki, one of the individuals most responsible for cultivating Zen in the West, states:

> Zen has nothing to teach us in the way of intellectual analysis; nor has it any set doctrines which are imposed on its followers for acceptance. . . . If I am asked, then, what Zen teaches, I would answer Zen teaches nothing. Whatever teachings there are in Zen, they come out of one's own mind.[1]

Of course, Zen does have a worldview, and most Zenists are in agreement on a number of teachings about such things as the nature of man, God, "salvation," etc. Suzuki's point is that Zen and its goal of *satori* are a subjective experience. One does not need to *believe* anything in order to experience the "enlightenment" Zen offers. This enlightenment involves looking at yourself and the world in a new way. It cannot come about through teaching or belief, but it must be directly experienced. Once we experience it, our entire outlook is transformed.

Prior to enlightenment, we perceive the world in ignorance and distortion. We perceive the world has having good and evil, subject and object, life and death: as duality. However, when we experience *satori,* we see reality as it truly is—One Entity. R. F. Sasaki states:

> God . . . the universe and man are one indissoluble existence, one total whole. Only THIS —capital THIS—is. Anything and everything that appears to us as an individual entity or phenomenon, whether it be a planet or an item, a mouse or a man, is but a temporary manifestation of THIS in form . . . .[2]

In other words, there is no validity to such concepts as good and evil, subject and object, God and man, etc. for everything is One united essence, everything is a whole.

In Zen, enlightenment is achieved through meditation *(Zazen)* on paradoxical questions or statements *(koans).* The purpose of the *koan* is to open the mind to "truth," to help it achieve *satori.* As perceiving things in a dualistic sense is "evil," the *koan* helps break down the mind to the point where it can begin to reorder its perception. "The koan . . . is only intended to synthesize or transcend . . . the dualism of the senses. So long as the mind is not free to perceive a sound produced by one hand [clapping], it is limited and divided against itself."[3]

Looking at the world logically, morally, reasonably, or scientifically must be overthrown. Only then will we experience freedom. The following is a common *koan:* "When your mind is not dwelling on the dualism of good and evil, what is your original face before you were born?" Huang Po indicates the impact of Zen:

> The single aim of the true Zen follower is to train his mind that all thought processes based on the dualism inseparable from "ordinary" life are transcended, their place being taken by the Intuitive Knowledge which, for the first time, reveals to a man what he really is. If All if One, then knowledge of a being's true self nature—his original Self—is equally a knowledge of all-nature, the nature of everything in the universe.[4]

For all practical purposes, the individual perceives himself as one with the ultimate reality, or as part of God. His experience of *satori* is so beyond the world of normal things that it brings a conviction of having "found reality." Of course, such a belief has serious consequences. Huang Po, for example, was concerned about such concepts as virtue, lest people be led astray into dualism. Christmas Humphreys stated:

> *Satori* is utterly impersonal . . . sufficient unto itself, its own authority . . . without any sense of separateness there is no need of benevolence or of love for one's fellow men. When I and my Father are one, why seek that one?[5]

The *Hsin-hsin Ming* states:

> If you want to get to the plain truth, be not concerned with right and wrong. The conflict between right and wrong is the sickness of the mind.[6]

Biblical Comparison

Zen, obviously, is opposed to a Christian worldview. However, Zen is especially opposed to the Biblical revelation, presenting as it does moral absolutes and the need for personal salvation from sin and death. The following quotations demonstrate how Zen teachers have recognized the incompatibility of the two systems. D. T. Suzuki states:

> The world is God and God is the world.... When Buddhists make reference to God, God must not be taken in the Biblical sense.[7]
>
> Therefore, in Zen, God is neither denied nor insisted upon; only there is in Zen no such God as has been conceived by Jewish and Christian minds... make obeisance to the camellia now in full bloom, and worship it if you like, Zen would say.... All those pious deeds considered to be meritorious or sanctifying by most so-called religiously minded people are artificialities in the eyes of Zen.[8]

Sasaki states:

> The great verities that Zen, with Buddhism, takes as basic are diametrically opposed to those the Hebraic-Christian religions have always assumed to be absolute.[9]

Alan Watts, the famous popularizer and prophet of Western Zen, stated:

> The new life for Christianity begins just as soon as someone can get up in church and say, "Wash out your mouth every time you say Jesus!" and, "The crucifixion gives eternal life" because it is the giving up of God as an object to be possessed, known, and held to for one's own safety... to cling to Jesus is therefore to worship a christ uncrucified, an idol instead of the living God.[10]

In *The Clatter of a Broken Tile,* Sokei-An states: "Neither one's own nature nor anything else that appears before one needs changing." But the Bible states:

> God is now declaring to all men that all everywhere should repent [change their minds and turn to Christ], because he has fixed a day in which he will judge the world in righteousness through a Man whom he has appointed, having furnished proof to all men by raising Him from the dead (Acts 17:30-31).

Psychoanalyst Eric Fromm stated:

> I truly follow God's will if I forget about God.[11]

Zen, then, is ultimately a system of self-salvation, a belief that, in reality, the individual is part of the absolute, part of God. There is no room for Christian morality, Jesus Christ as savior, a personal God, or heaven, or hell, unless it be in Christianity. However, the *experience* is so unique, it is to the Zenist everything.

> Only when you have no thing in your mind and no mind in things are you vacant and spiritual, empty and marvellous.[12]
>
> The answer, the eternal home, will never, never be found so long as you are seeking it, for the simple reason that it is you yourself—not the self you are aware of and that you can love or hate, but the one that always vanishes when you look for it . . . . This is why the mystics call the highest knowledge unknowing.[13]
>
> . . . we have to fix our will on the void, to will the void . . . this void is fuller than all fulness . . . . This nothingness is not unreal. Compared with it everything in existence is unreal.[14]

A major difficulty in dialogue with Zen members is one of semantics. For the Zenist, "one who knows does not speak and he who speaks does not know." A clear, prayerful presentation of the Gospel, relying on the Holy Spirit to do the work of conviction, is fundamental.

One can also appeal to a sense of morality of right and wrong, which God has placed in all men, and point out the nihilistic implications of Zen. The lack of final answers may be underscored, as compared with the Christian's full assurance of salvation and absolute truth (John 14:6; I John 5:13). For example, Suzuki states that even *after* enlightenment, we still "know not definitely what the ultimate purport of life is . . . ."[15]

Contradictions Among Zen Scholars

Contradictions among top Zen scholars can be noted: e.g., D. T. Suzuki states:

> Without it *(satori)* there is no Zen, for the life of Zen begins with the "opening of satori."[16]

Yet Shunryu Suzuki states of *satori:*

> It's not that *satori* is unimportant, but it's not the part of Zen that needs to be stressed.[17]

D. T. Suzuki even admits:

> . . . even among the Zen masters themselves, there is a great deal of discrepancy, which is quite disconcerting. What one asserts another flatly denies or makes a sarcastic remark about it . . . .[18]

As is true for many religious sects, the person involved is convinced of the truth of the religion because of his *experiences*—usually mystical—which *he* equates with proof. A discussion on the inability of experience alone (apart from God's true revelation) to convey truth may be helpful. Proverbs 12:15, 21:2, 3:5-6, and 14:12 are applicable (e.g., 14:12 —"There is a way which seems right to a man, but its end is the way of death.") The Zen devotee can be challenged to read the Gospels, as even Alan Watts, a Western apostle of Zen, stated of Jesus Christ:

> Even to atheists he is the supremely good man, the exemplar and moral authority with whom no one may disagree.[19]

Tucker Callaway records an interesting discussion he had with D. T. Suzuki, a discussion which points out the difficulty even the most devoted Zen teacher has with his own philosophy:

> Toward the end of the interview with Daisetz Suzuki, I said that while Buddhism accepts all things, just as they are, as good, Jesus-people

find things imperfect and therefore strive to change them. To this Suzuki surprisingly replied, "Yes, that's the good side of Christianity. Buddhists accept everything as it is, perhaps. That is bad. They don't go out of their way to do good .... Buddhism has a great deal to learn from Christianity."[20]

Callaway points out the implications:

> It is difficult for me not to believe he meant this seriously. It seemed to me that at that moment he departed from his Zen presuppositions and expressed a genuine value judgment. Whether he did, or whether he remained Only-mind viewing himself, me, and the entire interview with complete detachment, the value judgment he articulated is crucial.
>
> From the Zen point of view, not going out of one's way to do good is evidence of Enlightenment, as also would be not going out of one's way not to do good. Picking and choosing and the urge to "do good" are evidences of Ignorance. The freedom of the Zen Way is the freedom not to choose. But the freedom of the Jesus Way denies one the freedom not to choose. . . . If Suzuki seriously meant what he said . . . he, at least for that moment, was off the Zen way . . . .[21]

References for Chapter 7

1. D.T. Suzuki, "What is Zen" in R. Sohl and A. Carr (eds.) *The Gospel According to Zen* (N.Y. Mentor), 1970, pp. 13-14.
2. R.F. Sasaki, "Zen: A Method for Religious Awakening" in N.W. Ross (ed.), *The World of Zen: An East-West Anthology* (New York: Vintage Books), 1960, p. 18.
3. D.T. Suzuki, "The Koan," N.W. Ross, *op. cit.*, p.51.
4. John Blofeld (translator) "The Zen Teaching of Huang Po on the Transmission of the Mind," N.W. Ross, *op. cit.*, p. 67.
5. N.W. Ross, *op. cit.*, "Christmas Humphreys on Satori," p. 47.
6. Ross, *op. cit.*, p. 335.
7. D.T. Suzuki, "The Awakening of a New Consciousness in Zen," N.W. Ross, *op. cit.*, pp. 228-229.
8. D.T. Suzuki, "What is Zen," Sohl and Carr, *op. cit.*, p. 15.
9. Ross, *op. cit.*, p. 17.
10. Alan Watts "Wash Out Your Mouth," Sohl and Carr, *op. cit.*, pp. 16-17.
11. Fromm, "Zen Buddhism and Psychoanalysis," Ross, *op. cit.*, p. 252.
12. Sohl and Carr, *op. cit.*, p. 52.
13. *Ibid*, p. 115.
14. Simon Weil, "Gravity and Grace," Ross, *op. cit.*, p. 288.
15. D.T. Suzuki, "The Sense of Zen," Ross, *op. cit.*, pp. 39-40.
16. Sohl and Carr, p. 33.
17. Shunryu Suzuki, *Zen Mind, Beginner's Mind* (New York Wetherhill), 1976, p. 9.
18. Ross, *op. cit.*, p. 54.
19. Sohl and Carr, p. 16.

20. Tucker Callaway, *Zen Way—Jesus Way* (Rutland, VT: Charles Tuttle) 1976, pp. 238-239, 148.
21. *Ibid,* p. 239.

Chapter 7 Bibliography

Christian Treatments of Zen

1. Walter Martin, *Kingdom of the Cults* (Minneapolis: Bethany) 1965, Chapter 10—"Zen Buddhism."
2. Lit-Sen Chang, *Zen Existentialism: The Spiritual Decline of the West,* (Nutley, NJ: Presbyterian and Reformed), 1969.
3. Tucker N. Callaway, *Zen Way—Jesus Way,* (Rutland, VT: Charles Tuttle), 1976. (Although a Christian, this author spent years in Zazen—something we feel is not to be recommended.)

Chapter 8

Yoga and the Occult

We have seen that TM is basically a form of Hinduism. What about yoga? Is it just an innocent form of relaxing the body and mind? Or is it like TM a subtle form of imported Hinduism?

The goal of yoga is the same as Hinduism—Hindu God-realization, i.e., for the yoga devotee to realize that he is one with Brahman, the highest impersonal Hindu God.[1] The physical exercises of yoga are designed to prepare the body for the psychospiritual change vital to inculcating this idea into the consciousness and being of the person. Hence talk of separating yoga practice from theory is meaningless. From a Christian perspective, whether the two can safely be divided is doubtful. "I do yoga, but Hinduism isn't involved," is an incorrect statement. Those who do "yoga exercises" alone run the risk of spiritual warfare entering their lives.

The different schools of yoga overlap in their beliefs and practices, and hence various Eastern disciplines may incorporate parts of karma, japa, laya, raja, mantra, jnana, bhakti, or hatha yoga.[2] For example, TM's Maharishi calls TM karma yoga, and the karma yoga of the Bhagavad Gita involves an unattached, disinterested performance of one's duties. One detaches himself from his acts and their consequences, acts impersonally, without desire, and hence absolves his karma. This is TM, One continues to act, but in detachment.[3,4]

Yoga and Magic

We should note with the authority Avalon that yoga and magic go hand in hand.[5] Meditation is the operative principle of yoga.

In the authoritative yoga literature, there are invariably warnings about the dangers of yoga practice without first gaining vigorous moral, mental, or sometimes physical prerequisites (Yama and Niyama). This is largely neglected by many today.

Shree Purohit Swami warns:

> People forget that Yama and Niyama form the foundation, and unless it is firmly laid, they should not practice postures and breathing exercises. In India and Europe, I came across some three hundred people who suffered permanently from wrong practices, the doctors on examination found that there was nothing organically wrong and consequently could not prescribe.[6]

H. Rieker warns: "Yoga is not a trifling jest if we consider that any misunderstanding in the practice of yoga can mean death or insanity," and, that in Kundalini (hatha) yoga, if the breath is "prematurely exhausted, there is immediate danger of death for the yogi."[7]

It is symptomatic that in the West we do yoga to *achieve* what the East requires as basic prerequisites for *even starting* yoga; *physical and mental health*. Yoga is never really removed from its culture (Hinduism) and theory (occultic), and those who think they are doing only postures and breathing exercises are courting serious dangers. Swami Prabhavananda's *Yoga and Mysticism* lists brain injury, incurable disease, and insanity as potential hazards of wrong yoga practice; Rieker lists cancer of the throat, death, "all kinds of ailments," blackouts, strange trance states, or insanity from even "the slightest mistake

....."⁸ Once we really embark upon yoga, however, the evasion of a single requirement can turn supposed nectar into poison.

Body Disorder, Disease, and even Madness

E. Wood warns of "the imminent risk of most serious bodily disorder, disease, and even madness." Many people have brought upon themselves incurable illness and even madness by neglecting Hatha Yoga prerequisites, and "by any mistake there arises cough, asthma, head, eye, and ear pains, and many other diseases."*ᵃ The Hatha Yoga Pradipika (2:15) says:

> Just as lions, elephants, and tigers are tamed, so the prana [breath—actually *prana* is the supposed omnipresent substance behind the breath] should be kept under control. Otherwise it can kill the practitioner.

Yoga texts have many such warnings. One can see the problems involved when Wood says: "All Hatha Yogas are extremely dangerous," and urges use of a different form of yoga, raja yoga, while Rieker says: "Mastery of Hatha Yoga is only a preliminary to the mastery of raja yoga."⁹

The various schools of yoga (hatha, raja, jnana, bhakti, karma, japa, laya, etc.) are not always easily separated, hence it is difficult to define them precisely. Insofar as yoga is defined or thought of as totally safe, we should not expect to hear much of harmful cases, for their cause is thought to be elsewhere.

Yoga is really pure occultism, as any number of yoga and occult texts prove.¹⁰ Occult abilities are very common from yoga practice, and the numerous dangers of occultism are evident from many studies.¹¹ The yoga scholar and Sanskrit authority, Mishra, states:

> In conclusion, it may be said that behind every psychic investigation, behind mysticism, occultism, etc., knowingly or unknowingly, the yoga system is present.¹²

Kundalini and Yoga

Kundalini is thought of as a female serpent or goddess lying dormant at the base of the spine. When aroused via yoga, she travels up the spine, opening the chakras (psychic centers), and so leads to union with Brahman. "Traditionally she is known as Durga the creatrix, Chandi the fierce and bloodthirsty, and Kali the destroyer. She is also Bhajangi the serpent. As Chandli or Kali, she has a garland of skulls around her neck and drinks human blood."[13] One does not fool around carelessly with Kundalini—unless they care for terrible body pain and heat, deteriorating health, numerous forms of insanity, or sudden death.[14]

Shree Purohit Swami experienced near insanity, ate the leaves of two entire nimba trees, devoured insipid mudra leaves, and could not sit or stand. He mentions one yogi who had the fire rage for six to eight months, another who had to sit under cold tap water eight hours a day.[15] Gopi Krishna, founder of one of the several Kundalini research centers in the world, records his kundalini experience:

> It was variable for many years, painful, obsessive, even phantasmic. I have passed through almost all the states of different mediumistic, psychotic, and other types of mind, for sometime I was hovering between sanity and insanity. I was writing in many languages, some of which I never knew [the mediumistic ability of automatic writing].[16]

He believes most schizophrenics and manic depressives probably represent malfunctioning kundalini, notes the ease with which it produces mental derangement, and mentions his personal encounters with cases of kundalini-caused insanity. He notes that in India it is widely known that Hatha Yoga practices can lead to insanity.[17]

> The power, when aroused in a body not attuned to it with the help of various disciplines or not genetically mature for it, can lead to awful mental states, to almost every form of mental disorder, from hardly noticeable aberrations to

the most horrible forms of insanity, to neuroses and paranoia, to megalomania, and, by causing tormenting pressure on reproductive organs, to an all-consuming sexual thirst that is never assuaged.[18]

It is noteworthy that kundalini, mediumistic, and possession states have common characteristics, including various occult manifestations and the demonic succubae.[19] In light of the above, the tremendous increase of interest in Kundalini yoga is a very serious state of affairs. (There are some yogis who believe that the bizarre and fatal cases of spontaneous human combustion—people bursting into flames—are the result of malfunctioning Kundalini.)

Kundalini and Demonic Activity

Kundalini is generally thought to be aroused only by specific procedures, with specific accompanying signs. Yet many occult groups use different methods to arouse kundalini (e.g., Edgar Cayce's method is not Avalon's[20]), but the results are similar, showing that arousal occurs in various ways. Hence "kundalini" may serve as a guise for demonic activity, allowing demons to achieve their purposes by various methods. It generally takes several years for Kundalini to reach the top chakra, though spontaneous or accidental arousal is not to be ruled out. Rieker states that: "Kundalini is the mainstay of all yoga practices."[21] Avalon says all mantras are manifestations of Kundalini, being the basis of arousing her.[22] (He also notes that mantras are psychic powers which lend themselves to impartial use, "A man may be injured or killed by Mantra."[23]) This is the occult power of black magic where the occultist can injure or kill others. Dr. Koch, in *Between Christ and Satan,* lists several examples. Even TM's Maharishi describes what sounds very much like TM-induced kundalini.[24] Both TM and kundalini have produced the following: sexual arousal to the point of free prostitution, blackouts, surges of power, past-lives experiences, demonic and insane states, temporary respiration stoppage, astral projection, the development of "soma," occult powers including an opening to the astral world, use of the akashic records, spirit contact, and extreme paranoia. There is a similarity in claims and in description of mental states attained through the practice of both TM and kundalini arousal (bliss, merging or unity, enhanced perception, ego dissolution, mystical contemplation, union in Brahman, etc.). There are also similar practices used (mantra meditation, sensory withdrawal, nostril breathing), and, finally, both involve an identity change.[25]

On the matter of sexual arousal, a severe warning is necessary in light of this generation's combination of sex and eastern spirituality. Sri Krishna Prem says, "It is safer to play with dynamite than to practice the yoga of meditation" without complete control of inner and outer sex drives. A. Avalon warns that intercourse during the early stages of Hatha Yoga "is likely to prove fatal."[26] Finally, David Fetcho, who comes out of an extensive background in tantric yoga theory and practice states:

> At first glance it is difficult to pinpoint such a thing as "kundalini arousal" in TM. However, if we look in depth at one central feature of the practice, the initiation, as well as some of the less publicized techniques which are taught by the movement, we may be led to conclude that TM, as a yoga technique, is indeed involved with stimulating the psychic kundalini, whether practitioners believe in the existence of it or not.

This indicates that even the ignorant use of eastern spiritual disciplines does not nulify their impact. Whether or not one believes in Hinduism, yoga practice will have its influence in one's life. Clearly, the Christian should avoid all forms of yoga activity. Old fashioned cardiovascular exercise is quite adequate.

References for Chapter 8

1. Rieker, *The Yoga of Light* (Los Angeles: Dawn House) 1974, p. 135; Maharishi, *Transcendental Meditation*, p. 249; Vishnudevananda, *The Complete Illustrated Book of Yoga* (NY: Pocket Books) 1972, p. ix, 7-9.
2. A. Avalon, *The Serpent Power* (NY: Dover) 1974, p. 185-6; Wood, *The Seven Schools of Yoga* (Wheaton, IL: Quest) 1974.
3. M. Eliade, *Yoga, Immortality and Freedom* (1973), p. 153-61.
4. Yogi, *On the Bhagavad Gita*, pp. 319-20.
5. Avalon, *op. cit.*, p. 186-204.
6. Patanjali, *Aphorisms of Yoga*, (London: Faber), 1973; pp. 56-7 cf. Feuernstein and Miller, *Yoga and Beyond* (NY: Schocken), 1972, pp. 7-8, 27-8.
7. Rieker, *op. cit.*, p. 9, 134.
8. Prabhavananda, *Yoga and Mysticism* (Hollywood, CA: Vedanta Press) 1972, pp. 18-19; Rieker, *op. cit.*, pp. 30, 79, 96, 111-12.
8a. Wood, *op. cit.*, p. 14.
9. Wood, *op. cit.*, p. 79; Rieker, *op. cit.*, p. 128.
10. R.S. Mishra, *Yoga Sutras* (Garden City, NY: Anchor) 1973, pp. 132, 136-7, 295-399; Wood, *op. cit.*, pp. 112-13; Mishra, *Fundamentals of Yoga* (Garden City, NY: Anchor) 1974, pp. 2-3, Ch. 17-19, 26-7; J. Brennan, *Astral Doorways* (NY: Samuel Weiser) 1971, pp. 98, 29; H. Chaudhuri, *Philosophy of Meditation* (San Francisco: Cultural Integration Fellowship) 1974, pp. 50-51.
11. K. Koch, *Christian Counseling and Occultism* (Grand Rapids, MI: Kregel), 1972; Montgomery (ed.), *Demon Possession* (Minneapolis, MN: Bethany) 1975, etc.
12. Mishra, *op. cit.*, p. 138.
13. Gopi Krishna, *The Awakening of Kundalini* (NY: Dutton) 1975, p. 13.

14. Rieker, *op. cit.*, p. 134; Vishnudevananda, *op. cit.*, p. 328; Hisey, *op. cit.*, p. 146; White, *Everything You Always Wanted to Know About TM*, p. 99.
15. Patanjali, *op. cit.*, pp. 57-8.
16. Gopi Krishna, *The Awakening of Kundalini* (NY: Dutton) 1975.
17. *Ibid.*, pp. 14, 33, 37.
18. *Ibid.*, p. 14.
19. *Ibid.*, pp. 19, 37, 47, 82, 94, 120, 123; Rieker, *op. cit.*, pp. 49, 78, 102; J.M. Riviere, *Tantric Yoga* (NY: Samuel Weiser) 1973, pp. 64, 68; A. Avalon, *op. cit.*, pp. 83-4, 242.
20. ARE (Association for Research and Enlightenment, Virginia Beach, VA) circulating file on Kundalini; Baker, *op. cit.*, p. 69, *ARE Journal*, Nov. 1975, pp. 259-63; Puryear, Thurston, *Meditation and the Mind of Man* (Virginia Beach, VA: ARE Press) 1975, p. 80.
21. Rieker, *op. cit.*, p. 101.
22. Avalon, *op. cit.*, pp. 83, 225.
23. *Ibid.*, pp. 83-4, cf. note 2.
24. Maharishi, *On the Bhagavad Gita*, p. 410.
25. J.M. Riviere, *Tantric Yoga* (NY: Samuel Weiser) 1973, pp. 64, 68; Krishna, *op. cit.*, pp. 14, 47, 94-100; Hammond, *We Are All Healers* (NY: Ballantine) 1974, pp. 268-9; TM puja, "The Holy Tradition"; *ARE Journal*, Nov. 1975, p. 263; White, *Everything You Always Wanted to Know About TM*, pp. 97-9, 127; Vishnudevananda, *op. cit.*, p. 294; Yogi, *Transcendental Meditation*, p. 33; M. Eliade, *Patanjali and Yoga* (NY: Schocken) 1975, p. 193; H. Chaudhuri, *op. cit.*, pp. 68, 74-7; Avalon, *op cit.*, pp. 7-10, 18, 19, 127, 144; Rieker, *op. cit.*, p. 133; Prabhavananda, *op. cit.*, pp. 32, 35, 41, 68, Ch. 3; Norvell, *The Miracle Power of Transcendental Meditation* (NY: Barnes & Noble) 1974, p. 117, etc.; Rieker, *op. cit.*, pp. 79, 92, 144, 146, 91, 97, 148; Krishna, *op. cit.*, pp. viii, 16, 26, 43-5, 14, 47, 66-7, 72-4, 82, 87-93; Avalon, *op. cit.*, pp. iii, 9, 81-2, 204-8, 214, 222-8, 246-8, 279-80, 291-3, 254-5, 282-3.
26. Avalon, *op. cit.*, p. 190; Prem, *op. cit.*, p. 53.

Chapter 9

Reincarnation—Yes or No

We have considered some of the better known Eastern religions. Now we briefly examine two teachings that have gained widespread acceptance in the West. First we look at Reincarnation, and in our next chapter we talk about Life after Death.

Does the Bible teach reincarnation? Many people believe so. With the advent of the East, such an attitude is increasingly popular. However, the biblical doctrine of salvation and the idea of reincarnation are really based on entirely *opposite* principles.

Self-Improvement Through Many Lives?

Reincarnation teaches that we pay for ("atone" for) our own sins by self-improvement through many lives, based on karmic law. If we do evil in this life, we pay for it in the next. However, we can slowly perfect ourselves and eventually everyone will reach the goal of "perfection," "salvation," or "liberation." On the other hand, the Bible says we have only *one* life in which to attain salvation (Hebrews 9:27)—not even two, let alone thousands or millions. As fallen creatures, we are incapable of *ever* being good enough or improving ourselves sufficiently to meet

God's holy standard, which is complete perfection. God can require no less.

This is the purpose for the unique (John 3:16, 18) one-time incarnation of Jesus Christ, to pay the penalty for man's sin, because man couldn't meet God's perfect standards by his own ability. Christ died in our place and took the penalty for our sins. Note that Christ is never to die again (Rom. 6:9), and He was manifested only *once* (Heb. 9:25-28). The Bible says that self-improvement, or salvation based on human effort alone (e.g., reincarnation), is a hopeless path and will never take us to God (Galations 1:8, 3:24). Because He accomplished full salvation *for us*, we have no need to perfect ourselves (Heb. 10:14). The statements of Jesus Himself and the writers of the New Testament are clear. Christ came to die for the world's sins, so that through faith (not works) men could come to God. No one can claim that he is better than someone else (Eph. 2:8-9; Luke 24:25,46; I Peter 2:24, 4:1; Heb. 2:9,10,18, 9:26). The crucifixion of Jesus was planned from eternity past (Acts 2:23), and it was foretold 1,000 and again 700 years prior to the event (Psalm 22 and Isaiah 53). If it were possible for man to save himself, then God was wrong in judging Jesus in our place, and that is hardly a plausible option.

In fact, the resurrection of Christ disproves reincarnation. God says that the penalty of sin is death—physical death as well as spiritual separation from Him. Men die because they sin. (Perfect men would not die.) The very fact that Christ rose from the dead—and this *is* an historical fact, by all standards of historical judgment and legal evidence[1]—proves that all sins were paid for. Otherwise He would still be dead. So much as one "unpaid-for" sin, throughout all human history, would have kept Jesus in the grave (Romans 4:25). Christ died because He took the penalty for our sin—which was death. He was resurrected because the entire penalty for our sin was paid. Therefore, eternal life, a perfect and personal existence forever with an infinitely perfect God, is potentially available to anyone who will believe in Christ: "For God so loved the world that He gave His only Son, that whoever believes in Him might not perish but have everlasting life" (John 3:16).[2]

Hence, at its roots, reincarnation is opposed to the Biblical message. Yet people do have what they feel are genuine reincarnation experiences. It is curious that the occult text *Oahspe,* says these are experiences implanted into the mind by evil spirits for their play. This provides a logical explanation for geniune (i.e., "validated") past-lives experiences.

On a more scholarly level, even Dr. Ian Stevenson, perhaps the foremost secular authority on reincarnation in the world, declares that the "possession" hypothesis of explaining past-lives experiences is a distinct possibility *(Twenty Cases Suggestive of Reincarnation,* p. 377). Whereas he feels some cases are unaccountable by the possession hypothesis, we, on the other hand, are convinced that no case we have encountered is unexplainable according to demonic capacities. This includes such phenomena (offered as "proof") as the similar birthmarks on newborn babies corresponding to those on the recently deceased person whose spirit now purportedly entered the baby. The fetus can be marked in the womb as a consequence of the occult practices of its parents, rather than a previous life. While such things are rare, they do occur. For example, Levine in *The Strange World of the Hare Krishna* reports on one child born with red *telak* birthmarks on its forehead. (The telak are chalk markings carefully drawn on the forehead by devotees symbolizing their submission to Krishna.) Swami Rama was born with a hole in his ear, as prophesied by his guru, etc.

Reincarnation and occultism have long been close friends and nearly all occult schools teach reincarnation. These experiences fall into the realm of spiritual warfare (Ephesians 6) and represent an attempt to lull people into a false belief that there is no coming judgment (Acts 17:31), but merely a progression into the next life, which is supposed to be better.[3]

Validated reincarnation experiences are implanted into

the mind via occult power, and are very real to the individual who undergoes them. The fallen angels, having been around a long time, would find it easy to select an experience out of a dead person's past and implant it into a living person's consciousness. Some feel these experiences are proof of reincarnation, but even with the experiences, the theory has numerous flaws, most of them admitted by reincarnationists. First, it has shown no evidence of working throughout all of man's history, i.e., things should be improving, but, if anything, the world is worse off than ever. Actual proof is impossible by its very nature (subjective, generally indefinite experiences that are difficult to confirm).

There are also numerous internal contradictions and a variety of opposing theories, some of which contradict others. For example, is transmigration (into animal life) or progression (remaining human) the true view of reincarnation? By empirical testing, there is no way to tell which theory—if any—is correct. Reincarnation has an uncertain historical origin, most likely Hinduist. (The popular explanation of Egypt and/or a belief that Egyptians believed the idea appears to be refuted by their burial practices. Why preserve the body when the spirit will simply select another?) Its association with negative things like the occult increases the possibility that these are purposefully deceptive experiences. In fact, reincarnation experiences are rarely found apart from either a spiritistic environment and/or altered states of consciousness. People who have such experiences often end up producing information in a trance state, from one of their so-called past lives, the content of which is always unbiblical. This is an obvious problem when the available evidence points to the truth and validity of the Bible.

India's Suffering and Reincarnation

Historically, India, the country that has believed in reincarnation the most, has suffered the most. If reincarnation is fact, the opposite should be true. Also, the vast majority of people never even remember a single past life. If they did, they would more readily accept their suffering for their previous sins in humility, knowing their humble attitude and good deeds would assure them of a better life next time. To the extent that suffering (which is the *payment* for past evil) and ignorance of their past life and misdeeds *causes* people to do evil, the theory is a failure and self-defeating.

Other problems include:

1. In karmic law it is a sin to *stop* the suffering of others; hence a fatalistic acceptance of suffering and evil is the result.

2. Cases of possession may occur during the reincarnation trance experience.

3. How can the inviolate law of karma be held "in suspension" for several lifetimes?

4. If ignorance of reincarnation is a hindrance to spiritual progress, as taught by Edgar Cayce and others, why would the soul, prior to inhabiting a body, cause itself to forget about reincarnation, thus hindering the very progress it is trying to make?

5. The evidence for it almost always stems from altered or abnormal states of consciousness (hypnosis, drugs, occultism), which are clearly capable of demonic intrusion and manipulation.

6. Its Western form is simply an extension of the scientifically bankrupt[3] theory of evolution. Occultist Dr. Cerminara says: "The theory of reincarnation is really the familiar scientific theory of evolution on a psychological and cosmic level."[4] (Possibly no two theories have had more of a combined destructive effect on humankind in the last one hundred years.)

7. The "spirits" at seances are more than willing to give information on reincarnation, and the reasoning goes that they should know, for they are between incarnations. However, their information is often contradictory.

Jesus, the One Perfect Man, Repudiated the Idea of Reincarnation

Finally, for as long as the human race has existed, history records no perfect man except Jesus Christ, and He repudiated the idea of reincarnation. Hence, the only perfect man ever to live has denied its validity (John 9:1-3). (The possibility of sinning in the womb was reputedly a teaching of some rabbis, hence the disciples' question. However, Jesus' clear response is to deny any possibility of reincarnation. See also Matt. 25:46; Rev. 20:10-15.)

Even reincarnationists claim Jesus was more advanced than anyone else—so if anyone would know whether the theory is true, He should. Also, the Biblical records, for which there exists a great amount of evidence, universally oppose reincarnation: e.g., Phil. 1:21,23; II Cor. 5:1,4,8; Heb.9:27, 10:12; Acts 7:59, 17:31; Luke 23:44 (How could a *thief* reincarnate to a high life?!); Psalm 78:39; II Sam. 12:23; John 3:3,4 (obviously not physical); II Cor. 6:2; Gal. 1:8-9, 2:16,21, 3:2,3,10-13,24; etc.

Philippians 1:21,23: "For me to live is Christ, to die is . . . " cyclic reincarnation? *No!:* **"Gain."** "It is far better to depart and . . . " come back to earth in another life? *No!:* " **. . . be with Christ!**"

II Corinthians 5:1,4,8: "To be absent from the body is to be at home with God."

Romans 5:6; Hebrews 9:26: Christ died for our sins—all of them. *One* sacrifice for *all time* (Heb. 10:12). There is no need for us to purge our own sins by several rebirths under the "laws" of karma. They are already taken care of.

Hebrews 9:27: "It is given for every man to die *once* and then comes . . . " reincarnation? *No!:* **"Judgment."** (This verse does *not* say to die *once in each lifetime,* as reincarnationists *reinterpret* it.)

Acts 17:31: There is a coming day of judgment for the whole world. Reincarnation does not believe in a "day of judgment."

Matthew 8:29: Even the demons are aware of it.

II Kings 2:11: Elijah never saw death. It is strange that the very one who, to reincarnationists, gives evidence of their doctrine, in the Bible, never passed through the ordinary channel of death: an unorthodox reincarnation! But even their beliefs are erroneous. Jesus referred to John the Baptist as "Elijah which was to come" (Matt. 11:14). However, in Luke 1:17, it is explained that John was to go before the Messiah in the *spirit* and *power* of Elijah, which is quite different from *being* Elijah. In Matt. 17:3, the disciples saw Elijah as *Elijah,* not as John the Baptist. If John were Elijah, Elijah could not return. He would no longer exist. Jesus thus could not have meant that John the Baptist was Elijah reincarnated. Elijah was still "alive and kicking" as Elijah. Also, in John 1:21, John the Baptist himself stated explicitly that he was not Elijah. (If he could not remember whether or not he was Elijah, he could not have been so dogmatic.) In Matt. 11:14 ("If you care to accept it, this *is* Elijah who was to come."), the "is" is not literal, as when Jesus said of the bread, "This is my body." What Jesus meant was that John the Baptist was the fulfillment of Malachi 4, the messianic forerunner who was to be like Elijah, which he was.

Acts 7:59: Stephen called upon the Lord and said, "Lord Jesus, receive my spirit." He was going into the presence of Jesus (i.e., God, the Ultimate—one cannot go any higher) right *then.* He did not have to go through tens or hundreds or thousands of reincarnations. Also, Jesus was standing up, waiting to receive him.

Luke 23:44: Jesus said to the thief on the cross (a man who, in reincarnationist philosophy, would certainly be reincarnated into a worse life, and one who would undergo many reincarnations yet), "**Today** thou shalt be with me in **Paradise**."

The Bible Opposes Reincarnation

Reincarnation is a very subtle diversion of Satan. It renders ineffectual the major Christian doctrines. If one believes fully in reincarnation, to believe in Jesus as personal Savior is meaningless. Once people believe in reincarnation, there is no fear or expectation of judgment in the next life. Reincarnation denies the Bible at nearly every key doctrine:

Christianity	Reincarnation
Believes in judgment that is eternal, following man's death. God judges us.	States we have many lives, even thousands, to perfect ourselves. We only judge ourselves.
Believes in the atonement of Jesus Christ for our sins.	States we need no savior, therefore denies the necessity of salvation; there is no need for it, according to the nature of "reality."
Believes in the existence of hell as a place, eternal.	States everyone will be "saved" *(absorbed into the divine)* in the end.
Believes in the deity of Christ.	Vague and contradictory views on "God." States there is no need for Jesus to be God—He was just more advanced ("He's been through more incarnations") than most.
Believes in the existence of personal Devil or Satan, and fallen evil spirits—demons.	All evil is a result of man's choosing. Satan is devised by human institution. Evil spirits are held to be regressed human spirits between incarnations, not demons.
Believes in the *Bible* as God's *only* Word to mankind.	Opposes Biblical concepts: e.g., Heb. 9:27. *All* religious Scriptures or writings are communications from God or the spirit world to help man.
Believes in a personal God, revealed as the Trinity of Father, Son, and Holy Spirit.	Denies a personal triune God. Ultimate reality is often impersonal karmic law.

Believes in Heaven as a distinct, eternal place.	Various progressive spirit-realms.
Believes in the sinlessness of Christ.	Denies it; no one is perfect (some may say Christ has *now* reached perfection, but that He was a sinner like everyone else, beforehand).
Believes in the physical eternal resurrection of Jesus Christ.	Denies it; he will come back in another reincarnation, or he has now no need to come back at all.
Believes in personal resurrection and immortality.	The individual person is forever gone upon the next reincarnation.

Finally, the moral implications of reincarnation are considerable. Only three of several will be discussed:

1. Repeatedly in occult literature, we have seen this concept used to justify abortion (the fetus does not become "alive" until the spirit enters it, usually at delivery, never at conception or during the first six months); in fact, spiritistic communications often encourage abortion because the baby is "dead flesh" until delivery. Only "wanted" babies should be allowed to live; only mature parents, etc. should have children. Hence the doctrine leads to irresponsibility and even fornication.
2. Adultery and divorce. This is really an attack on the family unit. Oftentimes people are counselled by spirit guides, reincarnationists, or psychic therapists, to commit adultery or to get divorced, because they did not marry their proper "soul-mate," i.e., one they had lived with in a previous life. If they wish to advance spiritually, they must now join with this new partner or "suffer" the karmic consequences. We have read so many cases of adultery and divorce that resulted because of this teaching that it is clearly a very serious matter. It is also often used as a convenient justification for sexual immorality and for escape from a poor marriage.

3. A tendency toward bisexuality and homosexuality. Male and female roles are transitory, not permanent. Each of us has lived for millions of lives as members of the *opposite* sex. Males may be told they have a female spirit which has chosen to live in their current body and vice versa. Therefore, heterosexual relations are only one possibility. This is one (of several) reasons why so many eastern gurus are bisexual. (Such a view also denies God's created order as given in the book of Genesis.)

Reincarnation is one of the more wicked ideas that has surfaced in the history of human thought. Christians should reject it utterly. It is not surprising to Christians that parapsychology strongly advocates it.

References for Chapter 9

1. Josh McDowell, *Evidence that Demands a Verdict*; Frank Morrison, *Who Moved the Stone?*; M. Green, *Man Alive*; James Orr, *The Resurrection*.
2. For evidences, see J. McDowell, *Evidence that Demands a Verdict*; H. Morris, *Many Infallible Proofs*; F. Schaeffer, *He is There and He is Not Silent*; W. Smith, *Therefore Stand*; Purtill, *Reasons to Believe*.
3. E.g., R.L. Wyson, *The Creation-Evolution Controversy* (East Lansing, MI: Inquiry Press) 1976; J.F. Coppedge, *Evolution, Possible or Impossible* (Grand Rapids, MI: Zondervan) 1975.
4. G. Cerminara, *Insights for the Age of Aquarius* (Wheaton, IL: Quest) 1976, p. 4.

Chapter 10

Is There Life After Death?

In late 1976, *Psychology Today* stated:
> Death is in vogue as a topic of books, seminars, scholarly articles, and classes at every level from college down to elementary school.[1]

A recent Gallup Poll reported that 73% of Americans believe in life after death.[2] Our concern here is defining the correct nature of death and the afterlife. As indicated in chapter six of Weldon's *The Transcendental Explosion* ("The Manson Factor"), the manner in which a culture views death greatly conditions its quality of life.

There is an increasing sociological trend today to view death in a benign, and therefore, nonbiblical sense (I Cor. 15:26). This is in part a result of the increase in eastern and occult movements. However, there is another factor which aims at lending "scientific" validity to the view that death is for everyone something good, a "spiritual advancement" of sorts. This is the "clinical death" research currently being undertaken by several scientists, most notably Drs. Elizabeth Kubler-Ross and Raymond Moody. Dr. Moody has already published his findings in *Life After Life* and *Reflections on Life After Life*.

Clinical Death Phenomena

The Basic "clinical death" phenomena is that some people who are brought back from clinical death have reported being alive the entire time they were "dead." This occurs among people with a wide diversity of religious belief—from atheist to Hindu. Dr. Moody reports on 50 such cases in his book and details the experience. This may vary considerably, but in essence it involves being out of the body and having nonverbal communications with various spirits (e.g., dead friends and relatives) or a "being of light." This entity is very warm and loving and involves the "dead" person in an evaluation of his life by showing an instantaneous playback of the major events in his life.

At some point the person finds himself approaching a barrier or border which he is not allowed to cross over. He is told he must go back to earth, for his time for death has not yet come. The individuals' experience in this other state of existence is so peaceful and joyful that they desperately do not want to return, but find themselves back in their bodies anyway. They awaken in this world, only to find they had been pronounced dead, but were fortunately revived.

There are many questions which need answering here. As space is limited, we refer the reader to Weldon's book *Is There Life After Death* (Harvest House Publishers) which answers these questions in more detail. Tal Brookes' *The Other Side of Death* is also recommended. We can only point out some of the more important considerations. First, these people have not experienced true biological death, i.e., the irreversible loss of vital functions.[3] They were all revived. Judgment does not occur until some time after true irreversible biological death (Heb. 9:27). "Clinical death" is the absence of *detectable* vital signs. Because our machines do not pick up life, does *not* mean it is not there.

Of special concern is the personal impact of these experiences. Nearly without exception, they take away the fear of death. Dr. Moody states:

In some form or another, almost every person has expressed to me the thought that he is no longer afraid of death.[4]

A False View of the Afterlife

In so doing, such experiences provide a person with a false view of the afterlife. Scripture is very clear that *only* the believer in Christ need not fear death (I Cor. 15:54-57). For others, death brings judgment and eternal separation from God (Heb. 9:27; Matt. 25:46). In fact, fear of death and the conviction of coming judgment (Acts 17:30-31; John 16:8; Heb. 2:2,3,15) is part of that which persuades men to consider Christ. What these supposed "after-death" experiences do is to give non-Christians a false security that everything is in order in their lives, and they need not repent. If the after-death state is so blissful, there is nothing to fear in death and nothing to be saved *from*. Hence it is clear that these experiences oppose the Biblical view of death.

It should be pointed out that not every dying person has experiences of this type. Most have none at all, and of those that do, not all are glorious, peaceful ones—some are hellish.[5] However, there are enough cases reported to assume that we are dealing with purposeful deception. These experiences are what we would expect to find occurring in the realm of spiritual warfare (Ephesians 6).

First of all, the experience itself is deceptive. God says that death is an *enemy* to be overcome, not a friend (Ezekiel 33:11; I Cor. 15:26). Physical death is a result of God's judgment upon sin, and for unbelievers it leads to *spiritual* death (eternal separation from God). It does not lead to blissful joy and peace on some other plane of existence, as these spiritistically-inclined experiences would have us believe (Romans 5:12; Genesis 2:17; Revelation 20:10-15).

Second, the actions of the "being of light," whom many people "run into," indicate this entity is *neither* Jesus Christ nor a holy angel.[6]

Third, the dead friends and relatives many people meet cannot really be dead, for Scripture tells us the unsaved dead are confined and in agony ("the Lord knows how to keep the unrighteous under punishment for the day of judgment"), and the saved dead are with Christ (II Peter 2:9; Luke 16:19-31; Acts 1:25; II Cor. 5:8; Phil. 1:23).

Fourth, there is a clear parallel to occult phenomena in these experiences. Thousands of mediums and psychics express the same view about death as represented in these episodes. Considering the importance of the subject of death, as well as the existence of spiritual warfare, this cannot be coincidental. Mediumistic and other occult views of death stem from personal out-of-the-body experiences and communication with spirit-guides, "ascended Masters," etc.[7] Knowledgeable Christians know that these spirit guides, as well as the "dead" that are contacted in seances, are in fact demons impersonating them to deceive people about the afterlife. This is borne out in part by the testimony of former mediums.[8] That many non-Christians who have these experiences meet up with their "dead friends and relatives" is most informative in light of the fact that demons seek to imitate the dead. The famous 18th century medium and biblical antagonist, Emanuel Swedenborg, chronicles many personal experiences similar to the clinical death ones from his own out-of-the-body travels.[9]

The world-famous trance medium Arthur Ford had a "clinical death" experience that was identical almost point for point with the composite experience detailed by Moody.[10] Ford was responsible for getting tens of thousands of people interested in the occult and declared he was "sent back" with a mission to help "remove for all time the fear of death."[11] He was given this "mission" by the spirits he encountered, and it is *precisely the impact* of the clinical death experiences.

Granted that any sustained out-of-the-body experience might tend to make a person believe in the ability to "survive" bodily death, but the interpretation placed upon these experiences is very misleading (assuming they are genuine). That interpretation results largely from meeting "the dead" and the "being of light" who are all living happily on "the other side." Another important factor is that those who research these experiences often end up involved in the occult, and that occultists in general find confirmation of their views of death in the clinical death experiences.

Monroe, Kubler-Ross, and Moody

The three key people currently involved in clinical death or out-of-the-body research—Robert Monroe, Dr. Kubler-Ross (considered *the* authority on death), and Dr. Moody—are all involved in the occult, and all have spirit guides.[12] (Kubler-Ross has some half a dozen.) Much more could be said, and we refer the reader to Mr. Weldon's book for details. However, our research indicates strongly that what we are dealing with here is a demonic deception designed to confirm "scientifically" a false view of death. This is not to say that the experience is necessarily unreal, or that a Christian could not have an experience out of the body—indeed, a few do. However, they are of a different quality, nature, and outcome than the non-Christian ones.[13] Our concern is that Christians should not trust in *any* spiritual experiences that are not in accord with God's Word, or to *allow any seemingly* innocuous, neutral, or genuine experience to add additional theological insight upon which the Bible itself does not comment. Far too many Christians are giving credence to all "Christian" experiences of this type, some of which the authors know to be false.

George Ritchie's *Return From Tomorrow* (Chosen Books) is purportedly a Christian clinical death experience. Yet from personal conversations with Dr. Ritchie, Mr. Weldon knows he believes in reincarnation, numerous chances for salvation after death, that the Bible is not the final authority and highly unreliable, that Paul was a latent homosexual, that Christ does not condemn those who have not believed in Him, that the church of Jesus Christ *must* be involved in psychical research, limited contact with the dead, and supports occult groups like Edgar Cayce's Association for Research and Enlightenment and the Arthur Ford instituted Spiritual Frontiers Fellowship, both of which advocate mediumism. His death experience itself could not have come from God or Christ because it denies Scripture (e.g., it presents the spiritistic view of regressive human spirits lingering about the earth as "ghosts;" dead men's spirits possessing live men's bodies; realms of progression in the afterlife; seeing Christ in non-Christians; second chance salvation; "works" salvation; etc. Yet a respected Christian publisher, knowing Dr. Ritchie's views, published the book anyway. Many of the other new "Christian" books analyzing this phenomena also need to be viewed with caution. When experiences, even Christian ones, are used to add new data about life after death where Scripture itself is silent or contrary, the line must be drawn. The apostle Paul had an experience perhaps "out of the body" (he couldn't tell). What he did say was that he was not permitted to communicate the details of the experience (II Cor. 12). This is in contrast to today's experiences.

One other unfortunate result of these experiences, as more scientists become interested in the phenomena, is the possibility of a "scientific" necromancy developing under the guise of death research. Because they involve contact with the dead, these experiences can be used to promote a "legitimate scientific" basis to study mediumism. If *dying* people experience contact with the dead, how can "scientific objectivity" be retained if we refuse to study *living* contact with the dead—i.e., through mediumism? Again, this is clearly forbidden by God, and it is severly condemned in His Word (Deut. 18:10-12; Lev. 19:26,31).

The overall attitude that has developed because of these reported experiences cannot help but lead to increasing acceptance because they tell people what they want to hear —"You will live forever, and there are no consequences." As Christians we need to present to them the *Biblical* truths of God's love and forgiveness (if they will trust Christ) and of His severe judgment (if they do not).

True vs. False Spiritual Gifts

There are a number of practices which, acccording to

the Bible, are legitimate as expressions of divine spiritual gifts, but Satan will also counterfeit those gifts. As Maxwell Shyte puts it: "tongues, interpretation, and prophecy are what they have in seances! Satan is a good counterfeiter." Perhaps it should be stressed that counterfeiting can only take place when there is also the possibility of a genuine activity. The word "counterfeit" necessarily means that somewhere there is a *genuine* as well. Demonic practices do not mean there are no genuine "spiritual gifts." However, there is clearly a need to be aware that there are Satanic counterfeits.

Another type of counterfeiting occurs when witches and warlocks (strictly, witches are female; wizards or warlocks are male) are able to give healing. Witchdoctors in Africa and other places are demon-possessed mediums who can perform cures at times. However, their cures are likely to be temporary, and the illness may reappear in a worse state, or even return in its original form. With the Christian believer, when sickness is caused by demon influence (and we saw that this is not the only cause of illness), the demon can be dealt with and the healing will be permanent unless that believer goes back to his earlier involvement.

If we accept this concept of counterfeits being associated with evil spirits, even some of the remarkable prophecies about the future become less mysterious. Stan Baldwin discusses a number of these "prophecies" and points out that some of them actually involve sinister activities such as assassination. He argues that many prophecies are declarations of a Satanic intent, sometimes even as to the very place where one of his subjects would commit the particular crime. When the plan is successful the "prophecy" is fulfilled. It is also a fact that many predictions about the future are simply lucky guesses, and often it is the one *accurate* prediction—in a *thousand inaccurate* ones— that makes the headlines. If enough events are predicted, at least one of them might come to pass. Those who hear of that particular "fulfillment" are likely to be fully persuaded as to the reality of the prophetic powers of the person who so "prophesied."

"Speaking With the Dead" is a Satanic Counterfeit

Clearly another counterfeit operation relates to supposed communion with the dead. Sometimes the evidence of communion with departed friends or relatives seems to be very convincing, but again the Bible tells us that Satan can change himself into an angel of light, and that his servants can, too (II Cor. 11). The Bible teaching is that there are legions of fallen angels who serve Satan, and it seems possible that some of these actually accompany individuals, learning all about them, even knowing such things as their voice pattern.

One of the best examples of a man falling into a Satanic delusion relating to his contact with someone who had died was the late Bishop Pike. He wrote a book entitled *The Other Side* which was serialized in *Look* magazine and was also promoted on U.S. television. One result was that occultism was given a real boost. Pike had previously rejected the Biblical teaching of life beyond the grave, but now he claimed that the evidence of his contacts with his son forced him to change his viewpoint. He had noticed the occurrence of various physical activities which made him think his son was trying to contact him, so he consulted a medium. Over a period of time, he was involved with several mediums as they conducted seances; and he had conversation with a being that was supposed to be his son (who also denied Christ as the means of salvation). He was told intimate details which could not normally have been known to the medium, and Pike was convinced that the speaker was in fact his dead son.

At first sight, this explanation (that Pike himself accepted) seemed to be the only logical one—that it *was* his son. However, this is certainly not the teaching of the Bible, teaching which he, as a theologian, would presumably have known.

Known Cases of "Fake" Communicating with the Dead

We have said that Satan is shown in the Bible in one role as an angel of light, and the following comment from

Stan Baldwin's *Games Satan Plays* is relevant:

> One documented case should serve to point up the wide margin for error in the Bishop's thinking. A certain medium, Mrs. Blanche Cooler, supposedly communicated with the spirit of a man killed in battle; his name was Gordon Davies. The spirit, purporting to be Davies and speaking in a voice that sounded like his, described some unusual features of a house, foretold the future, and gave accurate information that was unknown to any of the participants in the seance and therefore was not a result of thought transference from them. This time, however, events proved the communication was not from the departed Davies, because he had not departed. He turned up alive and was shown to have had nothing whatever to do with the seance! What explanation can there be for such things? The Bible teaches that there is a company of fallen spirits which, to use an especially appropriate term, bedevil men. One such spirit enabled the girl described in Acts 16 to foretell the future. Obviously, she was not a fraud, for after the spirit left her, she could no longer bring her masters gain by telling fortunes—a result that would not have come about if she were only faking from the start.

Stan Baldwin goes on to suggest that it would not be a problem for a demon spirit to continually observe an individual during his lifetime and then to impersonate that individual after his death. He would be able to imitate his voice and to tell personal details about his life. He suggests that as this can be done so effectively in the entertainment field, why cannot it be done in the world of the spirits?

Dangerous "Entertainment"

Undoubtedly it can be done—and it is all too true that this is not the only intrusion into the realm of entertainment by demonic beings. Many people who become involved in seances and spiritism start out merely seeking "kicks," in a new form of entertainment or thrills. However, the seance is eventually found to be a trap, and spiritism is a snare.

Entertainment there is, so the literature declares. There is also entertainment in big game hunting, in lion taming, and in crossing the Niagara on a tightrope. Each has its attendant dangers, however, and clearly there are very real dangers in seeking contact with evil spirits.

References for Chapter 10

1. *Psychology Today,* September, 1976.
2. *National Observer,* May 15, 1976.
3. Moody, *Life After Life* (Atlanta, GA: Mockingbird) 1976, p. 103.
4. Moody, p. 68.
5. K. Osis, *Deathbed Observations by Physicians and Nurses,* (NY: Parapsychology Foundation), 1961.
6. Weldon, *Is There Life After Death?* (Irvine, CA: Harvest House) 1977.
7. *Seth Speaks,* by Jane Roberts is one example.
8. e.g., R. Gasson, *The Challenging Counterfeit,* B. Ernest, *I Talked With Spirits.*
9. E. Swedenborg, *Heaven and Its Wonders and Hell,* Swedenborg Foundation, 1940, p. 447-9.
10. A. Ford, *The Life Beyond Death* (NY: Putnams Sons) 1971, Ch. 8.
11. *Ibid.*
12. *Journal of the Spiritual Counterfeits Project,* April, 1977; Thanatology Article, P.O. Box 2418, Berkeley, CA.
13. Weldon, *Is There Life After Death?* (Irvine, Harvest House) 1977.

Chapter 10 Bibliography

1. Weldon and Levitt, *Is There Life After Death?* (Harvest House, 1977).
2. *Journal of the Spiritual Counterfeits Project,* April, 1977, "Thanatology: Death and Dying," P.O. Box 2418, Berkeley, CA.
3. Gerald C. Studer, *After Death, What?* (Herald Press, 1976).
4. Articles on Death, Hell, Judgment, the Intermediate State, etc. from the *Zondervan Pictorial Encyclopedia of the Bible, The New Bible Dictionary, Ungers Bible Dictionary,* and *Bakers Dictionary of Theology.*

Conclusion to Part I

A Tremendous Upsurge in Occult Interest

Though our generation has experienced a tremendous upsurge in occult interest, history shows there have been numerous occult revivals throughout past ages. To show the continuity of occult revivals, we quote from an article "Black Magic as an Unsuspected Source of the Increase in Insanity," in *Current Opinion* of June, 1914 (Vol. 56):

> Something very like a "craze" for "psychism" is spreading through all ranks of society, the result being an accentuation of the increase in morbidity, in neurasthenia, and in downright insanity. Such is the gist of a warning uttered by Doctor J. Godfrey Raupert, who has investigated psychical subjects in Europe and America. The tendency to occultism has been encouraged, he says, by men of science, by exalted personages at various courts and by disinterested inquirers.
>
> The "fad" has spread to the humbler ranks of society. The end of these studies and experiments is in many cases, Doctor Raupert says, the sanitarium or the asylum. Yet, in spite of the frightful danger, there is no attempt to check the propaganda.

All classes of society dabble in these mysteries, which would baffle a Freud of Vienna. Among the intellectuals, we read further, are thousands of men and women who, after abandoning Christianity, have, in search for some kind of spiritual life, plunged into "occult science." Society women and shop-girls, clergymen in large numbers, city clerks and young men with a smattering of self-taught culture, are rushing to seances, crystal gazing, and the invocation of spirits to an extent incredible to one who has not kept track of this cause of emotional disturbance.

Over sixty years earlier, in 1851, there were an estimated 1,200 mediums in Cincinnati, Ohio, alone.[1] This was only three years after the celebrated spiritualist revival of 1848.

An Unprecedented Occult Revival

However, this is not to say our age is a typical one. A wide variety of commentators seem to feel we are in a time of unprecedented occult revival. Although the figure seems too high, a Roper poll of 1977 reportedly indicated occult involvement of all types, direct and indirect, involving 114,000,000. We must show those who need help how they may get it and urge them toward sensible spirituality. People do not have to directly experience the demonic to realize the existence of its counterpart. Those who have found the only available deliverance recognize that it comes only from turning one's life over to Christ, stopping all occult involvement, and breaking all occult ties.

Rationalists and skeptics would be doubtful both of the existence of the demonic and of the idea that deliverance comes only through Christ. However, even the materialistic views of atheists cannot survive, once they experience Satanic power. The British scholar Os Guinness recalls the impact of the occult power on those with the limited materialist view of the world:

> I would only say that for many people who come through L'Abri [a spiritual retreat center

in Switzerland], the reality of these things has become only too real, far too real. And the various times when we have had somebody heavily involved, who has let out the power of the occult into the room, the most shaken invariably are the atheists. I remember a satanist who came to one of our discussions and started speaking about these things. And suddenly like this, like a rush, something just gripped you at the back of the neck. And you really felt the power of evil strongly in the room: totally different to any other experience—like something running up your spine or anything like that—totally different. And the most shaken people in the room were the atheists, and some of them just staggered out into the darkness, crying. It just didn't fit into their worldview—it shook them rigid, and they had no explanation.[2]

When we speak of sensible spirituality, again, we do not refer to the trend toward the East. Oriental metaphysics and its spiritual methodology are often indistinguishable from their western occult counterparts. In fact, most eastern religions are occult systems, hence the term "occult" incorporates these as well. If we examine today's spiritual supermarket of gods, gurus, and kundalini power, we find much that is *insensible,* and little wisdom. The self-potential or "growth" movements—e.g., est, various mind-control groups, etc., only serve to dehumanize people and provide an easy rationale for cruel, immoral, or narcissistic behavior.

Self-Image Eroded

Those who try to find a positive self-image in such movements will only find a dark despair that will further erode any self-worth they started with. Hedonistic groups, such as Nichiren Shoshu Buddhism, or anarchistic cults, such as Anton LeVay's church of Satan, provide only temporary houses for a hollow indulgence. More traditional eastern movements, such as transcendental meditation, yoga, and Vedanta, do little more in the long run than insulate one against the world of morality and the joy of creativity.

Groups such as these—and there are scores of them—will never help people find the desires they long for—meaning, love, peace, joy, challenge, and a personal relationship with God. The end of occult involvement is ruined lives and shattered minds. Those so involved often die in agony, with a sense of somehow being deceived, but they cannot grasp the how or why. Pride, self-delusion, and active supernaturalism kept them from the truth. The authoritarian personality of the new age psyche has been evident in all ages, but today it is predominant.

Thankfully, there are some on the frontiers of the "new consciousness" movement who question the trend. Eric Utne, quoted earlier, remarks:

> Spiritual seeking has clearly reached the proportions of a national trend. Everyone seems to be looking for the answer. So were the people of Germany during the 20's when there was widespread fascination with the occult and a higher rate of Indian gurus per capita than even in the U.S. today.
>
> I ask myself, "Are we, at the *New Age Journal,* in the vanguard of a great social awakening, or are we blindly leading a rush to judgment? Are these times truly unprecedented, or is the New Age simply this season's version of life's same old soap opera? How can we gain a sense of history and measure of common sense? Where have we come from, who are we, where are we going?"[3]

Social Consequences

Occult revivals have social consequences. The drug use, anarchism, sexual perversity, social indifference (or hostility), egoist solipsism, and economic parasitism produced by many of these groups cannot foster responsible members of society. The hundreds of eastern and occult religions in our country will, sooner than we think seriously degrade our quality of life—economically, morally, and spiritually. Ideas have consequences; they produce fruit, and the monist-pantheist-animist nature of these groups will seep into our children and those who make the laws and judgments of the land, and then they will dismantle and shatter our culture. Such issues encompass meaningful survival; they relate to the status of our future and to the quality of our future life.

References for
Conclusion to Part I

1. Slater Brown, *The Heyday of Spiritualism* (NY: Pocket Books) 1972, p. 159.
2. Os Guinness, cassette tape, "The Encircling Eyes."
3. Issue No. 8, p. 2.

Part II
Power From The Stars? — Untapped and Non-Physical Energy Sources?

Chapter 11

The False Claims of Astrology

We have considered intrusions from the East, but the story does not end there. False teachings are coming at us from all directions—even supposedly from the heavens. We consider this as we briefly examine the false claims of astrology.

Some of the facts about astrology are startling. It is estimated that there are 10,000 people who work fulltime in astrology in the United States of America, with close to 200,000 working parttime. The sale of astrology magazines totals a million copies a year, and three out of every four daily newspapers in the United States include horoscopes. Clothing and jewelry are commonly engraved with Signs of the Zodiac, and it is possible to buy computerized forecasts for a few dollars. Increasing numbers of even young students are actively engaged in this revised practice of supposedly ascertaining future events. Even some M.D.'s are recommending it. Norman Shealy in his *Occult Medicine Can Save Your Life* (sic) actually urges that astrology courses be required teaching in the nation's medical schools.

Astrology has become a religion; for many people it has filled what was previously a vacuum. We live in an age when the established Church has, to a great extent, been put to one side, and for many people a newfound interest in astrology fills the gap. However, that is not the only reason for the popularity of astrology. People are insecure and anxious; if they will not believe in the Bible and the hope of the Church in Jesus Christ, then there is likely to be a misplaced readiness to turn to stargazing in order to find out something about the future.

Others are arguing that we are in the age of space exploration and that the stars have their messages for us. Their argument is that if, before very long, we are to be in direct contact with beings from other planets, then we ought to know what we can about the hosts of heaven.

Astrology in Babylonia

Astrology was taken seriously as long ago as the time of the Sumerians in ancient Babylonia, dating around 3000 B.C. It was early believed that the planets were gods, and some of the ancients noticed that the planets moved around the fixed stars. This implied that there was tremendous power somehow associated with the constellations. It was also noticed that they resembled certain animals and other shapes. Twelve constellations were marked off, known as the Zodiac. The twelve were called Aries the ram, Taurus the Bull, Gemini the Twins, Cancer the Crab, Leo the Lion, Virgo the Virgin, Libra the Scales, Scorpio the Scorpion, Sagittarius the Archer, Capricorn the Goat, Aquarius the Water Bearer, and Pisces the Fish. To these *im*personal bodies, *personal* powers—and even homes— were attributed. The gods were all supposed to live in houses, with the various houses ruled by these twelve Signs of the Zodiac.

The signs were supposed to have a very great effect on people's characters and attitudes toward life. Each person was especially influenced by two different signs—first, the sign under which he was born, and secondly, the sign that was rising on the eastern horizon at the moment of his birth. Astrologists tell us that the sun actually moves backwards through the Zodiac, and it takes about 2,200 years to pass through each of the signs. These periods of time are called solar ages.

However, astronomers tell us that astrologers are quite astray in their calculations. The present astrological pattern was worked out about 130 B.C., at the instigation of the Hellenistic ruler, Ptolemy. At that time, it was commonly believed that the stars and the planets revolved around the earth. The fact is that, since that time, the sun has constantly shifted its apparent orbit through the various stars, and now the Zodiac has very considerably shifted out of the astrological timetable. Put in simple terms, this means that everybody is a sign of the Zodiac behind the pattern set according to astrological tables!

It is clearly relevant in the present discussion to notice that the planets Uranus, Neptune, and Pluto were unknown to the early Babylonians, or even to the Greeks at the time that the Signs of the Zodiac were formulated—in fact, Pluto was discovered only in 1930. However, this has not troubled astrologers very much, and they have been able to find convenient ways of incorporating these planets into their schemes.

Influence on a Newborn Baby?

Astrologers also ignore the fact that stars have a beginning and a termination and are not fixed and unaltered in their positions, and therefore they could not have a virtually eternal influence.

According to the astrologers, when a baby is born, at that moment a tiny but very influential part of the cosmic influence (influx) flows into his body and soul; this determines the whole pattern of his life upon earth. If two babies were born in the one hospital at the same moment of time, they would live virtually identical lives. According to this theory, earth is at the center of the whole solar system and the heavenly bodies rise and fall around the earth constantly. A person's horoscope is like the chart that navigators use. Astrologers rely for those horoscopes upon a series of astronomical charts that are known as the Ephemerides. These are supposed to tell what the profile of the sky is from any particular point on earth at a particular time—such charts have been kept since the late 17th century A.D.

The influence of the planets is decided by such profound statements (actually they are absurdities!) as how fast a planet is moving, and how bright or dim it is, and even what color it is. Our intellectual life is supposedly linked to Mercury, our love life with Venus, our courage and aggressiveness with Mars (so if Mars is in the wrong position we will be very timid). The big Roman god Jupiter—the largest planet—will affect our wealth and social status, while mysterious Saturn will have its effect in the troubles of our lives. Uranus deals with our changes, while Neptune affects our dreams and impressions—it is supposed to be the watery planet, and watery things are changing their shape all the time. The newly found Pluto is ignored by some, but by others it is regarded as the name for the Roman god of the underworld, and therefore has sinister influences on our lives. The planets can also convey, so the argument goes, opposite effects, depending on whether or not the planet was in a favorable position at the time of our birth.

The sun and moon are linked as well. The sun is supposed to have its influence on our growth and health, as well as on our vitality and our will. The Selenians (the moon-influenced people) are supposed to be dreamy and romantic. All these planets have a cumulative effect on the individual (so their story goes), but even more important according to astrologers, is the importance of the particular constellation through which the sun was passing at the moment of one's birth.

Absurdities With Astrology

There are other ways in which astrology is clearly foolishness. We have said that it is based on the belief that the earth is the center of the universe, and that all the planets, including the sun, revolve around the earth. It deals with a supposed line along which the sun revolves around the earth, this line being broken into 12 equal parts through which the constellations (the signs of the zodiac) move in succession. This actually means that areas near the poles would be unaffected by astrology for weeks on end when the sun's rays do not reach them.

As there are also important "aspects" associated with the angles made by the planets with the earth, one would need to know the exact latitude and longitude of his birth, and the exact moment he was born. Thus horoscopes that bring all the members of any sign group together (e.g., Scorpios) for a day's reading are necessarily false by the very bases of astrology itself. Another paradox is made clear when we think of identical twins or other multiple births—sometimes one dies at birth or soon afterward and the other lives on for many years. This is an embarrassment to astrology. In any case, if the stars really do have the influences that astrologers claim, it surely would be at the time of conception rather than of birth. It is easily established that the information given by astrologers is quite contradictory at times. People in the millions are following the daily suggestions; but if they were to compare different horoscopes, they would very often find quite opposite advice given for a particular day.

In *Bewitched by The Occult,* some interesting examples are given where horoscopes were compared on a particular day—these being the horoscopes presented by leading astrologers. On one day Virgos were told that they should stay at home, while another astrologer told them that they should go out to the theater. Different pieces of advice were also given to Capricorns—one astrologer told them to be flexible in their thinking; while a second said that caution should be the keynote; a third wrote that they were able to expand and should do so; and a fourth said that if a person was to do something, he should get into it and do it at once. Undoubtedly it is very confusing when the leading exponents read the signs as having opposite interpretations.

The same book goes on to tell of various prophecies which simply have not come to pass. Jeane Dixon is quoted as saying on October 20, 1968, that she stood by her New Year's prediction that Mrs. Jackie Kennedy would not marry in the near future—Mrs. Kennedy married again the next day. The volume quotes the American Society for Psychological Research as stating, "There is no evidence that astrology has any value whatever in revealing the past, the present, or the future fate of any human being, and there is not the slightest evidence for believing that social events can be predicted by astrology."

Undoubtedly, the Christian is warned in the Bible against dabbling in astrology. The Old Testament prophets constantly spoke against such activities. Deuteronomy 18:10-12 is one place where it is made very clear that the judgment of God is on all those who use divination or "observe times" in this way. Those verses state that all who do these things are an abomination unto the Lord. The Scriptures make it very clear that their prognostications are false, as when Isaiah mocked the Chaldeans, implying that the predictions of the stargazers were useless (Isaiah 47:13).

Houses of the Sky—And Precessions

One interesting text on the occult is *The Occult Conceit* by Owen S. Rachleff, Assistant Professor in Liberal Studies at New York University, where he teaches courses on the occult and religion. He has an elaborate statement relating to the "houses of the sky" which are supposed to have influence over the life, death, health, and happiness of human beings. He sees this as a clever invention by astrologers to cope with the problem of precession—which is the subtle shift that takes place in the direction of the axis of rotation of the earth. Because of this, constellations have shifted from where they were 2,000 years ago when the Hellenistic Ptolemy put out his scheme in the Tetrabiblos, about 130 B.C. Since that time, each sign in relation to the earth has moved to the west by about 30 degrees.

Astronomers constantly correct their findings, recognizing the fact of precession, but astrologers have fabricated this concept of "houses" as a way of overcoming the embarrassment caused to their theories by precession. They argue that through these solar houses the constellations are still able to have the same influences they had 2,000 years ago, despite the problems caused by precession.

Rachleff takes the argument even further. He talks about the supposed length of time light takes to come from the nearest star—4.3 light years. He suggests, "Considering the enormous distances of light years and the uncanny illusions of time and space they encompass, and adding to that the faulty perception of the human eye, how can anyone take seriously the influx of a constellation?" Rachleff goes on to show some of the inconsistencies in the IBM horoscope about his own future. He is to beware of the possibility of his appearing arrogant, but then it speaks of his tendency toward complete self-effacement which causes him to be apprehensive and retiring—a contrast to the earlier statements. He is also told that he is enamored of everything, and then he learns that it is feared he may suffer from a "relative inability to love" (p.26). Similar contradictions are stated about his personal ambitions.

Rachleff draws many other conclusions and makes many thought-provoking statements. He states, "The current craze for the occult suggests, it seems to me, a clear and present danger." He states that the danger is becoming increasingly evident with immature persons, both young and old, who are prepared to "govern their lives by the archaic principles of witchcraft and magic, or to conduct their personal affairs and business on the unfounded bases of astrology, numerology, and the Tarot cards" (p. IX).

Some of his comments are very relevant for today. He talks about the present craze for "states of consciousness, the emphasis on intense eroticism and anti-social behavior, and the secrecy and elitism characteristic of occultists throughout recorded time . . ." (p. XI). He talks about their negative ambitions and the religion of the revolutionary.

As an illustration of how far out the so-called astrological ages are, Rachleff makes the point that "the highly vaunted "Age of Aquarius" is, according to popular count, due to begin on March 21, 2000, and with it we may expect the "dawning" of a remarkably communicative, orderly, peaceful, and romantic 2,000 years." He goes on to say, "Astronomers at the Hayden Planetarium have poured cold water over the imminence of the Aquarian millennium. According to their quite conclusive calculations, the so-called age of Aquarius will not dawn until around A.D. 2570" (p.38). He goes on to show that Carroll Righter, a popular American astrologer with a column appearing in over 300 newspapers, has declared that the age of Aquarius actually began in 1904.

Fitting the Facts to Horoscopes

Rachleff tells of a very interesting experiment in which an identical horoscope was mailed to over 100 persons who had given their natal information to a post office box number. The recipients had 12 different birth periods represented by their birth dates, and their varieties were as opposite as could be expected, through Leo and Cancer. Each person was told that the horoscope sent out pertained only to that one person, and basically they accepted it as such. He tells us that "many admired its pertinence and exactitude" (p.38). The fact is, if enough information is given, we are able to find ways in which it fits our own experiences.

The Christian who believes in the Bible as the Word of God will see a dangerous Satanic subterfuge in all this, for a Christian can know true guidance from the Word of God. The Holy Spirit of God is the One Who does have direct influence on a person's life and can lead that person into the knowledge of the Will of God for his life. This is a vastly different proposition from the hoaxes and spurious "guidance" associated with the modern false religion of astrology. Astrology offers a panacea for all ills and an antidote for all that is wrong in the world around us.

The fact is, astrology and many other modern teachings are demonic attempts to turn men from the truth. Satan has always been anxious to confirm falsehood—that was shown right at the beginning, in the Garden of Eden, as we read at Genesis 3:4. Running parallel with this was slander of God Himself—and even in the New Testament the same tactic was used as men said that Jesus was guilty of blasphemy (John 8:44). Satan will do his best to blind men's eyes and to keep the knowledge of the saving Gospel from him (II Corinthians 4:4). The Bible clearly teaches that there are demons and false worship associated with Satan and his fallen spirits (I Timothy 4:1,2; 1 John 4:1-6; etc.). Satan is anxious to enslave men to himself, and part of the tactic is to turn their eyes from the truth. Astrology, together with many false religions rampant today, is part of his overall tactic.

Chapter 12

An Ancient Art In a Modern World

We have said that, traditionally, astrology is linked with the anceint Babylonians, and that it has had worldwide implications for many centuries. Even some of the great monuments of the past, such as Stonehenge, Easter Island, and centers in various South American countries, have links with the beliefs of people about the movements of the sun and other heavenly bodies. When we read of "the hitching place of the sun" and the religious ceremonies in which people were engaged because of the sun's supposed association with fertility and prosperity, we see another aspect of ancient astrology in more recent guise. The Great Pyramid of Cheops, just outside modern Cairo, is probably the most impressive reminder of the importance that ancient people placed on the movements of the stars in relation to man's good fortune. In a number of established ways, it shows that early in man's history he placed great stress on the movements of heavenly bodies.

There were other important evidences of the worship of the moon and the planets. Those great ziggurats (temple towers) that can still be seen in ruins at Ur, Kish, Borsippa, and other sites in Iraq, are continuing reminders of the association of the ancient world with astrology. Some of their knowledge continues on in practical use today, for even in modern times we have basically followed the Chaldean pattern of twelve months per year and twelve divisions of the day (they had double hours—a day was divided into 12, not 24 hours). Their calculation for one year was amazingly close to our own, even though they took it to be the time the sun went around the earth, instead of the earth going around the sun.

These points demonstrate the remarkable knowledge the Babylonians had of astronomy; as a science, astronomy is very different from the distortions linked with astrology. Astrology is at best a young stepsister to astronomy; it is drastically corrupted from the older, scientific knowledge of astronomy.

The Hebrew people were in direct contact with the Babylonians from time to time, and the Hebrew prophets knew the dangers to their people of syncretism (the absorbing of other cultures into their own). They warned against Babylonian astrology, star-gazers, and various forms of divination and magic associated with these people under whom they were eventually in captivity.

The False Worship of Baal
Through the Centuries to New Testament Times

At times the people listened to God's prophets, and blessings resulted. At other times they went their own way, with tragic consequences. At every period of their history the worship of heavenly bodies, and the gods associated with them, was a serious cultural problem. That is shown for mankind in general as early as the incident of the Tower of Babel, with its top inscribed in honor of the heavenly bodies. Moon worship must have been a real problem for the family of Abraham, living as they did in the city of Ur with its worship of Nannar, the moon god.

Later, Joshua challenged the tribes to choose between the Mesopotamian gods and the gods of Canaan—though he himself declared that he would serve the Lord, the true God. The people chose to follow Joshua's lead—away from idolatry—but the problem was a serious one. Baal, the Storm God of the Canaanites, was prominent in the religion of a number of Israel's neighbors at various times of history, not only at the conquest of Canaan, but later also. Thus Baal was "Bel" to Isaiah (Isaiah 46:1), and the Canaanite fertility goddess, Ashtaroth, was "the Queen of the Heavens" to Jeremiah.

Prophet after prophet warned against these false deities; but their continuing presence through so many centuries indicates that they were a major source of opposition to the true God. Astrology offered guidance for the future, as well as wisdom for the present. It was a false "tree of knowledge," intruding into areas that were forbidden to man—then and now. Moses warned against them; so did Joshua; so did Elijah, and Isaiah, and Jeremiah; and so did Paul in New Testament times.

Jesus rebuked those who wanted him to perform "a sign from heaven" (Luke 11:16), and then he warned them of the folly of suggesting that He Himself was utilizing the power of Baal (Beelzebub is a form of Baal, prince of the demons). The Apostle Paul also referred to the Jewish practice of seeking after signs (I Corinthians 1:22); in this they were influenced by the subtle continuance and intrusion of Babylonian religion in the form of astrology.

The Tower of Babel in a Continuing Form

The fact is, the false worship identified with the Tower of Babel has lived on. Astrology became a part of the religion of the Babylonian Empire, and even though the Medes and Persians under Cyrus conquered the Babylonians, the religion of the Babylonians had dramatic effects on their conquerors and their successors.

The gods supposedly gave men wisdom and prosperity, but there was a moral and spiritual price to pay. Both religious prostitution and sodomy were carried out in honor of Ishtar, the Babylonian goddess of love. There was a high rate of infant mortality, supposedly because of the demons lurking ready to snatch newborn babies. Omens from the gods were taken very seriously; treading on a lizard, giving birth to a deformed baby, seeing an unusual bird sitting above a roof, would all be taken as significant. There were dream books to explain the meaning of dreams.

As we study all this we find clear links between astrology and animism, both in Babylonia and Assyria, for both peoples took over each other's gods. The gods of the Zodiac were represented by animals, and these and the powers associated with the elements were likewise revered. The worship of the heavenly bodies was logical to this people, so it was just as logical to worship earthly counterparts.

Only the Hebrews were monotheists in the true sense of the word, for all other ancient peoples thought there were many gods. Even the famous Pharaoh Akhen-aton of Egypt, who tried to insist on the worship of Ra the Sun God, also insisted that he, too, be worshipped—a radically different approach from that of Moses. The Hebrews knew only one God, and throughout their history they have taken an especially strong stand against gods of the sun, the moon, and the stars, and false worship associated with those bodies. They included astrology in the category of false religion.

The later Greeks and Romans also became thoroughly indoctrinated with astrology: the Greeks made much of the four elements (air, earth, water, and fire), and these in turn were symbols of astrology. They were worshipped as deities. There were also hosts of demonic powers associated with these elements—the principalities and powers to which the Apostle Paul referred at Ephesians 6:12. The Christian should not fear these "rulers of darkness," for Christ has released us from them. Like the Babylonians and the Assyrians, the Romans were renowned for their insistence on signs and omens. Great decisions were supposed to lead to successful outcomes only if those portents were favorable. The internal organs of various animals were carefully studied, with a seriousness that had spread through the centuries. It clearly stemmed from Babylon, where they associated both heavenly bodies and animals of earth. Spiritually the Tower of Babel was continuing as a mockery of things divine. The signs of the stars were studied by the Romans almost as religiously as they are today.

We say "almost," for the Romans did not have their hundreds of newspapers with daily charts of astrological predictions. This is a relatively new phenomenon, at least in its intensity. How has it come about? The answer is simple. As we have said elsewhere in this book, the East has invaded the West. *Babylon has come to stay*—no longer a visitor, or even a stranger to be laughed at, or to be ridiculed by "the wise." According to the Bible (Rev. 14:8), Babylon's influence by the end time had spread to all nations. In the realm of religion and spiritual values, that influence has been established through astrology.

The Romans partook of Babylon's spiritual "fornication." Then the great Gospel of Christianity came against it like a flood, and Jesus told His followers that they would be "free indeed." The Apostle Paul and others took up the song of victory through Christ's death, and this was followed by the spread of the Christian writings of the New Testament. The Gospel itself, and the new inspired writings, were eventually widely accepted in the West, and for centuries the occult had little sway. The Bible was not studied by the masses through many years of "the dark ages," but basically it was accepted as the Divine Book. If the future could be known, it would be through that Book: that was the common belief in those centuries of the West where Christianity had spread and had become accepted as the "official" religion.

Christianity was not so accepted in all countries. It is an interesting fact that with the coming of Christianity, the East invaded the West, and wonderful blessing has followed through the centuries. "The gentle influence of Christ" has permeated western cultures in ways of which we are not always aware. It can even be seen in the Constitutions of many so-called western countries with their emphasis on democratic principles, justice, and the equality of men. Conversely, eastern nations which early rejected Christianity have suffered reverses and problems with their cultures that might well have been avoided if their attitude to the Gospel had been different. The West has been blessed even socially by its acceptance of Christian principles.

Then began an "Age of Doubt and Confusion," coming to its climax in the 20th century. Various cultural changes took place—some more subtle than others. Dare we say it? Television has been one—and let it be immediately said that television has tremendous potential for social and other good. Nevertheless, one dramatic side effect of this channel of communication has been to change the whole structure of our society. To some extent, *visitors* in the home have become a nuisance—we wanted to watch "Dallas"—or was it "Barnaby Jones?" Social patterns have become different—we no longer need to go out for our entertainment: we merely turn on the TV.

The argument then goes, "Why bother going to Church? We can watch it on TV." To many this is a serious argument, and sometimes they do in fact watch a Church service—but it is likely to lose out against a much more entertaining program. The habit of church-going—especially on a Sunday evening—has to a great extent given over to film watching.

The same is true for other Church-oriented activities. It is much easier and more relaxing to sit in an easy chair than to go to a mid-week Church service. All this is very understandable, but it means that the person-to-person relationship which is one of the functions of the church has been put to one side. Instead of a living relationship, for many people the remote invitation offered by a screen has taken its place.

All this is highly relevant for the increasing status of astrology in western society today. It is only this generation of "the West" that has taken astrology so seriously—the same generation that has seen the birth of television, and for many, the reduction of "the Church" to the status of just another social institution. It is the same generation that has seen the increasing emphasis on astrological charts with their guidance for the day according to the stars.

Guidance: Light or Night?

Therein lies a great pattern of change. We have said that previous generations sought their guidance from the Bible. That is not to say they all believed in the Bible; nor do all those who read their horoscopes today really believe they are thereby learning about the future. Yet it is true that for many the point of reference has changed; the horoscope has replaced the Bible.

The tragedy is—as we have seen—astrology is so empty and foolish. On the other hand, the Bible is the inspired Word of God. The prophecies of astrology are vague, and generally they do not come to pass. There are exceptions, because if enough predictions are made, some are sure to happen—and of course, those few are the ones that will get all the publicity. Usually the false prophecies are quietly forgotten.

As opposed to that, the Bible prophecies have been demonstrated as accurate time and time again. Jesus was to be born in Bethlehem, to be a great light in Galilee, to heal the sick, to give hearing to the deaf and sight to the blind, to die by crucifixion, and to rise from the dead (among numerous other prophecies, all of which He fulfilled while on earth.) The prophets themselves have been found to be sound historians, for over and over again it has been proven that their writings were actually set against the backgrounds claimed for them—sometimes hundreds of years before the fulfillment of the events to which they pointed.

The *realities* of the Christian faith are there for those who are prepared and willing to see. They offer spiritual satisfaction. By contrast, astrology is a meaningless vacuum. The choice is between light and night: The Bible offers light, while astrology offers only the darkness of night. The wise man will choose that Book of which it can still be said, "Thy Word is a lamp unto my feet and a light unto my path" (Psalm 119:105).

Chapter 13

Did Astronauts Visit Earth In Ancient Times?

We have considered the false claims of astrology and related concepts. What about the claims that earth has been visited by astronauts from other planets?

Clifford Wilson has written extensively in this area *(Crash Go the Chariots, The Chariots Still Crash,* and *War of the Chariots).*

Pyramidology

In *War of the Chariots* he deals with many topics, including the Pyramids of Egypt, "Pyramidology," the Easter Island statues, the Nazca lines, the supposed heart transplants of ancient times, how the Dogon tribe in Africa knew about Sirius the Dog Star, the Kayapo Indians and their straw suits, Australian cave drawings, the Piri Re'is map, Stonehenge, the Bermuda Triangle, the so-called "Electrified Ark," Ezekiel's vision, and many others.

The following survey of some of von Daniken's errors is taken by permission from *War of the Chariots* (Master Books, 1979), which is the record of Clifford Wilson's widely-publicized debate with Erich von Daniken, author of *Chariots of the Gods.* Von Daniken's influence has been vast, his books selling over 30,000,000 copies. We stress here the unreliability of his use of data and of his writings in general.

Many other points could be made to show the unacceptability of von Daniken's writings. Each point could be elaborated, but we have exhausted our space.

1. The Incas were not in Peru until 1200 A.D., not 3000 B.C. as von Daniken claims. Dr. Ann Kendall has worked in the area for ten years and is an expert on Inca building techniques. In "The Case of the Ancient Astronauts" she shows that the Incas were expert stone workers and superb administrators. She commented that it was absolutely nonsense to think of the Incas and primitive people in the same way. In Sacsahuaman alone they organized 20,000 people per annum for their mighty construction works. (Von Daniken refers to the 200-ton stone there as being 20,000 tons! *[Chariots of the Gods,* p. 22].)
2. Even a cursory reading of the Gilgamesh Epic would dispel such ideas of von Daniken as nuclear radiation being the poisonous breath that slew Enkidu.
3. The Sumerian King List was not perpetuated on seals and coins, but on clay tablets.
4. The fall of man and original sin are interpreted as man's lapse into having sex with animals.
5. The angels who saved Lot were robots, according to von Daniken.
6. Genesis 28:12 telling us about "Jacob's ladder" may be an account of loading material into a space ship.

John Weldon has taken the following points from the evidence given in *Some Trust in Chariots*, B. Thiering and E. Castle, eds. The text used is the Corgi paperback edition, 1971, London. The book is a collection of 16 essays by specialists in various fields. The page numbers shown below are first von Daniken's *Chariots of the Gods?* (Bantam ed.), then Castle's book.

7. The "Helwan cloth" does *not* require a modern special factory with great technical know-how in order to make it (page 27 Bantam ed.). The process was known 2,000 years ago (page 8).

8. The structure of the blocks of the Great Pyramid is limestone (soft), not granite (hard). (Von Daniken page 85, Castle page 10).
9. The "nonexistent" rope (page 101) can be seen in Cairo and several other museums. The nonexistent rollers, grain, and huts are also well attested. (Castle pages 10-11,35.)
10. The ancient Egyptians *did* import wood (page 97), from at least 9 different countries. (Castle page 11.)
11. The original height of the Pyramid of Cheops was 481.4 feet, not 490 (page 102; Castle page 11).
12. The area of the base of the Pyramid of Cheops divided by twice its height *does not* give *pi* (pages 99;12).
13. The stone blocks were *not* joined to a thousandth of an inch (pages 11; 12).
14. Granite was cut and used, sparingly, in early Egyptian dynasties (pages 5; 11).
15. The blocks of the Cheops Pyramid averaged 2½ tons, *not* 12 tons (page 84, Castle).
16. Modern engineers *could* build a copy of Cheops; it could easily have been built in the lifetime of a Pharaoh, not 664 years; von Daniken's mathematical calculations are erroneous (pages 100,101,179; Castle page 85). (The Japanese have recently proved it can be done, with their widely publicized modern construction of a small pyramid in Egypt.)
17. Von Daniken's numbers relating to the Mayan calendar accuracy are at odds with each other (pages 125,75; and Castle page 16).
18. The Greenbank Formula is *not* "far removed from mere speculation" (page 141 Bantam). There is considerable uncertainty regarding six of the seven factors in the formula, relating to the doubts about the existence of planets. The values chosen for "L" at the conference were based on much guesswork and were *less than 20, not more than 40,* as von Daniken claims (page 166). "No one really knows the value of most of the factors" (Castle page 17).
19. Velikovsky claimed that Venus came from *Jupiter,*

not Mars (page 155; Castle page 18).
20. Von Daniken says that the remains of an electric battery were found in Mesopotamia. (Castle page 37.)
21. Elephantinos in Greek does not mean "elephant," it means "ivory." The island that he says looks like an elephant from the air, does not. (Page 85; Castle pp. 37, 38.)
22. The Egyptian mummification technique was not imparted by astronauts who knew how to raise the dead (Castle page 38).
23. The Olmec sculpture heads are displayed in museums and *can* be transported—one was recently transported thousands of miles to New York for a special exhibition. (Page 117; Castle page 51.)
24. The most ancient text on Teotihuacan is not "ancient," but is from the end of the 16th century A.D. It does *not* mention that the gods assembled there to discuss mankind before *homo sapiens* existed. (Page 120; Castle page 53.)
25. The tall statues on top of the Pyramid of Tlahuizcalpantecuhtli are wearing feathered headdresses, *not* space helmets; protective breastplates worn in war, *not* advanced units; and the "communication devices" are atlatls or spear throwers. (Film; Castle page 53.)
26. The two wells at Chichen Itza are neither identical, nor perfectly round. The wells are formed naturally when a limestone land-surface collapses over underground water. They were not caused by meteorites or rockets blasting off. (Pages 126-7; Castle page 54.)
27. The line drawing in *Return To The Stars* (now *Gods From Outer Space)* depicts Toltec, not Mayan priests performing sacrifice to the sun god who required human hearts to sustain it and keep it on its course through the heavens. It does not refer to a misunderstood surgical technique of the space visitors. (Page 87 *Gods From Outer Space;* Castle pages 54-5.)
28. The Aztec drum huehuetl is not a space vehicle (film) and their other type of drum, teponaztli, does not depict a circular space ship. (Film and *Return To The*

Stars; Castle page 55.)

29. The Toltec god Quetzalcoatl is *earlier* in origin than the Mayan god Kukulcan, and the accounts of Quetzalcoatl are Toltec, not Mayan. The Mayans describe only Kukulcan. (Pages 127-8; Castle page 56.)
30. The representations of winged gods in Egypt are obviously bird wings, not rocket wings. (Castle page 72.)
31. Von Daniken's statements referring to the third, fifth, seventh, and eighth tablets of the Gilgamesh Epic are *not* in the Epic itself. (Pages 66 ff; Castle page 76.)
32. The evidence von Daniken gives to support the Sumerian Flood story over the Biblical one disproves his own argument. (Page 40; Castle page 77.)
33. All the cuneiform texts from Ur do *not* tell about gods. "I know of no cuneiform text from any city which would match the author's description of what occurs in every Ur text." "No part of this description of the Ur texts finds any basis in fact." (Page 40; Castle pages 78-9.)
34. Sumerian gods *were* represented in anthropomorphic form. (Page 42; Castle pages 79 and 11.)
35. "From the point of view of the Mesopotamian evidence this book is so full of error, misstatement, untruth, as to be worthless" (Dr. Noel Weeks in Castle, page 80).

Errors Relating to Light Years

36. His computation of the number of miles in a light year is off by a factor of 60. (Page 15; Castle page 119.) Also, in *Gods From Outer Space* (Bantam, page 4), *it would take 160,000 years, not 80, to reach the nearest star.*
37. He gives no direct instance of an "artifact from space" (Castle, page 119).
38. Scientists *do not* know that tachyons *"must"* exist (Bantam, page 116). They *may* exist (Castle, page 121).
39. Mars did not once possess an advanced civilization,

nor is Phobos an artificial satellite. (Page 154; Castle page 15.)
40. Jonathan Swift does *not* give "precise" data about Mars' two moons—he is off by a large factor. (Pages 152-3; Castle page 18.)
41. In quoting Einstein's theory of relativity in one place to support his theory (pages 22-3, 165), he undermines his argument in other places (pages 164; Castle page 18).
42. If the "gods" are so advanced, as von Daniken claims, why are the pictures he uses similar to *our* technology? (Page 97; Castle pages 20-21.)
43. Von Daniken admits: "The Pentateuch . . . is a mine of information for my theory, so long as the texts are read imaginatively, with the eyes of a man living in the age of space travel." (Unfortunately, too many other authors are attempting to do the same.) However, how can he trust something he himself believes is unreliable? "The Old Testament is a wonderful collection of laws and practical instructions for civilization, of myths and bits of genuine history" *(Gods From Outer Space,* Bantam 1974, page 155). In *Chariots of The Gods?* he remarks: "The Bible is full of . . . contradictions" (Bantam 1973, page 40). So how do "myths" and "contradictions" support his theory?
44. "The millions of people all over the world (including China) who are obviously eager to accept his [von Daniken's] theories make up one of the most amazing phenomena of a world that seems to be looking for new gods to worship." "The great geographical religions—Hinduism, Christianity, Islam—may well be 'passe'," says von Daniken. "I expect that a new religion will arise, a religion of the unknown, indescribably, indefinable, something we cannot understand" *(Newsweek,* October 8, 1973, page 104).
45. "A potentially viable scientific hypothesis should be capable of standing upon its own feet, relying upon the observed data and carefully formulated, logically derived inferences which themselves are capable of inde-

pendent analysis." (Phillip Grause, *Some Trust in Chariots,* page 118.)

46. In von Daniken's third book, *Gold of The Gods,* he claims to have seen a vast zoo or underground depository of gold animal statues and gold leaf documents in caves beneath Peru and Ecuador. *Newsweek* (above) comments: "Juan Moricz, a Hungarian-born Argentine adventurer who claims to have discovered the Ecuadorian caves, says von Daniken was never actually inside them."

47. Dr. Edwin M. Yamauchi (Specialist in Ancient History, Professor of History at Miami University, Oxford, Ohio) writes in *Eternity* magazine of January, 1974:

    No matter how appealing they may be to the uninformed reader, his suggestions are incredibly wild speculations without any factual basis .... His remarks about Egypt and the Egyptians betray ignorance about even the most elementary facts.

    Von Daniken's misuse of evidence from Mesopotamia borders on madness.

48. Yamauchi remarks that von Daniken does not appear to have even an elementary orientation to ancient history.

49. Carl Sagan (Professor of Astronomy and Director of the Laboratory for Planetary Studies at Cornell University):

    The book *[Chariots of The Gods?*—Ed.] is absolutely dreadful. The only thing worse is the ABC documentary on the subject ("Ancient Astronauts"). ABC's program had every conceivable error. (In *Science News,* Nov. 3, 1973, p. 35.)

50. Dr. Herbert Alexander, Professor of Archaeology at Simon Fraser University in Burnaby, British Columbia commented that "almost nothing in von Daniken's book, related to Archaeology, is factually correct."

(In pamphlet from Bible Science Association, Vancouver.)

Much more could be added. The evidence is surely overwhelming. Erich von Daniken's books should *not* be taken seriously.

That "Astronaut" About to Blast Off

At the debate with von Daniken, a question was asked about the Palenque "astronauts." As this is one of his most forceful arguments, the following critique is highly relevant.

In *Chariots Of The Gods?* (pp. 100-101) von Daniken has this to say:

> There sits a human being, with the upper part of his body bent forward like a racing motorcyclist; today any child could identify his vehicle as a rocket . . . . The crouching being himself is manipulating a number of undefinable controls and has the heel of his left foot on a kind of pedal. His clothing is appropriate: short trousers with a broad belt . . . . And there it is with the usual indentations and tubes, and something like antennae on top. Our space traveller—he is clearly depicted as one—is not only bent forward tensely, he is also looking intently at an apparatus hanging in front of his face.

In that same context von Daniken argues that if this example is not accepted as proof by scholars, then we must doubt their integrity. He even tells us, "A generally unprejudiced look at this picture would make even the most die-hard skeptic stop and think." What nonsense!

What Are The Facts?

1. The original relief comes from a tomb at the Mayan ceremonial center of Palenque in Mexico. It is carved on the lid of a sarcophagus.
2. It was found in 1954, and not 1935 as von Daniken originally claimed.
3. The astronaut has bare feet, and possibly no jacket

at all. We can count his toes—the first bare-footed astronaut? And why no protective gloves on his hands?

4. He is wearing the usual Mayan shorts, and this means that parts of his legs are also not covered.
5. We wonder why he has other typical Mayan-type clothing, including anklets, bracelets, and necklace.
6. His head is outside the so-called rocket.
7. His antenna is no more than the usual Mayan hairdo.
8. The national bird of Guatemala, the quetzal bird, is perched on the top of the "rocket."
9. Serpents are depicted . . . space travellers also?
10. The rocket is actually a throne-chair, with its various components, such as side arm-rest and supporting back, easily recognized.
11. Such thrones were used by Mayans and other dignitaries of neighboring peoples for transport across the country by relays of slaves.
12. These dignitaries had to travel many miles, and for the sake of comfort would sit at various angles, such as reclining as shown in this picture.
13. The inscription is dated to approximately A.D. 683, based on interpretation of accompanying Mayan glyphs. At other sites von Daniken's single visits by astronauts are supposed to have taken place at much earlier times.
14. In a debate with this author in Melbourne he had stated that there was only one visit, though later he has suggested that there were more. (His so-called "third visit" in historical times was "in Biblical times" which appears to extend to 683 A.D.!)
15. We actually know the name of the ruler—Pacal.
16. In von Danikens picture the "astronaut" has his head protruding outside the so-called rocket—it is just as well the rocket is in fact only a throne chair after all! Otherwise it would be blasted off, if Mr. von Daniken's hypothesis were correct.
17. Beneath the seat of the "astronaut" is the "earth monster" who is supposedly the guardian of the under-

world. This is a typical relief and has nothing to do with astronauts. It is a ruler honored at his death.
18. The ruler's skeleton was actually found inside the sarcophagus. (Perhaps the rocket didn't fire after all!)
19. In this scene he is depicted as being in a state of suspension between two worlds, the living and the dead. His so-called helmet is a representation of a corn plant. It is all fitting as religious symbolism on the lid of the dead man's sarcophagus. Now he is taking a dignified journey, with the traditional symbols of heaven and earth around him.
20. The Temple of the Inscriptions at Palenque was in fact a royal tomb. The scene carved on the stone slab actually has considerable religious significance. Nature worship was a basic part of Mayan religion, with corn plants and various fruits important in the understanding of the resurrection of the dead. This pointed on to the promise of immortality for man.
21. Jade was found on the ankles, wrists, and neck of the man inside the sarcophagus—and this contradicts von Daniken's claim in *Chariots Of The Gods?* that jade comes only from China. Jade has been found at other sites, such as some in Mexico and North America.
22. Von Daniken says that "today any child would identify his vehicle as a rocket," and refers to the "darting flame" at the tail. This actually is a two-headed serpent draped over the corn plant symbol and some large corn leaves. The "darting flame" probably represents the roots of the corn plant.
23. "It is not our fault that the stone relief from Palenque exists," says von Daniken on the very last page of *Chariots Of The Gods?* That is true, and its very existence gives the opportunity for an honest reappraisal by von Daniken *if* he really believes this is an astronaut figure, which it clearly is not.
24. A comparison of the same figure in *Chariots Of The Gods?* and then in *According To The Evidence* shows that von Daniken has turned the picture 90° in the

second book, and now the "astronaut's" seat is at a right angle to the floor!
25. Von Daniken has also cropped the picture, so that the arms and back-rest can no longer be seen. One wonders if he has a closed mind against explanations that oppose his pet theories. A systematic analysis of all of Erich von Daniken's mistakes would take another book, and that is not necessary.

Frankly, we have been forced to some regrettable conclusions about his writings. We have been surprised and disturbed at the man's nonscholarly approach to what surely should be a scholarly exercise. Again, comparison of the two pictures (first in *Chariots of the Gods?* and then in *According To The Evidence*) shows that the second is cropped. It has been strongly pointed out to him that this is *not* a space vehicle, and that the design of the chair can be clearly traced. Now the picture is cropped in the later book—there is no chair visible for the discerning researcher to see.

Von Daniken protests at the way he has been attacked, but this example illustrates why.

Von Daniken's Literary Style

What then do we say as we end this survey? Some conclusions are listed below.

Erich von Daniken's own conclusions cannot be taken seriously, nor can his hypotheses be substantiated.

Scientists and other scholars are attacked, their integrity denied, their learning put casually to one side. Instead of such supposedly wrongly-based traditional views, the reader is encouraged by von Daniken to accept *his* views as the authority. He openly acknowledges that he has no formal tertiary education, and identifies himself with the reader as one of those who knows only too well that the scholars have some sort of a conspiracy. They allegedly have secret conferences, distort facts, and refuse to change their point of view when the evidence so demands—even to the point of daring to call von Daniken's own theory "nonsense."

There is little systematic treatment of a subject: indeed, his writings teem with hundreds of subjects. Erich von Daniken tries to speak for archaeologists and historians, astronomers and engineers, cartographers and mathematicians, physicists and physicians—and, of course, theologians. A chapter in *Chariots of the Gods?* highlights the question, "Was God An Astronaut?"

Mysteries are collected, and now they are no longer mysteries—for von Daniken has one simple answer to all those problems . . . Easter Island and the Pyramids . . . the Mayas and the Incas. He says astronauts have visited earth, taught the primitive earth-dwellers certain essential skills, then moved back to where they came from—whether it was Mars, the Pleiades, or some other unknown destination. Von Daniken suggests each of these three, so we do have some measure of choice! On his first Australian visit he stated that "they" were still on their way back to their home "out there." On his latest lecture tour in Australia, he claims there were *three* such visits in prehistorical and ancient times. He changes like the proverbial wind!

How Not to Write!

Erich von Daniken introduces extraneous arguments from which he makes suppositions that are subtly close to the point discussed, but in fact he is guilty of *non sequiturs* (logical fallacies): he draws conclusions that are totally unwarranted by his argumentation.

He confuses time periods, bringing thousands of years together as though they dealt with simultaneous events.

He has a large number of uncorroborated statements.

He correlates cultures that are in fact separated by great distances of both time and space.

He does not recognize the native intelligence of humans in all ages and in all cultures.

He refuses to utilize "Occam's razor," the principle that the simplest explanation is usually the one to accept.

He acknowledges that he puts out some things "to be provocative," an unacceptable approach if he is to be taken seriously.

He contradicts his own statements from time to time.

He builds way-out conjectures on "mysteries" that are very often mysteries of his own making.

He takes unconnected facts and channels them into his own preconceived hypotheses, weaving a semblance of connection around facts and incidents that are not related.

He accepts only facts that suit those hypotheses.

He distorts evidence to make it fit those hypotheses.

He brushes aside opposing evidence.

He belittles scholarship when that scholarship is opposed to his own hypotheses.

He flatters his readers—*"They* know better!"—and presumes they are with him against supposedly inflexible scholars.

He confuses chronological and geographic data.

He ignores the great technological achievement of men who lived thousands of years ago—those achievements can be accounted for only by astronaut intervention, he says.

He appears to know little of great engineering and other activities of our forefathers.

However, Erich von Daniken *has* sensed the human urge for an explanation "from beyond," and has shown very real "psychological" discernment and commercial acumen. He reaches masses of people by his superficially exciting explanations, especially by his insistence on otherworld visitors.

Man is so created that he has a desire to find what is beyond himself, a god or gods whose power is greater than that of man himself. For the one who rejects the God of the Bible, Erich von Daniken offers a plausible, but totally unconvincing alternative. Something similar can be seen in the Old Testament as the Israelites turned to Baal when they did not want to accept the holy standards of Yahweh. Baal was a false god of the heavens, the god of lightning and thunder. The parallels are closer than might at first be obvious.

His writings are blasphemous and dangerous because of their seeming challenge to spiritual realities. They are unfortunate as an affront to scholarship because of their subtle overtones that suggest new learning, but they use methodology, techniques, and even facts in ways that actually distort scholarship.

Why is Von Daniken Accepted?

Erich von Daniken is accepted by thousands because:
1. He offers a new theology.
2. He opposes scholars and scholarship, in such a way as to identify readers with himself—"We know better," is his flattering style.
3. He offers delusion instead of reality to a world unwilling to accept spiritual verities, but forced to reject a materialistic concept of evolution.
4. He offers a new "answer" to life's beginnings.
5. He offers a new challenge of space life to a newly space-conscious generation.
6. His writings have coincided with an increased "respectability" of the U.F.O. phenomenon.
7. He replaces the frustrations of science by a pseudoscience, complete with "von Danikenisms" and mumbo-jumbo jargon.
8. Science has failed as a religion, and for many people von Daniken's plausible (but highly erroneous) hypotheses have filled the vacuum with nonsensical conjectures.
9. Not only does he offer a new creation, a new "god," and a new "science," he also offers a new religion, with empty hypotheses that should be rejected by all men of truth.

The Truth in a Nutshell

Carl Sagan was right when he wrote in the foreword to *The Space Gods Revealed*. "The popularity of von Daniken must, I think, be theological in origin."

The fact is, von Daniken's real attack is not only against archaeology, science, and scholarship. Ultimately that real attack, subtle as it is, is against:

The Bible

ANCIENT ASTRONAUTS/MODERN UFO's

The God of the Bible
The creation recorded in the Bible
The Christ of the Bible
The hope offered by the Bible

His case has failed, and his hypotheses have in no way detracted from the truths of the Bible nor from the teachings of Him Who said:

> I am the Way, the Truth, and the Life; no man comes to the Father, except through Me.
> (John 14:6)

What About UFO's Today?

On October 17, 1973, at 11:00 p.m., a mother of seven children woke from a sound sleep by the hysterical cries of her young son. He was terrified by a "skeleton" in the house. Looking to where he was pointing, she saw a strange figure, 4½ feet tall wearing a phosphorescent blue suit with the head encased in a helmet. Shortly, she and four of her seven children were purportedly taken aboard a UFO where they were herded into a large bright room. The mother was then taken to another room where she was given a complete physical (including gynecological) examination by a strange looking humanoid. Needles were inserted into her head and she was asked many questions.

It appeared as if this creature and the others like it were wearing masks created to look human. They had no ears, but had pincher-like hands. The feet were rounded and shaped like club feet.

Next, the mother and two of her children were placed under hypnosis by a very human-looking entity. While under hypnosis she could observe events around her, but was completely immobile. Her main concern during all this was for her children's safety, although she was also quite indignant at the treatment she had received. She experienced that the beings had no feelings at all for humans, as both she and her children were treated like animals. At times, she felt that the beings were taking her thoughts. She does believe, however, that this kind of phenomena (UFO abductions) are an ongoing activity of the alleged aliens she encountered.

Such is a typical close encounter experience with purported UFO creatures, as revealed through hypnotic regression (Lorenzen, *Encounters With UFO Occupants,* 1976, pp. 340-342).

Experiences of this type (and there are several thousand claimed experiences worldwide) bring to the forefront the issue of UFO's. What are they? Are they real or hoaxes? Are they extraterrestrial or some other known or unknown phenomena? As both authors have published books independently and jointly on this topic, they are familiar with the various argumentation used in support/denial of the many theories put forth to explain this strange phenomenon. The explanations include naturalistic theories (Menzel, Klass), collective unconscious theories (Clark, Coleman), extraterrestrial theories (the majority of UFO researchers), and occult theories (Weldon, Wilson, *et al).* In attempting an analysis of these phenomena, several facts can be noted. First, 80-90% of all sightings will be found to have a natural or normal explanation. Any number of factors may cause people to misperceive aerial phenomena. Second, although some have made excellent attempts at consigning the unexplained residue to known phenomena (e.g., Phillip Klass, *UFO's Explained)*, there remains a residue of genuine unexplained aerial phenomena which is often related to bizarre experiences of humans. Third, an explanation for the phenomena cannot be found in typical "lights-in-the-sky" sightings, but rather in the close encounter experiences people claim to have with UFO's and their occupants. These include close encounters of the third kind (e.g., "chance" happening upon a landed UFO with occupants about), contactee experiences (continued occult communication with UFO entities), and purported UFO abductions, where people report forced removal into a UFO. Our fourth fact is that the various official and unofficial investigations (the U.S. Air Force's Projects *Sign, Grudge,* and *Bluebook;* the Condon Report; Civilian investigations by the four major U.S. organizations NICAP, APRO, MUFON, and CUFOS; the CIA and other Defense Department investigations; the French Government's on-going study, etc.) have not satisfactorily defined the phenomena. Fifth, the UFO phenomena and experiences are of a psychic and spiritistic nature. Sixth, it is highly unlikely that the phenomenon taken as a whole is representative of extraterrestrial activity. Indeed from the viewpoint of purely naturalistic evolutionary theories, it is mathematically impossible.

We believe this phenomenon is occultic, and specifically, demonic. An in-depth examination of the phenomenon leads us to conclude there are various "levels of reality" to the UFO experience depending on its nature (i.e., whether it is a sighting, close encounter, abduction, or contactee experience). UFO abductions are not real events; they are implanted into the mind, but experienced as totally real (as in stage hypnotism). Other UFO experiences are real in that an actual space-time phenomenon may be present, although here, as well, the mind is capable of manipulation.

In broadly examining the world of the occult, we find about half a dozen characteristics that are predominant.

1. The contacting of a higher or supernatural entity, generally, but not always, while in a partial or full trance state, as in mediumism. This contact may or may not involve possession and may be precipitated by the person or by the entity.
2. The contact is often made through supernatural occult means—ouija board, automatic writing, altered states of consciousness, astral projections, yoga, hypnosis, etc.
3. The occurrence of both physical manifestations and violations of physical law.
4. Harmful physical-psychological effects.
5. Messages with a nonbiblical content.
6. Either the person has an occult background and/or psychic abilities before contact, or develops them soon after.
7. A "psychic transformation or illumination" is experienced, usually involving a new metaphysical and nonbiblical outlook.

In our text *Close Encounters: A Better Explanation* (Master Books, 1978), we have examined UFO phenomena in light of these occult characteristics and found a close harmony (Chapters 8, 9, and Appendix A). We have also examined the powers of angelic beings (demons are simply rebellious and immoral angels) as given in the Bible and compared them with UFO phenomena (Chapter 10). We have noted that other researchers have actively cited demonic/occult parallels to UFO's (Chapter 2). We have discussed some of their evil activities and their motives and methods (Chapters 3, 5, 6, and 14). Overall, in light of our own research and that of others, we have come to five conclusions.

1. The UFO's are not extraterrestrial, but originate on this planet.
2. They have been with us throughout all of human history, although assuming different guises.
3. They are clearly capable of evil and deception, although they often feign benevolence.
4. They operate on both the physical and psychic planes, primarily the latter.
5. They are nearly one and the same with occult phenomena.

The significant point is that the above five tenets are exactly and precisely what is expected in the demonic theory.

Although UFO's offer many men a humanistic hope of "salvation from the stars," we must caution them that personal involvement is hazardous, as we have documented.

Obviously, this brief introduction leaves many questions unanswered, and we must refer the reader to our book for a more complete analysis.

Chapter 13 Bibliography

1. Weldon, *Encounters with UFO's,* 1977; (*UFO's: What on Earth is Happening* [New York: Bantam], 1976) Irvine, CA. Harvest House, 1975.
2. Wilson, *UFO's and their Mission Impossible* (New York: Signet) 1975.
3. Weldon and Wilson, *Close Encounters: A Better Explanation* (San Diego, Master Books), 1978.
4. Segrave, Kelly, *Sons of God Return* (Old Tappan, NJ: Spire), 1975.
5. Alexander and Albrecht, "UFO's: Is Science Fiction Coming True?" *SCP Journal,* August, 1977, P.O. Box 2418, Berkeley, CA 94702.
6. Allnut, Frank, *Infinite Encounters: The Real Forces Behind the UFO Phenomena* (Spire 1978).
7. Hymers, R.L., *Encounters of the Fourth Kind* (Bible Voice) 1976.

Chapter 14

Energy Forces and Holistic Health

We have rejected the so-called influences of astrology. We have seen that UFO's involve demonic activity—a form of occult energy. There are various other ways in which humans are involved in seemingly innocent activities that are in fact highly dangerous.

"New" energy forces are in this category, and the following three chapters are perhaps among the most crucial in this book. For one thing, our findings and conclusions in this area will to a large extent determine our attitudes toward the majority of holistic health practices and the movement itself, as well as related fields utilizing similar concepts. If there is one key uniting element within the holistic movement, it is the idea of energy—not energy as we know it (gravitational, electromagnetic, or nuclear), but an unknown "psychic" energy which is purported to be resident within us all and uniting each person to the cosmos.

Untapped Human Potential?

Promoters of the holistic health and human potential movements have begun to view psychicism as the true doorway to the untapped human potential. They see most of our problems as the result of the misalignment of the latent and natural, but scientifically undetectable energy within. To have perfect health, this energy must be realigned—be it through channeling, acupressure, applied kinesiology, or one of the other numerous methods. Even if this unknown energy *is* a key to the holistic health movement, we must point out that historically it also has been the key to the occult as well, and we wish to examine the interrelationships here.

Some of the more reputable books dealing with the subject are all somewhat involved with the occult. They are *Future Science; Healers and the Healing Process; The Realms of Healing; In Search of the Healing Energy;* and *The Holistic Health Handbook*. We should mention that possibly this, or some other type of energy, does exist in a structural form in the human body—we do not wish to deny something or label something occult in the evil sense if it is not truly so. Historically, Christians have labelled some things occult which were later proven to be understood by science. *Occult* involves "hidden." We usually use the term in the sense of direct or indirect involvement with demonic supernaturalism. However, simply because a teaching is occult (in the sense of "secret" or "hidden" in meaning) does not demand that it be *false*. It could be argued that the belief in the spirit world is an "occult" view that, Biblically speaking, we know is true. *It is the interpretation of possible phenomena—and whether or not we should be involved with them—that is the important question*. From Biblical revelation, we know the occult worldview (involving a particular interpretation of man, God, salvation, the cosmos, etc.) is wrong. However, what about their views of energy—are they also wrong? More importantly, how have such views on energy *influenced* or *conditioned* their other beliefs?

The occult (in the sense we are thinking of it) is forbidden by God because (1) it involves direct contact with forces alien and hostile to Him (this is why idolatry is so strongly condemned—the reality of the demonic *behind* the idol); and (2) because it involves things secret or hidden. God says certain things belong to Him alone ("The secret things belong to the Lord our God," Deut. 29:29.). Man is to avoid them entirely.

If such energy as occultists speak of exists (apart from any necessary demonic connection—and we are by no means convinced that it does), then delving into this area is forbidden. This is not so much because the energy concepts are wrong or erroneous (perhaps they are merely twisted as to their true nature—as so much in the occult is), but because they will be (1) misinterpreted, with serious consequences in such areas as the nature of salvation and God; and (2) *coexist* with the demonic world, i.e., with demons and their activities. God did not make us in such a way that we can function either safely or effectively in such an environment, even if it were neutral, which it clearly is not. Who knows what demons can do in their own environment or what interrelationships exist, or can be manufactured between their world and ours? We were not made to fly around in astral realms. Granted the existence of the demonic, one is playing in an astral pig pen, filled with evil, cunning, and hostility.

Even Daniel Had to RECEIVE Extra Power

We were also not made with the intellectual capacities to separate the good (or neutral) from the evil, or the true from the false, etc., in the occult realm or teachings. For example, the prophet Daniel was a brilliant, wise, and Godly young man. However, even he had to be given additional special wisdom from God to be able to have discernment in occult matters (Daniel 1:17-20). (His "involvement" in Babylonian occultism is clearly an exception to the Biblical norm of avoiding the occult entirely. It was required because of circumstances relating to the Babylonian captivity and God's purpose for Daniel in his influence upon the Babylonian and Persian empire.) Thus involvement in the occult will always produce faulty conclusions because man, being a fallen creature, does not have the necessary equipment or abilities to sort out such matters.

Two examples will suffice to show the problems here:

(1) the idea of a universal energy (which we *could* define as God—in part) proves either we are all One or we are all part of God. Therefore man is not separate from God, but *is* God and needs no redemption. This is exactly the conclusion people have come to by experiencing occult states of mind and occult traveling. Such a view is deceptive from the standpoint of the Gospel. (2) Some argue that this energy appears to be neutral and can/should, therefore, be used by man for man's (evolutionary-spiritual) advancement. Such a view completely leaves out the demonic. Jesus said that Satan, a liar and murderer from the beginning, comes *only* to destroy (John 10:10). How can men guarantee themselves freedom from injury or deception?

Also, the question with which we are dealing here is of a different nature than previous cases of mislabelled phenomena. It is important to realize this. The difference between (a) the energy now under discussion and (b) the previously "secret," almost entirely unknown, but later-discovered *sciences,* is that in the *former* (a), people are almost entirely investigating psychics and their powers, then interrelating them with historical magic and occultism. The other (b) deals in purely scientific realms and does *not* bring the occult into the laboratory.

Scientific and Occult Contrasted

Electricity, magnetism, and quantum physics were all discovered through scientific principles based on previous science, not through occult principles based on occult experiences. This is a crucial distinction. The fact that quantum physics is producing paradoxes *does not* give us the right to assume that it, therefore, (1) scientifically validates the occult—it does *not;* or (2) because there are some similarities between *theoretical* physics and the occult, we can therefore investigate the occult with impunity. The recent research purporting to connect the eastern-occult view and science, (e.g., *The Tao of Physics, the Dancing Wu Li Masters, Stalking the Wild Pendulum,* etc.) deals more with appearance than reality. Also, some, if not many, of the "new consciousness" scientists who support a merger of science and eastern metaphysics are themselves involved in eastern-occult philosophy and practice. They are, therefore, only too happy to justify their activities by molding science into conformity to their worldview. The issue is how much of the purported relationship is real and how much has been contrived or unnecessarily extrapolated? More conventional scientists are so far unimpressed with the data purporting to show a relationship.

When all is said and done, the key question, which to some degree answers all others, is, "Can researchers, Christian or non-Christian, involve themselves in experimental research into this energy with *assurance* they will not thereby involve themselves in the occult, i.e., demonic?" Our extensive research into this topic leads us to conclude that further investigation in this area could be hazardous and should be avoided.

It is not always easy to determine *when* there is involvement with it. Thus, for example, speaking strictly neurophysiologically, acupuncture appears to be a neutral tool, useful for dealing with chronic pain in *some* individuals. However, *if* it is tied with an occult energy philosophy and a practitioner of that worldview, then it may be easy to find oneself involved in the psychic realm. A psychic can often make a neutral practice or tool occultic. This happens a great deal with what are termed radionic devices. The device itself has no power (although many can think so); the psychic effects come from the psychic ability of the practitioner, not the device (dowsing rods, pendulums, Abram's black box, etc). Radionics is really a form of occult psychometry, "aided by" a mechanical apparatus. Eventually the apparatus is dispensed with, but the psychic abilities remain. Hence in the field of health, *who* is doing the doctoring is of vital concern. As far as possible energy systems are concerned, there are far too many unknowns in this entire area, and too close a tie into historic and contemporary occultism to make investigation of this area safe. Having given such a warning, we now examine these problems in some detail.

The Basic Concept of Holistic Health and How It is Used

Dr. Tiller of Stanford suggests: "From experiments on telepathy, psychokinesis, manual healers, and traveling clairvoyance, we seem to be dealing with *new energy fields* completely different from those known to us via conventional science."[1]

Is there a revolutionary "new" principle in nature, heretofore unrecognized by science? Does an unknown, neutral energy flow throughout the universe? Is this energy behind the various manifestations of psychic power? Does man contain within himself a latent, structured form of this energy, thereby uniting him to the universe? Is this energy Divine? Can we develop and utilize it by turning within? Such are a few of the questions being raised today, sometimes by scientists, but mostly by parapsychologists.

Such questions have been answered in the affirmative by occultists of all generations. But why has the holistic health movement been so preoccupied with them? The answer is found in the sources of the holistic health movement itself. As so much of the movement is derived from eastern-occult presuppositions and metaphysics (dating to antiquity), it is hardly surprising to find the same questions being generated. Nor will it be surprising to see affirmative answers given to them as the movement advances to maturity in worldview of its historical parent—as is already the case in some circles. As White states: "These and other [primitive-animist, eastern-occult] traditions claim to recognize and in some cases control a vital cosmic energy underlying paranormal phenomena. It seems likely to some investigators of the paranormal that important clues for understanding the physics of paranormal phenomena can be found through scholarly examination of the documents and oral traditions of these ancient esoteric-occult paths."[2] (We should warn the reader here that reading occult books can be dangerous, and we do not advocate it in the slightest.)

A good introductory statement on the holistic health

worldview is by Elizabeth Kent, Assistant Editor of *The Yoga Journal,* which is heavily involved in the movement:

> At a very real and basic level, the holistic practitioner recognized the interconnectedness of all life in the continuous dance of the atoms and sees the individual as an integral part of a vast energy field that includes dimensions and levels of reality we can but dimly fathom. Holism, then, embraces the old and the new, the physicist and the mystic. It is a total way of looking at ourselves and our relationship to the larger Self, the universe . . . we are . . . little mini-universes imbued with a healing power that most of us have yet to tap.[3]

Bernard Green states flatly: "Holistic Therapy offers everyone the opportunity to develop psychic abilities."[4]

With long roots reaching into historic eastern and occult doctrines, it is not surprising that a central tenet of the holistic health movement conforms to their teaching on the deity of man.

You Are Divine (According to the Holistic Health Movement)

As TM promoter Dr. Harold Bloomfield told the 2,000-member 1978 San Diego National Holistic Health Conference: "In your essential nature you are divine and that's a major focus of our holistic health movement."

At the 1977 national conference, Sufi Pir Vilayat Khan expressed similar sentiments when he said that the motto of the New Age, part and parcel with the holistic health movement, is, "the awakening of humanity to the divinity of Man."[5] A year earlier at the 1976 conference, Dr. Jack Gibb stated "the absolute assumption that a lot of us are making in the holistic health movement is that . . . I believe I am God and I believe that you are [God]."[6]

In the first holistic health conference in 1975, William McGarey, whose holistic health research is based on the spiritistic Edgar Cayce readings, stated that everyone's core nature was Divine.[7] Along with this occult attitude often comes other antibiblical themes. George Emery said at the 1978 San Diego Conference: "Jesus did not come to die," but to provide spiritual (emotional) wholeness for man.

From its inception, the holistic health movement has proclaimed that man is God. *The pathway to this divinity is this "new" concept of energy.* A representative sampling of statements by holistic health practitioners will give us an idea of the various forms and qualities the concept can take. Rev. Jack Lindquist refers to "the healing power of the Universe, which many call God."[8] James Fadiman states: "We are primarily energy—or magnetic, or whatever [else] you like—forms around which matter adheres. Our primary nature is not physical."[9]

Ruth Robertson refers to "The intelligence that infuses all nature . . . the healing energy . . . the energy we call love."[10] Evarts Loomis, M.D.: "The life of man, in all its phases, is inseparably linked with every other form of life. Health and disease are due to the balance or imbalance of the living forces that compose the universe. Expanded (i.e., psychic) consciousness depends upon the inflow of primal energies variously referred to by different cultures as the Logos, Prana, Chi, Buddha Nature . . . cosmic energy, etc." ". . . finally the duality disappears into wholeness that says, *We are all one* . . . ."[11]

William Tiller discusses the implications of this new energy and his belief that there is a logical succession downward (to finer levels of reality) from matter to chemistry to conventional energy fields, to nonconventional energy fields; "Underlying that is a frame of mind that is embedded in the frame of spirit; all is embedded in the divine."

> One is that there are new energies which we have never dealt with before in physics; second, that we have within our organisms sensory capacities for cognition of these energies; third, at some level of the universe, we are all connected . . . fourth, time, space, and matter are all mutable. We can perceive events out of our fixed location in space: that's remote viewing [clair-

voyance]. We can perceive events out of our fixed location in time: that's precognition [divination]. Some people can materialize and dematerialize objects. If one can do it, eventually all will do it. Fifth, it appears that, whatever we think of as reality, it isn't what we perceive at the level of the five physical senses. We perceive a relative reality, but it isn't an absolute reality, which is something beyond. Sixth, it appears that at this point in time we (mankind) are developing another sensory network at a tremendous pace because the [occult] phenomena that used to be so exceptional in our previous history are now occuring by the tens of thousands every day.[12]

"The Universal Life Force" from the Occult

What Dr. Tiller has described are some of the implications and consequences of the new energies, essentially, eastern-occult doctrines; in their order: (1) parapsychology (science and the occult), (2) latent psychic powers in everyone, (3) universalism, monism, pantheism, (4) occult powers, (5) *maya,* the Hindu idea the world is an illusion, (6) a planetary occult transformation-evolution.

The Center for Integral Medicine, a group of medical professionals in Pacific Palisades, California, states: "Members of the Center view the universal life force as a benevolent process that stimulates and supports human development."[13] The Energy Rhythm House, sponsored by the Mandala Society, declares in a brochure that its theme is "the correspondence of the Rhythms of energy between the natural world, the universe, and the microcosm, man." Its activities are "designed toward helping man to become sensitive to the vibrations of these energy rhythms inside of himself." The Association for Holistic Health defines holistic health as, in part, "becoming aware of higher levels of consciousness."[14]

George Meek, surveying 10 years of research by 14 investigators on the energy underlying psychic healing and surgery states:

> These findings constitute a veritable Pandora's box filled with phenomena that will force us, when confronted, to rethink our concepts of the universe and the nature of man's mind and spirit, as well as the cosmic energies manifesting through him .... Fundamental changes in psychology, medicine, science, and religion will be suggested by this new knowledge once it has been refined, developed, and utilized."[15]

All these statements not only presuppose the existence of a cosmic energy, but that it is neutral or benevolent and applicable to man's use and control. These are unwise and even dangerous assumptions. *We have no reason to believe that this energy is truly part of God's creation and subject to heretofore unknown laws.* It has the characteristics of demonic energy, and as such it will always elude scientific grasp (while simultaneously being available to occultists), because it is something related to, or part of a living, thinking, mobile entity and is entirely "other-worldly," or supernatural.

Coddington, in an historical examination of this energy begins by stating:

> The search for a specific unknown energy, an energy with the power to heal, has obsessed the human mind and spirit since the beginning of civilization. For centuries men of genius have tried to harness this strange, enigmatic force and enlist it to the aid of science. Thus far it has remained slightly out of grasp, eluding its would-be captors with an almost capricious tenacity and always escaping definition.

She concludes at the end of her book, "In essence it continues to be a mystery...."[16] Interestingly, she points to a very intriguing characteristic of this energy: "Frequently related to certain powers of the mind and *portrayed as having an intelligence of its own,* the phenomenon began to emerge as part of consciousness itself."[17]

(Emphasis added.)

Is there any other energy we know of which can be described as having an intelligence of its own? Are we really dealing here with "new" dead energy, or with something old, but alive? Is it an entirely impersonal law, or more closely related to personal intelligence? As White and Krippner state: "There is still no absolute proof that energy . . . is involved in these unusual events . . . . Although the words 'new' and 'revolutionary' may occur frequently . . . bear in mind that many of the new phenomena have probably been known to humanity for millenia and that Western science is only now 'catching up' to what various other traditions have recognized in different ways from early times. The phenomena are only new to science—not to the totality of human knowledge."[18]

Why is this true? Is it because any systematic attempt at investigation fails, until science is redefined? Why have we not discovered them as *science* until now? Is it because of the western world's increasing acceptance of the occult—as in parapsychology?

The Importance of the Concept of Nonphysical Energy

The idea of a nonphysical energy which somehow unites man and the cosmos is central to the majority of techniques found within the holistic health movement: Acupuncture and acupressure (related forms of acupressure include shiatsu, Jin Shin Do, Tsubo Therapy, "Touch for Health" (involving applied kinesiology), yoga acupressure, Do' in, G-Jo, Jin Shin Jyutsu, and several others),[19] homeopathy, Reichian therapy, polarity therapy, yoga, applied kinesiology, and many others. While there are variations in name, theory, and use of this energy, the basic idea of a still unknown, yet essential energy, with connections to the cosmos, is evident in all these techniques.

There are two very broad categories of use involving this energy: one where the energy is *passively* acted upon, and another where it is *actively* used. In the former, e.g., various acutherapies, it is supposedly misalignment of this energy which leads to illness. The argument is that most, if not all, illness can be traced to this energy misalignment, and the various therapies seek to realign and properly integrate it with the whole person. Among psychics, this same energy is used to perform various psychic feats. Hence, there is a more active, outward use of the energy.

Although the former categories see the energy as innate and part of the spiritual nature of man, the latter mostly view it as an energy coming into them from an outside source and see themselves as channels of some higher power. These two categories are anything *but* clearly divided—e.g., yoga (with *innate* prana) develops psychic powers (an *outward* force). In fact, in yoga it is the prana itself, channelled from the universe, which, when properly channelled through yoga breathing and exercises, develops "cosmic consciousness" and the psychic powers that attend it.

In the former broad category, there may be the view of a tight interrelationship between the outward energy of the universe and its coming or acting upon the energy in the body.

For example, Nui Gung (a Chinese form of healing) employs the projection of energy *into* the body. It is rather difficult to make distinctions with such various forms of energy, as they are so closely bound together in history, theory, and practice. The fact that we know so little about how these nontraditional or alternate "medical" therapies function is probably explained by the fact that so many of them are tied to this enigmatic energy concept.

The task is to discern its origin—whether the energy is natural, divine, demonic, or some combination. For example, there is the possibility of (1) God's omnipresent "substance" (energy); (2) man's existence *in* God (Acts 17); (3) demonic use of their own energy—or man's; (4) the environment; (5) some heretofore undiscovered energy.

In Chapter 16 we will attempt to answer this question by looking at the history, various manifestations, and uses of this energy, the nature of man, and the worldview implied by its existence. We will also examine the fruit it has borne in man's use of it. We should note that only one of the above five categories seems capable of consistent strategic activity on behalf of spiritual warfare.

A Realignment of Energy?

Although it is difficult for many people to believe that these various practices could possibly be related to spiritual warfare—even the demonic (they are clearly related, at least potentially, to the occult)—we must ask a question. The basic premise of most is the idea of a realignment of energy to produce health. Most "followers" believe that, regardless of the name, the same energy is being dealt with. Reflexology and other forms of acupressure seem innocent enough (regardless of how effective they may or may not be)—i.e., touching various body points in order to supposedly realign supposed energy. *But,* in yoga we find *prana* being purposely directed for *religious*—not merely anatomical— purposes, and psychic powers invariably result from sustained yoga practice. Psychic healers utilize their energy to do psychic feats.

If this energy can be so used (obviously demonically) in these cases, then why cannot the energy called *Chi* in Acupuncture or orgone in Reichian therapy—and on down the list—also be used in a similar manner whether or not they exist? Could not the *idea* of such energy, even if it did not exist, become a cover for covert spiritistic activity? There is another consequence of this idea of latent energy—it turns people to an energy source within themselves for satisfaction and meaning in life. Because the energy is usually thought of as divine, it insulates one from the Gospel. Being already "divine," we do not need divine help.

Also, the very idea suggests the possibility of untapped psychic potential, and one who believes he has this energy potential inside himself is much more likely to try to develop its power (particularly within the metaphysical context of most holistic healing teachings), than one who does not believe it exists. It points to power within, as opposed to the Christian view of power from God Who is apart from and outside man. For example, several books and movements advocate a process which deliberately energizes the *chakras* (yoga's purported psychic centers) as a means to develop psychic powers. In fact, *many holistic healing groups utilize the manipulation or release of energy only as a prelude to psychic or spiritual (occult) awakening.*

Man will always try to develop such energy, whether because of lust for power, personal problems, dissatisfaction with life, curiosity, or some other reason. It will point him inward toward self-sufficiency rather than outward for salvation from Christ.

It should also be pointed out that historically, revelation of a nonphysical anatomy came through psychic means (whether acupuncture *meridians,* nadirs, yogic *chakras,* etc.).

Appendix to Chapter 14

Evidences for the Occult Nature of the Holistic Health Movement

Because of the current popularity of the holistic health movement, the following appendix is relevant:

A. Various articles on occultism from the first four major conferences (1975-78) sponsored by the Association for Holistic Health/Mandala Society. (The first four journals contain scores of references to occult ideas/topics, etc.)

1. "Applying Edgar Cayce readings to the Daily Clinical Practice of Medicine"
2. "Cancer Research Based on Readings Given by Cosmic Awareness"
3. "The Qabilistic Model of Wholeness"
4. "Clairvoyant Diagnosis"
5. "Altering Consciousness"
6. "An Electronographic Study of Psychic States Obtained by Yoga"
7. "Psychic Diagnosis ' (utilizing spirit guides)
8. "Creating Miracles—Side Effects of Holistic Health" (utilizing the spirit-written *Course in Miracles*)

9. "Scientific Applications for Altered States of Consciousness"
10. "Experiencing Spiritual Healing—A [Psychic] Healing Service" (with medium Olga Worrall)

In addition each conference had numerous workshops involving occult topics led by psychics, e.g., "Developing psychic abilities in the diagnostic process," Robert Leichtman; "Scientific Evidence of Psychic Phenomenon," Valerie Hunt and Rosalyn Bruyere (a spiritist); etc.

B. Apparently, few of the holistic health centers around the country are uninvolved with the occult, at least to some degree. The 1,164 entries of holistically-oriented groups in the resource guide *Holistic Dimensions in Healing* are overflowing with an eastern-occult orientation. Also, perusal of literature collected over the last two years indicates courses taught in various forms of divination (e.g., I Ching), psychic healing, astrology, yoga, spiritism, shamanism, cultivation of trance states, etc. Considered together, virtually no aspect of the occult is left out.

C. Large bibliographies on the movement invariably include a significant number (sometimes a majority) of occult books.

D. Various sundry data.
   1. *The Holistic Health Handbook*, one of the definitive texts within the movement states on page 14: "Although most holistic practitioners avoid rigid dogma, they do seem to agree there are certain universal laws, which provide a common framework for the movement. These concepts emerge as consistent themes throughout the articles, and readily suggest the outlines of a holistic health philosophy." *Eastern Concepts With the Holistic Health Movement.* Three of these major themes are: (1) an acceptance of a generalized eastern-occult worldview over the western; (2) a wholly pragmatic attitude—of primary importance is that the treatment works—an absolutely suicidal spiritual stance, given the

ENERGY FORCES AND HOLISTIC HEALTH

biblical reality of spiritual warfare and the indefinite nature of the energy with which they are working (little concern is expressed about *how* a technique works or the source of the energy); and (3) the Universal Life Energy.

Other themes include:

a. reincarnation/karma
b. spiritism/shamanism
c. man is part of God, or is himself God
d. yoga practice
e. the expansion of consciousness through meditation and cultivation of altered states of consciousness
f. hope for the dawning new age of spiritual evolution and psychic awareness. (There is even a section on psychic shiatsu.)

Interestingly, the demon Seth (e.g., *The Seth Material, Seth Speaks,* etc.) showed up in several places in the handbook—once in an article on psychic Patricia Sun, a powerful psychic who demonstrates her "healing sounds" at conferences about the country. "I don't even make the sounds unless I've worked with everyone enough to get them to a certain state of [psychic] openness. Much of what I do is intended to open people enough so that they can receive the sounds when I make them" (p. 277). Patricia Sun's sounds are possibly not human. They certainly don't *sound* human. It turns out that one day she was listening to tapes by Seth II (a cousin of Seth who makes rare appearances through Seth's medium, Jane Roberts). He gave a lecture on sound, and then at the end of the tape Patricia Sun notes that "his voice goes off into the same sound as the one I make" (p. 275).

It's not particularly surprising that Seth should make the sounds of the holistic health movement—we are simply surprised at the extent to which he keeps popping up in so many different contexts.

2. The holistically oriented Academy of Parapsychol-

ogy and Medicine was founded by a psychic dream; its President, Robert Bradley, who pioneered natural childbirth in the U.S., says, "I'm a great believer in spirit guidance.... The talks I give, the ideas I have on natural childbirth came to me either in sleep or from direct spirit communication."[20] He is a medium: the academy's purpose is to promote psychic healing.
3. A partial list of major speakers at holistic health conferences who are either mediums or psychic healers, or promote them, are: Robert Bradley, Olga Worrall, Paul Solomon (whose spirits told him to instruct his daughter in astral projection—"I assure you I am not a psychic," he says), Patricia Sun, William and Gladys McGary, Robert Leichtman, Rolling Thunder, Elizabeth Kubler-Ross, Thelma Moss, Dolores Kreiger, Irving Oyle, Norman Shealy, Jim Polidora, Valerie Hunt, Rosalyn Bruyer, Alan Levin, Gerald Jampolsky, Marcus Bach, Henry and Evelyn Allen, William Tiller, George Emery, Vernon Craig, and John Ervin. Probably 80-90% of the speakers at national holistic health conferences support the occult in one way or another.
4. *New Realities Magazine* (the old *Psychic*), which specializes in many forms of occultism, has subtitled itself: "The Holistic Health and Human Potential Magazine."
5. *The Psychic Yellow Pages* is a guide to 130 people and organizations in Northern California. The holistic health section lists several people and organizations. It is clear, if this is a representative sampling, that many of the holistic health practitioners of various therapies have psychic powers. Most all were involved in "energy channeling."

Christian Holistic Health?

We should also note that there *is* room for a distinctively Christian holistic health. Providing the eastern-occult methods and philosophy of the movement are disregarded, *what remains is sound* (e.g., preventive medicine, less reliance on drugs and surgery, advocating more personal responsibility for one's health, treating the cause instead of the symptom, etc.). Paul Reisser, M.D., and John Weldon have both critically analyzed the occult nature of the holistic health movement and provided a sound alternative based on biblical philosophy in their book, *The Holistic Healers: A Candid Look at the Old Occultism in the New Medicine* (1982).

References for Chapter 14

1. Tiller, "New Fields, New Laws" White & Krippner, *Future Science,* p. 29.
2. *Psychic,* Feb., 1976, p. 38.
3. Elizabeth Kent, "Toward Holism," *Yoga Journal,* July-Aug. 1977, p. 6.
4. "Holistic Living—The Key to Psychic Power," *Fate,* Jan., 1979, p. 64.
5. *The Journal of Holistic Health III* (San Diego, Mandala Society), p. 23.
6. *The Journal of Holistic Health II* (San Diego, Mandala Society), p. 44.
7. *Ibid.,* Vol. 1, p. 49.
8. *Ibid.,* Vol. 2, p. 5.
9. *Ibid.,* p. 13.
10. *Ibid.,* p. 70.
11. *Ibid.,* p. 71, 73.
12. *Ibid.,* Vol. 3, p. 46.
13. Brochure from the Center, "A Healing Center"—A Preliminary Prospectus.
14. Brochure from "The Association for Holistic Health," 1977.
15. Meek (ed.), *Healers and the Healing Process* (Wheaton, IL: Theosophical) 1977, p. 10.
16. Coddington, *In Search of the Healing Energy* (NY: Warner) 1978, p. 12, 182.
17. *Ibid.,* p. 12.
18. Coddington, *op. cit.,* p. 26-27.
19. *The Acupressure News* (Santa Monica, CA), Vol. 2, No. 2, p. 4, 15.
20. Bradley, "The Need for the Academy of Parapsychology

and Medicine" in the *Varieties of Healing Experience* (Academy of Parapsychology and Medicine), (Denver, CO, Box 18541), pp. 100-101.

Introduction to Chapter 15

In the holistic health field, there are vital issues through which to sort. Not unexpectedly, many of the so-called "cures" in this diverse field do not result from the specific kind of treatment undertaken, but from other sources. These include experimenter bias or personal expectation, e.g. it is possible that mental optimism may trigger an immune system response resulting in physical improvement. The therapy itself, though not responsible for the improvement, may appear to be the source of the improvement. If the therapy has occultic, unscientific, or unbiblical aspects, the possible "cure" is not worth the risk.

In many of the holistic practices we find psychic associations which are unsettling. The founder of Polarity Therapy, Dr. Randolph Stone, was a member of the occult Radhasoami sect and author of the occult-oriented *The Mystic Bible*.[1] The founder of Psychosynthesis, Robert Assagioli, was for several years an Italian representative for the occultic Alice Bailey movement/Lucius Trust-Arcana.[2] Bernard Jenson, founder of Iridology, calls the occult sect of the Rosecrucians his "spiritual abode," and uses a form of astrology in his practice.[3]

It is thus crucial that one fully investigate any therapy contemplated—from inception, through philosophy and treatment, to consequences. Spiritual discernment is needed today in areas that are not usually considered spiritual. This chapter provides information about where such discernment is needed.

[1] Punjab, India: Radha Soami Satsang Beas, 1977.
[2] Alice Bailey, *The Unfinished Autobiography,* p. 224-225.
[3] Interview: *Rays From the Rose Cross,* May, 1978, p. 226-229.

Chapter 15

The New Medicine

There is today a virtual explosion of "new" methods and techniques of diagnosis and healing. Many of these are not in fact new, but have been practiced for hundreds, even thousands of years. In fact, we suspect that most of them date from antiquity, although their historical counterparts would involve certain cultural variations and obviously, sometimes technological limitations. We do not set out to cover all of them, and the ones we have included are discussed in summary fashion, as entire books have been written on each. *As nearly all of these methods are controversial, more exhaustive research on our part could possibly alter our conclusions on any topic, and* **hence these are preliminary findings.** In any unknown area, particularly where the occult may be involved, we advocate caution and wisdom. In some of the following areas, clearly occult elements exist, and hence, these are to be studiously avoided.

The major alternative medical techniques are acupuncture, acupressure and sonopuncture, iridology, witchcraft, chromotherapy, sound therapy, kinesiology, radionics, astrologic medicine, chiropractics, orgonomy and bioenergetics, biofeedback, alphagenics and meditation, hypnotic regression (reincarnation therapy) the various body therapies (reflexology and zone therapy, polarity therapy, Rolfing, the Alexander Technique, functional integration, Do'in, Shiatsu, etc.), homeopathy, kirilian photography, and nutrition and herbology. Many of these depend on oriental philosophy which presupposes the idea of a universal energy which flows through humans and may be manipulated with the proper techniques. If the "energy flow" is obstructed or out of alignment, disease can result, and the proper energy flow must be restored (or so it is alleged). It is as if illness is not really caused by degeneration, sin, poor living, or man's finiteness, but by misalignment of the universal energy. If we could keep this energy functioning properly, we could perhaps live forever. Man is a god unto himself, as flowing through him is the ultimate reality, the universal energy. Man is not so much (morally) fallen as, simply, ignorant of the universe about him. Energy, not Christ, is the point of contact with the Divine (or, ultimate reality). Acupuncture and its related systems, most of the body therapies, and orgonomy are examples of such systems that are dependent on the idea of a universal energy. It is not uncommon to see this energy referred to in divine terms. Hence the pantheistic and unbiblical implications of these techniques are rather obvious. Nearly every system we discuss is to some degree related to either eastern philosophy or the occult. For example, many people are unaware that there may be occult elements in homeopathy, chiropractic, applied kinesiology, and oriental massage. As eastern cultures are generally occult, any technique relying upon their philosophies or worldview must be approached with caution. Clearly nonscientific methods should be avoided. There is always the *possibility* that *a few* of these alternate systems may have a scientific base or in some ways be neutral and useful. In analyzing any unknown area we should ask the following questions:

1. Does the method depend in any way upon the psychic sensitivity of the "healer?" Is it possible to distinguish between (a) techniques that demand psychic sensitivity to work at all, and (b) techniques which use the therapy

only as a vehicle for occult powers? For example, in areas of borderline medicine or anatomy (or the psychic anatomy of the eastern philosophies) how is the line drawn between unknown anatomical function and psychic working? Even some chiropractors depend on psychic sensitivity to do their work.
2. If the philosophical or religious basis of the technique is eastern or occult, to what extent, and how does this influence or affect the technique itself? Does the method *depend upon* a certain underlying religious philosophy in order to operate successfully? This is possible, for example with the martial arts. How does this influence or affect the outcome of the treatment?
3. Has the technique been proven through the scientific method, and is it generally accepted by the medical community?
4. Where areas of both science and the occult are present, can the latter be entirely removed without destroying the effectiveness of the former, and the treatment?
5. In areas of borderline science where it is unclear exactly where science ends and the occult begins, are the benefits to be gained worth the risk of possible involvement in the occult? (We say no.)

Distinguishing occult elements in many areas today can be difficult. Sometimes, a subject can, on the surface seem to be legitimate, yet a study of its history opens up clear occult ties. This causes one to suspect the founder's motives, as well as the ultimate impact the technique will have upon a person, regardless of any temporary benefit. It can be very difficult to know just how to assess such a treatment, although we would advise caution. The problem is partially one of degree of the legitimacy of a concept like "the occult of today being the science of the future." Also, many entirely neutral inventions have come from occult sources (e.g., the xerox machine). How can we make wise decisions here? Obviously using a xerox machine is fine. However, much of parapsychology's "new technology" is clearly psychometric in nature, i.e., ultimately depending on the psychic powers of the operator, rather than the apparatus itself. Until a great deal of scientific testing is done (which we cannot endorse, because it may involve the experimenters in the occult), we cannot know what is psychometric and what is neutral. Hence, many of these areas are extremely difficult to decide upon, and there may be no easy answers. Our conclusion is easy enough, although some will reject it as overly cautious: if there is a suspicion of anything occult, it is wiser to abstain from involvement. For us, to advocate any other position, knowing the consequences of occult involvement, is irresponsible.

Unfortunately, we cannot answer all of the above five questions in relation to each of the alternate medicines. Much more research would need to be done. The reader may wish to consult Weldon and Reisser's *Holistic Health and Occult Medicine* (1982) for a more in-depth treatment of some of these areas. What we are providing here is an introduction to these areas and pointing out certain data and implications that may not be well known. We hope this will help the reader to better understand the trend of these techniques. Obviously, in any borderline area treatment the reader is considering, we would urge that he take the time to answer the above five questions to his own satisfaction before undertaking the treatment. One of the most important areas here would be prayer and seeking others' counsel. Rushing into some new technique simply because "it works" is foolhardy. One must know *why* it works and with what else the treatment is associated. After all, the *drawing* power of the occult is that it *does* work. But the consequences are a radical disintegration of the person involved—psychologically, spiritually, and even physically, oftentimes resulting in suicide, psychoses, or death.

With these preliminary (and cautionary) statements, we now turn to an introduction of the various medical alternatives.

Iridology

Iridology is the diagnosis of the state of the physical body through the condition of the iris. It has been used by some German physicians for decades. Although the opinions about this technique vary from the totally fraudulent to extraordinary, at least ten different systems of eye diagnosis exist. Exactly where the truth lies is difficult to state, but iridology seems to offer a combination of both pseudoscience and the occult, depending upon how it is defined and which system you are talking about. It is true that certain physiological conditions can have a visible effect on the iris, as in certain forms of rheumatism. But is it possible that the detailed charts assigning a small segment of the iris to corresponding anatomical regions could have some merit? This is still doubted by the vast majority of physicians. The chart most often used was devised by naturopath-chiropractor Bernard Jensen of Los Angeles, who based it upon his examination of 250,000 eyes. His book, *The Science and Practice of Iridology* (1948) is one of the standard works on the subject.

According to Jessica Maxwell, author of *The Eye-Body Connection,* a self-help book on iridology, the "basis for iridology is the neurooptic reflex, an intimate marriage of the estimated half million nerve filaments of the iris with the cervical ganglia of the sympathetic nervous system. The neurooptic reflex turns the iris into an organic, etch-a-sketch that monitors impressions from all over the body as they come in."[1] She says the only exception is when an organ is surgically removed, as then its corresponding iris reflex point freezes in its presurgery condition and never changes again. As defined by optometrist Dr. James Carter, O.D.:

> Iridology or iris diagnosis is the art and science practiced through the observation of the texture, pigmentation, and density of the iris whereby the physical condition and activity of all special organs and/or systems of the body are directly and most profoundly observed. Structural defects, chemical imbalances, toxemias, inherent weaknesses and predispositions, tensions, endocrine disorders, et al, are observed through direct iris examination. The location and stage of in-

flammation and often the etiology or cause can likewise be determined. Reflex responses to diseases in other areas are most readily detected. The basic premise from which the above definition is derived is that each organ or tissue area of the body has a corresponding locus within the iris, which undergoes "microinflammatory" change simultaneous with the change at the organ level during its imbalance or disease states.[1a]

According to International Iridologists in Escondido, California, there are an estimated 10,000 practitioners in Europe and 1,000 in the U.S. The popular press is carrying more and more articles on iridology, much of it of a doubtful nature. For example, purported recent studies by Russian scientists, as reported in the *National Enquirer* of May 23, 1978, (which is often not accurate) were said to indicate a possible medical base for iridology. In a study of over 1,800 people, Dr. Eugeni Velkoven, head of the department of neurology at Patrice Lumumba People's Friendship University, and Dr. Fyodor Romashov stated they had charted positions of spots on the iris which directly correspond to over 90 areas in the body. "We were able to check the positions of the spots on the iris against the confirmed diseases of 1,273 patients. Without exception, the positions of the spots directly corresponded to specific areas of the diseases." The irises of 603 healthy people showed no spots, and they believe they can diagnose with 100% accuracy if spots are present. (The spots tell the location of the disease, not the kind.)

According to proponents, iridology cannot name a specific disease, but it does record past physical changes and warns of various trouble spots within the body, e.g., heart lungs, back, sinuses, etc. It has apparently been practiced for centuries. Dr. Carter states the first book published on the subject was *Chiromatica Medica* by Philippus Meyen (Germany, 1670). More recent studies include Ignatz von Peczely, *Discoveries in the Field of Natural Science and Medicine* (Hungary, 1880); Nils Liljequist, *Diagnosis from the Eye* (Sweden, 1883); Henry Lahn, *Iridology, The Diagnosis from the Eye* (U.S., 1904); Bernard Jensen, *The Science and Practice of Iridology*, (U.S., 1948); and T. Krieges, *Fundamental Basis of Iris Diagnosis*, (England, 1969).

Until recently, iridology has been the almost exclusive domain of chiropractors and naturopaths. However, some physicians are becoming interested in the topic, particularly, it seems, those with a certain metaphysical bent, e.g., Dr. James Carter. It was largely a result of Jensen's book that Carter became interested in studying iridology and he eventually became a "convert." He is now in the forefront of recent developments indicating a possible change in attitudes brewing in some circles. He has taught iridology to numerous doctors in the San Francisco area and is conducting studies at San Francisco General Hospital. The research there involves "several double blind studies on the accuracy and reproducibility of the schematic or homunculus (miniature body) relationship of the iris fibres and the body, and also some study into the possible pathways involved in iris changes as a result of systemic disease."[2] However, as we have said, iridology is rejected by most scientists because it has little scientific basis. Dr. Kurt Koch received a reply from opthalmologist Dr. Velhaged in answer to his question on this.

> On behalf of the medical faculty I am replying to your question on eye-diagnosis. It must first of all be said that it has nothing to do with the exact sciences. We are dealing here rather with a wild conglomeration of pseudoscientific expressions and more or less superstitiously-based theories, to put it mildly. For example, some eye-diagnosticians claim that through looking at a person's eyes they can say if the patient's grandfather died from a stroke, or if the patient himself will commit suicide. Others even go as far as predicting whether the suicide will be a bloodless one or not! Starting from the anatomically based fact that each organ of the body

is furnished with nerves and also with so-called "life nerves," the eye-diagnostician maintains that each mental quality and characteristic is localized by means of sympathetic fibres in particular areas of the irises, and that a mere fleck in the iris is sufficient to prove that the patient has a poor liver, or is envious and greedy, and so on.

Eye-diagnosis can be traced back to astrology and originated in China. It has frequently been the subject of whole series of tests and has been found to be completely untenable. In the medical science of ophthalmology it is recognized that many common illnesses can be diagnosed from the state of the eyes, but in these cases the illnesses are known to affect the eyes directly. A negative result is thus no indication that the body is in a state of health, but within limits a consideration of the state of the eyes can be a help in the diagnosis. It is true that one can actually see part of the brain tissue by looking at the optic nerve, and that the blood vessels of the eye are sufficiently exposed to allow one to see the circulation of the blood. However, this is not the same as having all the organs of the body represented in the irises.[3]

Dr. Koch is less concerned with the anatomical than the theological aspects. He points out there is clearly a mediumistic form of eye-diagnosis which can have serious consequences for the person on whom it is practiced. He gives several examples.[4] It may involve occult elements other than psychic diagnosis, e.g., fortune telling. Dr. Koch says that in about 6 of the 10 forms, it does not appear to harm one's faith, however he is concerned that people be warned of the occult aspects. He states:

> Many of our healers and occult practitioners use eye-diagnosis mediumistically rather than medically. That means that they are only interested in the iris as a mediumistic contact. In this way the human eye serves a psychometric pur-

pose in much the same way as hand lines do when a fortune-teller uses them as contact material or as an "intuition stimulant." When this is the case, eye-diagnosis becomes a form of fortune-telling. Because of this, these eye-diagnosticians are often very successful. Indeed some of them with little or no medical training can diagnose illness with 100% accuracy.[5]

Dr. Carter, who as we have said, is at the forefront of research in this area, may also possibly be promoting the psychic aspects. When asked whether or not a psychic aspect was involved, he replied:

> Intuitive skills do come into play here, and whether we want to call this "psychic" ability or not (it remains to be defined . . . what do we mean by "psychic?" Is that just a paranormal state? It is very easy to label it as such.) We may find that these skills are just a further progression of the conscious ability of an individual . . . a kind of hyperconscious or ultraconscious state.[6]

Dr. Carter also employs a kind of syncretism with iridology, which is easy to do. He has attempted to integrate it with oriental medical philosophy, as well as biochemical and nutritional concepts. Medical science has not paid too much attention to iridology because it felt scientific studies to refute quackery were unnecessary. With the increased interest in iridology, the medical establishment began to change its mind. Thus one of the first scientific studies done was reported in the September 28, 1979, issue of the *Journal of the American Medical Association*. The researchers gave iridology its best shot. Two of the three iridologists had been "using the technique as their primary method of analysis of patients for more than 40 years;" one of them was the most famous iridologist in the world, Dr. Bernard Jensen. After giving the iridologists every chance for proving the usefulness of their technique, they failed miserably. The researchers' conclusions are worth reading carefully. The test dealt with detection of kidney disease.

The 2.5% level of renal disease diagnostic accuracy with iridology—only 11 of 20 patients with disease are correctly identified, while 421 normal people are identified as having disease—does not warrant reliance on this technique in the detection of renal disease.

Clearly, none of the six observers in this study derived data of clinical importance or significance. Yet, the negative implications are significant. Iridology is a practice of growing interest among those turning to holistic health care and alternative methods. Offering the dual attraction of simplicity and mystique, it provides to some people a welcome alternative to the often painful and indisposing diagnostic procedures of traditional medicine . . . .

The results of this study show that there is no value in iridology as a screening technique for detecting or diagnosing kidney disease. Patients should seek other, more traditional diagnostic means to draw conclusions in conjunction with their iris examination. Beyond this, one must question the negative value. There is the serious potential psychological harm to the subject of carrying the burden of detected "disease." Of greater interest to physicians is the false-negative "analysis." One of the observers (an iridologist), who employs the technique and draws conclusions based on it, correctly identified only 26% of the patients undergoing dialysis as having kidney disease. Physicians are well aware of the harm that can come to these patients if they were to rely on iridology and thereby go without proper treatment.

In conclusion, there is no simple classification on iridology. Some forms are clearly occult. Others combine elements of eastern philosophy. It is doubtful that it has any *scientific* diagnostic ability, but as is true with a great deal of the holistic health movement, it also is often integrated with the worldview and practices of the individual doctor. If the doctor is psychic, some accurate (occult) diagnoses may be given, but again this would result from the psychic capacity of the physician, not the sensitivity of the iris.

Chromotherapy

Colors are used in healing in a similar manner to the way numbers are used in numerology. Colors and numbers are completely neutral, but when placed into an occult system, become tools for occult use. As Dr. Blair states, "Chromotherapy, the practice of healing with color, has long been a part of occult medicine."[7] As an example, we could note its use by H. P. Blavatsky, a strong medium and founder of the Theosophical Society. Psychics who use aura diagnosis may utilize its alleged color patterns as a means of detecting physical problems. Occultist Corinne Heline, author of dozens of books and a heretical magnum opus on "Esoteric Christianity" states that truly effective color healing requires occult powers: that "thorough diagnosis requires the powers of extended [occult] vision whereby the patient's aura may be examined and the lack of a specific color accurately noted."[8] She also brings to light the association between astrology and chromotherapy. Each of the signs of the Zodiac has its own (occultly perceived) color and corresponding anatomical regions. Color therapy works best in conjunction with casting horoscope charts:

> All color treatments, when used in conjunction with the harmonious aspects by transit of their corresponding planets, will produce quicker and more lasting effects, particularly if the individual horoscope is also taken into consideration.[9]

Obviously chromotherapy is a pseudoscience lacking any scientific basis. For example, if we examine several advocates of the practice we find divergent views on the primary healing color. To Heline it was yellow, orange, rose, green, or lavender, to Edgar Cayce, green, and to Wallace and

Henkin, either gold or orange.[10] Heline further digresses into primitive medicine by even relating all diseases to one of the "four elements"—fire, air, water, and earth:

> We have noted that the twelve signs of the zodiac are divided into four triplicities correlating to the four elements in nature and also that these same divisions correlate to man's lower quartenary or the threefold body, together with mind, which constitute the composite vehicle in which the Ego functions on earth. The same fourfold classification pertains to diseases, all of which fall into one or another of these four groupings.
>
> To illustrate, infirmities caused by alcoholic excesses, fevers, high blood pressure, and that most dreaded disease of all human scourges, cancer, all come under the element of Fire. All forms of insanity and drug excesses relate to the Air element. Diseases of the stomach, digestive tract, the assimilative and glandular systems come under the Water element. All abnormal growths and malformations of the body belong to the element of Earth.[11]

Occultists have always tried both to deny and escape the effects of the Fall and to have mastery over the environment themselves, even the cosmos. Rather than *turn* to God, they wish to *become* Him. This is why the occult has concentrated so heavily upon disease, death, and the future—all conditions over which man has no control. We can see this hope is evident in chromotherapy, as well. Note also the antimedical bias, so often a form of cult religion (Christian Science, Jehovah's Witnesses, etc.).

> The New Age preventive against epidemics, which will replace the present barbaric custom of vaccination will be the scientific use of color. Each ductless gland, for example, possesses what we may call a "color power" which is the energy radiation visible to extended etheric vision. When properly focused, this color power will

> overcome and eradicate certain diseases caused by a lack of the stimulus native to that color .... When the color flow is sufficiently powerful, the body will become immune to the particular malady under consideration.[12]

Once man has control over disease, death, and the cosmos, he will be as God is. As an example of the occult nature of chromotherapy, we note one of its treatments, "bathing in color:"

> The occult student should be able to do much for himself through color visualization. "Bathing in color" is not mere fancy, but fact. Regular periods of daily meditation in which the affected organs are flooded with the color necessary for their re-invigoration will be found to be most beneficial, both from a physical standpoint and in the cultivation of powers of concentration and visualization.
>
> The envelope of Life Spirit [universal life] which encircles the earth, bears the healing yellow ray of the Christ. Immersing the physical body in a bath of this Christ ray is most efficacious in healing maladies of mind and body.[13]

Without wishing to deny the possibility that colors may affect health in some unknown or indirect way (certain colors may be individually emotionally soothing), or that there may be unknown aspects about the nature of color (can LSD users "hear" color?), it is still true that chromotherapy is occult and involves entering a forbidden domain requiring psychic sensitivity. Dr. Koch states:

> Colour therapy is a speciality of New Zealand. It is basically a form of radiesthesia which we have described more fully in the section on the use of a rod and pendulum. We must again say to the rationalists that this is not just a pack of lies and all a matter of fake. Healings actually do take place. Yes, it does help people—but the price is high.
>
> All methods of healing involve the ideas of

> diagnosis and therapy. Well, what does this entail in the case of colour therapy? For diagnosing they use a divining rod, or a pendulum, or a mechanical pendulum called a motor skopus. The diagnosis is based upon mediumistic powers and not on the scientific background which colour therapists actually claim.[14]

He then lists several case histories involving the psychometric use of color therapy, e.g., "color therapists" who could diagnose the illnesses of people in other countries via a hair, handkerchief, etc. One person simply had to concentrate in his mind and immediately perceived the illness. Obviously such knowledge is not determined by color, but by occult means. Dr. Koch also states:

> Having come across and observed mediumistic forces for over 35 years of work as a Christian counsellor I can say that although these forces are not to be directly equated with the demonic, they are in fact an open door to the devil's work. And as I have said, I have seen what these forces can induce in a person who has contact with them, and the evil effect they can have on one's Christian faith, character, and psychic health. For this reason I cannot warn people too strongly against the use of colour therapy and similar practices.
>
> Much confusion has been caused in New Zealand through preachers of the gospel either actively or passively using colour therapy. Why do Christians dabble with such forces instead of calling on the Lord for healing or for the gifts of the Holy Spirit?[15]

Witchcraft

Occult healing is fairly common among witches and in covens. Witch Justine Glass in her *Witchcraft, the Sixth Sense* gives several examples.[16] The title of her book is yet another example of the concealment of psychic powers under the guise or pretense of latent human potential: the supernormal abilities of witches allegedly are not unnatural or demonic, they are simply a sixth sense into which we can all tap. However, witches are also known for contact with their "familiar" (spirit guides), and although some witches may think their powers are latent, they are not. Witches also make use of psychometry in their healing.

Sound Therapy

There is a fair amount of research being conducted on sound waves and their impact on the human body. There are about 50,000 ultrasonic therapy units in use by physicians and physical therapists which are used to relieve pain and promote healing in muscles and joints.[17] The Food and Drug Administration recently issued mandatory safety standards due to "wide discrepancies made for the equipment and its actual performance, which ranged from production of too little energy to provide effective treatment to too much, causing burns, swelling, and nerve damage."[18]

It is indisputable that sound can greatly effect people, as shown by an incident recorded by Dr. Blair:

> A French engineer, Professor Gavraud, nearly quit his job at the top of a Marseilles office block due to perpetual illness until he discovered that because of its particular proportions and materials, his office was resonating at an inaudible frequency to an air-conditioning plant in a neighboring building. The frequency was making him sick, but he was able to cure himself simply by recovering his walls with a less resonant material. Gavraud became fascinated by sound, and, intrigued by the whole range of low frequencies produced by the French police whistle with a pea in it, he built a giant six-foot version of it powered by compressed air. The unfortunate technician who first tested this whistle died instantly, a post mortem revealing that his internal organs had been thoroughly scrambled by the sound.[19]

We see no harm in using sound waves as therapy, provided they are used under competent medical supervision. However, there is also a need for caution, as this is a relatively new field. Of greatest concern to us is the occult use of sound, using sound as a vehicle for occult purposes. Dr. Blair states:

> But if resonance is not contingent on volume so much as on pitch, it is the dimensions and proportions in frequency which remind us again of the occult traditions. In both Mexico and Peru there is a legend which tells that the ancient peoples were scientists of "sound," with which skill they had no need of technological impedimenta. They could split massive stone slabs along precise harmonic lines with sound alone, and then "resonate" them into position. Thus the vast and precisely laid temples of Uxmal and Machu Pichu were raised and patterned—according to this legend—in symphonies of sound. Their religion recognized each individual as having a particular note and pitch. With the "sound knowledge," a man could be "purified" and raised by vibrationary mantras or, conversely, slain by a single note. An echo of this is found in the "kiai" of the Samurai warriors in medieval Japan. The biologist Dr. Lyall Watson suggests that when uttered at the correct pitch, the kiai " . . . produces partial paralysis by a reaction that suddenly lowers the arterial blood pressure."[20]

Blair's reference to notes literally killing people is reminiscent of Yoga authority A. Avalon's conviction that "A man may be killed or injured by Mantra."[21] Mantras are special words believed to be imbued with occult powers and used in eastern meditation. Almost always they have corresponding *devas* (gods or spirits) which accompany them and help the meditator accomplish his purposes of gaining power, wealth, control over others, etc.[22] In essence, we have here a form of ceremonial magic—magicians often use certain "words of power" to obtain their desires through ritual (culminating in possession by the spirit). Apparently, within the spirit world, the use of certain words is a known accepted method of contact and reciprocation. The mantra is used to empty the mind, attract the spirit, and when he is possessed, the magician bids the spirit to do his will.[23] In this case, the spoken mantra itself has no power, but the spirit who places himself behind it. The mantra has become a focalization for occult power.

Dr. George W. Peters, Professor and Chairman of the Department of World Missions of Dallas Theological Seminary, declares in Montgomery's (ed.) *Demon Possession* (Bethany, 1976, pp. 199-201):

> It is my impression that the focalization of demonic powers in objects and practices is the secret of "magical" powers of charms and fetishes. Here also is the secret of the potency of the "curse" in witchcraft, sorcery, the evil eye, etc. Let no one imagine that words do not carry power, that they cannot become embodiments of dynamics. It is so with the Word of God. His Word is power-bearing. It is a living and powerful Word. Can the opposite be true also? Can words become bearers of destructive forces? Can the curse carry paralyzing effects and the power of death? . . .
>
> Two things, however, are clear. First, the Bible realizes the reality of evil in these practices. It does so not because they are superstitions and pagan cultural and religious "hang-overs," but because they are *embodiments of evil*. Second, the Bible condemns such practices without compromise and apology.

A more direct relationship between sound itself and the occult involves the use of special sounds containing certain rhythms and pitches. Music has been used for millenia in primitive tribes (usually combined with drugs) to enter altered states of consciousness for spiritistic purposes.

Today we are seeing an unfortunate resurgence of this, particularly among the young. It is claimed that some rock musicians are mediums who have produced albums designed to foster spirit contact. Some mediums have received instructions from "the other side" in how to produce the right sound for the right purpose—be it helping to develop psychic powers, spiritism, inducing astral projections, etc. In other words, in listening to these records, it is the sound itself (and not the spirit) which induces an altered state of consciousness for a variety of occult purposes. To give some examples, in his M-5000 clinics, Robert Monroe uses taped sounds to induce astral projection and help "prepare" people for death or to explore the "astral" realm. He has reportedly received the instructions on this program from the spirit world.[24] The "Inter-Dimensional Music" through IASOS (the musician) is used to aid meditation, produce psychic highs (altered states), and establish spirit contact—in fact the spirits state that the music draws them, they enjoy it so much. Unfortunately, a particularly dangerous method is marketed by "The American Research Team" of Beverly Hills, California. A partial list given by the group indicates that at least 60 colleges, universities, high schools, hospitals, counseling centers, and psychic research institutes are using their "astral sound tape." According to their brochure, it is an exceptionally easy way to induce astral projection, develop psychic powers, experience hallucinations, etc. Marketed as an "autogenic training device," it has even been adopted as a required text in the psychology/nursing department at Metropolitan Community College in Minneapolis, Minnesota. The American Research Team states:

> Recent experiments prove that out-of-body experiences can be induced by simply listening to certain sounds ... these sounds, known as "Astral Sounds" have triggered out-of-body experiences in persons who have tried many other methods that have failed, others report seeing visions of light, colors, designs, symbols, pictures, hallucinations, peak experiences in

higher awareness, and an opening of tremendous psychic ability.[25]

Formerly, it was necessary to utilize the help of a spirit-guide, or some other relatively involved means of inducing astral projection. With the use of the "new technology" of parapsychology (again, often developed by instructions from "the other side"), being introduced to the world of the occult is as simple as listening to a cassette tape. There are numerous other esoteric uses of sound, e.g., Dr. Steven Halpern's "psychoacoustic/meditative music," or psychic Patricia Sun using her own almost nonhuman sounds in her seminars as a means to enter meditative states and manipulate psychic energy. Essentially, our concern is not the use of music to relax or calm yourself down, but the use of music to induce altered (abnormal) states of consciousness, spirit contact, or music used as a vehicle for occult-eastern metaphysics. There is some difficulty as to whether the sounds themselves produce the effects, whether they are a cover for various forms of thinly disguised spiritism, or whether they operate in conjunction with each other. (When mediums have received instructions from "the other side" in how to produce psychic music, it is apparently in a manner similar to the Rosemary Brown phenomena. This involves her receiving musical dictation (in this case compositions) from the spirit world. Naturally, the spirits doing the dictating are opposed to Christianity.[26])

Kinesiology

True Kinesiology is a legitimate medical branch of physiology. However, there exists an unscientific practice of the same name, which we hereafter discuss, which causes a great deal of confusion. *Applied* kinesiology is the practice of testing "energy flows" in the human body by finding and treating "muscle imbalances." Supposedly, a problem with one muscle can affect the functioning of the entire individual. Muscles are "tested" by applying pressure to them to see if they are "weak." Or the person holds a bag of sugar in one hand to prove the "overdose" weakens the muscles in the right side of the body and that sugar is bad for you (think what holding a bag of heroin must do!). If weak muscles are found, they are strengthened by what can be termed psychic methods. Particular points on the body will be touched—some lightly, some with a fair amount of pressure, and meridian therapy is applied—tracing imaginary lines up and down the body that supposedly correspond to the acupuncture meridians (reminiscent of nineteenth century occultic Mesmerist hand passes [See *Psychic Diagnosis, Healing, and Surgery* by **John Weldon (Moody Press, 1981)**]). Involved is the idea that each muscle has a related organ, so that a weak muscle may indicate trouble in the related organ. Hence by tracing the organ's appropriate meridian line from beginning to end, the organ is prevented from developing trouble.

Applied kinesiology was reinvented by Chiropractor George Goodheart in 1963, who combined techniques of his own work with ancient oriental practices. It is fairly exclusively the domain of chiropractors. Included in modern kinesiology are the theory and practices of acupuncture, massage, acupressure, the very dangerous occult system of Kundalini yoga, and polarity therapy.

Underlying applied kinesiology is the concept of the "life force" of *chi,* which is derived from our environment, respiration, and nutrition and is circulated through the body via meridians. Meridians are said to be detectable electronically, thermatically, and radioactively, however, they are normally invisible—although *with training* they can be felt, and some psychics even claim to see them.

Chi supposedly flows through the 12 meridians over a period of 24 hours, the corresponding organs (or anatomical sections) receiving their maximum flow at opposite times. As the effective functioning of each is in part dependent on chi, any blockage of a meridian results in blockage of energy to that organ, or anatomical section, resulting in disease.

There are numerous difficulties with the theory of applied kinesiology, many related to its nonphysical aspects.
1. Regarding the ideas behind the sugar test, which, incidentally, doesn't work all the time and probably results

from a temporary reduction in the muscle of lactic acid (which requires time to build up again), there is no evidence to indicate a normal substance can affect muscles or organs simply by being held next to it. If this were true, our anatomy should be nearly shattered by now, for every time one uses bug spray, or holds a cocktail at a party, our opposite side suffers the effects. Are we now suppose to have a scientific reason why it's not safe to carry "Sir Walter Raleigh" in a pouch?

2. **Medically speaking, applied kinesiology and all the related systems**, despite their prominence in the holistic health movement, only attack the symptoms, not the real cause of illness.
3. Illness, stress, drugs, etc., allegedly cause the chi flow to reverse—hence, in order to correct it, meridian lines must be traced backwards from end to beginning. This is more closely aligned with magic than anything scientific.
4. If the theory is truly correct, applied kinesiology, acupuncture, etc., should not only be able to prevent an organ from being diseased, but also to cure it. Theoretically, it should prevent death. If we were all to use it properly, we should not degenerate and finally die. In fact, this was the basis of the Taoist psychosomatic techniques used in ancient China. Immortality was held to be achievable by applied kinesiology, various occult practices, and yoga.[27]
5. Rethinking past emotional traumas supposedly causes muscular weaknesses, which can be relieved by holding a designated area of the head while having the patient keep reliving the process, until the patient is no longer so upset, thus supposedly abolishing the weakness. This has little to do with anything physical—it is a mild form of implosion therapy. If the muscle is improved, it is due to reduced anxiety because of reliving the experience, not pressure on the head.

Of greater concern is the relationship being developed by applied kinesiology and yoga, particularly kundalini yoga. Yoga is an acknowledged powerful eastern form of occultism.[28] This form of hatha yoga is exceptionally dangerous, and as acknowledged by yoga authorities, even the slightest mistake can produce serious illness, insanity, or death. (See Chapter 8 on Yoga.) However, there is an apparent relationship between all these eastern-occult techniques—yoga, acupuncture, applied kinesiology, etc. This is why kundalini symptoms (mimicking psychoses) can be stimulated through acupuncture and massage.[29] It is very clear that the system of kundalini yoga is pure occultism. Despite some western pronouncements to the contrary, eastern yogis call it such. It produces the "psychic transformation" of Vedantic Hinduism that alters one's concept of self and the world to conform with the nondualist Hindu worldview; it develops psychic powers; it can easily establish spirit contact; cause possession; etc. A recent article in *The Kundalini Quarterly*,[30] "Yoga and Kinesiology, Studies in the Physical Processes of Kundalini Yoga," by Jaswant Singh Khalsa, M.D., pointed out the correspondences. Dr. Khalsa says of kinesiology:

> This Western discipline is now providing new insights as to the mechanism of Kundalini Yoga.
>
> The muscle testing techniques of applied Kinesiology have wide application in the study of Yogic methodology. The terminology and approach of the two sciences are different, but many of their insights are mutually supportive.
>
> Many yogic exercises affect the muscle balance of the pelvis. Yet the formulation of these yogic exercises differs from physical therapy or other forms of Western rehabilitative or preventive exercise, because they were formulated to affect organ function and energy flow, as well as body structure and muscle balance.
>
> Yogic asanas are an example of movement or exercise used to induce energy changes in the body. This idea is a very ancient one—it is the basis of the Tai Chi Ch'uan and Eurhythmy (the therapeutic dance movements described by Rudolf Steiner).

Applied Kinesiology is an investigative and therapeutic complement to the use of Kundalini Yoga.

Acupuncture

We believe that the (limited) effectiveness of acupuncture is related to functioning of the physical body, not to mystical Life Energy concepts. While the specific reasons for this are discussed in some detail in Dr. Paul Reisser and John Weldon's *The Holistic Healers: A Candid Look at the Old Occultism in the New Medicine,* an excerpt from that book (pub. 1982) may prove useful for those considering treatment.

The Bottom Line: Some Guidelines for Evaluation. Our look at the mystical roots of acupuncture, acupressure, applied kinesiology, and the rest of Chinese medicine has revealed that, in many situations, patients are being treated on the basis of religious beliefs rather than physiologic principles. However, some questions remain when we come to specific cases. For example, we have frequently been asked questions such as whether someone should have acupuncture for chronic back pain, or whether a particular technique is sound, occultic, or somewhere in between. The issues, unfortunately, are not purely medical or scientific, but have spiritual implications, as well. After much study and reflection, we have arrived at some guidelines which we apply to individual cases. Our considerations are both scientific and biblical.

First, we propose that entry into the realm of ancient Chinese medicine be made for only one specific reason: The treatment of chronic pain with counter-stimulation therapy, such as needling or electrical stimulation, when other methods have failed, or are only partially successful. The problem should be evaluated thoroughly using standard medical approaches, and the individual(s) who carry out the treatment should be trained in conventional anatomy and physiology. An example might be a patient who is receiving acupuncture on a trial basis for chronic pain (such as from a low back injury), by an anesthesiologist in the setting of a university pain center. We feel it important that the therapist be thinking in terms of mechanisms in the nervous system, rather than in terms of meridians and Life Energy. This may seem like a trivial distinction when one is merely seeking pain relief, but "energy balancers" are much less likely to stay within the realm of known physiology, and more likely to inject their mysticism into the therapy session.

The use of acupuncture for treating other medical problems, such as high blood pressure, hearing loss, obesity, etc., has not been validated, to our knowledge, by any *controlled* study, and is extremely suspect. We emphasize the word "controlled" because of the problems we saw in the claims made for "miraculous cures" in China: no one was counting the cases which failed, or were they considering what other factors might have contributed to the success. Therapists who treat such problems with needling or other stimulation are in the twilight zone of medicine, and usually are working from a mystical perspective—which brings us to our second guideline.

We strongly urge that any therapists who claim to be manipulating invisible energies (Ch'i, "Life Energy," or whatever), whether using needles, touch, hand passes, arm-pulling, or any other manuever, be strictly avoided.

Why such a hard-nosed stand? For two reasons.

Objection No. 1: The Abandonment of the Brain. We have seen how the invoking of Life Energy, especially in the spin-offs of applied kinesiology, throws critical thinking to the wind. *Therapists who use techniques such as applied kinesiology are operating totally outside of the realm of objective knowledge about the human body.* Their "science" is based on conjecture, subjective impressions, unreliable data, and most importantly, the precepts of Taoism. They stand totally separate from the scientific community. You will never see muscle testing written up in *Scientific American,* recognized by the National Institutes of Health, or given the time of day by any reputable scientific body. We challenge anyone who is involved in these therapies to take a hard look at their assumptions, and thoroughly examine the evidence for their truthfulness.

Objection No. 2: The Metaphysics. Our look at Jin Shin Do provided an example of a different problem: the general orientation of the literature which promotes the doctrines of Ch'i and meridians. The overwhelming majority of authors express a distinct spiritual perspective, which is *always* a variation on eastern mysticism or New Consciousness themes. We have seen no exceptions to date. John Thie, originator of Touch for Health, proclaims in *Science of Mind* magazine that "we are all one with the universe." Iona Teegarden and her spirit guide tell us how Jin Shin Do can open psychic centers and experience the "Universal Flow" which is love and magic. Dr. Hiroshi Motoyama, a Japanese physician, acupuncturist, psychic, and psychic researcher, is actively seeking to unify ancient Chinese medicine, East Indian Kundalini yoga, and virtually all other psychic/mystical experiences into a single "science of consciousness." Psychic healer and medium, Rosalyn Lee Bruyere, whom we will discuss elsewhere, "sees" auras, chakras, and meridians, and manipulates the latter two in her practice; under the direction of two "spirit guides" who instruct her regularly, she teaches a strikingly all-encompassing blend of psychic healing, spiritism, reincarnation, and eastern mysticism. The pattern is unmistakable. *There is no neutral "science" of Life Energy and meridians, but rather a highly developed mystical system with strong ties to the psychic realm.*

What does that mean? It means that "energy" therapists, whether they realize it or not, are carrying out a form of religious practice and conditioning their patients to accept its teachings. Indeed, some therapists actually enter a trance-like state in order to become a "channel" to direct Ch'i (or whatever they choose to call "Life Energy") into the patient. The idea of the healer "injecting" invisible energy into another person may seem innocuous to most (and even silly to some), but the results may be anything but trivial. Brooks Alexander, codirector of the Spiritual Counterfeits Project, warns that:

It is not difficult to see that . . . psychic

manipulation could turn an otherwise benign form of treatment into a spiritual booby trap. The nature of the doctor-patient relationship implicitly involves a kind of trust in and submission to the healer on many levels. For a Christian to accept the passive stance of "patient" before a practitioner who exercises spiritual power (either in his own right or as a channel for other influences) could easily result in spiri**tual derangement or bondage.**

We thus find it particularly unsettling to see many members of the evangelical Christian community having their "energies balanced" by "therapists" who claim a Christian commitment, and who feel that they are not involved in any questionable practices. In the Southern California area, we know of many Christians, including some in the ministry (as well as some celebrities) who regularly take part in energy-balancing therapy, usually in conjunction with nutritional counseling. Their practitioners claim that Ch'i, yin and yang, and meridians are a neutral component of God's creation (similar to electricity and radio waves), which are available for anyone to use—but they ignore the roots of these practices.

The products of a truly neutral science—the technologies of electronics, biochemistry, and so on—can be validated and used by all, for whatever purpose, regardless of belief system. But the "technology" of Life Energy stands on quicksand when examined by noncommitted observers, because it falls outside of the boundaries of "neutral" science. Instead, its boundaries are defined by its sources and its promoters: The mystics, the psychics, and the leaders of the New Consciousness.

Christian energy balancers present us with the paradox claiming reliance on scripture as their guide, but carrying out the practices of an occultic/mystical system. Most are sincere in their desire to help their patients. Unfortunately, they are lacking in discernment, failing to see the implications of the ideas they are promoting. Some are even dabbling in the psychic realm, diagnosing disease through hand passes or over long distances, claiming that this is a natural by-product of their sensitivity to Life Energy.

To those energy balancers who profess to be Christians, we offer a challenge and a warning: take a long look at the world of Chinese medicine, and then decide whether or not you belong there. Do you feel comfortable as a part of the New Consciousness movement, promoting Taoist philosophy, participating in a mystical system whose basic message is that "All is One" in the universe and helping usher in the "New Age of miracles and magic?" If so, then continue what you are doing, but understand that you are part of a movement whose very core is incompatible with the teachings of the scriptures. On the other hand, if you do not see yourself as a Taoist mystic, then you should stop acting as one.

Those seeking help should be extremely cautious in the selection of treatment for their ailments, and equally, if not more important, select the person who administers that treatment with even greater care.

Sonopuncture

This is the manipulation of "body energy" by sound, rather than needles. The acupuncture philosophy undergirds it, and the only difference is that tuning forks are used in place of needles. New age occultist and osteopath, Irving Oyle, author of *Magic, Mysticism, and Modern Medicine*, is one loud proponent. He recalls the First International conference on Bioplasmic Energy held in 1972 in Moscow. One professor reported on a reversal of bone tumors "by means of low intensity laser radiation into the acupuncture system" and proposed the existence of a 4th circulatory system in the body which is pure energy—similar to the Chinese chi and yogic prana.[31] Oyle tells us the idea operating here is that the acupuncture system responds to *any* appropriate stimuli:

> Acupuncture means puncturing with a needle; sonopuncture means puncturing with sound. What I'm beginning to think is that the acupuncture system—this fourth circulatory system in the body—responds to nonspecific stimuli. It

> doesn't matter how you stimulate it. You can shine a light on it, beam a high-frequency sound into it, stick a needle in it, rub it, burn it, stare at it—it doesn't matter how you put energy into it. There's nothing special about sonopuncture except that it's easy and doesn't require any fancy tools. All you need is a tuning fork.[32]

Of course, the problem is just this—many psychics do "stare" at energy centers in the body and "heal" by psychic power. If acupuncture works apart from needles or other mechanical means, and the energy can be manipulated by concentration and hand passes alone, then we are dealing here with magic (i.e., occultism)—the needles, etc., aren't vital—"the psychometric factor" is. *It is important to realize at least the possibility of a number of the alternate medical technologies being psychometric in nature to one degree or another.*

Radionics

Radionics, psychotronics, etc., involve the occult use of technology (various devices) and are not really dealing in heretofore undiscovered areas of neutral energy, but rather are dependent on the psychic ability of the operator. For example, radiaesthesia is a form of psychometry (not always recognized or admitted) aided by a mechanical apparatus—a diving rod, pendulum, abram's box, or any one of the numerous machines used for such work coming under the modern title of radionics or radiaesthesia. It is worth noting the conclusions of the Theosophical Research Center in its publication, *The Mystery of Healing*.

> It is now admitted by those who use the various types of diagnostic machines associated with radiaesthesia that for successful work it is necessary to have present a human operator of a special type [i.e., one with occult abilities]. It is also well known that some operators are more proficient than others, while in the case of certain people, the machine will not work at all.[33]

This corresponds well to the fact of some psychics being

more powerful than others, and that some people cannot work these machines, e.g., this is true for many occult tools, such as the ouija board. Oftentimes, if a Christian is present and praying for Satan to be bound, the machines won't even work for a psychic.

Astrologic Medicine

It is not our concern here to discuss the many facets of astrology; (1) the scientific and theological case against astrology;[34] (2) the possibility of a pre-Fall legitimate use for astrology, subsequently corrupted by the occult, and which could possibly account for some if its effectiveness even today;[35] (3) the extent to which its correct functioning today depends upon a mediumistic ability[36] or the fact that there are interconnections that exist between heaven and earth.[37] These areas have been discussed elsewhere. Our concern is to first point out that all forms of astrology are occult—in fact astrology provides a "justification" for many forms of the occult.

Keith Thomas states in his *Religion and the Decline and Fall of Magic:*

> First, we must emphasize the interrelatedness of the main magical beliefs. The links between magic, astrology, and witchcraft were both intellectual and practical. On the intellectual level, astrology provided a coherent justification for geomancy, palmistry, physiognomy, and similar activities. "All these skills of divination are rooted and grounded upon astrology," declared Cornelius Agrippa. By postulating correspondences between the heavenly bodies and earthly substances, the palmists and physiognomists assigned different parts of the face or hand to different signs of the zodiac. Geomancy employed the twelve astrological houses and, according to the leading textbook on the subject, was "none other thing but astrology." Alchemy also divided up the metals between the planets and could be described as mere "kitchen magic or

chimney astrology." The astrological choice of times was important, not only for alchemical operations, but also for the ritual gathering of magical herbs and the conjuration of spirits. According to Robert Fludd, even the choice of ingredients for the weapon-salve had to be determined by astrological investigation; while the witch Ellen Green confessed in 1619 that her spirits came to suck her blood at certain phases of the moon.

The intellectual links between these different beliefs were emphasized by their practical associations with each other. The astrologers themselves were often men of wide-ranging activity. Forman practiced astrology, geomancy, medicine, divination by facial moles, alchemy, and conjuring. Ashmole's activities were equally diverse. Richard Saunders wrote a series of textbooks on chiromancy and physiognomy. Even Lilly, who did more than anyone to "purify" astrology, also practiced conventional medicine, spirit-raising, treasure-hunting, and the conjuration of angels and fairies. It is not surprising that a clergyman preaching to the Society of Astrologers in 1649 felt it necessary to warn his hearers to stick to their last: "Some falling by the ill practice of your lawful art have become, of magi, magicians, and, of wise men, wizards."

The links between magic and astrology illustrate the way in which the various types of magical or semi-magical belief propped each other up. Like the cunning men, the astrologers dealt with many patients who thought themselves bewitched and hence helped to sustain the belief in witchcraft. Indeed both Richard Saunders and Joseph Blagrave went so far as to declare that astrological diagnosis was the only sure way by which witchcraft could be discovered.[38]

Paracelsus, the foremost occultist of his time (born 1493)

and a precursor to the New Age holistic health physician vigorously integrated medicine and the occult. He was an alchemist, animist, diviner, and homeopathist. Astrology was one of the methods he used for divination. There also appears to be a relationship between astrologic influences and the ideas of a universal energy. Paracelsus, like Mesmer (who did his doctoral thesis on "The Influence of the Planets on the Human Body") believed in a "vital force" radiating around man that could be made to act at a distance. The concept of universal (interrelated) energy provides the basis for an interrelationship among the stars and man. Interestingly, in yoga there exists the idea of *prana,* the universal energy. This becomes tied to astrology, for example, in Garrison, who integrates the use of yogic postures and breathing (prana) techniques for each Zodiacal sign. For him, yoga and medical astrology go hand in hand, (although Hinduism has a system entirely contrary to the western system of astrology.)[38]

Although the best Christian discussion of astrology is to be found in Bjornstad and Johnson's *Stars, Signs, and Salvation in the Age of Aquarius,* our central concern here is to discuss the medical use of astrology. Astrology has numerous functions in relation to the medical field, e.g., for diagnosis, the best time to have an operation, etc. Omar Garrison, the author of *Medical Astrology* defines its function within medicine:

> Medical astrology is the art of determining from an individual's horoscope the diseases and infirmities to which he is predisposed.
>
> The stellar patterns at the time of birth are believed to indicate potential illnesses which may be triggered by transits of the planets over sensitive areas of the natal chart during the ensuing years . . . .
>
> [However], even when dormant physical disorders are clearly evident in the birth chart, the native may live his whole life without the inherent defects ever becoming active. In fact, one of the chief aims of medical astrology is to *prevent*

the occurrence of ill health during those periods in a person's life when his progressed horoscope shows that he will be subject to unusually discordant planetary influences.

In the area of preventive medical examination, an expertly cast horoscope can be especially helpful. For example, the medical astrologer, knowing that a prominent and afflicted Jupiter is associated with liver trouble, can determine from other planetary aspects whether and when a disease involving that organ will become manifest. An enzyme test in the laboratory, on the other hand, can diagnose the difficulty only after it has taken hold.

The same is true for all other disease entities. Each has a corresponding planetary formula and birth-chart constant, which alert a healer skilled in astrology, enabling him to make an earlier and sometimes more accurate diagnosis than the physician who relies upon observation of symptoms, laboratory tests, and the patient's medical history.[39]

Manolesco states:

> Each zodiacal sign encompasses a definite body area, and rulership over the organs and members of the body is given to the planets. Each sign has physical, mental, and emotional characteristics that have much bearing on the physiological and also the pathological tendencies of the ruling planet. The ruling planet in turn bestows a certain individual temperament upon the native according to his birth sign.[40]

Diagnosis has long been one of the main uses of astrology, and this dubious practice is not only in use today, but increasing. According to Garrison, "A growing number of doctors are quietly availing themselves of astrology as a diagnostic aid, even though they still find it professionally unwise to let the fact be known. Some have themselves become proficient in casting horoscopes; others rely upon consultants."⁴¹ C. Norman Shealy, M.D., in his *Occult Medicine Can Save Your Life*, adds his approval:

> I believe astrology is a science of considerable value in medicine, even though it has fallen into both disrepute and disrespect.
>
> I sincerely believe that astrology can do a good deal to improve medical care. I feel we ought to bring this science back to the medical school, to the training of young doctors.⁴²

Unfortunately, Shealy and the others who advocate such a position never mention the serious emotional and spiritual harm following the use of astrology.⁴³

There are serious difficulties in medical astrology of which we can mention only a few. Even astrologers have admitted it is an area "fraught with many pitfalls."⁴⁴ One area is the moral and legal. In his book, *Scientific Astrology*, Manolesco refers to the legal problems in which such people can find themselves. One astrologer advised a patient against his child's appendectomy, only to have the child die as a result. The problem is compounded by the fact that *very* few astrologers have any medical background. They still believe their occult art is precise enough to give them the expertise of a physician. Whether or not they have that expertise, they are willing to assume the responsibility. It also needs to be pointed out that *no evidence exists* that planets or their patterns influence disease in any sense, let alone that one's birth chart can determine when and where disease or death is likely to occur. As Garrison states:

> Accurate diagnosis of disease by an interpretation of radical and progressed horoscopes requires not only long experience and great skill in astrology but a basic knowledge of medicine as well. Few practicing astrologers today can lay honest claim to such expertise.⁴⁵
>
> Astrologers of the past had one striking characteristic in common—the cocksure way they predicted the exact time of such vital events as fatal accidents and death.

> Either they were in possession of data not available to us today or they based their prognoses upon some form of extrasensory perception. In either case, there is no evidence to show that their record of accuracy was something to be envied.[46]

He also tells us that, "It has been reported, but none too reliably, that Pluto governs the widely discussed nucleic acids, DNA and RNA, which control the body's enzyme patterns . . . . " Unfortunately, "There are not yet available sufficient data concerning the physiological effects of Pluto to present in detail a reliable guide to astrodiagnosis" (p. 182).

Occult science marches on!

Chiropractic

Please Note: We state at the beginning—and it will be reiterated throughout this segment—that *we do not* label all chiropractic medicine as "occult," nor do we adhere to the "throwing out the baby with the bath water" principle. We ask you to withhold hasty judgment and read this entire section, giving it your serious consideration. But we must point out the questionable origins of chiropractics and emphasize once again to *know your practitioner.* If he is dabbling in the psychic realm, it will likely be used in his treatments. Take all possible precautions to avoid becoming involved in such treatments.

Chiropractic was developed in the late 1800's by D. D. Palmer, a magnetic healer. The following assessments and interviews with chiropractors indicate that its success at times may possibly depend upon a psychic sensitivity. A late 1976 article in *Psychic Magazine* stated:

> It does, however, seem to be influenced by the mental or emotional state of the healer, a fact indicated by Dr. Grad's experiment and some further tests made by Sr. Smith, and attested to by most "spiritually" oriented healers, who feel that they need to be attuned to the patient and to the healing source, whatever it may be, before

they are able to help others.[47]

The basic idea behind the practice is that most diseases result from misaligned vertebrae, which results in nerve pressure. To many, the hand contact is as important as the spinal adjustment, perhaps in some cases a testimony to its origin from a magnetic healer—or perhaps merely a sense of well-being due to the establishment of sympathetic physical contact. Magnetic healers attempt to alter the "electromagnetic" (or "Life") field by removing harmful or adding beneficial "substances" or "energy," in much the same way that many psychic healers claim to restore etheric imbalances or "realign" energy. The following extended discussion in *Psychic* magazine gives us an idea of the psychic component that may be found in chiropractic (note the possible hereditary factors in the Palmer family).

> "There is always an energy transfer from doctor to patient," says Bill [Streiff], Jr. "It's a nerve transference, I believe, which works with the nerve energy released by the adjustment. In this way the patient receives energy from me and is also able to release more of his own. Touch is extremely important in healing; it gets you about as close to the patient as you can get."

Another advantage that actual body contact with the patient seems to give the manually-oriented healer is a heightening of his intuitive, or psychic abilities in the areas both of diagnosis and of correction of a problem. For example, many "magnetic" or "spiritual" healers claim that they can feel sensations of heat, coolness, prickling, or heaviness when they touch the afflicted part of a patient's body. These sensations are usually heightened during the healing process and may even be experienced by the sufferer, as well.

Many chiropractors, in palpating, or manually checking a patient's spine, can sense the heat released by nerve pressure with their fingertips, as well as feeling swelling or actual bone displacement.

"This close contact gives intuitive flashes in diagnosing," Bill Streiff, Jr., claims, "unless you close off your mind. I work this way all the time. And usually I can back up my psychic flashes with proof, by checking it out further."

"Just to give you an example," adds Bill, Sr., "if a patient with flu walks into the room, I can usually 'feel' it, as soon as I lay my hands on him. The body talks to you, if you listen to it."

Rob Butts' method of arriving at a diagnosis follows the same intuitive pattern.

"I just relax and ask within myself where I should work first, and in what way. I am frequently led to some part of the body and later I may wonder why in the world I went there. Academically, that shouldn't have been the point, and yet it worked. I don't usually try to explain my method of diagnosis to the patient, in this case." He adds, with a grin, "If they ask me why I did what I did, I tell them that the potato in my back pocket told me to!

"It seems to me that a chiropractic physician, in general, is more inclined to use intuitive, or psychic, factors in healing. Whether this is because he works with his hand on the body, where the energy vibrations come through, or whether this type of individual just has a tendency to go into chiropractic, I'm not sure."

Dr. Butts feels that most chiropractors, if they don't start out with psychic ability, tend to develop it as they go along, even though they may simply think of it as "hunches" that prove accurate. Because they work close to their patients, with considerable personal involvement, they set up an energy flow which allows more intuitive feeling to come through.

B. J. Palmer, the son of D. D. Palmer, and

an instructor for many years at Palmer College, taught the concept of "innate intelligence," which he claimed each individual possessed and which was the force which made a person sick or well. Although this idea is still included in the college's chiropractic training, students are not obligated to accept it, although, "... those who don't are missing the boat, in my opinion," says Bill Streiff, Sr.

"For example, when I talk to a patient, I usually say that 'we' are treating him. He may not know what I'm talking about, but that 'we' is me, the physical, and me, the innate intelligence. Sometimes I'm aware of the actual presence of the innate in the room—not only my own innate, but the patient's as well. This is when I get my best results.

Some chiropractors make additional use of the hands by incorporating various massaging techniques into their practice. "Sometimes I use needles," explains Rob Butts, "since they can accomplish more in a shorter time, and mine is a country practice, where people may have to travel long distances to get here. But, if time allows, or the patient is hesitant about the needles, I use my fingers, massaging the acupuncture points.

"Sometimes I treat the acupoints with different fingers of either the right or left hand, because I'm after an electrical response, and the fingers have a positive and negative energy value. So, I can stimulate these points in less time by using a certain finger, because of its electrical value. The body is basically positively charged on the right side and negatively charged on the left. Each hand has both positively and negatively charged fingers. The palm is positive, the back of the hand, negative, and the left hand is the mirror image of the right, with the electrical values also reversed. All this has been proven by electronic instrumentation. The thumb, middle, and little fingers are all positive, but more so on the right hand than on the left. The fingers next to the thumb and little finger are negative on both hands, but more so on the left. This definitely involves an electromagnetic type of healing,"[46]

We close this preliminary discussion with the following verbatim analysis of chiropractic by Elliot Miller, a researcher at the Christian Research Institute (used by permission). It is presented here as one researcher's tentative reaction to the above, as well as for its discussion on the potential occultic aspects of Chiropractic. It is also interesting to note that at one major Chiropractic school which Dr. Reisser visited, many of the students had become involved in the psychic world.

The Occultic Roots of Chiropractic
by Elliot Miller

While reading a manuscript of John Weldon's on the holistic health movement, I was shocked to see chiropractic listed right along with acupuncture, yoga, and many other occult techniques for aligning oneself with "cosmic energy" (occult power). I had never heard chiropractic associated with the occult before, and what's more, my step-grandfather was a chiropractor (and a very good, gentle man, I might add!), and I unquestioningly received chiropractic "adjustments" throughout my childhood, seemingly with no adverse effects (though I can't recall any time that they really helped either). I thought that perhaps Mr. Weldon had not done his homework thoroughly enough, and so I decided that I would get down to the bottom of this by investigating the matter myself.

First I consulted three encyclopedias, and then I found a book, *Chiropractic Speaks Out—A Reply to Medical Propaganda, Bigotry, and Ignorance,* by Chester A. Wilk, D.C. In none of these did I find any evidence that a nonphysical or occultic energy is implied in chiropractic theory. I did find that energy, and the belief that disease is caused when the flow of energy is obstructed, form the theoretical foundation for chiropractic. However, I saw no indication that this energy is believed to be anything more than very natural nervous energy. I was beginning to think I might have to write Mr. Weldon a letter and point this out to him.

At this point I was fortunate enough to locate *The Chiropractic Story,* by Marcus Bach. Marcus Bach is a researcher/author with whom I am very familiar. He is a liberal authority on cults and religious movements of all kinds, a promoter of the holistic health movement, and a strong supporter of occultism in many of its forms. I knew that if there were any occultism in chiropractic's roots, Bach could be counted on to unearth it.

But could I rely on a mystic such as Bach to give chiropractic a fair representation? I found that the book was written due to the encouragement of chiropractors, who had heard Bach speak on essentially the same things he wrote of in his book, at chiropractic conventions in Los Angeles and elsewhere. I observed that the book was placed in the library where I obtained it by the Auxiliary to the Academy of Missouri Chiropractors. Additionally, it should be noted that the most substantial information I did find in the book came directly from quotes of the two central personalities in the history of chiropractic; its founder D. D. Palmer, and his energetic son, B.J.

Moving through the book I was enjoying myself, as Bach is a fine writer and a personable man, though I always disagree with his conclusions. Then, at page 102, my eyes froze over the following paragraphs:

> While trying to find my way out of these dilemmas, I took a new look at the basic chiropractic concept of Innate. This philosophy, which insisted that the primal source of energy or vital force (Innate) is directed through the nervous system, had been mentioned to me long ago by Dr. Stacy. Innate, for him no less than for me, was but another name for the spirit of life, or God. Innate was that power which kept the complicated autonomic system functioning. Innate was Infinite Life expressing itself through an individual for a specific period in time and space.
>
> D. D. Palmer had described Innate as "a segment

of that Intelligence which fills the universe." He made a distinction between two manifestations of this Intelligence, referring to one as "Educated" and to the other as "Innate." While these two manifestations were considered distinctive, they were also complementary. Educated Intelligence, according to the doctrine of chiropractic's founder, began with our physical life and ended with its death. It revealed itself through our sensory perceptions and was a conscious, mental function. Innate Intelligence, on the other hand, existed before the physical body was born and continued after it was laid aside. It expressed itself through a spiritual force and was super-conscious. Educated Intelligence was limited, Innate Intelligence unlimited. Educated Intelligence had to think and plan, Innate was intuitive, instinctive, immortal.

"Educated Intelligence and Innate," said D. D. Palmer, "assist each other, more or less. At times they are antagonistic. Educated is concerned with acquired experience during life, and Innate with experience obtained during a period that is co-extensive with the existence of invertebrates."

Educated Intelligence clearly had its areas of control over Innate, as in bodily functions which respond to impulses of the brain; Innate had its areas of control over Educated Intelligence, as in the case of supplying Educated with vital force. Vital force was necessary for all bodily functions. Normally expressed in matter, this vital force was physiological; deviating from normal, it was pathological.

To anyone familiar with occultic philosophy it is clear at this point that Palmer's "Innate" (God) is not the personal God of the Judaeo-Christian tradition, but the impersonal "force" of eastern and occultic mysticism. Occultism holds that God is Mind, and all reality is an expression (and thus part of) that Mind. Palmer refers to the same concept here when he speaks of "that Intelligence which fills the universe." It is disturbing to realize that the entire practice of chiropractic was inspired by this occultic conception of reality, and developed in correspondence to it.

The theory behind chiropractic is that if the structural and neurological aspects of the body are properly aligned, "Innate's vital force," an intelligent entity that has a will to be well, will keep the body healthy. As Palmer put it:

> An intelligent force which I saw fit to name Innate, usually known as Spirit, creates and continues life when vital organs are in a condition to be acted upon by it. This intelligent life-force uses the material of the universe in proportion as it is in a condition to be utilized (p. 227).

And of course, the "condition to be utilized" is achieved, when needed, through chiropractic.

Where did Palmer get this occultic conception of the universe, upon which he based his chiropractic theory? The answer lies in his acceptance and practice of "magnetic healing." Bach writes of Palmer in those days before he discovered chiropractic:

> I pictured D. D. as the mental healer that he was in the days when the influence of men like Mesmer and Quimby was widespread and experimental (p. 97).

Of course, the association of Anton Mesmer and Phineas Quimby, and their ideas to the occult is well known. Palmer wrote:

> All observers realize that we are surrounded with an aura; that we pass from our bodies a subtle, invisible substance known as magnetism; that this emanation may be either repellant or attractive (p. 225).

D. D. speculated that this energy was transmitted from the brain through the nerves to give power to the organs, and that disease occurred when this process was disrupted by vertebral subluxations. Referring to Palmer's acceptance of this occult philosophy of energy, Bach writes: "It was out of this line of reasoning that chiropractic was established" (p. 226).

The success of chiropractic in the twentieth century is due much less to its founder than it is to the efforts of his son B.J. B.J. Palmer not only grasped the philosophical and therapeutic speculations of his father, but he promoted them on a worldwide scale with vision, skill, and drive that his father lacked.

B.J. was a man driven by the power of "Innate." He believed

"All roads that lead to God are good" (pp. 158, 220—thus implying that there are many roads to God), was a Mason (p. 220), and leaned toward a belief in reincarnation (p. 162). He was interested in Buddhism (p. 163), the occult, and demonstrated powerful occultic powers himself. He had enjoyed Bach's work, and so in 1950 sent Bach a letter in which he expounded his philosophy of "Innate," and invited him to his home for dinner so that they might discuss the matter further. During their time together Bach personally experienced B.J.'s psychic powers. After B.J. made a statement indicating he knew what Bach was thinking, Bach was both "disturbed and thrilled."

> I knew now what was meant by the statement of a chiropractor friend who once said, "You do not engage in verbal conversation with this man, for he *thinks* his way into your mind and to protect yourself you must think your way into his." This was quite right. He was a receiving and sending station, turned on, tuned in, seeing with an inner eye, listening with an inner ear, speaking with an inner voice.
>
> I thought of my research into the field of psychism and the moment this subject flashed to mind, I heard B.J. exclaim with frightening accuracy, "No, Marcus, spiritualism is not the thing I am talking about! I know you are interested in it. So am I. But most of it is bunko!"
>
> What kind of an extrasensory man was this? How literally was one to take this "lasso" that he said he tossed out to take people in? (p. 161).

The excerpt from B.J.'s letter that Bach includes in his book gives such a clear insight into both the philosophy of Innate, and the spiritual dynamic that controlled B.J., that it seems worth including in full here:

> . . . But most of all he wanted to talk to me about Innate Intelligence. "A child is born," his letter said, "and at the time of birth the fetus becomes an independent unit. A certain *something* takes possession of that body. What is *it*? What is this *something* that takes full and complete command of *that matter* and which changes it from inert inanimate matter to an

active functional boy or girl, and makes it live to fulfill a predetermined, predestined pattern, possessing a universal law of species, duplicating millions of others who have come and gone, and other millions to follow, an intellectuality which has spanned centuries in millions of living things, man included? We call *that something* Universal Intelligence, God, Jehovah, many names. *WE* call it *Innate Intelligence.*"
His "we" as I have said, always meant "B.J.," his theorizing always revolved around Innate. His wish apparently was to tap the thinking of other minds and use them as a sounding board for his speculations.

He went on to say, *"Inside* your brain, beyond and behind you, Marcus Bach, is another intellectuality, personality, which built Marcus Bach in utero before he *was* Marcus Bach, which was gathered by trial and error, through millions of years in millions of people of all sects, creeds, colors, countries, many of whom also tried to find out what made *other men* tick. To do this they built creeds, sects, drew color lines, set country boundaries, devised tabu and kapu customs. But the *internal mentality* is *so much greater* than the external education that it is like the sands of the seashore to a grain of sand."

A page later he came to the heart of the matter and the philosophy which ruled his life and mind. He put it this way, "The *external* seeking and searching accumulative *education* of Marcus Bach is superficial. It is *outside* you and limited in scope to an understanding of even yourself. But in and behind this *surface Marcus Bach* is the deeper, inner resources which are unlimited, and which remain unexplored as the *inside inner* of your life. *Educated* man lives by virtue of what he receives from *outside-in* and *below-upward*. The natural, normal, healthy, *internal* living man thrives by virtue of what he receives from *above-down* and *inside-out*. Listen, Marcus Bach, in what I have just said lies *the* difference between ordinary men and the people you have referred to as great in your books. These people *found themselves* by minimizing the *outer* man and maximizing the *inner* man which flows from *above-down, inside-out*.

"Most men kick off the throne the real *inner fellow* who controls, directs, governs *all of them inside,* giving the throne instead to *all the world outside* them. To open the gate between the *outer* insignificant fellow by subjugation, is to bring into action the one *inner*fellow by evolution. *If* the *outer* fellow listens to the voice of the *inner* fellow he will receive ideas of great value, live them, permit them to act through the *outer* fellow, raising him *up* to loftier heights by contrast to the small *outer* fellow who limits his observations to his *external* self and others like him, for he sees in others only what he sees in himself: the limitations of education of the *outer* world as viewed by the limited scope of his horizons of his *outer* senses."

This inspirational writing went on and on through ten typewritten pages and the ideas surged forth as from a fountain overflowing, as if the mind that generated them knew no limitation, as if the writer *"We"* were actually and literally a composite of God and Man. The letter bore the notification that it was written at 4:30 A.M. It was typed on blue stationary which carried across the top of the page an engraving of the Palmer School replete with radio antennas and giving a bold suggestion of the Palmer empire which Innate had built. But the point of the letter was an invitation for me to come to Davenport for a visit with B.J. and to "have dinner with *us* in our 100-year-old home." "If you are not afraid of heretics," the letter said, "come and be *our* guest" (pp. 139-141).

When Bach visited him at his home, B.J. went on to say:

"The master maker of the human body did not create you and then run off and leave you masterless. He stayed on the job as *Innate*, as the *Fellow*

> *Within,* as nerve transmission controlling every function of life, as Spirit from Above-Down, Inside-Out, expressing, creating, exploring, directing you in every field and phase of experience so that your home is truly the world and the world is your home." The application of this principle to chiropractic became the heart of B.J.'s discourse during this my first visit with him.

And, from the Christian perspective, the application of this "principle" (the occult nature of which B.J. has so graciously clarified for us) to chiropractic raises serious questions about the spiritual safety of submitting to the practice.

To what do we attribute the growth of chiropractic? Historians would single out B.J. Palmer as by far the most instrumental human force behind the movement. Yet B.J. himself would not receive this credit. He attributed his accomplishments to a living spiritual entity that worked through him. As can be adduced from B.J.'s comments above, he was controlled, directed, and governed by the *"Inner Fellow."* He received his ideas by listening to the "inner fellow's" voice. Truly he could speak of himself as "we," for there was a spiritual person inside of him, empowering and directing his every move. As Bach wrote: "He spoke as the spirit moved him . . . spoke of his life's destiny, to be and prove the power of Innate Intelligence working through the channel of man. That was his theme if there was one" (p.121). B.J. told Bach: *"I have achieved* nothing. I do nothing. It is *Innate* that does the work" (p. 162).

Some of these statements sound similar to Jesus' affirmation that the signs He performed were worked through the Father's power, and not His (John 5:19,30; 8:28; 12:49; 14:10). However, by the pantheistic, impersonal conception of God that he preached, we know that whatever spirit was controlling Palmer, it wasn't the *Holy* Spirit. As difficult as it is for those of us with backgrounds of personal experience with chiropractic to acknowledge, it appears clear that the demonic powers have offered full support to the promotion of the chiropractic movement, no doubt with the hope that all who submit to the treatment will also submit control of their lives to the "fellow within."

To what extent has this occurred? The fact that I, a researcher of the occult, had for years never heard chiropractic associated with the occult suggests the possibility that the practice's attendant philosophy of "Innate" has been dropped by many of today's chiropractors. B.J. himself said, almost thirty years ago:

> Chiprac*tic* must un-brainwash the public and demonstrate that health comes from Inside-Out. But first *we* must un-brainwash the chiprac*tor,* too many of whom have themselves not caught the idea that the vertebral adjustment releases Innate, works in harmony with Innate, becomes a partner with Innate in effecting the cure (p. 165).

The fact that the roots of chiropractic are clearly tied to occultic philosophy does not of itself disprove that the practice has a biological basis for healing. Though to a great extent the medical world looks upon chiropractic with scorn, who am I to say that vertebral subluxations cannot cause disease? Speaking of holistic health methods (of which chiropractic was a forerunner in this country), Weldon writes in his manuscript:

> Perhaps this [demonic] idea was to involve a *true* concept—or part of one—that offers practical help (one that works) with a *false* philosophy and worldview? Never underestimate the power (drawing and sustaining) of a worldview that *heals,* or one that seems to provide answers to the gnawing riddle of man's existence. The final answer to the forms of acutherapies *may* be ultimately found in known scientific laws and processes, rather than in unknown occult ones, or in metaphysics. However, we believe this is doubtful.

Perhaps what Weldon describes here is true in the case of chiropractic. Perhaps Satan, knowing that the proper distribution of nervous energy to the body's organs is vital to health, revealed this to the occultist D. D. Palmer *along with* an explanation for the success of the method that, if accepted, would dethrone a Biblical worldview and enthrone an occultic one.

Where there is an expectation (on the part of the chiropractor or the patient) for the power of "Innate" to flow, there is an open door for demonic energy and deception to be unleashed.

The spiritual danger of any Christian submitting himself to this is obvious. *If it can be demonstrated that chiropractic has a scientific basis for healing, then where no thoughts of "Innate" or any occultic "force" are entertained, it would seem possible to separate the occultic roots from the method and benefit from the treatment.* (Emphasis added.)

Orgonomy and Various Bioenergetic Therapies

Orgonomy was developed by Wilhelm Reich, who as a student specialized in psychoanalysis under Freud. One of his basic theories involves what is termed "character [or bodily] armour." In this theory, usually "bioenergy" flows freely about the body, as well as the universe. However this energy can become obstructed in the body. This happens through character defenses which block and concentrate the energy in certain areas. This is termed "armoring" and as the energy is not flowing freely, emotional and physical problems result. In "therapy," character defenses are uncovered and the energy can flow freely. Reich termed the energy "orgone," and for him it was sexual.

Although a student of Freud, he differed from the latter in believing sexual desires should be freely released rather than controlled. After all, if the universal energy is sexual, how could nature ever place restrictions on its use? Hence neurosis could not be cured apart from transferring sexual energies (the orgone—from orgasm) to realistic sexual objects. As a result, he advocated premarital sex for "problem adolescents," and extramarital sex for troubled mariages. In essence Reich's theories are a convenient rationalization for sexual sin. While the name Freud is connected with sex, Reich was the real radical. Orgonomy is only one example, but it is rather amazing how many of the modern "therapies" fall into the same category of little more than complex rationalizations for hedonism, or living any way one wants to. Reich believed that man was only at peace with himself when drained of all sexual energies—the uninhibited orgasm was the road to both personal and societal freedom and happiness. Reich's theories are discussed in his *The Function of the Orgasm*. His "therapy" sessions were forerunners of the modern sex "therapy" clinics (e.g., the International Professional Surrogates Association) which provide professional sexual partners for people with sex problems. Techniques to improve orgasms were developed in such sessions. "Inadequate" orgasms left surplus energy in the body that caused secondary and often unhealthy drives. Again, Reich believed that "bioenergy" in the healthy adult travels freely about the body. When emotions are held in, muscles become tight, blocking the energy flow. This "armoring" greatly reduces the level of bioenergy and can lead to poor health, emotional problems, and disease. Free sex is the means to insure proper flow of the "bioenergy." In his *Sexual Revolution,* he discusses how the "regressive" sexual norms of western society were responsible for so many social problems. Hence, Orgone became the human manifestation of the basic energy of the universe. Reich believed this energy could be isolated and accumulated, and in 1939 he started building and selling "orgone accumulators," which eventually led to his arrest and imprisonment in 1957. He believed that these accumulators could have some therapeutic effects on cancer, arthritis, and other diseases. The FDA investigated his claims for many years and attempted to duplicate his results by having various institutes test the validity of the orgone theory. Their failure to do so may indicate a psychometric effect which itself can indicate demonic influence. Modern sympathetic Reichians have duplicated some of his work, but it seems unsympathetic researchers cannot. Reich died in jail the year of his arrest and is today a modern hero among neo-Reichian therapists who give him credit for discovering the correlation between sex energy and the "universal energy."

Reich also believed that the accumulation of orgone in the body (named DOR—Dangerous ORgone) could be removed by a device called the "DOR buster," which draws off excess orgone. (He also devised a "cloud buster" which destroyed black clouds of DOR that mysteriously hung over his laboratory.) Reich was also heavily involved with UFO research, and this is one more tie-in to the demonic. Our other books on UFO's have documented that UFO's and UFO entities are manifestations of the demonic. Jerome Eden's books, *Orgone Energy* and *Planet in Trouble—The UFO Assault on Earth*, discuss Reich's relationship to UFO's. (Eden is also the author of *Animal Magnetism and the Life Energy* and states that orgone and animal magnetism are part of the same universal energy.)

It is uncertain whether Reich was a UFO contactee (in personal contact with UFO's or their "occupants"), although a respected researcher, John Keel, labels him as such and states he derived his orgone theories from the UFO entities themselves.[49] It is perhaps more accurate to state he verified his orgone theory from UFO contact,[50] although it is clear that "UFO entities" could have been supervising his work "behind the scenes" for many years (even decades) before contact was purportedly made (apparently in 1954). This "invisible supervision" is common among occultists and presents a problem in determining the true origin of the many modern discoveries within the "new [occult] technology" field by parapsychologists and occult scientists.

Reich has had an influence among many modern therapies—Dichter's depth psychology, Perle's Gestalt therapy, transactional analysis, encounter therapy, etc. Therapies directly derived from Reich's theories include Ida Rolf's Structural Integration (Rolfing) and Alexander Lowen's *Bioenergetics*. Lowen was a student of Reich's and became a practicing Reichian Therapist for 2 years. However, Reichian therapy didn't work for him—"Despite my having successfully completed Reichian therapy, I was aware that I still had many chronic muscular tensions in my body that prevented me from experiencing the joyfulness I longed for."[51] He wanted a "still richer and fuller sexual experience" and it was out of this desire, and after more "research," bioenergetics was developed.[52]

Both the failure of Reichian therapy and its many unbiblical branches indicate the truth of the biblical statement that a bad tree cannot bear good fruit (Matthew 7). One particular offshoot of Reich's work is of interest due to a similarity to the Mesmerists' hand passes (and resultant emotional outbreaks) and the various healing methods utilizing rod passes. Pyramid "technology" seems to lie in a similar camp. W. Edward Mann, author of *Orgone, Reich, and Eros* states:

> One recent [homemade] version has the individual sitting or lying under an orgone blanket; a metal funnel perhaps a foot or two long, connected with BX cables is placed near supposed armored areas of the body. The therapist passes the head of the device back and forth over the patient's body for about fifteen minutes in a treatment. When successful, this device draws off DOR and excites energy movement. At times it can result in outbreaks of strong emotions locked in by the bodily armoring and thus facilitates therapy.[53]

Practicing orgonomist Barbara Koopman, M.D., Ph.D., writing in the foreword to Jerome Eden's *Animal Magnetism* declares:

> Mr. Eden has rightly, in my opinion, placed magnetism in the realm of orgonotic phenomena, as discovered by Wilhelm Reich, the founder of Orgonomy. What is common to both Orgonomy and mesmerism is the use of the cosmic life energy, which Reich called orgone, albeit the working techniques of the two modalities are quite different and should not be confused.
>
> As a practicing Orgonomist, I am intrigued by the red thread running through all these energetically-based techniques—magnetism, acupuncture, psychic healing, vivaxis, dowsing, hypnotism, biofeedback—in that all appear to be working directly with cosmic energy and the orgone energy field, or "aura," as it is termed in the esoteric literature. . . .[54]
>
> As for animal magnetism itself, I do believe it has a kinship with hypnosis. (I think Mr. Eden

would agree.) However, Mr. Eden emphasizes the absence of verbal induction and the use of "physical" (energetic, really) techniques, such as hand passes. My personal guess is that a dual process unfolds: the charging up of the subject's energy field to a high pitch, the source of the charge being the fields of the magnetizer and his helpers (sometimes a chain of people backing him up), often augmented by devices similar to Reich's orac (orgone accumulator); the literal pulling out of stasis energy (what Reich termed DOR or deadly orgone radiation) from the organism by means of hand passes. Actual touching was not necessary and merely combing through the aura sufficed. Mr. Eden's observations about the operator's being grounded in water and the analogy to Reich's medical DOR-buster apparatus is well taken.

One could guess that the practitioners of magnetism must have been endowed with extremely powerful energy fields in order to be able to withstand the depletion of their charge and the absorption of toxic emanations from their patients.

There are countless examples of psychic healers one could cite—the occult literature abounds in them. Some, like the Kahunas, avoid depletion by what they regard as a process of channeling atmospheric energy into their subjects and directing it as if it had intelligence.[55]

Biofeedback, Alphagenics, and Meditation

Biofeedback utilizes scientific instruments (e.g., the EEG and EMG or electromyograph) to allow a person to recognize and to an extent control certain otherwise unconscious or automatic internal functions of the body (heart beat, muscular tension, blood pressure, etc.). It also allows one to recognize certain mental states of consciousness. Alphagenics (and similar methods of the commercial mind-training courses) are used to achieve similar results—although neither identical nor as precise—without the use of instruments. Biofeedback may be a useful tool for therapy. We say *may* be, because psychic events sometimes occur in *all* types of biofeedback training. This is not to say every person who uses it for physiological conditioning has these experiences. It is simply to note that there are unknown variables, perhaps person specific, which indicate caution is advisable. If it is a safe tool, there are still important guidelines to be followed. First, it must be handled by qualified personnel. Those who are into parapsychology and other forms of the occult should not be sought after as biofeedback instructors. Second, proper instrumentation must be used or serious consequences can result. One alpha machine being sold taught people how to replicate an epileptic brain wave pattern.[56] Whereas biofeedback may be useful in treating tension-related and other ailments, our concern here is to examine its occult uses. (The authors have, however, encountered Christians for whom biofeedback would not work, i.e., they were unable to replicate certain brainwave patterns or levels.) The most popular function of biofeedback is to develop altered states of consciousness. In fact, it can be used to enter mental levels which mediums find most useful in contacting the spirit world. The alpha level of biofeedback promotes a state of receptivity and passiveness, also essential conditions for mediumism.[57]

There is nothing necessarily occult in the underlying principle of biofeedback—that the mind can be used to partially regulate the body. The brain naturally controls a significant portion of the body's physiology, and the mind is more than the brain. Biofeedback *in part* is simply an extended application (perhaps overextended) of Proverbs: "As a man *thinks* [mind] in his heart, so is he [mind-body]. Psychosomatic medicine has proven the importance of the mind's impact on the body. The problem of biofeedback is twofold: First, since the basic idea involves *mind* control of the body, it is difficult not to extend this into mind-experimentation in general. This opens up the realm of the occult. The very fact that it is often used for occult purposes is to the point. There *is* no safety valve or hedge against using biofeedback (via the occult) to "better the mind," as well as the body. In fact, given the premises of the human potential movement, this is a natural follow through. Second, we are concerned over the underlying philosophy of the biofeedback-autogenic researchers. Because it is a combination of human potential and new consciousness thinking, the researchers feel that everything they discover during biofeedback experimentation is part of the innate powers of man. If psychic powers result from biofeedback-induced altered states of consciousness, then they must be innate untapped human potential. The blinders of evolutionary thinking (man is all there is; man must advance upwards; we are on the verge of a major evolutionary shift—a quantum leap in consciousness-expansion) not only condition man to accept psychic powers as *natural* progress, but allow no room for even the existence of demons, let alone the possibility of demonic intervention subtly masquerading as evolutionary advancement. Such ideas are not even momentarily entertained. In our research, we were continually amazed at how often this humanistic spiritual naivete' kept recurring. As Dr. North states in his brilliant *None Dare Call It Witchcraft:*

> But there is more of the occult than meets the eye of some of the antiestablishment experimenters. The possibility of *animism*—demonic interference in the experiments—is never acknowledged, either by the orthodox scientists (who conveniently dismiss all signs of the abnormal) or the parascientists (who do not want hostile, supernatural forces to interfere in *their* sympathetic creativity). There is a whole new zone of research for Christian scientists to clarify—disentangling long-ignored patterns of God's creation from the activity of demons. The non-Christian investigators are powerless to sort out facts from theory when demons tinker with the meters.[58]

Such an attitude bias as described by Dr. North is extremely counterproductive and provides the demonic world with the best cover they have (and historically the most frequently used)—invisibility. Needless to say, invisibility produces control. Even with the more "orthodox" biofeedback researchers (Barbara Brown, Elmer Green), their experimentation tends to cause a movement into eastern or occult types of thinking. Both Brown and Green advocate exploring altered states of consciousness as a possible prelude to evolutionary advancement of individual or social consciousnes. From her biofeedback experiments, Barbara Brown has synthesized the philosophy of the East (monism/pantheism) and West (materialism) and is convinced that "there *is* a universal consciousness." Optimum personal functioning involves taking the best of both worlds.[59]

Dr. Elmer Green's research is perhaps the prototype of the ability of biofeedback to synthesize science and the occult. His book, *Beyond Biofeedback,* is a clear indication of the occult use of biofeedback. He says that ESP and parapsychological phenomena sometimes occur in *all* types of biofeedback experimentation, even though they may not be the goals of the training.[60] Although he disagrees with the hypnotic methods utilized by almost all of the commercial mind-training programs, (indeed he notes they can cause possession or even psychoses) he states: "Hypnotic programming for ESP [which can involve a form of biofeedback] bears a similarity to some of the methods used for development of trance mediumship, especially the 'possession by spirits' of low-grade mediumship."[61] Here we encounter an area of concern for those individuals who could trigger, or "open up" this susceptibility even though there was no intent to do so. Biofeedback, therefore, could be particularly dangerous for these people, i.e., those who have some occult involvement to four generations in their family history. The studies of Kurt Koch have indicated that individuals with such a family history are more likely to be susceptible to psychic influences or involvement. (See Koch's *Christian Counselling and Occultism.)* Unfortunately, there is often no way of knowing who these

THE NEW MEDICINE

people are. How many people today know if their grandfather was a dowser or even if they themselves were "charmed" at a young age? A related problem is that those individuals who develop these abilities will see them as positive advancement—rather than the result of an occult curse. Of interest, too, is Dr. Green's view that "hypnosis and parapsychology are not necessarily two separate subjects."[62] He also discusses the occult and "medical" uses of the mind-training courses (actually much of this is magic):

   a. A person can "go down" into his own "unconscious" and while in that deep "level" can program his own physiological and psychological processes so that various diseases in him that have not yielded to standard medical treatment can be brought under control.
   b. While at his deep "level," a person can become aware of physical, emotional, and mental states and diseases in other people and can correctly diagnose ailments.
   c. While at his "level," a person can learn to manipulate the physical, emotional, and mental natures of other persons, sick or healthy, and thereby modify their behavior.
   d. While at this "level," a person can learn to manipulate nature so that coincidences, "accidents," or lack of accidents, can come under his control. This is, essentially, a promise of psychokinetic powers.[63]

Unfortunately, even Dr. Green, while labelling much of the commercial use of hypnosis (though it is not acknowledged as such) in mind-training courses as dangerous, still refers to the "safe" path of yoga and the "safe" development of psychic powers, when in fact, *yoga is extremely dangerous and there is no such thing as the "safe" development of psychic powers.*[64] (See appropriate sections.) Because of the fallen nature of man, even the "normal" use of power nearly always corrupts in some form or another. *Supernormal* power, therefore, is not an *"evolutionary advancement,"* it is a *deadly entrapment,* and it represents a dual dimension of fallenness—human plus the demonic. Psychic powers can be used for any purpose—even for evil. What is unknown to most people is that there is no "good" use of psychic abilities. It is all contact with demonic powers. If human history proves man cannot handle normal power well, how much less supernatural power? The very fact that much of occultism (including yoga, hypnosis, and mind training) boasts of the *control* you can exert over others (causing them to do things they ordinarily would not) is evidence of the seriousness of the matter. This control *does* work and has been responsible for innumerable tragedies.

In summary, the nonoccult use of biofeedback represents a useful tool if it is used in a purely scientific, physiological, responsible way. Unfortunately, however, even nonoccult researchers have advocated its use for expanding consciousness. It appears that in the long run this method will have a usefulness, but will be the recipient of much abuse and result in a great deal of emotional and spiritual malaise.

A discussion of meditation is another book entirely and is tied together with both the occult use of biofeedback and the mind-training courses. There are many varieties, and all of them save one (the biblical instruction on meditation) involve an occult or potentially occult usage. Meditation is a common method of developing mediumship. The attempt to cultivate altered states of consciousness (ASC's) is always hazardous, and there is no guarantee the door to the spirit world will not be opened. The most popular current form, Transcendental Meditation, is a representative example of the eastern and much western meditation, and unknown to most is that it is potentially quite dangerous. Insanity, possession, apathy, psychic insulation against true spirituality, and a high suicide rate are a few of the consequences. There are also serious cultural implications of TM. Interested readers should refer to Chapters 5 and 6 herein or coauthor Weldon's, *The Transcendental Explosion,* for documentation.[65]

Hypnotic regression

The use of hypnotic regression into past lives, or "reincarnation therapy" is currently on the increase among professionals. The general idea involved is that many of our psychological and physical problems result from negative experiences in other lifetimes. Representative of the trend is Dr. Edith Fiore's *You Have Been Here Before—A Psychologist Looks at Past Lives* and Marcia Moore's *Hypersentience*. A few examples in these books involve: (a) a woman with a strong impulse to jump overboard when on a ship and a phobia of getting lost at sea. Naturally, her reincarnation therapy uncovered past lives involving being a sailor lost at sea and refusing to jump off a sinking ship and being drowned; (b) a woman with a fear of the color red discovers that in another life she saw her mother bleeding to death after being stabbed; (c) another woman's phobia of trains goes back to seeing her sister crushed to death under a train. Nearly all patients with a chronic weight problem have had another life in which they nearly or actually starved to death (of course!). Chronic headaches are due to being shot, clubbed, guillotined, hanged, scalped, etc.— some severe injury to the neck or head in a past life. Much of this sounds like the brutally sadistic case histories discussed in Scientology founder L. Ron Hubbard's *Have You Lived Before This Life?* For some reason, reincarnation cases often seem to concentrate on the morbid.

What are we to make of all this? Much more could be said than we have room for, but a few key points should be noted.

First, hypnosis is by no means above suspicion. Hypnosis clearly has a strong occult tie-in. Our reasons for distrusting the use of hypnosis involve: (1) its possible similarity to the forbidden biblical practice of charming;[66] (2) its historic origin to the occult in both the East (yoga) and West (Spiritist movement); (3) the fact that a wide variety of occult powers can be developed from hypnosis; (4) often past lives "pop-up" during standard hypnotic regression, even when there is no expectation or searching for them; (5) cases of possession that have resulted; (6) the will must be surrendered to another person; (7) a similarity to mediumistic trance states; (8) we know too little about either the mind, hypnosis, or the spirit world to say unequivocally it is a generally safe practice.

Second, reincarnation itself is an occult doctrine. All the "evidence" for it comes only from occult sources—mediums, spirit guides, trance states (hypnosis), etc. Reincarnation is entirely opposed to the biblical worldview—in fact they are totally opposite systems. Reincarnation goes a long way toward insulating people against biblical salvation[67] and provides a justification for a great deal of evil (see Chapter 9 herein), confuses sex roles, and generally involves people in the occult. Considering these facts—the biblical view that "it is given for every many to die once and then comes judgment" (Hebrews 9:27); plus the known powers of biblical demons (extensive knowledge of past history, the implanting of false experiences into the mind, etc.)—the only really plausible explanation for genuine past lives episodes lies in the demonic realm.

Body Therapies: The Mediums of Muscles and Massage—Zone Therapy and Reflexology

Zone therapy teaches there are 10 zones in the body which govern other corresponding anatomical sections, or organs and their functions. (Reflexology is one aspect of Zone therapy that deals primarily with the feet.) For example, if one wishes to cure a heart ailment, the heart "zone" is found in a certain portion of the sole of the foot. When pressure is applied to the zone, the condition (pain, tension, etc.) is supposedly relieved. Reportedly (similar to acupressure), strong and consistent application of pressure will cause an anesthetic condition in the corresponding section (zone analgesia). According to Lipson, the big toe is particularly important (as it was in the ancient tradition of mystical Zoroastrianism), since it is purportedly connected to the mind, as well as coordinating harmony and rhythm in the body.[68] Underlying zone therapy is the idea that crystal deposits accumulate at nerve endings "affecting the ability of nerves to ground the electrical impulses which pass through them. The result of the therapeutic methods is to rub out these crystaline deposits, thus enabling the nerves to ground in the places of the body which gave pain or discomfort."[69]

It is interesting to note that although zone therapy uses many massage points that do *not* correspond to the meridians of acupressure, it has similar results.[70]

Other similar (and dissimilar) techniques include Functional Integration or the Feldenkrais method (named after its founder), the Alexander Method, Rolfing, Do'In, Shiatsu, and polarity therapy. Most of them incorporate massage techniques.[71] Psychic experiences are also reported in them variously. *Functional Integration* involves 1,000 physical-meditative exercises (with 40 variations each) which are designed to "virtually rebuild the human frame"[72] via neural repatterning, to expand the consciousness and to heighten or integrate the interrelationships and functions of mind and body. Sometimes called Western Yoga, it was developed by physicist Moshe Feldenkrais, author of *Awareness Through Movement* and *Body and Mature Behavior*. A knee injury led him to study anatomy and physiology and to spend two years studying yoga with Kuvalayananda in India.[73] Its application to yoga is primarily one of enhancement, although both techniques utilize a "state of [inner] attention [which is] a functioning of the nervous system that is of radically different order than normal conscious activity."[74]

The Alexander Method involves a rearranging of the skeletal-muscular system by changing the harmful ways that we move and rest (improper posture, etc.) in order to cure various physical and mental problems. *Rolfing* is based upon Wilhelm Reich's theory of "character armor" —that the "consciousness" can be found in the body as well as the brain, and that energy blockages cause lots of problems. "Because mind and body are interconnected, the results of past traumatic experiences show themselves in a person's posture . . . ." Through deep muscle massage—

which may be painful, even torturous, these blocks can be broken down and a harmonious mind-body system achieved. (The physical massage causes emotional release hence it is an emotional as well as physical treatment.) Lande warns:

> Because of the vehemence with which the massage is applied, it is important when seeking this treatment to choose skilled practitioners.[75]

Do'in is an ancient oriental, possibly occult teaching. Do'in teaches that an individual is most harmonious with himself and his environment when he is able to receive the proper mixture of finite and infinite stimuli or impulses of the universe. The infinite vibrations can only be received by those who are "properly attuned." (Most likely, "proper attunement" would involve some occult training.) These infinite vibrations "are contained in an electromagnetic energy or *ki,* which is received at the various pressure points and transmitted along the body's meridians."[76] A fully healthy body has *ki* circulating freely about it. Do'in helps the flow remain unobstructed. Supposedly, if an organ is not working properly, its meridian points become painful, even before any trouble signs show up in the organ. This pain is evidence that the *ki* is obstructed in these areas and thus hampering the natural flow. Do'in massage "calms the accumulated energy and rejuvenates the flow."[77] It claims to be able to cure any pain or disease, no matter how progressed, but the cure will be permanent only if the patient "studies, understands, and maintains a macrobiotic way of life."[78] (As with Edgar Cayce, health here is tied to maintaining a certain philosophy, i.e., a nonbiblical worldview.)

Shiatsu involves massage to treat various illnesses. It is somewhat similar to zone therapy in that pressure applied to certain areas distinct from the ailing areas can "cure" them. It is unlike zone therapy in that it usually applies pressure *near* the affected zone, and has some dissimilar correspondences—e.g., in zone therapy, the heart is strengthened by pressure on a certain area of the foot; in Shiatsu, pressure on the left hand is what works.[79] *Polarity*

Therapy (previously mentioned in connection with kinesiology) is based on man having both positive and negative energy within him. Massage is used to change the energy pattern and polarity of the body. The right side of the body is charged with "positive sun heat energy" and the left with "cooling moon receptive (negative) energy."[80] An excess of either requires readjustment of the energy pattern. The healer may tap the power of his heart chakra (yogic psychic center) by putting one hand over it and the other on the affected area. Again, many of these methods can have psychic elements and/or lead to psychic experiences (see the section on psychic Shiatsu in *The Holistic Health Handbook,* Berkeley, CA: And/Or Press, 1978).

Homeopathy

Homeopathy is a rather fascinating topic—it apparently works (sometimes), although no one knows how or why. Webster defines homeopathy as: "A system of medical practice that treats a disease esp. by the administration of minute doses of a remedy that would in *healthy* persons produce symptoms of the disease treated." It was developed by Samuel Hahnemann (1755-1843), and it has a prominent role in much of the holistic health movement. Since little is known about how it works, it is not surprising to find divergent views among homeopaths—even about the basic theory. Hence Bill Gray, M.D., refers to the "like cures like" theory—that microdilution (greatly reduced amounts) of the same substance which causes the illness will cure it.[81] These are called Succussed High Dilutions (SHD's). On the other hand, Victor Margutti, M.D., states: "The basic factor in homeopathy is not the use of small doses, as many unknowing people believe, but rather the use of qualitatively altered substances which are hence capable of efficacy in small amounts."[82] Even further, Dr. Michaud says you can use just about *anything* to cure ailments, it does not have to be the same substance (a radionic function?) Homeopathy is a strange mixture of odd elements—unknown energy concepts, cures effected as if by magic, a required (?) sensitivity to personality types (more concern with psychology than anatomy), etc. According to some, we must be dealing with an energy concept here because nothing else can account for the fact that cures are still effected after SHD's, which in essence leave none of the original substance in the treatment. Homeopath Dr. Jacques Michaud elaborates on this strange effect:

> Dilution means diminishing the quantity of the substance, according to a geometric progression, to the point where there are no more detectable molecules, and even beyond. But although there's less and less matter as dilution increases, there's more and more energy.
>
> As for succussion, it consists in energizing the bottle between two successive dilutions, which facilitates disintegration of molecules. Complex physical phenomena are involved here, but clinical experiments have shown the importance of this process.
>
> In homeopathy, the wealth of therapeutic resources is infinite. There are no foreseeable limits because anything can be a remedy and can be used with all possible and imaginable dilutions. For example, a woman came to consult me because she had an allergy. I found that she was allergic to a product used for cleansing soil. I put some of it into a bottle and sent it to a laboratory. It's become a useful homeopathic remedy in other cases.
>
> So we have an infinite range available to us. A homeopathic doctor usually knows and uses only a few hundred remedies. That's nothing compared to the possibilities that could be exploited if there were medical research in homeopathy. But even now the wealth of homeopathic therapy goes far beyond what's offered by allopathy, which seems to us a meager, narrow form of therapy.[83]

Dr. Margutti quotes David Mock of the University of Oklahoma Medical Center as noting the effect of nonexistent mercuric chloride:

> The effect of microdoses of mercuric chloride in distilled water used were in the order of 10^{-71}, the term *microdoses* seems almost gross, for in terms of contemporary physical thought, *not a single molecule of the mercuric chlorides should be present in the test solutions.*[84]

He then notes that "Barnard and Stephenson point out that succussion . . . 'dilutions' of 10^{-70} have noted clinical responses . . . ." He says the most plausible way to explain this is by the (occultist) Pythagorean idea "that the reality of things lies more in their form than in their material . . . ." Whether homeopathy involves "balancing the etheric body" as Blair suggests,[85] or as yet unknown physical or spiritual laws remains to be seen. Margutti believes that it is the form and subchemical (etheric?) nature of the substance that allows for small changes that are the causative factor. Hence presumably the "original substance" remains, but in changed form and is thus not perceptible. Whether this is the case, or whether the SHD's leave "imprints" of the original substance that in some sense persist beyond the physical, is impossible to tell. Margutti seems to opt for both:

> The basic factor in homeopathy is not the use of small doses, as many unknowing people believe, but rather the use of qualitatively altered substances which are hence capable of efficacy in small amounts. This "qualitative-quantitative" factor, the basis of allergy, is well known to medicine, as illustrated by the "Pollen Diseases." Thus, in cytoplasmic molecular chemistry, the information content of the solute may reproduce itself separate from its chemical action. As this process may also occur in cellular fluids, it provides a hypothesis for explaining the clinical action of S.H.D.'s (Succussed High Dilutions) almost on an antigen-antibody basis. This may be likened to an "energy template" passing on its patterning long after the original

> embossing, but altering some with each successive act. Thus the change must be physical-spatial rather than chemical. In other words, since the imprint goes on far beyond the presence of the imprinting agent, it involves energy factors.
>
> There is also another factor to consider, i.e., the extreme biological importance of order in molecular structure. Thus specificity of proteins is determined by the exact order of amino acids in the polypeptide chain, and in drugs of similar chemical structure. Small changes in the spatial arrangements of the molecule can alter toxicity considerably. Quantum chemistry theory indicates that succussed high dilutions may act via the physico-dynamic structure of their solvent phase rather than the chemical properties of their dissolved solutes.[85a]

He also refers to osteopath Selye's fascinating observation that "glass objects regularly produce cancer when implanted under the skin of a rat. They fail to do so unless they have a certain shape."[86]

The concept of the "life force" is predominant in both holistic health and homeopathy. Margutti relates homeopathy to Burr's L-(for life) fields. Dr. Gray refers to a generalized life force that does the healing and states it has many names—chi, prana, spirit, etc. He gives the force almost a god-like power, providing, or course, it is stimulated by homeopathy. (In fact, he claims nonhomeopathic holistic health methods are essentially ineffective when dealing with chronic disease.) Not so with homeopathy:

> Homeopathy is a very systematic method of prescribing single substances which powerfully stimulate the life force to heal whatever is wrong with a person. It is, of course, highly effective in acute ailments, even viral illnesses such as influenza and hepatitis. Its greatest value, however, is in chronic diseases such as arthritis, allergies, asthma, colitis, ulcers, migraines, neurological diseases, diabetes, and cardiovascular prob-

lems, in which the proper homeopathic remedy can cure not only the specific chronic disease but also the inherited tendency to chronic disease in general. By "cure" the homeopath means relief from the ailment for life after being given one dose of one remedy (or at least only a very few remedies), and without being dependent on any regimen of activity, diet, or medication.[87]

Also of concern is the emphasis in homeopathy upon matching treatment to *personalities,* not diseases, and here we come into a more clearly discernible possibility of occultism. Michaud states: In homeopathy, we try to do that [recognize individual uniquenesses], which is why we have to put more stress on individual differences, and that leads to an interest in such things as astrology and acupuncture.[88] Dr. Gray states of a belladonna-treated fever:

This cure will occur regardless of whether the cause of the fever is strep throat, influenza, or meningitis, because the cure is matched to the individuality of the *person,* not of the disease.

He goes on to say:

So the basic task of the homeopath is to match *personalities.* The "personality" of the remedy is determined by the individual actions it has on normal people. Some people describe this "personality" as the manifestation of the "vibrational frequency" of the substance.

Then, the homeopath must discern in great detail and with deep sensitivity, what are the most unique aspects of the personality of his patients. Some of the kind of questions he might ask include: Compared to most people, are you . . . changeable or predictable? . . .mental, emotional, or physical? . . .introverted or extroverted? . . . high or low in self-confidence? . . . fastidious or sloppy? . . . leader or follower? . . . good with or afraid of responsibility? . . . warmblooded or chilly? . . . indoor or ourdoor type . . . athletic or sedentary? . . . Do you tend to crave or dislike sweets, sour, salt, meat, fat, milk, warm drinks, cold drinks? . . . And so on during an interview that can take 1 - 1½ hours or longer. When this matching of images is properly done, just a single dose of the remedy will produce a seemingly miraculous cure. How does this cure occur? As I said, we have no idea, but we do know the method of producing it.

What exactly are the homeopathic remedies? Again, we do not really know. We only know how to prepare them. In experimenting with various methods of preparing substances to be given to normal people, Hahnemann somehow came across a method of enhancing the curative powers of substances while preventing toxic effects. Initially the remedy is dissolved in alcohol from herbs, flowers, earth salts, and animal tissues. This is then diluted 1:10 to 1:100 in alcohol in a glass container and shaken very hard for a long time. That solution is further diluted and shaken. The more the substance is shaken and diluted in alcohol and glass (all four factors being absolutely essential), the greater the curative power that results. The incredible fact is that there is no limit to how many times the shaking and diluting can be done while increasing the curative potential. According to chemistry, 1:100 dilutions past 12 times no longer possess even one molecule of the original substance. In homeopathy, we consider 30 such dilutions a "low potency;" a "high potency" might go as high as 100,000 or 1,000,000 of the 1:100 dilutions, but as yet no limit has been found.

When we give a homeopathic remedy, what are we giving? Some kind of energy, life force itself? Nobody knows. All we know is that it works. If the "wrong" remedy is given (not a perfect match by the principle of "Like Cures

Like"), nothing at all happens—no cure, no side effects. But when the "right" remedy is found, and given as this infinitessimal "essence," it produces a profound and lasting cure, even of so-called incurable hereditary diseases.[89]

There are many other methods of "healing"—pyramidology, the various pendulum methods, stones and plants with supernatural healing abilities, etc. All of these methods are occult. For example, healing stones and plants are part of the animist cultures—those who believe a spirit indwells nearly everything. Amulets, fetishes, and talismans are made from stones considered to have psychic power behind them.[90] In essence, the spirits are the elements of power, not the plants or stones. A variation of the occult use of plants would involve a discussion of the Findhorn village, a "new age" community in Scotland comprised of a group of mediums who in return for their obeisance to the nature devas (various spirits) are able to produce giant forms of plants and vegetables. Analysis by soil experts has proven there is nothing in the soil to account for the rapid growth or giant forms of the plants—they are produced by energy from the "devas."

This concludes our admittedly brief trek through the alternative medicines. We find that most of them are occult or borderline occult and should be avoided (radionics, witchcraft, astrology, meditation, hypnotic regression, chromotherapy, etc.). Some may offer new possibilities for the advancement of medicine and treatment (medical sound therapy, certain massage methods). A few are neutral and can be used for good or evil (biofeedback). Some, while having a partial medical basis are at times a combination of occultism and faulty science (chiropractice, iridology, applied kinesiology). Others are a combination of the above and resist easy classification. Future research may uncover the fact that many of the alternative medicines are psychometric in function: they work (or the machines that accompany them) only because of the psychic sensitivity of the "healer"/operator.

The Spiritual Counterfeits Journal issue on Holistic Health had a particularly perceptive statement which concludes this section eloquently:

> The original purpose of this article was to answer the question: To what extent does the holistic health movement commonly recognize occult metaphysics and eastern mystical spiritual experience as an operating basis for its activities and its self-understanding? Most of the evidence available for inspection indicates that the answer can be given without qualification: Overwhelmingly. It appears that the movement as a whole is dominated, if not controlled, by a consistent and systematic form of spirituality that is radically antithetical to biblical Christianity.
>
> . . . The matter of *modality* (specific healing techniques) is quite a bit more complicated. The question is likely to be presented as, "Is it permissible for a Christian to submit to acupuncture (or Rolfing, or homeopathic medicine, or psychic surgery, etc.)?" Procedures such as psychic surgery and mediumistic diagnosis do not require much comment. In some of the less obvious cases, there are too many variables to permit generalized conclusions. However, some pertinent observations can be made.
>
> The first, and most important, is to realize that nearly all of the "holistic" techniques—biofeedback, acupuncture, meditation, and so forth—are brimful with subtle and complex spiritual implications which derive from the humanistic, occult, or religious worldviews of their originators. Most of them are designed to produce novel states of consciousness which are interpreted to the patient in ways that seem to validate those worldviews. *To the extent that these considerations are ignored or remain unanalyzed,* they are capable of eroding the intellectual and experien-

tial foundations of Christian faith. Indeed as Kenneth Pelletier candidly remarks, the reshaping of a meditator's worldview is part of a process that may well be *intrinsic* to the technique:

> A person entering into meditation has already in some sense committed himself to an accompanying philosophical system. This factor of the individual's attitude as he approaches meditation practice cannot be underestimated in understanding the positive effects of such practice.

As a practical matter the "accompanying philosophical system" will usually be conveyed by the person who administers the treatment. *His* role, then, is critical, and his spiritual stance (if it can be determined) may well settle the issue. In fact, the intellectual and philosophical factor may be less significant than the healer's direct spiritual or psychic relationship with his patient. Many holistic practitioners evidently rely on trance states or other altered states of consciousness in order to make their treatments "work."

For example, in describing the technique of massage in Oriental medicine, two experts emphasize that the process is expressed:

> . . . as an actual physical relationship, and entails a passage of "vital energy," "life essence," . . . or "Ki," as it is called, between the practitioner and patient . . . . Practitioners have described their conscious mental state as devoid of conceptual thought. This allows them to concentrate and channel their Ki strongly and evenly during treatment. By acting in this state of awareness, the practitioner . . . attempts to "stimulate" or "charge" the Ki of the other person by

channeling his own Ki into the patient.

It is not difficult to see that such psychic manipulation could turn an otherwise benign form of treatment into a spiritual booby trap. The nature of the doctor-patient relationship implicitly involves a kind of trust in and submission to the healer on many levels. For a Christian to accept the passive stance of "patient" before a practitioner who exercises spiritual power (either in his own right or as a channel for other influences) could easily result in spiritual derangement or bondage.

It is probable that none of the eastern or occult healing techniques are "neutral" in themselves, even when ostensibly divorced from overt philosophical statements; the metaphysical framework from which they emerge is so pervasive and encompassing that every detail of practice is intricately related to elements of the underlying belief system. As a result, the technique taken as a whole will carry overtones and implications of the metaphysical system from which it is derived, even if that system is not *explicitly* attached.

On the other hand, it may be possible to *neutralize* or even *revalue* some techniques by thoroughly grasping their philosophical derivations, analyzing those derivations carefully, and replacing them with a framework of biblical understanding. This would be a delicate and difficult undertaking, to say the least.

As a *movement,* holistic health presents a picture that is difficult to assess, partly because of its extent and complexity, partly because it is in a state of rapid change . . . .

The most significant and troublesome aspect of the movement, however, has to do with the admittedly religious basis that it has chosen for itself. The San Diego symposium made it blazingly clear that the holistic health movement believes its primary task is to proclaim that the occult-mystical worldview contains the only workable solution to the human predicament. However, this fact is rarely stated as plainly to outsiders as it was acknowledged in San Diego. Perhaps one reason for this evasion is that such a proclamation contains a number of uncomfortable implications . . . .

These qualities of religious zealotry are classic, and would hardly deserve our commentary were it not for two momentous facts:

1. The religious point of view embodied in the holistic movement is an integral part of the occult/mystical worldview that is making a coordinated thrust into every aspect of our cultural consciousness. It is not a fad, it will not go away, and it is fundamentally hostile to biblical Christianity.

2. A major part of the movement's strategy is based on an effort to bend the structures of government and public policy in its behalf—to enlist the state in the propagation of its religious vision for humanity. One speaker in San Diego announced that AHH president David Harris had recently been appointed to Senator Hayakawa's advisory board on health. Public funding is already being sought—and obtained—for teaching holistic concepts to various audiences, professional and otherwise. In these circumstances, it would be something of an understatement to say that this policy raises serious constitutional problems in terms of separation of church and state.

The ultimate weakness of the holistic concept, however, is one that only time and a confrontation with truth will reveal. Since it lacks any objective moral basis, holism in the occult/mystical sense can never comprehend authentic healing or its source.

> Be not wise in your own eyes; *fear the Lord and turn away from evil.* It will be healing to your flesh and refreshment to your bones [Prov. 3:7-8; italics added].[91]

References for Chapter 15

1. Jessica Maxwell, "What Your Eyes Tell You About Your Health," *Esquire,* January 1978, p. 56.
1a. E.M. Oakley, "Iridology: Your Eyes Reflect Your Health," *New Realities,* Vol. 1, No. 3, p. 50.
2. *Ibid.,* p. 52.
3. Kurt Koch, *The Devil's Alphabet,* p. 38-9.
4. *Ibid.,* pp. 40-42.
5. Koch, *Ibid.,* p. 40-41.
6. Oakley, *op. cit., New Realities,* p. 51-2.
7. Blair, *Rhythms of Vision,* p. 111.
8. Heline, *Healing and Regeneration Through Color,* p. 37.
9. *Ibid.,* p. 39, cf. 14-18.
10. Heline, *op. cit.,* p. 15, 37, 39; Stearn, *Edgar Cayce the Sleeping Prophet,* p. 84; Wallace and Henkin, *The Psychic Healing Book,* p. 24.
11. Heline, p. 33-4.
12. Heline, *op. cit.,* p. 37-8.
13. *Ibid.,* p. 37.
14. Koch, *The Devil's Alphabet,* p. 35.
15. *Ibid.,* p. 36.
16. Glass, *Witchcraft the Sixth Sense,* p. 123-4.
17. *Los Angeles Times,* 2/18/78
18. *Ibid.*
19. Blair, *op. cit.,* p. 117.
20. *Ibid.*
21. Arthur Avalon, *The Serpent Power.* (NY: Dover) 1974 p. 83-4.
22. Weldon, *The Transcendental Explosion,* appendix.
23. Conway, *Magic: An Occult Primer,* chapter on the Kabbalistic Master Ritual.
24. Weldon, *Is There Life After Death.* p. 93.
25. Brochure, "Astral Projection by Sound" from The

American Research Team, Beverly Hills, Calif.
26. Brown, *Unfinished Symphonies* (NY William & Morrow) 1971, eg. ch. 5.
27. Huard & Wong, *Oriental Methods of Mental and Physical Fitness* (NY Funk and Wagnalls) 1971, p. 51-2.
28. Weldon, *The Transcendental Explosion*, Appendix 2-3.
29. *New Age Journal,* March 1978, "Kundalini Casualties" p. 86.
30. Reprinted in *New Directions,* no. 20, Nov.-Dec., 1976, p. 36-44.
31. *Psychic,* Nov.-Dec., 1976, p. 17.
32. Alan Vaughan Interview: Irving Oyle, D.O., *Psychic,* Nov.-Dec., 1976, p. 18.
33. p. 63.
34. Gallant, *Astrology Sense or Nonsense?* (NY Doubleday, 1974); Jerome, *Astrology Disproved* (Buffalo NY Prometheus) 1977; Gauquelin, *Dreams and Illusions of Astrology* (Prometheus) 1979.
35. Ben Adams, *Astrology: The Ancient Conspiracy* (Bethany) 1963.
36. Wilson, *The Occult,* p. 250.
37. Gauquelin, *op. cit.*, ch. 8.
38. Keith Thomas, *Religion and the Decline and Fall of Magic,* "Some Interconnections," ch. 21, p. 631-32.
39. Garrison, *Medical Astrology,* pp. 11-13.
40. Manolesco, *Scientific Astrology,* p. 143.
41. Garrison, *op. cit.,* p. 13.
42. Shealy, *Occult Medicine Can Save Your Life,* p. 115, 118.
43. Koch, *The Devil's Alphabet; Between Christ and Satan; Satan's Devices,* pp. 18-21.
44. Manolesco, *Scientific Astrology,* p. 135.
45. Garrison, *op. cit.,* p. 147.
46. *Ibid.,* p. 165.
47. Goosen, "Touch Me, Heal Me" *Psychic,* Nov.-Dec. 1976, p. 11.
48. *Ibid.,* p. 12.
49. John Keel, *Operation Trojan Horse* (NY Putnam Sons) 1970, p. 279.
50. Lowen, *Bioenergetics,* p. 38.

51. *Ibid.*
52. *Ibid.*
53. W. Edward Mann, "Wilhelm Reich and Orgone Energy" in White and Krippner, *Future Science*, p. 113.
54. J. Eden, *Animal Magnetism and the Life Energy*, p. x.
55. *Ibid.*, p. xv-xvi.
56. Lande, *Lifestyles - Mindstyles*, p. 160.
57. *Ibid.*, p. 163.
58. North, *None Dare Call It Witchcraft*, p. 57-58.
59. Lande. *op. cit.*, p. 165.
60. Green, *Beyond Biofeedback*, p. 318.
61. *Ibid.*, p. 319.
62. *Ibid.*, p. 320.
63. *Ibid.*, p. 320.
64. Weldon, *Transcendental* app. 2-3; Dr. Koch's six books on the occult.
65. *Harvest House*, 1977.
66. *The Zondervan Pictorial Encyclopedia of the Bible*, Vol. 2, p. 304.
67. Weldon, *Transcendental*, appendix 4.
68. G. Lipson, *Beyond Yoga*, (NY: Jove) 1977, p. 101.
69. Most of these descriptions are from Lande, *op. cit.*, p. 174-182.
70. B.A. Goosen, "Touch Me, Heal Me," *Psychic,* Nov. 1976.
71. Lipson, *op. cit.*, p. 93.
72. Lipson, *op. cit.*, p. 174-5.
73. S. Cubley, "The Feldenkrais Technique and Yoga," *Yoga Journal*, Nov./Dec. 1976, p. 40-43.
74. *Ibid.*
75. Lande, *op. cit.*, p. 177.
76. *Ibid.*, p. 178.
77. *Ibid.*
78. *Ibid.*
79. *Ibid.*, p. 179.
80. V. Kulvinskas, *Survival into the 21st Century* (Wethersfield Conn, Omangod Press) 1975, p. 209.
81. Bill Grey, "The Role of Homeopathy in Holistic Health Practice," *Yoga Journal*, Nov./Dec., 1976, p. 44-6.
82. V.M. Margutti, "Homeopathy, Homeotherapeutics and

Modern Medicine," *The Journal of Holistic Health*, 1977, p. 88.
83. de Smedte, *et. al.*, *Lifearts*, pp. 141-3.
84. Margutti, *op. cit.*, p. 89.
85. Blair, p. 152.
85a. Margutti, *op. cit.*, p. 88-89.
86. *Ibid.*, p. 89.
87. Bill Grey, "The Role of Homeopathy in Holistic Health Practice," *Yoga Journal*, November-December, 1976, p. 45.
88. de Smedte, *Lifearts,* p. 142.
89. Grey, *op. cit.*, p. 46.
90. E.A. Wallace Budge, *Egyptian Magic,* ch. 2.
91. *SCP Journal,* "The Marriage of Science and Religion, special holistic health issue, from SCP, Box 2418, Berkeley, CA 94702, pp. 15-17.

Chapter 16

The "New" Energy Forces Are Very Old

Contrary to popular opinion (at least some), the startling new discoveries of psychic energy—put forth as evidence of a quantum burst in man's evolution—are in fact very old. Not only is the energy idea ancient, but in every age the concept has been tied to the occult, including our own age of "exciting new discoveries." For example, White and Kripper list about 90 different names for the same general energy idea. Although all 90 terms are not fully synonymous, and there is overlap and convergence among them, the basic idea of an unusual, unknown energy is central.

The date of origin of such theories begins with Hindu *prana* (3000 B.C.) and extends to Dr. Tiller's magneto-electricity (1973). Nearly every name of which we had some knowledge (25) was tied to the occult in one way or another. Another 25 were from animistic-spiritistic cultures. Hence, without any further research, we find that 50 of the names were integrally tied to the occult. Also, many if not nearly all of the individuals who put forth names for this energy (from 1650 to the present) were heavily involved in the occult, either as psychic researchers and parapsychologists (nearly all of whom attended seances) or mediums. The energy studied was nearly always associated with occultists and mediums.

Name	Active Involvement	Names Used
Viktor Inyushin, et al	Russian parapsychologists	Bioplasma, psychotronic energy, etc.
Charles Reicher	Psychic Researcher	ectoplasm
Henry Bulwer-Lytton	Psychic Researcher	Vril
H. P. Blavatsky	Medium, Theosophy founder	Astral light
Rudolf Steiner	Occultist	Etheric Formative Forces
Hereward Carrington	Psychic Researcher	Human fluid or vital magnetism
Paracelsus	Occultist	Munia or Mumia
Franz Anton Mesmer	Occultist	Animal magnetism
Robert Fludd	Rosicrucian (occultist)	Spiritus
William McDougall	President, Amer. Society Psych. Research; Society Psychic Research	Hormic energy
William Crooks (1811)	Psychic Researcher	Psychic force
Hans Dreisch	Psychic Researcher	Entelechy
J. B. Rhine	Psychic Researcher	Psi Faculty
Andrija Puharich	Medium	Psi Plasma
George De La Warr	Medium	Bio magnetism
Ambrose Worrall	Medium	Paraelectricity
Colin Wilson	Psychic Researcher	X-Factor
Eliphas Levi	Magus	Astral Light
W. E. Butler	Magus	Elemental Energy

In fact, White and Kripper imply that all their names stem from "prescientific and esoteric/occult tradition."¹ (In the above list a few have been added by the authors.)

Examining Five Examples

We shall examine five types of energy in more detail: Hindu (or yogic) *prana*; the *mana* of the Hawaiian/Polynesian Kahunas (Shamans or primitive mediums); Mesmer's *Animal Magnetism;* Von Reichenbach's *Od;* and Karagulla's *Higher Sense Perception.* We may not be able to state the exact nature of this energy, but by demonstrating its strong relationship to the occult we can at least point out three possibilities: (1) that depending on the topic, the energy is the energy of the demon itself (which may also involve a vampirism of human energy, a possible intermingling, as in ectoplasmic seances); (2) that the energy is actually or potentially usable by demons, i.e., if in fact it does not exist, it can be used as a guise for "neutral" energy; (3) as a philosophical justification for monism (the only reality is One divine energy), or pantheism (the universe and man are God). We should take note of the fact that hope of this power is to give man control over his destiny.

Prana. Prana is believed to be universal energy residing behind the material world (akasa), and it has 5 forms. All energy is a manifestation of it. Nikhilananada describes it in his *Vivekananda—The Yogas and Other Works* (1953) as "the infinite, omnipresent manifesting power of this universe." Yoga aims at the knowledge and control of prana, or pranayama, through the potentially lethal rising of the Kundalini, a snake believed to be residing at the base of the spine. When aroused through yoga, she travels upward, opening the chakras and giving psychic powers. (From the days of Genesis snakes have always been symbols of knowledge and power.) Perfect control of prana makes one God. One can have "infinite knowledge, infinite power, now."

> What power on earth would not be his? He would be able to move the sun and stars out of their places, to control everything in the universe from the atoms to the biggest suns. This is the end and aim of pranayama. When the yogi becomes perfect there will be nothing in nature not under his control. If he orders the gods or the souls of the departed to come, they will come at his bidding. All the forces of nature will obey him as slaves. . . .He who has controlled prana

has controlled his own mind and all the minds . . . and all the bodies that exist. . . .[2]

The aim of pranayama is to rouse the coiled-up power in the Muladhara [chakra], called the Kundalini [note: Kundalini rising can lead to possession or death and is extremely dangerous] . . . .Only for those who can go on farther with it [prana] will the Kundalini be aroused. Then the whole of nature will begin to change and the door of [psychic] knowledge will open. No more will you need to go to books for knowledge; your own mind will have become your book, containing infinite knowledge.[3]

Cases of healing from a distance are perfectly true. Prana can be transmitted to a very great distance.[4]

. . . when the balance of prana is disturbed, what we call disease is produced. To take away the superfluous prana, or to supply the prana that is wanting, will be to cure the disease.[5]

According to Vivekananda, all occult forces are accomplished through prana.

We see in every country sects that attempted the control of prana. In this country there are mind-healers, faith-healers, spiritualists (spiritists), Christian Scientists, hypnotists, and so on. If we examine these different sects, we shall find at the back of each is the control of prana, whether they know it or not. If you boil all the theories down, the residuum will be that. It is one and the same force they are manipulating . . . .Thus we see that pranayama includes all that is true even of spiritualism. Similarly, you will find that wherever any sect or body of people is trying to discover anything occult, mysterious, or hidden, they are really practicing some sort of yoga to control their prana. You will find that wherever there is any extraordinary display of power, it is the manifestation of prana.[6]

Regardless of what prana is, or even whether it exists as defined by Vivekananda, it is clear from the above that what is truly a demonic energy output in seances, witchcraft, psychokinesis, psi-healing, etc., *would* be defined as prana. Prana is therefore reducible to the demonic energy of occult manifestations. How many of the other "new" energy categories fall to a similar fate?

Mana. The word *huna* means secret or occult. A Kahuna (Polynesian Shaman) is the keeper or guardian of the occult. The Kahuna's power to do all kinds of miracles and practice magic—black or white—is accomplished through *mana,* the vital force of life. As described by Max Freedom Long in *The Secret Science Behind Miracles,* the Kahunas have a rather complex psychology-philosophy, involving a separate-etheric body for the low, middle, and high self. There is the use of an increasingly strong *mana* by each one, depending on the function, whether it be thinking or doing miracles.[7] The really big miracles are done by the *mana loa,* used by the "etheric body" of the "high self."

Similarities to Parapsychology

In many ways, Kahunas are reminiscent of modern parapsychologists. They have redefined and neutralized the demonic under the guise of human potential. As animists, they at least freely confess their belief in spiritism as well and state it is the spirits who use the *mana,* particularly in death magic. In the Kahuna system the High Self acts in an equivalent fashion to the spirit guide of a medium, although not viewed as such. Everything the spirit guide does for the medium, the High Self, utilizing *mana,* does for the Kahuna. Sometimes the Kahunas admit that the spirits of the dead make contact with the High Self and do various psychic feats (p.196). Like the energy behind Edgar Cayce's "unconscious," and the higher-self spiritism of the popular *A Course in Miracles,* the *mana* force of the Kahunas has a separate, independent consciousness and intelligence all its own.

Interestingly enough, the "higher self" concept is becoming increasingly prevalent today; even in academic circles. Even though the demonic remains completely hidden under the idea of higher self powers, the dynamics of spiritism are always manifested sooner or later. Robert Assagioli's psychosynthesis movement is one modern example where this concept is utilized. The psychosynthesis Workbook 2 (*(Synthesis 2)* contains an article by Stuart Miller "Dialogue With the Higher Self" which is clearly spiritistic, although carefully couched in neutral language (e.g., cf. p. 138). It is not surprising that the mind should be a guise for demonism. The mind is the natural focal point and target for demonic schemes. Humanistic and transpersonal psychology have thus laid a theoretical foundation for higher-self spiritism, i.e., spiritism under the guise of one's higher self. Psychology and the occult have had a tenuous partnership for a long time. The occultist Mesmer was held to be responsible for laying the foundation of modern psychiatry. Jung was a part-time occultist. E. Fuller Torrey, in *The Mind Game,* points out many numbers of similarities between the witch doctor and psychiatrist. *Occult Psychology, Psychiatry and Mysticism,* and *Psychoanalysis and the Occult* are three books which variously indicate the relationship and trends of an emerging occult psychology that will hide the demonic in the realm of the mind.

Three Spirits Inside Man?

Actually, the Kahunas see the three selves as being three spirits inside man—a less evolved lower spirit just up from the animal kingdom, a more evolved spirit, and a superconscious spirit, acting as a guardian angel. Interestingly, Long, in reference to Edgar Cayce, states: "This medium was used by a spirit doctor who was responsible for many amazing cures"—p. 348. Probably this is simply his analysis, but possibly he had access to additional information not well known. Given Long's familiarity with the occult and various spirit manifestations, his classification is still noteworthy.

Long uses the fact of *mana* to explain all the various miracles of psychic research—for him, like Vivekananda's prana, they are done by *mana* power. Long admits that even the lowest *mana* acts "almost as if it were itself conscioius" (p. 230), and that it does supernatural feats and obeys the Kahuna in an "almost human way" (p. 262).

As with prana, it is clear that the force Kahunas describe as *mana* is simply a synonym for demonic energy. Substitute the word spirit for *mana*, place the Kahuna in a modern spiritistic environment, and there would be little *essential* difference between the effects and actions of the spirit and the *mana*. They are quite similar.

Another interesting point Long mentions, which relates to other energy concepts, is the supposed ability of Kahunas to energize water with low *mana* for purposes of healing (p. 264). Anton Mesmer, father of modern hypnotism, would also charge a tub of water to transfer animal magnetism into his patients via iron rods. Similarly, "Christian" spiritist Olga Worral, in experiments done with a Dr. Miller at the famous Roman Catholic "healing" shrine at Lourdes found no healing properties in the water itself. However, when she "energized" it (she admits spirits work through her) "some very interesting things happened."[8] Again, all this points to a demonic use of energy, rather than a neutral latent energy source in man.

Animal Magnetism . . . and Mesmerism

Anton Mesmer, discoverer of our third energy example, animal magnetism, had an early interest in ESP and did his doctoral study on astrology. It was not infrequent for people who were "mesmerized" to experience spiritistic contacts and trance (somnambulist) states achieved through "the universal fluid, animal magnetism." Despite what some wish to deny, Mesmer was an occultist, although, like parapsychologists today, one with a more scientific orientation, and animal magnetism was an occult force.[9] Like mana and prana, animal magnetism is the power behind all occult manifestations. Dr. Vincent Buranelli states in his *The Wizard From Vienna:*

He began with the abililty of men and women, under the influence of animal magnetism, to activate strange powers wtihin themselves, to gain insights into cosmic truths hidden from most of humanity by a veil of ignorance. He had observed subjects, and the annals of Mesmerism recorded many more, who manifested super-normal powers. He could no longer be sure where the real sciences left off and the occult sciences began . . . . He had written in his doctoral dissertation and repeated in a series of writings, that hoary fallacies could be shown to have essential truth within them when interpreted scientifically—astrology, alchemy, oneiromancy (divination by dreams), divination. Now he will explain them through animal magnetism.[10]

He went on to investigate clairvoyant diagnosis and prognosis during trance, precognition, and general clairvoyance, telepathy, etc. He desired to know: Why is a man not always endowed with such powers? How can the powers best be developed? And most importantly, why do these powers occur most frequently and appear in their most developed form when the methods of animal magnetism are used?

In addition, the founder of homeopathy, Samuel Hahnemann, "was also a great defender of Mesmer's animal magnetism. In the *Organon* he stated it was a curative force and marvelous priceless gift of God to mankind."[11] After Mesmer died at 81 (as accurately predicted by a fortune teller), his friend and biographer Justinus Kerner became a leader of Mesmerism during the 19th century, utilizing Mesmeric trances as a means of mediumistic communication. His book about Frederike Hauffe, *The Seeress of Prevorst*, made the latter an important figure of European occultism. It was through the Mesmeric trance that she initially began contacting the dead, and Kerner surmised that the Mesmeric and spiritistic trance were one and the same.

Dr. Buranelli noted that "Mesmerian Spiritualism

flourished most abundantly in the United States. . . ."[12] He also documented that Mesmerism and its animal magnetism had a wide occult influence. For example, Phineas P. Quimby was a Mesmerist whose healing of Mary Baker Eddy led to the founding of Christian Science. Quimby based his healings on an unknown energy, which was developed for personal use only after much effort. (This is a common requirement for developing psychic abilities—unless one has a family history of occult involvement, it may take a long time to acquire them.) Quimby would first pray to an impersonal wisdom, and then contact would be made with a tremendous energy which allowed him to heal. Initially Quimby seems to have believed that spirits did a great deal of the work. However, he later changed his views to a belief in the power of the mind, reminiscent of modern "higher self" theories.

Helena Blavatsky, the potent mediumistic founder of Theosophy, was also in some manner indebted to Mesmerism (both Eddy and Blavatsky purportedly agreed that animal magnetism was "esoteric magic"). Blavatsky read Mesmer's works which gave her a foundation in mysticism, and she appropriated animal magnetism as a "carrier" of occult powers. Her spirit-written *Isis Unveiled* has many references to Mesmer, and according to Buranelli states: "Mesmerism is the most important branch of magic; and its phenomena are the effects of the universal agent which underlies all magic and has produced in all ages so-called miracles."[13]

Supposedly, in the years to follow, "scientific" Mesmerism became hypnosis, while occult Mesmerism has continued to this day in various occult groups. Yet distinguishing between occult and "scientific" mesmerism is like distinguishing between "scientific" and occult psychic powers. They are not so easily divided. In fact, no occult phenomena found in Mesmerism is lacking in hypnosis. The only difference between hypnosis and Mesmerism is that the former does not have the trappings of the latter —a universal fluid theory, iron tubs, etc. It appears that, in *essence* modern hypnotism *is* Mesmerism. Martin Ebon, fairly well respected as an occult authority, even connects the two: "The mesmeric, or hypnotic, trance bears a close resemblance to the mediumistic trance."[14]

In conclusion, animal magnetism is the same "unknown" energy utilized for psychic powers as mana and prana.

Od. "Od," (from the Norse God, Odin) was "discovered" by Baron Von Reichenbach. Utilizing experiments with some 300 "sensitives" (i.e., psychics), he discovered that all substances radiate their own quality of an omnipresent "Odic" force. This was evidenced by the psychic's ability to see odic emanations (a luminous glow) around magnets and crystals in a darkened room. According to magician W. E. Butler, Reichenbach's findings "have much of value for the practical magician . . . [and] certainly enter into all magical work."[15] In other words, the odic force is equivalent to the energy behind occult magic.

When we realize that many magicians (such as in Conway's *Magic: An Occult Primer)* view their energy as coming from spirits and demons, again the spiritistic connection is made (although in magic there is also a belief in an omnipresent "life force" linking the occultist's mind to the cosmic mind). Regardless, it is often the spirit, conjured up by ritual, who does the actual work. (Conway, p. 130-131.)

Reichenbach himself had been heavily involved in the study of Mesmerism for several decades. He discovered that those individuals who could perceive the od were easily placed into the somnambulistic trance, where spiritistic manifestations occurred. According to Mishlove, "The link between Mesmerism and spiritualism is most clearly evidenced by the researches of Baron Karl von Reichenbach . . . ."[16] He used the concept of odic force to explain much of the phenomena of spiritism. Colin Wilson, in the book, *The Occult,* states that it is clear "that this sensitivity to the 'odic' force is fundamentally of the same nature as the powers of psychics like [Peter] Hurkos or [Gerard] Croiset."[17] In other words, "od" is the power utilized by occultists.

Higher Sense Perception

Although not defined in the same manner as other energy concepts, Shafica Karagulla's term is included in our discussion, both because of her wide influence and as an example of a conceptual masking of the occult. In her book, *Breakthrough to Creativity,* Karagulla tells of the exciting discoveries of the "new powers" people are manifesting (defined as a possible evolutionary "mutation in consciousness"). The book attempts to entirely stay away from the occult—and she refuses to use even the term psychic. No doubt this is due to her desire to maintain her reputation as an orthodox scientist.

Other parapsychologists have the same general bias. Ebon notes: "One word that parapsychologists totally disdain, regardless of geography or nationality, is *occult*."[18] However, the truth of the matter is that despite her seeming desire to stay in new scientific frontiers, it is the old world of the occult again. (Parapsychologists have made the same attempt, valiantly, and failed as dismally.) In her book, psychics and mediums are called "sensitives," and occult powers are termed "Higher Sense Perception" (i.e., the ability to observe and experience hitherto unperceived dimensions of the environment).

In reading her book (despite her dislike for mediums—p. 40), it is clear that even though none of her sensitives were practicing (seance) mediums, they all had mediumistic abilities (e.g., psychic diagnosis/PK, psychometry, etc.). The powers she is investigating are no different from those found repeatedly in Fodor's *Encyclopedia of Psychic Science,* based largely on investigations of mediums. In fact, she notes that some of her subjects have a history of occultism in the family (cf. Ch. 8). This is a strong indication of the presence of demonism. (She fails to find a strong correlation here, most likely because her subjects' powers were derived through personal occult involvement rather than being hereditary.)

Probably due to Karagulla's avoidance of occult terminology, her book is used as a text or supplemental reading on many university campuses. Interestingly, it was a friend's challenge to read Joseph Millard's *Edgar Cayce—Mystery Man of Miracles* which revolutionized her outlook and made her very excited about studying people like Cayce:

> Were there other individuals like Cayce with perceptions beyond the range of the five senses? Could they be located and tested? Could I find the answer to this phenomenon of Higher Sense Perception: The lure of this new truth that might be discovered was irresistible. I began to seriously consider risking my reputation and my career to make a full time study of human beings with these strange and amazing talents.
>
> . . . I began cautiously to inquire among my friends about people with such exceptional gifts . . . . Eventually my tentative inquiries blossomed into a full-fledged scientific research project which has become my life work . . . . This will continue to be my life project.[19]

As in his impact on the life of Jess Stearn and dozens of others (and their influence), Edgar Cayce's occultism lives on—with all that accompanied him. Ultimately Karagulla's "H.S.P." is the old occult energy again. There are many other examples we could cite—e.g., Carrington's "human fluid" or "vital magnetism" which allegedly is responsible for "many [spiritistic] physical phenomena,"[20] etc.—but the point is made. All these energies are occult energies, i.e., tied directly or indirectly to demonism.

The Five Energies Examined Are Occult Energies

Thus, we have briefly examined five energies and found that all of them are occult energies which can be used by the spirit world. It is very likely this is true for every other similar energy concept ever put forth. The person who wishes to say that such energies are a new, neutral, scientific energy must tell us how they differ in essence from the old energy and the work done and/or energy utilized by demons in seances and other occult activities.

Some will say, "Well, there appears to be a great deal of circumstantial evidence for some kind of neutral or latent energy in man." That may or may not be true. Many things can *appear* to be true, but not be (e.g., a sunset). It is true that a spirit apparently utilizes some form of human material or energy in ectoplasmic manifestations. Mediums have been known to suffer the loss of up to half their weight during particularly strong manifestations, and the weight of the ectoplasmic form corresponds to the weight loss of the medium.[21] Does this prove the existence of an unknown latent neutral energy in man? *No!* As White and Krippner state:

> "Psychoenergetics" is used by some Soviet parapsychological investigators to describe their field of research. Again, it implies that the researchers are especially interested in the energetic aspects of psi phenomena, although there is still no absolute proof that energy, as physicists use the term, is involved in these unusual events.[22]

For example, some scientists claim that there is a great deal of evidence for evolution—but evolution has never occurred. It is absolutely a mathematical impossibility.[23] What has happened is that true data are molded into a presuppositional worldview—but the data would be better placed if there were no philosophical evolutionary bias.

In this matter of energy, the data are *fit into* an occult energy worldview. However, there is no evidence of a nonphysical energy system residing in the body. There is no biblical basis for the view that man and the cosmos are united by an energy force.

Then again, there is the problem of *misperception*. The omnipresence of God does not demand pantheism, but through a psychic misperception while in an altered state of consciousness, it perhaps can be mistaken for such. According to Teegarden, the Chinese acupuncture points were discovered in an occult state of mind—again, probably most of the nonphysical organized energy systems were so discovered—nadirs, chakras, etc., and as such they are to be viewed with skepticism. (For example, chakras are seen clairvoyantly by Indian yogis and some mediums. Therefore the concept was likely developed through psychic vision.) Teegarden, a yoga and acupressure instructor for 7 years, states:

> The Chinese meridian system was arrived at thousands of years ago by way of meditation, yoga, and paraclinical [i.e., occult] observation.[24]

He also notes that many forms of acupressure (Jin Shin Jyutsu, Jin Shin Do, Yogic acupressure, etc.) are related to or were arrived at through occult meditative means and may depend upon a psychic ability more than scientific knowledge.[25]

Yin-Yang

Similarly, scholar Kenneth Cohen notes that the mysterious energy "Ch'i" comes from the (Chinese) Taoist yoga system:

> Taoist yoga is based on a model of the human body as foreign to Western thought, as is Indian yoga. It comes on the one hand, from the shamanistic tradition, in which dance and ritual were used to contact the beneficent nature spirits. On the other hand, it comes from a very sophisticated system of meditation that began during the Warring States Period (4th century B.C.).[26]

Cohen notes that "This [Chi] energy is known to every culture," and that it has a philosophical relationship to the ultimate or divine energy. It is the energy uniting man to the cosmos: "As above, so below." Man contains within himself the universe.

The problem with all these various energy concepts is the real possibility of demonic entanglements. Perhaps the very things God does not want us to know, for sound reasons, are in some cases exactly the things that demons would reveal to us. Certainly this is true in divination. Great suffering has unnecessarily resulted where people knew, or believed they knew, the future. Many other seemingly innocent activities have led people directly into demonism. These occult energy forces are also "out" for the Christian who would follow his Lord.

References for Chapter 16

1. White & Krippner, *Future Science,* Appendix 1; Information on the individuals was derived from Fodor's *Encyclopedia of Psychic Science* (Secducus, NJ: Citadel) 1974, books by the various researchers (A. Puharich's *Uri* (NY, Bantam 1975), C. Wilson's *The Occult* (NY: Vintage) 1973, and J. Mishlove's *Roots of Consciousness* (NY: Random House) 1975.
2. Vivekananda, *The Yogas and Other Works* (NY: Ramakrishna and Vivekenanda Center) 1953, pp. 592-93, 598.
3. *Ibid.,* pp. 601, 605
4. *Ibid.,* p. 596.
5. *Ibid.,* p. 597.
6. *Ibid.,* pp. 593, 599.
7. Long, *The Secret Science Behind Miracles* (Marina del Rey, CA: DeVorss) 1954, pp. 139-40.
8. The Journal of Holistic Health III, *op. cit.,* p. 41.
9. Buranelli, *The Wizard from Vienna* (NY: Coward, Mc Cann & Geoghegan) 1975, p. 31, 140-143, Chapters 9-11, 13, 17-19.
10. *Ibid.,* pp. 190-191.
11. Coddington, *op. cit.,* p. 99.
12. Buranelli, *op. cit.,* p. 205.
13. *Ibid.,* p. 207.
14. Butler, "The Energy Behind True Magic" in White & Krippner *Future Science,* p. 94.
15. Ebon (ed.), *The Signet Handbook of Parapsychology,* p. 24.
16. Mishlove, *The Roots of Consciousness,* p. 64.
17. Wilson, *The Occult: A History,* p. 537.
18. Ebon (Ed.), *The Signet Handbook of Parapsychology* (NY: New American Library) 1978, p. 24.
19. Karagulla, *Breakthrough to Creativity* (Santa Monica, CA: DeVorss) 1967, p. 29-30.

20. Carrington, *Your Psychic Powers and How to Develop Them* (Van Nuys, CA: Newcastle) 1975, p. 226.
21. Fodor, *op. cit.*, "ectoplasm" article.
22. White & Krippner, *op. cit.*, p. 26.
23. Coppedge, *Evolution: Possible or Impossible?* (Grand Rapids, MI: Zondervan) 1975, Eden (Ed.) *Mathematical Challenges to the Neo-Darwinist Interpretation of Evolution* (Philadelphia: Wistar Press), 1967.
24. *The Acupressure News* (Santa Monica, CA), Summer, 1978, p. 6.
25. *Ibid.*, Spring 1978, p. 5, 15.
26. Kenneth Cohen, "Chi: Breath Energy" *Yoga Journal*, Jan. 1979, p. 18.

Chapter 17

A Satanic Counterpart to Conversion

Christian conversion is being born "from above" (John 3:3). Is it possibly, in part, an "operation" on the human spirit? Just as there can be a revitalizing of this "energy" (if we call it that, or assume this is what it is) by a "Divine operation" on the human spirit in Christian conversion (which obviously connects to the mind, i.e., ". . . but be ye transformed by the renewing of your mind . . ." Romans 12:2), there seems also to be a Satanic counterpart, or revitalizing of the human spirit (or energy) for occult purposes and powers. This takes place via the "psychic transformation" which happens to occultists and eastern religion practitioners of all varieties.

It is vital to realize that many, if not all, of these energy concepts are tied to such transformations via the physical regimen which attempts to manipulate or infuse this energy (physical yoga exercises; physical acupressure, manipulation, etc.). Yoga utilizes prana for Kundalini arousal. Chi is manipulated for merging with the universe and to attain immortality. Nicheren Shoshin Buddhists utilize "essential life" as a basis of ceremonial magic, etc.

In Christian conversion, a person is sovereignly made spiritually alive to *God* and His purposes—a new dimension is added to him, and he receives the Holy Spirit. In the occultist's case, the person is made spiritually, perhaps more appropriately, *psychically,* alive to *Satan* and his purposes.

Now, if they exist, would demons reveal the existence of nonphysical energy systems? Would they thus tie them to destructive philosophical/religious concepts? Chinese acupuncture comes with a certain worldview of the universe—yin and yang, dual elements which must be in harmony in the body. Its proponents contend that simply by maintaining this harmony, we can *live forever* (apart from biblical salvation). Yogic prana unites us to Brahman. Psychic energy unites us to the impersonal Divine. In all this, where has Christian salvation gone? The Chinese Taoist philosophy is anti-Judeo-Christian. Acupuncture theory is tied to Taoist philosophy, and as McGarey states:

> Their philosophical-religious concepts are seen to be the basis of the traditional [Chinese] medical approach to therapy, and it is doubtful if there will ever by a way in which the two can be separated.[1]

Therein lies the danger.

The Anti-Christian Worldview

Similarly, yogic prana is tied to the anti-Christian Vedanta worldview of Brahman realization, and the yogic nadirs (transmitting lines of prana) were also psychically revealed. According to Gopi Krishna, "for the ancient Indian adept, bioenergy or prana is the superintelligent cosmic life energy to which he owes his own existence and the existence of the world around him." Prana maintains his "ego bound flicker of consciousness" until he eventually becomes God.[1] Probably these nonphysical systems do not exist, but if perhaps they are partly true, the *idea* of them is being manipulated. Perhaps the idea was to involve a true concept—or part of one—that offers practical help (one that works) with a false philosophy and worldview. We should never underestimate the power (drawing and sustaining) of a worldview that promises the hope of healing, or one that seems to provide answers to the gnawing riddle of mankind's existence. The final answers to the forms of acutherapies *may* be ultimately found in known scientific laws and processes, rather than unknown occult ones. However, as we have said, this is doubtful.

But, it might be asked, what about the meridian energy system behind acupuncture, acupressure, and similar ideas? Cannot Chi and all these related concepts exist apart from any occult connection, philosophical or supernaturalist? Not really. White and Krippner state:

> In the Orient, the Chinese conception of Chi (ki in Japanese) was thought to be the intrinsic vital force throughout all creation. It is this life energy which acupuncture manipulates to maintain health and which can be concentrated through disciplines such as t'ai ch'i and akido to perform paranormal acts [hence no different from prana or animal magnetism]. According to Confucianism and Taoism, without Ch'i nothing can exist, and from it spring the yin and yang forces (making them divine) that are present in all living things. Paralleling this in the yogic tradition of India and Tibet is the notion of prana . . . .[3]

Psychic Hiroshi Motoyama has been involved in scientific research into psychic matters for a long time. The following statement is illuminating because it indicates the energy is not innate (note its origin), but derived, and also shows that Chinese ch'i is equivalent to Hindu prana. Motoyama believes this is the same power that mediums, psychics, psychic surgeons, and other occultists use:

> Through more than twenty years of yoga practice and the study of parapsychology, I have found that such paranormal phenomena as PK and ESP are caused by a higher dimensional energy, which tentatively we call psi-energy. Also through my research into the chakras and nadirs of yoga and the meridians of acupuncture, I have found that this psi-energy is ejected

> from the chakra and the points on the acupuncture meridians.... Through the chakras, *prana,* a higher dimensional vital energy force, *is received from the universe* [emphasis added] and converted into a kind of physical energy ....this (original) energy seems to be of a non-physical nature (refer to *The Non-Physical in the Correlation Between Mind and Body).* This psi-energy also appears to be the energy flowing through the meridians and/or that energy directly received through the chakras. I also believe that this psi-energy is what is called *prana* and *Ki* in ancient yoga and acupuncture texts.... If a chakra is [by yoga] thus awakened, a person can control the receiving and ejecting of energy through the chakra by *mental concentration.*[4]

Thus, since we know demons work through occultists (as many admit), the prana and Chi here are either direct demonic energy, or energy produced (vampirized) from the medium. In fact, Mishlove reports one case of pranic healing reported 70 years ago by Yogi Ramacharaka, who also named it "magnetic healing." He stated the healing was not to be done until a definite tingling sensation appeared at the fingertips. (The tingling sensation appears so often when spirits are on the scene that, for these authors, its presence [in an occult atmosphere] indicates the demonic.) Hence again, we have no way of distinguishing any difference between "prana" and demonic energy. In fact, reading Mishlove's discussion of pranic healing indicates it is equivalent to mediumistic healing.[5]

More About Holistic Health and the Occult

We have seen that the new energy of the holistic health movement is in fact very old occult energy. The spirit entity who works through psychic healer George Chapman states: "I draw energy from my medium and give healing rays."[6] (This suggests the possibility that human energy may be transformed by the spirit into a new type of "healing" energy.) If one examines modern spiritism—what happens and what it does—we find the same things occurring with all these other energy systems. In other words, a final conclusion would be *they are simply variations of whatever energy spiritism utilizes.*

From the testimony of thousands of psychics and mediums, we find the recurring claim that the energy either comes directly and entirely from their spirits, or that they work through and utilize energy from their human hosts. Many psychics advance to the belief that the energy comes entirely from their higher self. In this event, spirits willingly take a back seat, with more freedom to maneuver. It should be noted here that *the energy is not entirely, if at all, human.* Psychics universally claim to be channels for an outside energy. It may *interact* with something human, but the energy itself does not appear to be part of man's constitutional makeup in terms of a nonphysical energy.

The modern holistic health movement has not devised its idea of energy on its own. It has been borrowed from occult and eastern teachings and the research of parapsychology, which itself borrowed it from similar sources, plus mediumism. Practitioners within the movement, being tapped into occult traditions before it began in 1970, naturally brought such concepts with them into the holistic health camps.

Holistic medicine thrives in eastern-occult communities because its birthplace is there. Coddington notes that, "Holistic doctors, when they discuss the spiritual aspect of the body-mind-spirit triad, often sound more eastern than western in their approach."[7] For example, Dr. Paavo Airola in the June, 1977, issue of *Let's Live* magazine writes: "Our life on this planet . . . is just a short episode in the eternal divine plan of human development and progression—a schooling period aimed at improving and perfecting our human and divine characteristics."

Common Characteristics of Occult Energy

Several researchers have noted various common characteristics of this energy. They are:[8]
1. Science rejects it.

2. It can heal (more likely, this is appearance only and there is rather a transference from the organic to the psychic, and the illness is produced at a higher level).
3. It has properties similar to other types of energy (electricity, heat, light, magnetism, etc.), but is a distinct force unto itself and separate from them.
4. It can be "stored" inside inanimate materials—wood, stone, fetishes, etc. (e.g., inside idols).
5. It seems to penetrate everything.
6. It may accompany solar rays.
7. It can possess polarity and be reflected by mirrors.
8. It can be directed through or seem to emanate from the human body and is especially detectable at the fingertips and eyes.
9. It can fluctuate with weather conditions.
10. It can be controlled or utilized by the mind.
11. It enters into the dynamics of nearly all occult phenomena.
12. It can be used for evil and "good."
13. It can be conducted by other materials—wire, silk threads, etc.
14. It has been in existence since the dawn of history and is consistently tied to the occult.
15. It is basically synergetic. It has a basic negentropic (negative entropy, it does not wear out), formative, and organizing effect—i.e., it violates, or appears to violate the second law of thermodynamics (a proven law of science).
16. Denser materials conduct it better and faster. Metal refracts it (sometimes). Organic material absorbs it.
17. It can operate apart from the medium—e.g., cases when metal a psychic has touched continues bending long after the initial touch.
18. It is highly concentrated at certain geometrical points—chakras, nadirs, meridian points.
19. The energies will flow from one object to another. According to the Hawaiian Kahuna tradition, it is "sticky" so that an invisible stream of energy will always connect any two objects that have in any way

been connected in the past (thus providing the basis of sympathetic magic).
20. It is observable as ectoplasm, clouds or auras around the body, flames, pulsating points, spirals, a web of lines (Don Juan's "lines of the world," "etheric web" of occultists).
21. It can behave intelligently.

Considering parapsychological research with mediums, the broad spectrum of abilities claimed and feats done by mediums or psychics who admit their powers come from spirit guides, ascended masters, etc., few if any of the above characteristics are left out.

References for Chapter 17

1. McGarey, *Acupuncture & Body Energies* (Phoenix, AZ: Gabriel Press) 1974, p. 10.
2. Krishna, "Prana: The Traditional and the Modern View" in White & Krippner *op. cit.,* p. 85; See his book on Kundalini: plus Nikhilananda, *Vivekananda, op. cit.,* p. 597.
3. White & Krippner, *op. cit.,* p. 54.
4. Motoyama, "Physiological Measurements and New Instrumentation" in Meek, *op. cit.,* p. 150-51.
5. Mishlove, *op. cit.,* p. 152.
6. Meek, *op. cit.,* p. 38.
7. Coddington, *op. cit.,* p. 183.
8. Coddington, p. 15; White and Krippner, p. 55-6.

Chapter 18

Energy Forces and the Nature of Man

Having indicated that the "new" energy touted in the multifaceted world of psychicism is a very ancient occult energy, we now examine the nature of man and see if God's Word gives us clues as to whether or not there is a supernatural aspect to man. In other words, is the "new" energy (capable of doing all these miracles) resident within man, or is it not? Is it innate?

Latent Capacities: The Biblical View

First, we will examine the biblical view of man as to latent or potential supernatural capacities. Watchman Nee in his *Latent Power of the Soul* (all page notations are from the Christian Fellowship Publishers (NY) ed. 1972) puts forth the idea that in the original creation man had psychic or soul powers which became latent at the Fall. He feels that today, they can be released and used through demonic agency, and that even Christians can use this harmful soul power. We wish here to put forth some tentative criticisms of such a theory. While this theory does explain certain data, his arguments for such an idea are unconvincing and seem to lack any biblical base. In fact, his argumentation is often suspect, e.g., Adam and Eve hardly *required* psychic powers to fulfill God's commands to have dominion over the earth (pp. 14-17). He also engages in unjustified extensions of scriptural data; gives an aura of absolute truth to doubtful statements; and provides little evidence to support his claims (pp. 9-28). While such an idea cannot be ruled out, if it is true, it raises many serious questions—the godly Christian's use of latent psi, distinguishing spiritual gifts from psychic abilities, etc.

Of particular concern is Nee's somewhat arbitrary distinction between spirit and soul power. Soul power (or psychic power) is Satanic (p. 43, 65). Believers can use this power unknowingly and do much harm, e.g., in prayer for another Christian, a Christian can oppress and hypnotize him by soul power (p. 47). Pastors can preach using soul power and by implication harm their audiences (pp. 78, 83-4, 67, 60). The power of the human spirit, however, is the power used in conjunction with the Holy Spirit, to perform genuine miracles (p. 33). The Christian must never use soul power, yet Nee's methods for distinguishing soul vs. spirit power appear to be neither adequate nor convincing. Of primary importance is the question: Are such designations stated in scripture? If it is not stated that the soul is supernatural, can we assume it is? Is everyone potentially a psychic, as Nee and modern parapsychology declare? Or have the "findings" of modern parapsychology been given too much weight by some Christians? Nee says that it is, *"The evidence produced by modern parapsychology* [which] indicate that Adam had not lost his original power, only that he had it hidden in his soul" (p. 37, emphasis added). Even though he opposes it, Nee is fairly dependent on the findings of modern psychic research to support his thesis (pp. 38-40). Is such research to be trusted? Since when should Christians turn to occultists to find answers about spiritual issues? God has not revealed a great deal about this whole area—should we pursue it further, even using the findings of occultists to extrapolate on the nature of the soul? The fact is there is no biblical data to support the claim that Adam ever had supernatural powers to begin with. Is it wise to base so much of one's worldview upon something so uncertain?

An important issue is not that psychic powers are used by demons. We are in agreement there. The issue is the nature of man. If I believe my soul is natural, I will view myself in one way. If I believe it is supernatural, I will view myself in another way. If natural, I have no fear of wrongly using soul power, no fear of demonic collusion within my very soul. For example, when praying, I do not have to worry about whether or not I am *really* using psychic powers against others, as Nee suggests is possible (p. 47). This is something Nee *must* warn Christians against, because *his* view of the soul makes it a real possibility. For Nee, potentially *every* Christian could naively have a harmful psychic influence over others. The *power is there* without the demon.

On the other hand, if we view the soul as natural, then the power is not there without the demon. The demon must initiate something abnormal in the soul (rather than release its normal power) or perform the miracles on its own. If the soul is supernatural, then every Christian must be concerned about psychically harming others. Nee teaches that *every Christian has the potential to release his soul power* (p. 47). However, if this soul power does not exist, a Christian does not have to worry about releasing it. Thus, if my soul has latent psychic power, I at once have not only the fear, but the problem of how I am to be certain something is of God. However if I have only to trust in the Holy Spirit, my prayer life and preaching will bear fruit, and I will not worry about the possibility of directing a harmful psychic force outward toward people. *There is no latent power to be released.* Nee's viewpoint, on the other hand, tends to make psychic powers more "accessible" and "natural."

Scripture *never* says, "Don't unleash the latent power of your souls," or anything even remotely resembling that, and we *are* instructed to pray for one another. It does say that in regard to demons, *our war is against principalities and powers* (not our souls). The *flesh* wars against the soul (I Peter 2:11; Eph. 6). Scripture does say, "Resist the devil" (James 2). Nee claims that the living soul "possesses unthinkable supernatural powers" (p. 19); that Adam's power was, literally *one million times* greater than ours and that his latent power resides within us (p. 15, 26). "Today in each and every person who lives on earth lies this Adamic power, though it is confined in him and is not able to freely express itself. Yet such power is in every man's soul just as it was in Adam's soul at the beginning" (p. 20). If this is true, is there any way to distinguish the Satanic from the natural? It would seem that *all* occult powers become *potentially* natural.

Who are we to judge that this power cannot be released apart from Satanic intervention? (Again, Nee believes it can be—pp.23, 56.) And in parapsychology today, even technological means are being devised for just this purpose. If we do not keep a dividing line between the natural and the Satanic, how can we say in this case or that, that *any* occultist is demonic—if he may simply have developed *natural* capacities?

Could it not be argued that these powers can be released *naturally* by some faulty biopsychic mechanism disrupted at the Fall? And if such powers are believed to be natural, many people will develop them (as thousands are doing today), under the impression that they *are* natural. What can be wrong with developing *natural* powers? Why *must* they be demonic? Many will go on to deduce, as thousands already have, that such natural powers are a gift from God. Which psychic today does not claim their "gift" is from God? Who can criticize gifts from Heaven? "Every good thing bestowed and every perfect gift is from above, coming down from the Father of lights . . ." (James 1:17).

However, conversely, people would be more reluctant to develop what are believed to be *demonic* powers. In other words, *how* these powers (and energies) are viewed is very important. If it is latent, natural, or divine, people *will* develop them much more readily than if they are believed to be demonic.

It is relevant to comment in passing, that if man is still evolving, then these can be seen as a great evolutionary leap. However, if man is created and not evolving, no such justification exists. There is also the problem that these powers will be developed from wrong motives—pride, selfishness, the desire for power over others (which is actually the basis of occultism, anyway), etc.

Distinguishing Gifts of the Spirit

If what Nee says is true, how can we distinguish gifts of the Spirit from "natural" psychic powers? Or are they just "Spirit-opened-up" natural capacities? Remember, it is the "Christian"-oriented mediumistic groups (and not the true church of Christ) which teach that psychic powers are gifts of the Spirit. Obviously the Satanic power still operates, but if such powers are also in fact natural, there would be no way to be *certain* which are Satanic and which are natural. What of the Christians who claim to have psychic gifts? (Nee, himself, is telepathic; p. 66.) Can the use of soul and spirit power be so easily discerned by the average Christian?

Should the church adopt Nee's position? With Satan's craftiness, we can be certain he would utilize such an idea to his maximum benefit, by keeping any direct involvement of his own hidden, while inspiring long-term bondage. Satan would have us believe that psychic powers are natural and latent, not demonic and "received." Much evidence could be provided by him for a "5th field" of neutral psi energy available to man, through concepts like the Akashic records, travelling clairvoyance into the past, and the discovery of a *natural* psychic mechanism allowing such things. But what are the implications?

What if psychic trips into the past repeatedly uncovered "evidence" that the biblical records were falsely recorded in key crucial area—e.g., salvation by substitutionary atonement vs. karmic salvation? What if reputable people, under scientifically controlled conditions, all went into the past and reported similar findings? If this is all a neutral, natural talent, then who will believe the Bible? Even some mature believers, to say nothing of most naive Christians, would be seriously affected. Demons would be supervising the "findings," but the results would appear entirely neutral and historically accurate.

In fact, "psychic archaeology" is already making an appearance. Several books have been published on psychic visits into the past for archaeological purposes. (But why shouldn't demons be thoroughly acquainted with all the facts of history . . . they existed through it and, if all the facts were known, probably had an affect on much of it.) This is only one of many conceivable implications of allowing an overall concept of neutrality in the psychic realm. There are many others.

Supernatural Abilities—From God or Satan

What does the Bible seem to teach? Simply, that all truly supernatural abilities come from one of two sources: God or Satan. To redefine the "supernatural" as "supernormal," and thereby remove its miraculous character, is suspect. Notice the following arguments and scriptures in light of man having latent supernatural abilities. (Even if it be argued that *latent* psi is totally demonically initiated and directed, e.g., re: holistic health, this still undercuts any hope of *neutral* power resident in man.)

1. The miracles done by believers in the Bible are done entirely through spiritual *gifts*. The nature of a gift implies the person does not have the item before it is given. Were Elijah, Daniel, Elisha, etc., able to do miracles apart from God's power? Who were the disciples before Jesus gave them power and authority? Did these fishermen go around performing miracles? The greatest, most godly man alive, apart from Jesus, never did even one miracle (John 10:41—John the Baptist). The most humble man of his time, Moses, could do nothing apart from God. Jesus even says, "Apart from Me, you can do nothing" (John 15).
2. The Jewish worldview was that supernatural abilities were not resident within man (apart from the occult Kabbalistic worldview).
3. If psi powers were innate in everyone, anybody should be able to develop them, but they can be developed by

only a portion of the population. *Nowhere* in the Bible is man presented as having supernatural powers of the occult type, from his own nature ("higher self," etc.). On the contrary, supernatural power always comes from one of two sources—God or fallen angels. For those who hold to biblical authority, this speaks lucid volumes about the parapsychological-occult/holistic health idea of a latent, natural, neutral energy that can be developed. When such powers are developed, they are always developed within an occult worldview and occult circles (unless hereditary, and then this was true for the ancestors).

Note the thrust of the following Scriptures. Taken collectively, they strongly imply man has no latent psi:

1. Can a man walk on hot coals and his feet not be scorched? (Proverbs 6:28).
2. Regarding dream interpretation, Joseph stated to Pharaoh of the answer, "It is not in me; God will give Pharaoh a favorable answer" (Gen. 41:16). The book of Daniel is replete with God giving Daniel special abilities of knowledge and interpretation of visions and dreams. Apart from God, Daniel was helpless (Daniel 1:17,20; 2:27-30). Daniel states:

    But as for me, this mystery has not been revealed to me for any wisdom residing in me more than any other living man, but for the purpose of making the interpretation known to the king . . ." (Daniel 2:30).

3. Luke 5:17. Even Jesus, as a *perfect man,* could not do miracles. *"And the power of the Lord* was present for Him to perform healing." This is the "power that went out from Him" in Mark 5:30, Luke 8:46—it apparently was not latent. This has obvious implications for the theory of original unfallen man having psychic powers. As a perfect man, Jesus had to rely totally on the Holy Spirit for His miracles. (See also Matt. 12:28.)

    Jesus had to represent perfect humanity (unfallen Adam and Eve) and keep God's laws entirely as a man in order to truly live the perfect life for man in order to die for man. Hence, because He was a perfect man and unable to rely on His Divine powers (such would disqualify Him as being a true representative of man), He had to rely on the Spirit for His powers. That He did so, as our example, seems to indicate that He had no supernatural power as a perfect man—i.e., God did not create man that way in the beginning.

4. Exodus 3:20. Moses had no power but from God: "So I will stretch out *My hand* and strike Egypt with all *My miracles* which *I* shall do in the midst of it." Exodus 4:21. God (to Moses): "See that you perform before Pharaoh all the wonders *which I have put* in your power."
5. Acts 3:12. The healing of the lame beggar: "When Peter saw this [the people's amazement], he replied to the people, 'Men of Israel why do you marvel at this, or why do you gaze at us, *as if by our own power* or piety we had made him walk?' "
6. Acts 4:30. "While Thou dost extend *Thy hand* to heal."
7. Acts 14:3. "Therefore they spent a long time there speaking boldly with reliance upon the Lord, who was bearing witness to the word of his grace, *granting* that signs and wonders be done by their hands."
8. Acts 4:11,15. Concerning the attempt to worship Barnabas and Paul: "And when the multitude saw what Paul had done, [they said] . . . .'The gods have become like men and have come down to us . . . .' [But Paul said] 'Men, why are you doing these things? We are also men of the same nature as you . . . .' "
9. Acts 9:34. "And Peter said to him, 'Aeneas, *Jesus Christ* heals you . . . .' "
10. Acts 10:26. Concerning Cornelius' attempt to worship Peter: "Stand up, I too am just a man."
11. James 5:17. "Elijah was a man with a nature like ours, and he *prayed earnestly* . . . ." (and a miracle from God resulted).
12. Luke 10:19. Jesus said, "Behold *I* have given you

authority . . . and over all the power of the enemy . . . ."

Similar verses declaring miracles come from God—and not from man—are found in Acts 15:12; 16:16; 19:11; Romans 15:19; I Corinthians 12:9, 10, 28, 30; Mark 6:7.

Conversely, note the following biblical assessments of man. Do they sound like statements that man might become such as the psychics and higher self promoters teach, entirely in his own power?

> Psalm 39:5. ". . . my lifetime is as nothing in Thy sight. Surely every man at his best is mere breath. Surely every man walks about as a phantom."
>
> Jeremiah 17:5. "Thus says the Lord, Cursed is the man who trusts in mankind, and makes flesh his strength."
>
> Isaiah 2:22. "Stop regarding man, whose breath of life is in his nostrils, for why [lit. "in what] should he be esteemed?"
>
> Psalm 103:14-16. "For He himself knows our frame. He is mindful that we are but dust. As for man, his days are like grass. As a flower of the field, so he flourishes. When the wind has passed over it, it is no more; and its place acknowledges it no longer."

Characteristics of Godly Miracles

Biblically, Godly miracles have certain characteristics and requirements. They are performed through the power of God to glorify Him, edify the church, and validate the Gospel. (See Acts 14:3; Romans 15:19; Hebrews 2:4; I Corinthians 12:7, 14:12-13.) However, there are also miracles performed through the powers of evil, sometimes by imposters of Christ and *wrought in support of false religions.* (See Exodus 7:10-12,22; 8:7; Matthew 7:22; II Thessalonians 2:9; Revelation 16:14; Deut. 13:1,2; Matthew 24:24; Rev. 19:20; Acts 8:9-11.) They are not to be regarded (Deut. 13:3), and they deceive the ungodly (II Thessalonians 2:10-11; Rev. 13:14; 19:20). We see that when the slave girl had the demon cast out of her, she lost her supernatural powers (Acts 16:16-19). If her powers were latent and normal (part of her make-up), this should not have happened.

Parapsychologists like to boast that faith is not necessary to have a psychic perform before you. Biblically, faith in God generally *is* necessary—both in those who perform and receive: Matt. 17:20; 21:21; John 14:21; Acts 3:16; 6:8; Matthew 9:28; Mark 9:22-24; Acts 14:9. Also miracles are to be done *in the Name of Christ* (Mark 16:17; Acts 3:16; 4:30). Miracles are demanded by unbelievers (Matthew 12:38-39; 16:1; Luke 11:16, 29; 23:8), not by believers.

Biblically, as we can find no basis for man having latent psychic powers, on what basis can we say otherwise? Scripturally, the issue appears to be fairly clear. Even when demons draw power from their host, it appears that they utilize some normal, physical aspect of man *in an unknown manner,* rather than utilizing some unknown energy power that is latent within him.

Confirmation in Secular Sources

If the above is correct, can we find any secular confirmation? Note the following statements. All of them tend to support the view that man, in himself, is not supernatural.

1. It is a known fact that animist Shaman tribes attribute all the supernatural miracles to spirits. The Shaman receives powers from the spirits. This has been noted by many studies—e.g., anthropologist Harner's *Hallucinogens and Shamanism* and well-known authority Eliades' *Shamanism*.
2. The authority Idries Shah states of Hindu holy men who work miracles: "It is true that the Sadhus claim that their power comes exclusively from spirits; that they within themselves possess no special abilities except that of concentration."[1] Until the advent of parapsychology and because of its desire to validate itself by becoming "scientific" (therefore psi powers are not "apart" and supernatural but immanent and natural), all mediums and psychics said the same thing. Their powers were

not innate, but from spirits. Only recently, under the influence of parapsychologists, have many of them begun to view their powers as latent and natural.

3. Louis Jacolliot, Chief Justice of the French East Indies and Tahiti, states in his *Occult Science in India and Among the Ancients,* "What is the force which Hindus attribute to the pure Agasa fluid, under the direction of the spirits?"[2] The Indian psychics "produce at will the strangest phenomena, entirely contrary to what are conventionally called natural laws. With the aid of spirits, who are present at all their operations, as claimed by the Brahmins, they have the authority, as well as power, to evoke them."[3]

4. Charles Panati, in his *Supersenses,* refers to the research of Lawrence Le Shan who "has gone out into the field and observed Eastern and Western healers firsthand." Panati states: "But if the healers he studied had one thing in common, it was that they all felt they did not perform the healing themselves; a 'spirit' did it working through them. They felt they were merely passive agents . . . . "[4] This has been abundantly confirmed by the 10-year research of 16 worldwide investigators, reported on by Meek in *Healers and the Healing Process.*[5] The statement by medium Olga Worall, that "the power comes from personal spiritual sources [spirits], not from me,"[6] could be multiplied a thousand times from other occultists.

Summarizing our findings to date, we see that it is very difficult to find evidence for any latent, neutral energy of man.

1. It is not new, but is historically tied to occult energy and manifestations.
2. No evidence for it exists from science.
3. The Bible gives no support to man being supernatural.
4. Apart from God, all supernatural powers seem to arise from spirits.
5. No evidence exists that the energy concept in its scores of names (prana, mana, od, Chi, etc.) is different from energy introduced or utilized by spirits. Since it is never

detected physically (it is nonphysical), but only gives an effect during supernatural miracles, how is this different from saying, "A spirit did it"???

Appendix to Chapter 18

Problems Within Psychic Anatomies

It is true that there exists a wide divergence between the *claims* of alternate medicines (and its energy flows) and what, in fact, can be accomplished. Several of them claim to be able to heal virtually every disease or ailment—in fact this is consistent with the ancient teachings, as they taught the possibility of immortality itself.

One question we would like to examine is, just how many nonphysical components, organs, channels, and systems do we all seem to have?

1. Shealy notes the number of acupuncture points has increased with the centuries (it started with 12, plus 2 "regulating" points). "Some sources describe 295 points, others 365. Many others record totals running into the 600's or even the 700's and some talk of more than 1,000."[7] An article in *New Realities,* Volume 1, No. 4, p. 59 mentions 500.
2. Brown notes that the same problem plagued phrenologists; Franz Gall designated 28 bumps-in-the-head area. However, those phrenologists influenced by the animal magnetism theories of Mesmer ("phreno-magnetism") doubled or even tripled the number with such additions as profligacy, playfulness, patriotism, etc., so that their

topographical maps of the cranium were soon covered with a bewildering array of circumscribed areas, some almost invisibly minute."[8] And if this weren't enough, there are always more available: By means of Mesmeric experiments, the Rev. Laroy Sunderland "discovered no less than 150 new phrenologic organs."[9]
3. Swami Rama in his *Lectures on Yoga* states we all have between 72,000 and 326,000 nadirs.[10]
4. The *New Age Journal* of May, 1978, (p. 8) says we have between 6 and 13 chakras.

It appears evident that a great deal of the "healings" in holistic health today are purely psychological in origin and have little to do with purported knowledge of psychic anatomies. For example, a first cousin to acupressure is reflexology, or zone therapy, which divides the body into 10 zones or areas of influence. Yet "although it uses many massage points which do not correspond to the meridians of acupressure, it produces similar results."[11] Numerous such examples could be given.

The admission in the *Holistic Health Handbook* that not every new therapy will work for everyone—a consistent feature of the alternative medicines— indicates again a significant psychological and/or possible occult factor at work, rather than any realignment of legitimate non-physical energy.

References for Chapter 18

1. Shah, *Oriental Magic*, p. 123.
2. Jacolliot, *Occult Science in India and Among the Ancients*, (New Hyde Park, NY: University Books) 1971, p. 201.
3. *Ibid.*, p. 204.
4. Charles Panati, *Supersenses*, (NY: Quadrangle) 1974, p. 102.
5. Meek, *op. cit.*, p. 32, 51, 17, 80-81.
6. Krippner & Viloldo, *The Realms of Healing*, (Millbrae, CA: Celestial Arts) 1976.
7. Shealy, *Occult Medicines Can Save Your Life*, (NY: Bantam) 1977, p. 180.
8. Brown, *The Heyday of Spiritualism* (NY: Pocket Books), 1972, p. 25.
9. Fodor, *op. cit.*, p. 240.
10. Rama, *Lectures on Yoga* (Glenview, IL: Himalayan International Institute) 1976, p. 136.
11. *Psychic*, Nov. 1976, p. 12-13.

Chapter 19

Brainwashed by Choice ...(For a Fee!)

How "est" Breaks Down Defenses

These two chapters first appeared as an article by John Weldon in *Contemporary Christianity*. It is highly relevant to show yet another indoctrination strategy that has become deeply rooted in our Western culture and is growing at an alarming rate. It illustrates yet another supposed energy source. There is a difference in strategy, but ultimately there is a strong link with concepts already presented. Instead of messages, etc., from a supposedly divine source beyond human intelligence, now the human himself is seen as supposedly divine. We quote Erhard as stating, "You're god in your universe."

The Frightening World of "est"

Erhard Seminars Training (est), founded by Werner Erhard, is an intensive sixty-hour seminar of psychological indoctrination (brainwashing) designed to restructure a person's worldview. Though not started until 1971, the est organization has had a substantial impact for such a short history. *San Francisco* magazine has stated:

Est is making a serious bid to affect basic American institutions, and Werner Erhard's increasing influence has many people concerned. They see an effective, growing organization which has a strong political base.[1]

As of June, 1980, there were 250,000 est graduates. Werner Erhard has initiated an instruction program which he hopes will yield an additional ninety-one trainers in the next five years.[2] Since only *nine* trainers have taught 250,000 in less than nine years, est seems to be preparing for a tremendous expansion.

John Denver—An est Graduate

Among the prominent est graduates is John Denver, who wrote a song about est ("Looking for Space") and dedicated one of his albums to Erhard. Denver also sang the theme song for *I Want to Live*, a film used by est's Hunger Project. Valerie Harper, TV's Rhoda, praised est at the Emmy Awards before a national audience of 36 million. Other graduates include Yoko Ono, Roy Scheider, George Maharis, Richard Roundtree (of *Shaft* fame), Joanne Woodward, Jerry Rubin, and Cloris Leachman.

About 20 percent of est graduates are in the field of education. Erhard states, "The real thrust and goal of est is to put it in education." [3]

Est has been involved in giving seminars to prison inmates, and Erhard feels it is very important to train the police force as well.[4] He pays special attention to members of the clergy . . . they receive a 50 per cent discount. Since est is profoundly affecting the lives of thousands of people, we need to examine the multimillion dollar est business and see just exactly what it is for which people are paying $350.00.

Erhard Was Rosenberg

Werner Erhard was born as Jack Rosenberg in 1935. He changed his name after abandoning his wife and four children in 1960 (he made amends eleven years later). He also ran an automobile dealership under the name of Jack Frost and has been involved in several businesses, against one of which the State of California filed two lawsuits. The State charged that Grolier Society, Inc. used lies and trickery to persuade people to buy its encyclopedias, and the State won both cases. Erhard was a supervisor of salesmen.[5] During his stay with Grolier, he met several people in the San Francisco human awareness movement, one of whom was Dr. Leo Zeff, an LSD researcher and now on est's Advisory Board. Zeff and others led Erhard into Scientology. Erhard was also closely associated with Alex Everett, founder of Mind Dynamics, a self-hypnosis mind-control enterprise. Mind Dynamics was also sued by the State of California for fraudulent claims, although both Erhard and Everett had left the organization by the time of the suit.[6]

About three years after leaving his family, Erhard had a radical life-transforming experience. This was to eventually culminate (via other transformations and research) into the Seminars Training. Bartley's biography of Erhard indicates extensive occult involvement on Erhard's part prior to starting est;[7] he studied or became involved in numerous disciplines. Besides the aforementioned Scientology and Mind Dynamics, there were Zen Buddhism (Erhard has made trips to the East to study with Zen masters), hypnosis, Subud, yoga, Silva Mind Control, Psychocybernetics, Gestalt, encounter therapy, and transpersonal psychology. Est is the fruit of his "conversion" experience and personal research into these and other disciplines.[8]

The est Experience

Est is not concerned with giving people a temporary "high" that will wear off eventually. Erhard states, "We want nothing short of a total transformation—an alteration of substance, not a change in form," [9] and "See, all we want to do is change the notion of who you are." [10] He wants it all—your mind, your life, your soul. And he is often successful. Why does est "work"? Why do so many people say it radically changes their lives?

est "Conversion"

The experience transforms people because through intensive, at times brutal and cruel, physical and mental conditioning, the individual undergoes a "conversion episode" where the "old" way of viewing reality is supplanted with the est way. The seminar is designed to change a person's epistemology (i.e., their way of relating to reality) radically and permanently. People are "voluntarily" conditioned to the point of what we might call "epistemological vulnerability" (voluntarily brainwashed *out* of all they presently believe), and then the est philosophy is conveniently provided as "the" answer and "the" truth about life and how to live it. As one est trainer put it:

> We're gonna throw away your whole belief system.... We're gonna tear you down and put you back together.[11]

One graduate remarked, "Certainly we had been worn down to the point we were ready to accept it."[12]

People generally don't have any idea just what they are in for when they go to the seminar. Graduates are held to an agreement they make during the training *not* to divulge any information about the *techniques* of the seminar. If they *did* talk about it—the tensions, harassment, deliberately foul language, and trauma to which you might be subjected—many would not bother to attend. As it is, the "secret" elements of the training cannot help but arouse curiosity. Est is successful, despite its many negative aspects, because of the impact of its program—which destroys one way of looking at the world (the average way) and substitutes another view, in such a manner that the people undergo a genuine conversion experience, with new psychological insight about themselves.

Through various techniques, defense mechanisms and role playing are broken down and confronted, often in a very cold manner. People's reactions vary: some weep, some get sick, some beg for help but get none. Some become psychotic.[13] The experience is as intense as it is dependency-producing; that is, a person who goes through so much suffering in the process wants to make the experience "worth it all" (all the *trouble*, that is) and is much more inclined to "take the message." Est doesn't change everybody at the seminar, but it seems that its most susceptible victims would be those who are sensitive, psychologically or spiritually insecure, and "searching."

The seminar combines psychological insight and confrontation with a method of allowing emotional release and a sort of self-acceptance. Est combines the positive (commonsense psychology) with the negative (authoritarianism, manipulation, and so forth). Psychiatrist Joel Kovel remarks:

> In sum, est has discovered how to compress and intensify the basic psychotherapeutic maneuver of breaking down defenses. From one side of the tedium, haranguing and privation are battering resistance, while from the other the group experience leads a person to dissolve his or her individuality, and its stubborn arrogance, and to psychologically merge with the others in the room. The very size of the group, along with the technique of est, tends to keep those others in a rather undifferentiated state, hence promoting a sense of union with them. The result for the individual is a state of openness, receptivity—and weakened discrimination. Into the gap steps the est philosophy, embodied in the trainer, and behind him, Werner Erhard.[14]

However, the ultimate philosophical-religious system into which even the positive aspects of the training are molded (this being similar to the nihilistic Zen and nondualist [advaita] school of Vedanta Hinduism), ultimately negates any benefits, especially if the trainee attempts to live the philosophy consistently.[15]

The est "conversion" also gives its subjects a conviction that they are, in an ultimate sense, in control of their lives and circumstances, no matter what those circumstances are—since in fact they, as "God," created them. Herein lies one of the social implications of est: if each individual is "God," and thus created his or her own particular circumstances in life, then helping the poor, the underprivileged, the starving multitudes, and so forth, is a definite sin against the wisdom of the divine plan. No matter how erroneous, the belief that *you* are the Creator, God, and are in control of whatever happens to you, can be a security-producing factor. Especially for middle-upper class Americans: that great body of spiritually deprived people searching for identity and transcendence in a varuum of loneliness. To become convinced that you are *It*, The Divine, can give one a false impression that one's life has been stabilized, enhanced, and improved. This narcissistic ego stimulation is, in part, responsible for the est impact.

When Erhard speaks of responsibility, it is in the sense of acknowledgment of one's authorship of all situations; that is, as the Creator, but not in any moral sense. Est supporter Marcia Seligson elucidates how this idea of divine control (responsibility) affects her life:

> I run my body, it doesn't run me. I'm in charge here.... Personal responsibility is a potent force indeed, the sensation that one is the cause of one's life. For me, it is the focal wisdom of the training and becomes even more solidified as the weeks and months go by. To the extent that I embrace and own the principle, my life seems to be, in truth, clear and simple and in my grasp; to the degree that I still hang on to my victim beliefs (i.e., that things outside myself control me), things don't work out too well....[16]

During the Guest Seminar Leaders Program (for graduates) "you get to experience moving beyond your limits, to the point where you realize that, in fact, you have no limits."[17]

What is ironic is that the worldview implanted by est is even more meaningless than what most people began with. It is held on to only because there is nothing to go back to. That has all been done away with via the "training" (brainwashing). Fortunately, many trainees see est for what it is and do not allow themselves to be intimidated into a more destructive philosophy of life. But many others do not, and this is of concern. Est has a great potential for misuse. As one est brochure puts it, "Graduates have reported that the results of the trainings do not wear off." [18] Before going into specifics, we first need to document the est philosophy.

The est Philosophy

"I am here to explain what can't be explained," says Erhard,[19] transcending Zen. In *What's So* for October, 1974, there was the following box:

RULES ABOUT LIFE

by

Werner Erhard

1. Life has no rules
2.

Dr. Kovel remarks:
> The philosophy promoted by est is no more than basic human-potential subjectivism. To quote Erhard, "Consciousness is all there is, there *isn't* anything else." We live mechanically, by belief and intellect, instead of trusting to experience, to being.[20]

Blind to the reality of evil in the world, Erhard states:
> Life is always perfect just the way it is. When you realize that, then no matter how strongly it may appear to be otherwise, you know that whatever is happening right now will turn out all right. Knowing this, you are in a position to begin mastering life.[21]

Voytek Frykowsky: shot twice, hit over the head 13 times . . . stabbed 51 times.

Rosemary LaBianca: 41 knife wounds.

Leno LaBianca: 12 knife wounds, punctured with a fork 7 times, a knife in his throat, a fork in his stomach, and, on the wall, in his own blood, "DEATH TO PIGS." (From a book on the Manson family) [22]

Erhard says:

As you can see, this universe is perfect. Don't lie about it. You're god in your universe. You caused it. You pretended not to cause it so that you could play in it. . . . [23]

Manson believed he was God, too. Where did his "game" end up? One wishes it weren't true, but Erhard says: "What you're doing is what God wants you to do," and "If you keep saying it is the way it really is, eventually, your word is law in the universe." [24]

In a three-page analysis of a special "Evening with the Clergy" on November 12, 1975, Woody Wilson records Erhard's reaction to a crucial question:

A graduate asked what do we do about killers? He had a hard time accepting such people as being OK. In brief he [Erhard] answered that it is perhaps unwise to take this to its brutal extreme. It must work in the extreme, yes, but it is hard to take it right off. . . . You were forgiven in the first place, you have to realize that, he said, "Make the world be God, don't make part of it be God and part be not God." [25]

So Manson is God.

De-identification is Part of est

Another key concept of est is the idea of the illusion or *maya* of the world. The goal of most yoga and Hinduism is to get the person to realize that he or she is not a body. The body, the self (ego) is unreal. The real person is Self, Brahman, the Absolute. Maya, the illusion, deludes us into thinking we are not the Absolute. The sport or game of the impersonal Brahman (his *lila*) is to make us think we are something we aren't, that is, a separate body and personality. Erhard explains the est effect:

So the de-identification happens at all levels. The person de-identifies with his mind, deidentifies with his body, he de-identifies with his emotions, he de-identifies with his problems, he de-identifies with his maya, he begins to see that he is not the Play.[26]

Marcia Seligson recounts the final hours of the seminar:

The final point, arrived at after six hours of dissertation and questions, is that there is no objective reality, only reality by agreement, which is illusion, and that the sole reality is the experience that I create.[27]

According to Erhard, *my* Self equals *your* Self equals the *same* Self. All is One. "Self is all there is. I mean that's it." "To pay attention to personality is to pay attention to an illusion. . . ."[28]

The est Effect and its Potential for Misuse

Although we have briefly discussed est effects and their potential misuse, there are further important est effects that need to be noted. First, in many cases, the est experience seems to result in a distortion of common sense. Marcia Seligson notes that initially she was skeptical—after talking with est graduates and hearing Erhard, she had thoughts about Hitler, mass hypnosis, cultism, Manson, and so forth. She said, "It didn't seem just cuckoo, it seemed (----) dangerous," and "As far as I was concerned, est was the biggest rip-off. . . . And I would expose it." After the est training, we find that her initial impressions, which were fairly accurate, have undergone a transformation: "I think that est has been one of the truly powerful experiences in my life. And I love Werner Erhard."[29] She is now a member of est's Advisory Board.

Est is a subjective experience and people can "get" different things from it. "Getting it" is the term used by "estians" to describe what they learned from the seminar. Prison inmates are made to "get" that they enjoy being in prison; rape victims are made to "get" that this is their way of inducing sympathy.[30] Since each of us created our own circumstances, we must have wanted this or that to happen to us. As "God," we created our own life-conditions. To recongize this means to "take responsibility" for them.

There seems to be some things in common that people "get" from the seminar. The following statements by est graduates show the impact it can have. By and large, these elements recur in the literature: selfishness, fatalism, nihilism, hedonism, apathy, and a moral relativism.

Marcia Seligson says:
> The differences I can measure in myself are mostly attitudinal. Nothing overwhelms me as before: nothing seems tragic or permanent. . . .[31]

A businessman coldly replies:
> I take responsibility for the people that let me step on them, and don't feel guilty.[32]

Here we see a good example which shows that the est concept of responsibility is not necessarily tied to any moral values. In effect he is saying, "I acknowledge I created these situations to play in." This is "taking responsibility" in estian language. It has nothing whatsoever to do with blame or guilt or burden.[33]

Adelaide Bry, author of *Est: Sixty Hours that Transform Your Life*, reports on another est graduate:
> During the training, she *got* that she was frigid. She subsequently left her high-status and well-paying job to work full time producing pornography films.[34]

About a dozen books have been written on est and they sometimes contain personal accounts by its graduates:

Jane: It certainly isn't nearly as important for me to be right anymore as it used to be. . . . What is important to me is what is happening to me right now. And I don't give a (----) about tomorrow.[35]

Phil: It becomes apparent to you that the people whose lives aren't working are those who don't support that which supports them.[36]

Hans: I am so lazy these days. . . . I don't care that much if people don't buy my work. . . . That is their problem. . . . For the first time I am running into a problem about paying the rent. And it doesn't really bother me. A lot of people (est graduates) are seeing their marriages break up and they consider that as making their lives work.[36]

Jesse: Recently my father criticized me for not responding after my uncle had died. He thought I should have telephoned my aunt or sent a card. "You don't even care," he said. "I don't care," I told him.[38]

Unconcerned About the Future and Death

The following statements show that est tends to make one unconcerned about the future and death.

Dan: I know that things are going to be the way they are. The est training tells you that what you have to do about things is *nothing*.... The only thing there is, is right now.

I experienced no sadness when I was told my father had died. That was okay.

That is one of the things that makes life easier, things aren't significant. Nothing is. I got that my father's death really isn't significant.

Things have lost their significance, so I probably don't notice a lot of big things. I just notice my life is working a lot.[39]

What Dan is really saying is that the burden of normal social responsibilities and customs is now lifted from him. He is a lot happier being unconcerned about life's problems, because he now believes they don't really matter. As he says, nothing is significant. Robert Hargrove, in his book on est, recalls how, upon beginning to realize the world wasn't real after all, he had the sensation of someone lifting an enormous rock off his head.[40] Naturally, if nothing is real, or really matters, then the person is free to do whatever he or she wants and has no undesired commitments, obligations, or values to live by. Who, in our high-pressure society, *would not* feel great release upon truly believing (and thinking he has a *basis* for believing) that nothing really matters? All at once, one's social, financial, family, and job pressures are all gone.

Another graduate, Dale, reports his personal belief about est as simply "dangerous." He tells of a friend who had difficulties in school after taking est:

> He had a "so what" attitude and flunked out of school at the end of his second quarter. Est teaches you that if you have problems, you're chosen to have them. My friend thought he must have chosen to have problems at U.C. . . . but he never had any trouble before he took est.[41]

What we see here is evidence that est produces an apathy toward life. This is a logical result of the basically Vedantic philosophy of est: a belief in personal divinity, in God's game playing (lila), in the unreality of the world (maya), and so forth.

Is Murder Just *"Improper"*—Or Is It *Wrong?*

What is also of great concern is the instilling of relativistic morals from the est seminar. In the interviewing several graduates in depth, what always comes out in this area is a personal philosophy like this:

> We all live by agreement. We can choose to break these agreements. This is not really morally *wrong*, but it is improper. We should try to keep agreements. Hence, if a society says murder is wrong, we should abide by the agreement, even though it's probably more accurate to say murder is improper, rather than wrong. But equally, if society were to say murder is good, then it becomes correct behavior. The Roman slaughter of the Christians was proper because the agreement and consensus of the society *made* it proper. Were this true in Hitler's Germany, Hitler would have been acting properly.

No matter how optimistic estians are that they can change the world for the better, it appears that the system, when logically applied, opens the door for the suppression of minorities. As one est trainer, Rod, puts it:

> The universe works on agreement and reality is a function of agreement and agreement alone. . . . In order for something to have a value, it's gotta' be

out in the agreement.⁴²

Logically applied, if everyone hates Christ, then Christ is of no value. Or, if there is no agreement that Christ exists, He, in fact, does not exist. Hence, est would teach that Christ did *not* exist prior to the existence of the people who made him exist, the Christians.

The following dialogue of an est trainer during a session illuminates the est worldview. It is reported by graduate Robert Hargrove.

"So when you experience the truth, you know it's nothing but an illusion! . . ."

"Then how did all this stuff [the universe] get here?" someone asked.

"It never did," Rod said.

I was beginning to feel myself moving into a state of consciousness that I had previously experienced only in meditation. It was accompanied by the physical sensation that someone was lifting an enormous rock off the top of my head. . . .

"In the illusion that we call reality, there's no cause. It's effect! Effect! Effect!"

"Well, who created the universe?" Charlie asked.

"In your universe you're God," Rod said, "You caused it, and pretended not to cause it so you could play in it. And there are at least as many universes as there are people on this planet. It all comes out of your point of view." ⁴³

The Illusion of Becoming God

In other words, it is all an illusion, but by agreement I play the game ("take responsibility"). Then, as "God," I can do whatever I want without thinking there are any *real* consequences for my actions. I can play the game (live in the world) with immunity—not necessarily in the sense of breaking laws, because I created them, but in the sense that nothing is important or threatening unless I want it to be. And it wouldn't really be *wrong* to break laws, only "improper." In est, nothing is really immoral in the absolute sense.

The concept of "keeping agreements" is used to persuade people to stay at the seminar for the entire four days. Since 80 per cent of the effect is "gotten" on the fourth day, people have to be kept there somehow. So est paradoxically appeals to the *moral* notion of holding to an agreement. This is dishonest manipulation, to say the least. The people make the agreement before they are even told what will happen to them. One elderly woman who was shocked at the brutality of the trainer's language said that "if the doors hadn't been locked and if she hadn't made an agreement," she would have left.[44]

This woman should have left. The next morning she was back singing a dirty song through the microphone while the audience gave her a standing ovation. Her integrity was compromised. The woman's mistake was to keep the agreement in the first place. In est, trainers manipulate the audience through guilt and human weakness. However, once you know something is evil, you shouldn't stay around to watch it infiltrate your life—you should get up and walk away. Unfortunately, the level of control est trainers exert over the audience is so great, hardly anyone leaves, despite the offer of a refund several times (if they will leave at that point).

Est, along with Transcendental Meditation and all the other cults of Vedanta, has serious social implications. People care less about things that were once meaningful to them. They may use the philosophy to justify immoral behavior. They become dehumanized. If everyone agrees Hitler was cool, then he *was* cool, and so on. Help the sick? the poor? the downtrodden? This is wrong because as God, the poor and sick have chosen those conditions to experience and play with. Who am I to interfere with their choice? This is not too different from the caste system in India, which justifies the sickening conditions of millions on the basis of not interfering with the will of the Divine. Of course, I can also play the game of "social causes" if I want to. Even though the value of *everything* is equal (nothing), boredom is the result unless we *arbitrarily* make something more important than something else. In the Hunger Project est has created the game of making the reduction of starvation more important than world hunger.

The Hunger Project—An est Rip-Off

The Hunger Project, founded in 1977 by Werner Erhard, is a notable addition to the world's list of charity rip-offs.

Since Erhard teaches that people must claim authorship for their own particular circumstances in life, it may sound strange to hear Erhard and his followers say that they are personally taking responsibility to end world hunger. Remember, though, that est's "responsibility" does not involve a moral obligation to *do* anything. Erhard does not need to feed the hungry—he can move about in plush surroundings and assert his authorship of a positive world food situation.

Actress Valerie Harper, utilizing est double-talk, says that Hunger Project enrollees will create "a critical mass of agreement about an idea, and then out of that, things will manifest." [45] That is, if everyone aligns their thinking on the hunger issue, a "context will be created in which hunger cannot exist," and starvation will somehow end—a comforting thought for well-fed Americans.

Sending money to food relief organizations is considered by the Hunger Project to be a dehumanizing act. So almost none of the approximately $1 million collected by the Hunger Project has actually helped the hungry. Instead, the money is used to tell more Americans about the Hunger Project. As *Mother Jones* magazine observes in its recent exposé of the Hunger Project, "consciousness is everything; distribution of wealth and power, nothing." [46] Lester Brown who is widely respected in the field of world food problems, says that the Hunger Project has "probably collected more money in the name of hunger and done the least about hunger than any group I can think of." [47]

Although it is claimed that the Hunger Project is separate from the est organization, the two are intimately related. Almost all Hunger Project staffers are est graduates, and the rest are pressured to take the est training.[48]

The Hunger Project appears to have other aims besides

the elimination of world hunger. *Mother Jones* says that the Project is "a thinly veiled recruitment arm for est." And the hunger issue itself has been used to gather money for est. A "Hunger Project Seminar Series," for instance, costs $30.00 per enrollment, and the proceeds have gone directly to the est organization.[49]

As *Mother Jones* points out, est's Hunger Project is one of the first attempts by one of the new "self"-oriented groups to address a social issue. If the Hunger Project is any indication of what the future holds, the prospects for the poor look increasingly dim.

References for Chapter 19

1. R.C.D. Heck and J.L. Thompson, "Est: Salvation or Swindle?" *San Francisco,* January 1976, p. 22.
2. *Graduate Review,* August 1978, p. 10.
3. *East-West Journal,* September 1974.
4. *New Age Journal,* No. 8, p. 47.
5. Heck and Thompson, p. 70. According to an est statement, Erhard was not involved in any wrongdoing.
6. *Ibid.*
7. W.W. Bartley, *Werner Erhard: The Transformation of a Man: The Founding of Est* (New York: Clarkson Potter) 1978, p. 145.
8. *New Age Journal,* No. 7, pp. 18-20.
9. *What's So,* January 1975 (est brochure)
10. Adam Smith, "Powers of the Mind, Part II: The Est Experience," *New York,* 29 September 1975, p. 35.
11. *Psychology Today,* August 1975, p. 39.
12. *New York Daily News,* August 12, 1975.
13. *New Age Journal,* No. 7, p. 25.
14. Joel Kovel, *A Complete Guide to Therapy from Psychoanalysis to Behavior Modification* (New York: Pantheon Books) 1976, p. 172.
15. See John Welson, *The Transcendental Explosion* (Irvine, CA: Harvest House) 1976, Chap. 6.
16. *New Times,* October 18, 1974.
17. *What's So,* January 1975.
18. Werner Erhard, *What is the Purpose of Est Training* (1976).
19. *Newsweek,* February 17, 1975.
20. Kovel, *op. cit.,* p. 171.
21. *What's So,* January 1975.
22. V. Bugliosi, *Helter Skelter* (NY: Bantam), 1975, pp. 327, 330f.

23. Werner Erhard, *If God Had Meant Man to Fly, He Would Have Given Him Wings* (1974), p. 11.
24. *Ibid.*, last page and p. 2.
25. Woody Wilson, unpublished report on "An Evening with the Clergy," November 12, 1975.
26. *East-West Journal,* September 1974.
27. *New Times,* October 18, 1974.
28. *East-West Journal,* September 1974.
29. *New Times,* October 18, 1974.
30. Heck and Thompson, p. 20; cf. *San Francisco Chronicle,* December 3, 1974.
31. *New Times,* October 18, 1974.
32. Heck and Thompson, *op. cit.,* p. 22.
33. See the glossaries in Pat Marks *Est: The Movement and the Man* (NY: Playboy) 1976, and William Greene, *Est: Four Days to Make Your Life Work* (NY: Pocket) 1976.
34. *Book Digest,* July 1976, p. 144.
35. Donald Porter and Diane Taxon, *The Est Experience* (NY: Award) 1976, p. 57.
36. *Ibid.*, p. 94.
37. *Ibid.*, p. 62.
38. *Ibid.*, p. 51.
39. *Ibid.*, pp. 88-93.
40. Robert Hargrove, *Est: Making Life Work* (NY: Dell) 1976, p. 102.
41. Heck and Thompson, *op. cit.,* p. 23.
42. Hargrove, *op. cit.,* pp. 90, 92.
43. *Ibid.*, pp. 101-2.
44. Smith, *op. cit.,* p. 36.
45. Suzanne Gordon, "Let Them Eat Est," *Mother Jones,* December 1978, p. 44.
46. *Ibid.*, p. 43.
47. *Ibid.*, p. 52.
48. *Ibid.*, p. 50.
49. *Ibid.*, p. 42.

Chapter 20

The Potential Dangers of est

Stripping Defenses and Beliefs Leads to Trouble

Est does pose dangers for certain people. These dangers are more direct and immediate than the epistemological transformation est brings to any receptive participants. One danger is est-induced insanity. For example, T. George Harris writes in *Psychology Today:*

> Bruce Ogilvie in the Counseling Center at San Jose State University and a few other clinicians are treating est casualties. The stripping down of defense and belief leave some people in serious trouble.[1]

Psychiatrist Lloyd Moglen states:

> I've also seen several people who have become psychotic and had to be hospitalized.[2]

Erhard himself states that the est policy only discourages people who have a previous history of serious psychopathology, but that "we don't exclude them from participation."[3]

Three psychiatrists detailed in the *American Journal of Psychiatry* seven case histories of serious psychotic reactions among est participants (most requiring confinement and antipsychotic drugs). Six of the seven had no previous history of psychopathology among themselves or their respective families. While the psychiatrists did not wish to state that an exact cause-effect relationship existed, they were concerned enough about its possibility to issue a warning to the psychotherapeutic community.[4]

In discussions with est graduates, John Weldon has been told of another potential danger: that certain aspects of the training border on the occult. Reportedly, some people experience astral projection during certain exercises, and reincarnation experiences are fairly common.[5] Many of the est techniques are consciousness altering.

We have noted that est has a consuming interest in spreading its philosophy via the educational route. It is also relevant to mention the funding of est training for elementary school children, which is surely deplorable—there are few individuals more susceptible than young children. At the Sydney School in Castro Valley, California, the teachers who were est graduates instigated an est seminar training for their second and third graders. *San Francisco* magazine reported:

> ... the reaction of parents and children was mixed. Parents reported discipline problems with children after the training. The project chose not to repeat the training this year.[6]

Brainwashing

Est cannot be classified with the type of brainwashing employed by, say, the North Koreans. That in part utilizes torture and extreme and continued physical-sensory deprivation. However, the 1960 college edition of *Webster's New World Dictionary* defines brainwashing as if it were defining est methodology:

> To indoctrinate so intensively and thoroughly as to effect a radical transformation of beliefs and mental attitudes.

Perhaps implicit in this is the idea of involuntary confinement, something not true of est. People *choose* to go to the est seminars, regardless of how inadequately informed they may be. Many people do, however, see it as brainwashing. Mark Brewer, writing in *Psychology Today*, comments on the techniques:

> Such efforts, of course, are commonly known as brainwashing, which is precisely what the est experience is, and the result is usually a classic conversion.[7]

In the same article, San Francisco State University Professor Richard P. Marsh represents the case for est. He says est is *not* brainwashing, but he then proceeds to define brainwashing as the attempt "to confuse by sudden reversals of logic, to frighten and humiliate a captive subject in order to break his will and insinuate forcibly into his mind the belief system of his captor." *It seems that he is, for the most part, giving an excellent description of est.* Other writers also say est is brainwashing, and that the est techniques are similar to those described in William Sargent's book, *Battle for the Mind: A Physiology of Conversion and Brainwashing.*"[8]

William Green, author of *Est: Four Days to Make Your Life Work*, remarks:

> Everyone goes through a tremendous emotional upheaval. During that upheaval, the belief system of the trainees are very often cast aside. . . .[9]

Heck and Thompson state:

> A major step in the est training is negating any preexisting belief system.[10]

The question of brainwashing seems to depend on the degree of force/coercion used to effect this change of belief system. The evidence indicates that est should be labeled a mild form of brainwashing, or at least intensive indoctrination. Even pro-est writers have acknowledged the controversy. For example, Luke Rhinehart notes that, in his mind, the most substantial argument against est so far is "that the training is a form of brainwashing," although he feels this is not the case.[11] Even Erhard admits that the est techniques are "mind-blowing:" "You give it [the mind] something to deal with that it's incapable of handling." [12]

Let us say that we have no quarrel with any positive and

psychologically healthful insights that might be derived from est, nor with the obvious sincerity and goodwill of many est graduates. We only ask that they look at where the philosophy leads. Our main concern is the overall worldview which est imparts. If the philosophy of est were so good to begin with, would such drastic conversion measures be necessary to get us to adopt it? And the many benefits reported by est graduates have to be screened by a system capable of providing a legitimate value judgment on them. Any relativistic system is insufficient. If 50 million people say a stupid thing, it is still stupid. Reality and truth are not a function of agreement and experience alone. They are found only through the eternally immutable and righteous infinite personal God of the Judeo-Christian scriptures. Any beneficial changes est claims to bring must be judged in the light of this revelation. Est may give people the "freedom" to get divorces, quit their jobs, and feel like they are making progress. But are they?—Or are they simply running away from problems they will have to face later? Even valid psychological insights can be a problem when attached to the new est worldview, which is dehumanizing at its core.

est and Christianity

Intellect alone cannot easily withstand the onslaught of the training. Intellectual attackers often become yielded converts. Dr. Kovel remarks:

> The most sophisticated judgment in the world is no match for such [seminar] conditions—which indeed make their effect felt, not on the intellect, but on the soft space that yearning occupies behind the mask of reason. Numerous people who have undergone est tell of how they attempted to dispute the trainer, only to become confounded and yield. What such reports leave out is that the most powerful intellect necesarily becomes puerile under the conditions of the training. It is like playing tennis with your side of the court under water.[13]

Part of the reason for this is that in est, there is no absolute truth or objective reality. Reality is defined as experience which is the same as truth.[14] Everything is subjective. The problem here is that this leaves out two crucial factors entirely.

First, human experience can be tremendously deceptive. Second, there is the existence of demons who like nothing more than to give people genuine experiences which they use to "validate" false belief systems. All experience-oriented religions (Scientology, Nichiren Shoshu, Hare Krishna, TM, etc.) promote both human and Satanic deception with no absolute standard of judgment by which to check these experiences. Dr. Kurt Koch has noted that in his very extensive personal counseling experience, Satanic visions outnumber Christian ones by fifty to one.[15] "Jesus Christ" appears often in Mormon temples, thereby "validating" Mormon beliefs.[16] And on and on.

The Scriptures have numerous warnings about false experiences.[17] Scripture must stand in judgment of est, and not vice versa. Once people place something above Scripture, they open a Pandora's box, and it grieves us to see this occurring today in many churches. If we as Christians do not honor God's Word *as Jesus* honored it (as *fully* authoritative and trustworthy), then we and our children will suffer for it. Keeping in mind that a bad tree cannot bear good fruit, let us look at est in the light of God's Word, the Bible.

Scripture does not at all support the use of foul language. How can Christians sit through sixty hours of vile language? We are to *expose* the deeds of darkness, not participate in them.[18] God says, "Let no evil talk come out of youth mouths, but only such as is good for edifying . . ." (Eph. 4:29). In the *East-West Journal* of September, 1974, Erhard implies that Jesus Christ is dog excrement (using the four-letter equivalent). This is the same man who says, "I consider myself one of Christ's staunchest supporters."[19]

Erhard knows just where he stands, even though he and his followers state that est does not interfere with anyone's religious beliefs. He admits, "I would have been burned as a witch."

> Had I been in a religious order or any church or monastery, I definitely could not have done any of this. It would have been heresy.[20]

On another occasion Erhard solidified his position:

> For instance, I believe that the "belief" in God is the greatest barrier to God in the universe—the single greatest barrier. I would prefer someone who is ignorant to someone who believes in God. Because the belief in God is a total barrier, almost a total barrier to the experience of God.

An Unbiblical Concept of God

Erhard's concept of God is totally unbiblical. Scripture declares God to be an infinite person Who exists apart from his creation. Erhard denies this.

> To pay attention to personality is to pay attention to illusion or effects.
>
> That's all there is, there isn't anything but spirituality, which is just another word for God, because God is everything. Where isn't God?[22]

Although a Christian believer would be told est would not interfere with his religious beliefs, this is not true. The est belief system is designed to destroy the validity of the Christian worldview. Est is supposedly nonreligious, but since its purpose is to alter one's epistemology and instill a monist and/or pantheistic belief in personal divinity, est qualifies as religious. In the est philosophy, it is Christianity which is detrimental, even harmful, to growth and enlightenment. William Greene states:

> In the est training *you* are God. . . . Therefore you cannot look to any supreme being for special treatment, goodness, or award.[23]

Erhard himself states:

> We've been conditioned to look for answers outside ourselves. But that's not what people get from us. What they get is an experience of enlightenment, which is different from the belief system called salvation. If I get the idea that God is going to save me,

therefore I'm all right, that's salvation; if I get the
idea that nothing's going to save me, therefore I'm
all right, that's enlightenment.[24]

It is easy to see that est is opposed to the very core of Christianity. Anyone who believed the above would have no need whatever to turn to Christ. In the est philosophy, truth and reality are found in *experience* alone. "Belief" is detrimental. It is defined as "the act of placing trust or confidence in a concept or conviction and accepting it as Truth. Beliefs prevent an individual from experiencing life."[25] Hence, Christian faith or belief is, according to est, preventing one from experiencing life and is opposed to truth and reality. Christians are living a lie.

There is another crucial distinction between est and Christianity. This lies in the difference est makes between "help" and "assist." To assist is good; to help is bad. To *assist* someone is to lend support, recognizing that if you gave them no support, they could get along quite well without you. To *help* someone is "an admission that he or she is incapable of accomplishing the act alone. According to est, helping should be avoided."[26] This completely undercuts the Biblical concept of salvation by grace through faith. It is a Christian imperative that human beings recognize that they cannot "make it" alone. They need to trust in Jesus Christ, and Him only, for salvation. He alone died for our sins.[27] As one est trainer puts it, est attempts to "systematically cut off all hope . . . that any external sources will ever save you. . . ."[28] Hence, est and Christianity function on two entirely opposite principles. Est is a system of "self-salvation" that appeals to human ego and personal "divinity." Christianity recognizes only an agency outside of humanity, Jesus Christ, as its sole instrument of salvation. Erhard teaches self-glorification; Jesus teaches self-sacrifice.

In Conclusion

The est graduation booklet states:
Obviously the truth is what's so. Not so obviously, it's also so what.

Erhard and est graduates may say "so what" to all the evil and greed and wickedness and hate and terrible suffering in the world. Erhard can play his game as "God," telling us of our divinity while millions starve to death. Let him preach a belief that robs people of their values, morals, and dignity in the name of "enlightenment." The fact that he *does* sleep at night only lays bare the human capacity for deception. How valid are the words of Isaiah:

> Woe to those who call evil good and good evil, who put darkness for light and light for darkness, who put bitter for sweet and sweet for bitter! Woe to those who are wise in their own eyes, and shrewd in their own sight!... who acquit the guilty for a bribe, and deprive the innocent of his right! Therefore, as the tongue of fire devours the stubble, and as dry grass sinks down in the flame, so their root will be as rottenness, and their blossom go up like dust; for they have rejected the law of the Lord of hosts, and have despised the word of the Holy One of Israel.[29]

Perhaps the attitude est can instill in a person is best displayed by an est graduate who wrote to *Psychology Today* in response to a critical, but perceptive article.

"In response to Mark Brewer's article on est—so what?[30] Since nonestians aren't 'enlightened,' how can they possibly speak with authority on est?" Erhard displays the same attitude as his convert:

So est is evil, what's the point?
yea, I got that, now what?
So what?[31]

Erhard goes on to say to his graduates:

> Another thing. You do not *have* to accept any of the responsibility for any of the evil in the organization, nor do you have to make anyone else responsible. Everybody is absolved of *having to be* responsible for any of the evil. I have already taken 100% of the responsibility, so no one else *needs* to take any. I have already acknowledged being 100% causer and creator of every speck of evil in this organization—

as a matter of fact in institutionality and organization. I am telling you that I am 100% responsible. That's not manipulation, that's my experience. I am willing to have created all the evil in the organization. I am willing to and experience that I have.[32]

Finally, Erhard states paradoxically:

It's not my experience that people come out of est with this kind of, you know, "Everything is all right, it'll all turn out all right." It *is* all right, and it *will* turn out all right, and in the meantime, there are things that are outrageous and about these things, it's appropriate to be outraged.[33]

We could not agree more.

Reference for Chapter 20

1. *Psychology Today,* December 1975, p. 8.
2. *New Age Journal,* No. 7, p. 25.
3. *Ibid.*
4. *American Journal of Psychiatry,* March and November 1977.
5. Reported by advanced graduates who prefer anonymity. For a reincarnation analysis, see Weldon, *The Transcendental Explosion,* appendix 4.
6. Heck and Thompson, *op. cit.,* p. 22.
7. *Psychology Today,* August 1975, p. 39.
8. Heck and Thompson, *op. cit.,* p. 22.
9. Greene, *op. cit.,* p. 171; cf. p. 132.
10. Heck and Thompson, *op. cit.,* p. 71.
11. Luke Rhinehart, *The Book of Est* (NY: Holt Rinehard and Winston) 1976, pp. 259-60.
12. *New Age Journal,* No. 7, p. 28.
13. Kovel, *op. cit.,* p. 172.
14. Adelaide Bry, *Est: Sixty Hours that Transform Your Life* (NY: Avon) 1976, pp. 229-30; Greene, pp. 33-34; Marks, pp. 165-66.
15. Kurt Koch, *Christian Counseling and Occultism* (Grand Rapids, MI: Kregel) 1972, p. 63.
16. Told to the author by a practicing Mormon.
17. Jer. 17:9, 23:16; Ezek. 13:1-9; Col. 2:18; Gal. 1:8; Matt. 24:24; etc.
18. Eph. 5:11.
19. Woody Wilson, *op. cit.*
20. *East-West Journal,* September 1974.
21. *Ibid.*
22. *Ibid.*
23. Greene, *op. cit.,* p. 131.
24. *New Times,* October 18, 1974.

25. Greene, *op. cit.*, pp. 29-33, 131.
26. *Ibid.*, pp. 32, 29.
27. Eph. 2:8-9; Acts 4:12; John 14:6.
28. *San Francisco Chronicle,* December 3, 1974.
29. Isa. 5:20-21, 23-24.
30. *Psychology Today,* December 1975, p. 8.
31. *Graduate Review,* November 1976, p. 10.
32. *Ibid.*
33. *New Age Journal,* No. 7, p. 24.

Conclusion to Part II

The Consequences and Evil Design of Nonbiblical Supernaturalism

We have seen enough to realize that the supposed "power from the stars" is inherently evil. So also are the attempts to take over the minds of men by suggestions as to their own deity. Behind it all is an evil intelligence, the being named in the Bible as Satan. His nonbiblical supernaturalism is a *form* of godliness that denies the *true power* of godliness. His time is short and his pace has quickened.

Nat Freedland, writing in *The Occult Explosion,* says that "No modern, post-industrial society has ever experienced anything like this occult explosion."[1] Colin Wilson, author of *The Outsider,* one whose own skepticism toward the occult was altered by his research, writes in *The Occult: A History:* "It would probably be safe to say that there are now more witches in England and America than at any time since the Reformation."[2] (As late as 1965 the British authority Pennethorne Hughes remarked that witchcraft was "dying rapidly" and that in essence "the practice is over."[3])

Sybil Leek, encouraged by the success of her multimillion seller, *Diary of a Witch,* referred to the literally millions of people interested in witchcraft in her subsequent book, *The Complete Art of Witchcraft.* Anton LeVey refers to our era as "The Age of Satan" in his book, *The Satanic Rituals.*[4] H. Stanley Redgrove refers to the recent and "astonishing swing . . . back to magic and mysticism."[5] Authority C. A. Burland sums up what could be a worldwide assessment. In *Beyond Science,* he states, "At no time in the history of civilization has occultism in its various forms been so widely practiced as today."[6]

Even academic areas are being encroached upon by various forms and degrees of occult philosophy and technique: Psychology by parapsychology, transpersonal psychology, and new consciousness concepts; Medicine by the holistic health movement (incorporating eastern metaphysics, psychic healing and surgery, etc.); Science by speculation on theoretical physics and the occult use of technology for development of altered states of consciousness, psychic powers, and mediumship; Anthropology by sympathetic shamanistic studies; Theology by the study of occultism for its own sake (e.g., "Christian" parapsychology); etc.

The Erosion of Science

Science in general is being slowly eroded into occultism by parapsychology in the West (as we shall see in our next section) and its corresponding psychotronics and psychobiology in the Communist countries. When the communists study the occult, the Western military personnel must also react with proper defensive measures. For example, two recent studies (e.g., *Soviet and Czechoslovakian Parapsychology Research* and *Controlled Offensive Behavior —USSR)* released by the Defense Intelligence Agency indicate that the U.S. and U.S.S.R. are exploring the military potential of psychic power.

In discussing the occult, we must always guard against extremism—either fostering an interest in the topic or giving it too much or too little power. C. S. Lewis stated:

There are two equal and opposite errors into

> which our race can fall about the devils. One is to disbelieve in their existence. The other is to believe and to feel an excessive and unhealthy interest in them. They, themselves are equally pleased by both errors, and hail a materialist or a magician with the same delight.[7]

Concerning his own belief in the existence of literal demons—intelligent, but evil spirits—he said:

> It seems to me to explain a good many facts. It agrees with the plain sense of Scripture, the tradition of Christendom, and the beliefs of most men at most times. And it conflicts with nothing that any of the sciences has shown to be true.[8]

It is the underlying philosophy of our book that occult powers and methodology in all their forms (eastern or western, psychic or technological) represent in varying degrees contact with these demonic spirits. This contact can be overt (spiritist), covert (healing by psychic energy), acknowledged (black magic), or repressed (parapsychology). Such contact is always deeply consequential.

It is very clear that parapsychology (or psychotronics, bioenergetics, etc.) is simply a modern and "scientific" term for occultism in general.[9] This we shall document.

We emphasize that parapsychology is *not* the study of heretofore unnoticed innate natural powers of man—it is the study of historic occultism and demonism, much of it *redefined* as latent psi. The study of parapsychological literature (less the thousands of meaningless esp trials) displays this fact as a clear day displays the sun.

Both historical and modern occultism involve the same basic investigations and phenomena as parapsychology. The only difference is that modern parapsychology is more technically and scientifically oriented due to advances in instrumentation, technology, and scientific knowledge in general.

The Consequences of Occult Involvement

In this section, we wish to document the noticeable consequences of involvement in these areas. These dangers are not of the same type as, say, a high risk profession such as driving explosives. They are of a more serious nature and involve both direct and indirect, seen and unseen results, some of unimaginable torment. In our investigation, we have examined the findings of theologians, psychiatric professionals, parapsychologists, and occultists alike. We make no apology that we are sounding a severe warning to persons involved and to our society which has lately become so enamored with the topic.

Unfortunately, we will reap the consequences severalfold in the next generation, unless we wisely choose to cease our activity. That activity includes mediums, dabblers with ouija boards, tarot cards, astrology, and the I Ching . . . and parapsychologists conducting "scientific" investigations. Those who are so involved must understand that they *are not* advancing the cause of personal growth, spirituality, science, or society. These practices will affect their lives in a harmful way, and there can be severe consequences for their own children.

We are dealing with an area that is admittedly fraught with numerous dangers. Widespread ignorance of the facts, a presuppositional bias against the demonic, and an almost deadly naivete' about the supernatural has allowed people to jump eagerly into the occult. Normally cautious scientists are rushing full speed ahead into investigations, when even the occultists warn of serious consequences of a casual and undisciplined approach. Only someone who has spent the time necessary in researching this area of occult dangers can fully appreciate the damage now being done. Around the world there have been, and are, literally tens of millions of people who have suffered—large numbers having been driven to insanity and suicide as a result. Brazil alone has some 40 million spiritist practitioners and followers.

The Scripture calls Satan a "a liar and murderer from the beginning," and one who comes only to "kill and destroy" (John 8:44; 10:10). He is a being who takes pride in his name and lives up to his reputation well.

Defining the Occult

There are dozens of categories of various occult practices and phenomena. A generalized broad definition would be nonbiblical supernaturalism, as our chapter heading suggests. Dr. Kurt Koch divides these practices into three basic categories, which we have utilized and upon which we have expanded.[10]

I. ESP (Extrasensory Perception)
 A. Spiritism (mediumism, apparitions of the dead, ouija boards, trance speaking, various automatisms, i.e., automatic writing, painting, composing, etc.)
 B. Hyperaesthesia (heightened or supernatural capacities of perception, i.e., precognition, visionary dreams, telepathy, clairvoyance, clairsentience, clairaudience)
 C. Divination (fortune-telling, ouija boards, tarot cards, I Ching, palmistry, astrology, rod and pendulum, etc.)

II. ESI (Extrasensory Influence)
 A. Hypnosis
 B. Healing magnetism
 C. Magic charming
 D. Mental suggestion (psychokinesis [PK] or remote influence)
 E. Black and white magic
 F. Blood pacts
 G. Fetishism (the use of objects with magical powers)
 H. Incubi, succubae (intercourse with male and female demons)

III. Extrasensory Apparitions
 A. Seance materializations
 B. Independent materializations (poltergeists, UFO entities, "ascended masters," etc.)

In other works he discusses color therapy, death magic, occult forms of iridology (eye diagnosis), firewalking, freemasonry, letters of protection, mesmerism, etc. In general the basis of both occultism and parapsychology is the desire for an application of supernatural power and knowledge in opposition to God's revealed will. Someone may point out that in the past certain supernatural methods were used in the Bible which would be called occult today, e.g., the Urim and Thummin. These occasions are infrequent (even rare) in the Bible and were used by one person specially designated by God—*the prophet*. They served as a special means of communication with God. They were not available to the masses.

Just as portions of the law of Moses are no longer in use today because the reason they were needed is no longer present, so it is that these other supernatural methods are no longer available. They are not needed today. With God's written communication freely available in the Bible, the need for "Urim and Thummin" activities has passed.

The Importance of Semantics

It is crucial that we do not dilute the seriousness of occult involvement by redefining it into something else. Parapsychology and psychiatry often redefine dangerous occultism into harmless, natural, or neutral phenomena. Much of parapsychology actually hides the demonic. Camouflage has always been the best tactic of the father of lies. The devil never walks up to someone and says, "I am Satan. I wish to damn your soul." On the contrary:

> The devil is a many-sided and versatile demagogue. To the psychologist he says, "I will give you new knowledge and understanding." To the occultist, he will say, "I will give you the keys to the last secrets of creation." He confronts the religionist and the moralist with a mask of integrity and promises them the very help of heaven. And finally to the rationalist and the liberalist he says, "I am not there. I do not even exist."
>
> The devil is a skillful strategist. He is the master of every tactic of the battlefield. He befogs the front. He hides behind a camouflage of empty religious talk. He operates through the use of the latest scientific method. He success-

fully fires and launches his arguments on the social and humane plane. And his sole aim is to deceive, to entice, and to ensnare his victims.[12]

There are many examples of semantic distortion, both in psychiatry and parapsychology. Clearly demonic occurrences—by all historic, anthropological, and biblical criteria—are reinterpreted as "natural" subconscious manifestations. Demon possession may be viewed as an "hysteric multiple personality" or Jungian archetypes. Poltergeist phenomena are viewed as "recurrent spontaneous psychokinesis," not the often vicious demonic attacks they really are. (Parapsychologists are entirely ignorant of the hidden motives behind the milder poltergeist manifestations.) Semantics are important, because insofar as the true origin and cause of occult phenomena and resultant problems are not accurately discerned, helping the individual or society occultly subjected will not be possible.

Problems Beyond Finance

All the foreign aid in the world will not significantly change an occultly dominated culture. The problems are much deeper than financial—the people are economically depressed because of their regressive worldview fostered by occult involvement, not vice versa. No matter what the liberal optimists may say, the failures of their programs and a deeper analysis of the situation reveals the truth.[13] When occultism is defined as the progress of "evolutionary consciousness," as it is today, how can people recognize it as demonism? That which is demonic should be labeled as such, for our own protection. Edgar Cayce's son, Hugh Lynn Cayce, gives us an example of another kind of naive and simplistic approach. In his *Venture Inward,* he discusses automatic writing and ouija boards (both forms of mediumism), hallucinogenic drugs, and Scientology as dangerous paths to the "subconscious."

Yet he advocates mediumism, hypnosis, meditation, and the "safe" development of psychic abilities. How many of our children would still be living if we labeled our household poisons with bright flowers and added the smell of chocolate?

When ouija boards are supposedly not moved by demons, but by "imperceptible muscular movements" activated by the unconscious, the spirit is free to act undetected with impunity. Invisibility, or a "neutral" label, secures control.

Take another example, the practice of spiritism, i.e., mediumism or necromancy. We rarely hear the term "spiritism," which gives us an idea of what is involved (contact with spirits). We hear the much more respectable term, "spiritualism," which conveys the idea that the mediums and their activities are godly, spiritual activities. "White" magic, they tell us, is really the "good" use of magic as opposed to "black" magic—but needless to say, only the forms differ. Black magic uses spells and incantations, etc. to invoke demons. White magic uses the Name of the Trinity, Bible phrases, psalms, and Christian symbols, but both attempt the same thing—power over nature and the "gods" (spirits).

Dr. Koch notes that:

> The use of the names of the Trinity or of religious symbols is a fatal, beguiling mask and deception, to which many Christians readily fall victim.
>
> That black and white charms are really essentially equivalent appears first of all from the similar psychological effects attaching to them. Further, the equivalence of the procedures can easily be seen from a simple theological consideration. The charmer who seeks to force a cure, whether by God's help or that of the devil, stands in relation to these transcendent powers as one who would dispose over them. This is clear from Chapter 1 of the well-known charm book [title has been deleted by authors]. Here guidance is given as to how to subject the spirit helper to oneself and to become master of the transcendent powers. Theologically viewed, such a ven-

ture is the basic rebellion of man. Man gives orders to the transcendent power; man wants to have God at his disposal. This arrogance is the starting point of magic, which makes it easy for the theologian to understand the nature of magic conjuration processes.[14]

He also states:

It is a fact of pastoral experience that where black and white magic are practiced we find psychological disturbances in the family. This rule may have exceptions, although I have met with no exceptions in the case of active occultists.[15]

The same bias exists in psychiatry, when it is faced with the clearly supernatural. When they deny the very existence of occult subjections and oppression, they do great damage to their intended purpose—that of helping people solve their problems. What is true of occult oppression is also true of possession: it is redefined as hysteria, schizophrenia, etc.

Parapsychology, in its zealous attempt to be "scientific," has redefined the supernatural as the heretofore unknown natural and is paradoxically guilty of a rationalist, antisupernatural bias. Rarely do psychic researchers admit the existence of demonic influence in the phenomena they study. When the demonic remains hidden, there is no escape from its hold. We now turn to an in-depth examination of parapsychology.

References for Conclusion to Part II

1. Freedland, *The Occult Explosion* (Berkeley: Berkeley Medallion) 1972, p. 3.
2. Colin Wilson, *The Occult* (NY: Vintage) 1973, p. 32-3.
3. Os Guinness, *The Dust of Death* (Downers Grove, IL: Intervarsity) 1973, p. 278.
4. Sybil Leek, (World, 1971) p. 11; LeVay (Avon, 1972), p. 11.
5. H. Stanley Redgrove, *Magic and Mysticism* (NY: Citadel Press), 1972, p. 1x.
6. C.A. Burland, *Beyond Science* (NY: Grossett & Dunlap) 1972, p. 9.
7. C.S. Lewis, *Screwtape Letters,* (MacMillan), p. 3.
8. *Ibid.,* p. vii.
9. B.B. Wolman (Ed.), *Handbook of Parapsychology* (NY: Van Nostrand Reinhold Co.) 1977, p. 3-25.
10. Koch, *Christian Counseling and Occultism*, p. 17-18.
11. Gary North, *None Dare Call it Witchcraft* (New Rochele, NY: Arlington House) 1976, appendix B. "Table-Raising, Introduction to the Occult," p. 229.
12. Koch, *The Devil's Alphabet* (Grand Rapids, MI: Kregel) 1969, p. 7.
13. North, *op. cit.,* Ch. 8.
14. Koch, *Christian Counseling,* p. 136.
15. *Ibid.,* p. 152.

# Part III

Power From The Mind?
—Or A Controlled Mind?

Chapter 21

Parapsychology: The "Scientific" Study of Psi

Parapsychology is the "scientific" study of psi, or psychic events. It is often viewed as either a "new discovery" or as evidence of man's sudden evolving to a higher level (an evolutionary "mutation in consciousness"). Louisa Rhine, wife of the well-known "father" of scientific parapsychology, J. B. Rhine, states:

> One of the most significant advances of science is the discovery that psychic or psi ability is real.[1]

David Hammond, author and copublisher of *Psychic* magazine (now *New Realities),* reflects the evolutionary view: "What seems clear is that a giant leap forward in human evolution is being taken *now.* Evolution of the mind, along with the emergence of a psychic sense, has begun."[2]

A basic premise is that psychic abilities are solely natural and innate—although undeveloped—powers. *The Hand-*

book of Parapsychology reflects such a view, referring to psychic powers as "potentialities of the race," "latent human possibility," and "slumbering abilities within the self."[3] All view it as a new frontier of human knowledge.

The serious scientific research in parapsychology consistently attempts to draw a line between the occult and parapsychology, attempting to convince us that only the latter is a truly scientific field of study. We present a different point of view. The phenomena of parapsychology are not new, but very old. They *do not* involve heretofore unknown capacities, innately resident within man, just waiting to be uncovered or developed solely by man. Psychic abilities are initiated from and result from a force outside man. Parapsychology is not the study of a new scientific field: it is the study of the occult. Unless this is recognized, the number of respected scientists who are becoming occult adepts, spiritists, and magicians will continue to be seen as respected scientists, rather than occultists—which to varying degrees they are. Dictionary definitions of the occult indicate that these scientists study the occult—hence they may be labeled occultists, regardless of their disclaimers.

Throughout this section of our book, certain facts about parapsychology will be emphasized. It is of great importance that the following conclusions be noted, as they are at variance with the commonly accepted views on the topic.

The Claim of Parapsychology	The Data
1. Parapsychology involves a new field of scientific study.	1. Parapsychology is neither a new study nor true science, although it may use scientific methods. It is an attempt at the classification and quantification of occult powers and abilities that have existed throughout history. This is why experimental parapsychology has largely failed to make psi a scientific field

PARAPSYCHOLOGY: THE SCIENTIFIC STUDY OF PSI

	of study. Occultism will always remain beyond the field of true science.
2. Psi or psychic abilities are *innate* and *natural* capacities that can be developed solely by man through proper instruction.	2. Psi abilities are *unnatural,* and initiated by and involved with sources *apart from* man.
3. Although the study of parapsychology can be dangerous, if we use caution, wisdom and discernment we can study this area effectively and without harm. (This is the view generally presented by parapsychologists in *The Satan Trap: Dangers of the Occult.)*	3. *All* study of parapsychology is extremely consequential and to be avoided. Solely human discernment in this area is inadequate to deal with the complexities involved.
4. Research into parapsychology and its consequent practice can produce a wide variety of benefits to man.	4. *No* benefits will come from practices associated with this area of study. Rather a great deal of harm will come to those who personally involve themselves. By helping to move society more and more into the occult, our culture will eventually deteriorate to primitivism and superstition, with serious consequences in every area, including the spiritual, moral, and economic.
5. The Bible contains hundreds of parapsychological events and supports parapsychology. (Christian parapsychologists are particularly	5. The Bible contains hundreds of supernatural events and opposes the phenomena of parapsychology. It represents man as a nonsuper-

fond of this view.)	natural being, with truly supernatural events coming from one of two sources—God or Satan.
6. Parapsychology will advance the cause of true science.	6. Parapsychology may ruin true science.
7. Neutral, unbiased, and pure scientific experimentation and research into parapsychology is of a different nature and higher quality than lay research in this area. Given such conditions, we can safely study parapsychology neutrally.	7. Scientific "neutral" experimenters are subject to the same hazards as others delving into this area and are not exempt from the laws of God which ordain judgment upon those occultly involved.
8. From the viewpoint of Christian parapsychology, Christians should be open to helping advance this area of new horizons. The gifts of the Holy Spirit are none other than psychic abilities.	8. Christians are commanded to leave the occult alone entirely. The gifts of the Holy Spirit are in *opposition* to psychic abilities. They arise from a different source and have different outcomes and impact.
9. Parapsychology largely involves the study of a neutral impersonal energy or force.	9. Parapsychology *may* partially involve a neutral energy, but it is regulated and manifested by personal forces.

The Bias of Parapsychology

Many people are not aware that parapsychology has a recent history that extends over 130 years. Often times, a great deal about a movement can be determined by investigating its origins and ancestry. Some variations and refinements can take place, but what a movement was initially is often what it remains in principle. Scientific parapsychologists state that parapsychology has nothing whatsoever to do with the occult. What they mean is that no occult dogma or interpretations are required in parapsychological study. This is true to a point. However, we cannot say there are no occult dogma or interpretations found in parapsychology, as, in fact, there clearly are. Yet parapsychologists seek to imply that their study is entirely removed from the occult, and this is a false assessment. If the mother and father of parapsychology were occultic, the chances are good their offspring would be also.

If we examine the nonoccult claims put forth by psychic researchers, we will see a very clear, unscientific, and reprehensible dishonesty in operation. If there is one stigma parapsychologists have vowed to do away with, it is being classified as having anything to do with the occult. Again, Martin Ebon states:

> One word that parapsychologists totally disdain, regardless of geography or nationality, is occult. It is too closely linked with the field's not-quite-respectable antecedents. After all, no shipping tycoon likes to be reminded that his great grandfather was a pirate.[4]

Yet if we examine the assessments of those who have no emotional bias in this area, we find an entirely different view. Dr. Kurt Koch states simply, "Parapsychology is the science of occult phenomena."[5] Dr. Koch is an authority on the occult, having investigated it for fifty years and having counseled over 20,000 people who have suffered from involvement with it. If anyone knows what is and is not occult, he surely does.

However, both views cannot be true. Parapsychology either does or does not study the occult. It is not by chance that Dr. Koch's research work is entirely absent from the literature of parapsychology. This bias is similar to the way historians of Adolph Hitler refused to discuss or acknowledge the influence of evolution upon him for fear of being classed as antievolutionary.[6] Parapsychologists refuse to consider the phenomena they study as being occult, because of its justly deserved negative image and the damage this will do to their cause. In reality, among many parapsychologists real science and objectivity find little home. However, it is one thing to declare that parapsychology is occult. It is another to document it. We should note that while certain categories of the occult (e.g., astrology) are not studied by most scientific parapsychologists, taking the characteristic phenomena of the occult world as a whole, virtually nothing is left out.

Let us begin by first examining the disclaimers of parapsychologists: Louisa E. Rhine in *Psi: What Is It* states:
> Some ask about auras, UFO's, astrology, demonology, and other occult topics. None of these however is a proper parapsychological one.[7]

Witchcraft and Parapsychology

The ASPR's (American Society for Psychical Research) *Parapsychology: Sources of Information* declares that "contrary to uninformed popular opinion, parapsychology does not deal with astrology, numerology, tarot cards, theosophy, witchcraft, or other occult systems or practices —or, if so, only insofar as they empirically demonstrate that at their base some form of Psi is operating."[8] In other words, if witchcraft cannot demonstrate psi *in the laboratory,* it may be denied as parapsychological, even though it clearly demonstrates psi outside the laboratory. Thus we see that parapsychology and the occult do not differ in either nature or manifestation, but only in scientific laboratories.

It is interesting that, prior to the above quote, the book had discussed psychokinesis (which occurs in witchcraft and theosophy), precognition (which is the mainstay of numerology, astrology, and tarot cards), and telepathy and clairvoyance (which are common in seances) as legitimate fields of parapsychology. In fact, "Psi is also a useful concept in explaining much that happens in mediumship." But it is not occult! . . . *so they claim.*

As Ebon notes, "Parapsychology has long sought to free itself of magical associations, of too close a relationship with spiritistic and occult traditions."[9] Despite heroic efforts for over a century, these efforts have not succeeded. Perhaps this tells us something about the nature of parapsychology itself.

The authors of the traveling *Psi Search* exhibit and book by the same name spent five years investigating psi. They noted:

> Throughout this search for answers about psi we have become profoundly aware of how inextricably the subject of psychic phenomena is associated with a wide-ranging mass of esoteric, metaphysical, and occult belief.[10]

Yet they seemingly do not stop to consider the *reasons* for this association and, with blinders on, go on to state that psychic phenomena are not occult.

The difference between occultism and parapsychology is not one of nature, essence, characteristics, or manifestations. In this sense scientific parapsychology is the equivalent of occultism, though sometimes minus its worldview. The difference is merely in location of the events (laboratory) and scientific verification (replicable experimentation).

One sense in which parapsychologists believe they are nonoccultic is that scientific parapsychology has no dogma of belief, such as occultism has. This is only partially true. Some scientific parapsychologists resist certain occult beliefs, but most of them sooner or later *end up* adopting an essentially partial or fully occult philosophy in their personal outlook. This is a natural consequence of occult investigation. Dr. William Tiller, D. Scott Rogo, the early psychic investigators, Charles Tart, Karlis Osis, Rex Stanford, Shafica Karagulla, Edgar Mitchell, Thelma Moss, Milan Ryzl, etc. are all prominent parapsychologists or psychic researchers. Who among them does not express openness to or belief in various occult views or philosophy? In fact, it is certain that a number of parapsychologists will become active occultists. For example, this was true for Dr. Adrija Puharich who became a part-time medium through his study of Uri Geller. Hence the claim that parapsychology adopts no occult dogma is only a half-truth.

In the laboratory when a scientific attitude is dominant, this is generally true. In personal philosophy, it can be an entirely different matter.

References for Chapter 21

1. Louisa Rhine, *PSI—What is it—An Introduction to Parapsychology* (NY: Harper & Row) 1975, p. 2.
2. D. Hammond, "Psychic Evolution and You," *Psychic,* April 1976, p. 21.
3. Wolman (Ed.), *The Handbook of Parapsychology, op. cit,* p. xvii.
4. Ebon (Ed.), *The Signet Handbook of Parapsychology,* p. 18.
5. K. Koch, *Satan's Devices,* (Grand Rapids, MI: Kregel) 1978, p. 154.
6. R. Clark, *Darwin: Before and After* (Chicago: Moody) 1971, p. 117. See Chapter 6.
7. Louisa Rhine, *op. cit.,* p. 12.
8. R. White, L. Dale, *Parapsychology: Sources of Information,* (Metuchen, NJ: Scarecrow Press) 1973, p. 13.
9. Ebon, *Signet Handbook, op. cit.,* p. 1.
10. Bowles and Hynds, *PSI Search* (NY: Harper & Row) 1973, p. 3.

Chapter 22

The Occult History of Parapsychology

In the last half of the 19th century, Darwin's theory of evolution had done a greal deal to destroy belief in the existence of God, to say nothing of belief in the Bible. Many believed that God was no longer necessary to account for our existence, and so He was "dropped from consideration," as was His word. For them, there was no spiritual reality; there was no personal immortality; there was no salvation—only the chance occurrence of a brief life and then annihilation. Having previously had faith in the biblical view—now made unpalatable by evolution and rationalism—they turned to the occult in an attempt to bring a spiritual reality back into their lives. In this sense Darwinism was a necessary ingredient, compelling openness to and exploration of the occult. It even made some Christians encourage psychic research, hoping to bolster their faltering faith in the Bible.

During this time the spiritist movement (which had begun in 1848) was the predominant vehicle of occultism. Early investigators believed that if they could prove a medium really does communicate with the dead, the evidence of personal immortality and meaning to life could be revived. As John Randall states, the early founders of the Society for Psychic Research "had one thing in common: they were all seeking a way out of the mechanistic impasse into which nineteenth-century science had led them."[1]

Documentation of Occult Foundations

The following statements, taken from various reputable histories of parapsychology, clearly indicate that the source of inspiration for modern parapsychology was occultism, primarily in the form of mediumism and spiritism. The authoritative *Handbook of Parapsychology* ties the origins of parapsychology to two related historical movements: mesmerism and spiritism. In terms of much of the phenomena produced, mesmerism was a crude forerunner of spiritism and helped pave the way for it. Dr. Beloff, former President of the Parapsychological Association and Senior Lecturer at the University of Edinburgh in Scotland states:

> The other principal precursor of parapsychology in the nineteenth century was . . . spiritism. The movement . . . insured a steady flow of mysterious phenomena that cried out for investigation. No doubt its passage had been eased by the earlier conquests of the mesmerists. The role of trance medium fitted neatly the niche previously occupied by the somnambules [people who entered mesmeric trances], and not a few of those who began as mesmerists made the transition to spiritualism[2]

He notes that spiritism had a much greater impact on parapsychology than mesmerism, and that its principal idea, "that of communicating with the spirits of the deceased, stems from a venerable occult tradition—Shamans and witchdoctors were forerunners of the medium."

Gardner Murphy discusses some of the reasons for parapsychology's early dependence upon spiritism:

> But there are special reasons why modern psychical research made a heavy investment in time, thought, and funds, in studying the problem of mediumship. Modern spiritualism had

come into existence in the middle of the nineteenth century, and it was among the spiritualist mediums that many of the most interesting paranormal phenomena, phenomena involving telepathy, clairvoyance, and psychokinesis, appeared. There was, moreover, a deep-seated conviction among skeptics and intellectuals that the reality of existence beyond death was of enormous personal and philosophical importance to all serious persons, and was, moreover, a major issue with reference to the tenability or untenability of the widely held "materialism" of an agnostic era. The various kinds of evidence for survival beyond death, whether they derived from the study of apparitions and ghosts, from mediumship, or from the more complex lines of investigation to be discussed below, became for many the most important, the central problem of psychical research.[3]

Even J. B. Rhine states:

Most of the attention of those active in psychical research [the early term for parapsychology] during both the first and second periods [1876-1925] was given to the study of mediums, but on a somewhat declining scale over the years.[4]

According to Rhine, the decline set in because nothing could be scientifically demonstrated:

Actually, the dominant interest in psychical research circles during the half century already reviewed had been in mediumship and post mortum survival; and yet, in 1925, no scientific conclusion was even in sight to back them up. There was no successful method to follow [just as there is none today, another half century later].[5]

Psychic Societies

The history of the various societies for psychical research is littered with mediumistic contacts, both in the U.S. and Europe. According to Douglas,[5a] in 1869 the first serious investigation of spiritism was undertaken by the London Dialectical Society which appointed six subcommittees to investigate mediumship. In the 1870's the Phantasmological Society at Oxford and the Ghost Society at Cambridge also studied mediumism. In 1874 the first public meeting of the British National Association of Spiritualists commenced with most of the prominent spiritists of the time as members. In 1875 the Psychological Society was founded by the well-known spiritist Sergeant Cox.

In 1882 the British National Association of Spiritualists became what is today known as the famous Society for Psychical Research. In 1882, two-thirds of its membership was comprised of mediums. However, for the spiritualist members the society became too eager in its meticulous plans for experimentation—and too eager *not* to believe, apart from scientific proof. Within five years only one-third of the membership constituted mediums, and eventually the mediums abandoned the organization entirely. Despite the fraud uncovered and the skepticism of many researchers, there was still an underlying trust and reliance upon spiritism as the means through which psi and survival would eventually be proven. The SPR continued to investigate mediumship, but with no supporting members of that profession. Scientific investigation had been too restrictive and had actually limited their supernatural manifestations. Still the research of the SPR was heavily spiritistic for over 50 years. (To give an idea of the extent these researchers involved themselves in occultism—in 1922 alone SPR member Eric J. Dingwall boasted of attending over 300 seances.[6])

Dr. J. B. Rhine, dean of the experimentalists, notes the reliance on spiritism, and also that the change which took place in the 1930's did *not* stop investigation into the manifestations of spiritism. Indeed, in the 1930's parapsychological societies were still being founded by spiritists. The location of the investigations simply began to change: from seance room to laboratory. He also notes that *without mediumism,* parapsychology probably would never have started:

> The groping branch of psychical research, which down to the 1930's (i.e., for 60 years) had been largely the study of mediumship and spirit survival, changed almost abruptly to an emphasis on the abilities assumed in mediumship. These are now investigated as an important part of the nature, not just of the medium, but of all mankind. But had there not been the earlier powerful interest in survival [due to Darwinism], and the promotion of mediumship in serving that interest, the eventual emergence of the psi research era would probably have been indefinitely delayed.[7]

Rogo concurs: "The major precipitating factor in the development of psychical research was the spiritualist movement . . . ."[8] In other words, *the foundation of experimental psi* (i.e., scientific laboratory psi) *is the spontaneous psi of a wide variety of occultists*. (Spontaneous psi are psychic events which happen spontaneously outside the laboratory in the "home environment" of the psychic.)

It is probably true that if any parapsychologists were to be regarded as unrelated to the occult, it would be J. B. Rhine. Yet even his early work at Duke was with spiritism. He "could not resist trying to make it sound scientific if it actually was true."[9] The Rhines' primary interest was in survival after death, and the most logical way to investigate this was through mediumship.[10] Hence, at Harvard they worked with Walter Franklin Prince in his spiritistic investigations. However, the Rhines' research with the famous mediums Margery, Eileen Garrett, and others could not prove survival. There was no way to tell if the information was being received solely by clairvoyance and telepathy on the medium's part (from other human minds), rather than from a discarnate entity. Hence Rhine switched over to statistical methods in an attempt to first prove scientifically that esp existed. However, even today confirmation of his "scientific" research has not been dependable.

Kurtz states:

Although I have no doubts that Rhine is committed to an objective experimental methodology, I have substantive doubts about his views on clairvoyance, precognition, and PK. The problem here is that one may question not simply the reliability and significance of the data, but the conceptual framework itself. Rhine and others have performed tests in which they maintain that they have achieved above-chance runs. What are we to conclude at this point in history? Simply that and no more. ESP is not a proven fact, only a theory used to explain above-chance runs encountered in the laboratory. Here I submit that the most we can do is simply fall back on an operational definition: ESP is itself an elusive entity; It has no identifiable meaning beyond an operational interpretation.[11]

Bowles and Hynds state:

Both scientists and nonscientists alike find it disconcerting that not every researcher who tries to repeat one of the leading psi experiments can do so successfully. Psi critic Hansel lists unsuccessful attempts to repeat Rhine's ESP experiments by other researchers at Colgate University, Southern Methodist University, Brown University, and John Hopkins University.[12]

Although Rhine continued investigating occultists until his death, he did not believe the question of survival could ever be scientifically proven.

Philosophy and the Occult

Some of the most famous philosophers of the 19th century were members of the SPR and nearly all of them took part in the first-hand investigation of mediumship.[13] Henry Sedgwick examined numerous physical mediums in the 1870's. William James investigated and attended many Leonore Piper seances, "communicating" with his dead friend Richard Hodgson who himself studied Mrs. Piper for 20 years. Alfred Russel Wallace attended seances with the materialization medium Mrs. M. V. Ross. James Harvey Hyslop investigated virtually every form of mediumism and psychic phenomena and founded the American Society for Psychical Research in 1905. (The first society had disbanded.) William Romaine Newbold attended seances by Mrs. Piper (in which supposed communication from Sir Walter Scott stated that monkeys lived in caves on the sun!). Arthur James Balfour, F.C.S. Schiller, C. D. Broad, and several others all attended numerous seances in their investigations. However, philosophy was not the only profession that became fascinated with the occult. As Dr. Russel Goldfarb has shown, "Virtually every major or minor literary figure of the nineteenth century had immediate experience with spiritualism."[14] He claims that this is reflected in its influence upon their writings—be it Harriet Beecher Stowe, Hamlin Garlind, Dante Rossetti, Horace Greely, or Arthur Conan Doyle (of Sherlock Holmes fame). All these individuals attended seances and were supporters and/or believers.

Concluding, we should note that parapsychology was born investigating mediums and the occult, and although branching out considerably in the last 30 years, has to this day continued investigating occult phenomena.

Occult Phenomena Are the Lifeblood of Parapsychology

Rauscher declares:
> Rhine abandoned laboratory studies of life after death in the 1930's when he discovered that the methods of parapsychology did not enable him to differentiate between messages from discarnate entities, or spirits, and the telepathic or clairvoyant impressions of the mediums he had as subjects in his laboratory at Duke University in Durham, North Carolina. Outside the laboratory, research with mediums has gone on.[15]

Parapsychology may hold at bay the tide of occult dogma from most of its ranks. It may provide some evidence of essentially useless data in the laboratory. It may continue to call itself scientific and continue to redefine the occult. But no matter how "scientific" it attempts to be, it can never entirely remove itself from occultism. Occult phenomena and manifestations are its lifeblood. Its "major" advances have come from studies of psychics, not of normal individuals.

Remove every psychic and mediumistic subject from parapsychological laboratories. Disallow any phenomena found in mediumism to be studied. Allow only subjects who could provide reasonable evidence of no occult involvement in their family histories for four generations, and who themselves have never had any interest in any form of the occult.

Parapsychology would then cease to exist.

The History of Modern Parapsychology

	Early	Middle	Late
	In 1854 Robert Hares' investigations of mediumism were presented before the annual AAAS meeting.	In the 1930's J.B. Rhine began his experimental studies.	Current research is divided into early and middle period approaches.
Time Period	1854-1930	1930-1970+	1970-
Characteristics	Qualitative	Quantitative	Qualitative and Quantitative
	Spontaneous	Lab research	Technologic-occultic; electronic; spontaneous/experimental
	Spiritistic	Spiritistic, psychic and nonpsychic	Spiritistic, psychic, and nonpsychic, with a trend toward the former.
Analysis	Historic ties to the famous occultist John Dee in the 16th C; Swedenborgh in the 19th C. As a reaction against Darwinistic materialism, spiritism is seen as hope for proof of a spiritual reality and survival after death. Psychic phenomena viewed as mysterious occult ability of certain "sensitive" people (i.e., as supernatural).	Consistent ties to spiritism, but major attempt to prove psi extends throughout the general population. Comparatively little spiritistic phenomena produced in the lab. Occult phenomena studied but with a different purpose and interpretation. Psychic phenomena viewed as natural. Less acceptance of occult interpretation of data.	A movement back to historical occult roots and methodology (i.e., field research) begins, while strong ties remain to science and technology. Various hardware are devised to measure psi energy and events (random number generators, Tobiscopes, radionic devices, computer use, biometers, etc.).

References for Chapter 22

1. J. Randall, *Parapsychology and the Nature of Life* (NY: Harper Colophon) 1975, p. 67.
2. J. Beloff, "Historical Overview" in Wolman, *op. cit.*, p. 5.
3. Gardner Murphy, *Challenge of Psychical Research,* (NY: Harper-Colophon Books) 1970, p. 185.
4. Wolman, *op. cit.*, p. 27.
5. *Ibid.*, p. 29.   5a. See Douglas (below) p. 63-64.
6. E.J. Dingwall, "The Early World of Psychical Research—Some Personal Reminiscences." *Parapsychology Review,* Vol. 6, No. 5, p. 8.
7. J.B. Rhine, "A Century of Parapsychology" in Ebon (Ed.) *The Signet Handbook of Parapsychology,* p. 11.
8. D. Scott Rogo, *Parapsychology: A Century of Inquiry* (NY: Dell) 1975, p. 44.
9. *Ibid.*
10. L. Rhine, *op. cit.*, p. 32-33; Douglas, *Extra Sensory Powers,* (Woodstock, NJ: Overland) 1977, p. 252-3.
11. Paul Kurtz, *The Skeptical Inquirer,* Vol. 3, No. 2, p. 26-27.
12. Bowles and Hynds, *op. cit.*, p. 39.
13. J. F. Nicol, "Philosophers as Psychic Investigators," *Parapsychology Review,* Vol. 8, No. 2, p. 1-11.
14. Goldfarb, *Spiritualism and 19th Century Letters,* p. 139.
15. W.V. Rauscher in *The Signet Handbook of Parapsychology, op. cit.*, p. 164.

Chapter 23

The True Status of Parapsychology

Parapsychology has fought long and hard to gain even a small portion of scientific respectability. Given its origin and nature, it is surprising it has gained *any* respectability at all among scientists. Some naively state it is a true science. Some are overly gullible. This is true particularly of the media which has reported on psi "breakthroughs" which were either worthless or fraudulent. Even Dr. Jose Feola, President of the California Society of Psychic Research, states in the witchcraft journal, *Gnostica,* that the vast majority of psi research is a waste of time because of its fraudulent nature: "I agree: this conclusion is correct in over 95 per cent of the cases, based on my own experience."[1]

At best, parapsychology, like psychology, is a soft science. It can never be a hard science because of its occult nature. Yet even the label of soft science is not really accurate. Psychology and related soft sciences deal with that which is solely human: the human mind and its activities. Despite the commonly held, but false view that it too deals with the solely human (i.e., that psychic powers are innate and natural), parapsychology actually deals more with the nonhuman—i.e., the demonic. This can never be studied scientifically unless science becomes magic.

There has been a great amount of research and theorizing on all aspects of psi for over a century. Yet we still have *no* undisputed repeatable experiments and no known mechanism or methodology for psi. We probably never will, simply because the supernatural realm is of a different order, nature, and substance than the physical realm.

Parapsychology and the Occult: The Unity of the Phenomena

We have seen that despite the numerous denials by psychic researchers, parapsychology is the scientific (and not-so-scientific) study of occult phenomena. We have already briefly noted this earlier. In this chapter we wish to further elaborate and more fully document our conclusions. Parapsychologists, if they are honest, will admit that they study occult phenomena. The following assessment by R. J. Munson of the Institute for Parapsychology at Durham, North Carolina, is representative. In a review of Shepard's *The Encyclopedia of Occultism and Parapsychology* (1978), he states:

> While *the boundaries that separate parapsychology from occultism are somewhat nebulous in terms of the phenomena they cover,* it is not difficult to see how they differ in terms of the methods employed to study them. Whatever the phenomenological or historical likenesses of these fields, they are indelibly marked by their differences in objectivity. Both the occultist and the parapsychologist have their identities to gain by recognizing the significant differences between them. Bringing occultism and parapsychology together can only serve to confuse the distinction between metaphysical belief and scientific data.[2] [Emphasis added.]

We see here an admission that the occult and parapsychology study essentially the *same* phenomena, although by different means. In other words:

1. Parapsychologists and occultists approach the same

phenomena differently; one more scientifically than the other.
2. Occultists are personally involved in developing psychic powers, spirit contact, and a certain worldview. Parapsychologists should not be so involved. (But in actuality that is not always the case. Thus:)
3. Parapsychologists may or may not be involved in developing psychic powers, spirit contact, and a certain worldview.

Most (but not all) parapsychologists would take issue with point number three, stating that the central purpose of parapsychology is scientific investigation only, that little direct involvement in the occult is involved, and that parapsychologists do not adopt occult dogma. It is true that some have remained personally uninvolved in the occult, say, in spirit contact, even though they have studied mediums. It is also true that the publications of the more scientific organizations, e.g., the *Journal of Parapsychology* and the *Journal of the American Society for Psychical Research,* limit by definition what they consider valid areas of study. They will not study astrology, for example. However, they do issue reports on astrologic research, as long as it is "scientific" (ASPR Newsletter, April, 1979, p. 10).

God Forbids Scientific Investigation of the Occult

The areas they do study are still occult—they have simply purposely limited their scope as a means toward more scientific recognition. We intend to show in this chapter that while psi researchers may remain personally uninvolved, it may just as easily be true that parapsychologists can (and have) become occultists. The crucial issue here is that even *scientific* investigation of the occult is forbidden by God and carries with it penalties and consequences.

At what point does one become "uninvolved" in the occult? If one scientifically studies occult phenomena all day long and, due to his interest in it, is involved in reading occult literature, witnessing psychic demonstrations, etc., is he *personally* uninvolved in the occult? Do scientific parapsychologists stay scientific outside the laboratory? Is every "scientific psi" researcher a "spontaneous psi" researcher after 5:00 P.M.? It could hardly be otherwise. The real world is not a scientific laboratory. Therefore, in what ways are scientific psi researchers exposed to, opened to, and influenced by the occult outside their laboratories?

If we were to list all the phenomena involved with spiritistic seances, various occult rituals, shamanism, etc., and compare them to phenomena studied by parapsychologists as a whole, there would be little difference between the two. An examination of the Conference Proceedings and published journals and literature of any or every parapsychology organization clearly shows varying degrees of involvement in the occult. This is true from the first day of inception of these organizations. For example, some of the more clearly occult articles from recent issues of the scientifically-oriented ASPR include:

"A Communicator Unknown to Mediums and Sitters" (Jan., 1970)

"The Analysis of a Mediumistic Session by a New Method" (Oct., 1968)

"An Experiment with the Icelandic Medium, Hafsteinn Bjornsson" (April, 1979)

"Reincarnation, Astral Bodies, and Psi Components" (April, 1979)

"Eileen J. Garrett—An Appreciation" [Garrett is a medium] (July, 1971)

"Occult Books at the University of Pittsburgh" (July, 1971)

"The Raudive Voices" (Jan., 1974) [The Raudive phenomena involves communication with the dead through tape recorders.]

"The Sitoebondo Poltergeist" (Oct., 1973)

"The Vanished Man—A Psychometry Experiment with Eileen J. Garrett" (Jan., 1968)

"Automated Forced Choice Precognition Tests

with a Sensitive" (Oct., 1971)

"Is there a Case for Disembodied Survival?" (April, 1972)

All of the above articles deal with spiritism. Also, in the scientific psi societies as a whole, an increased interest in reincarnation research may be noted.

Psychical Research and Spiritism Linked

A good example of the distinctions and yet unity between the occult and parapsychology is given by Dr. Nandor Fodor in his *Encyclopedia of Psychic Science,* a one-half million word volume detailing parapsychological phenomena. He states:

> Psychic science embraces both psychical research and spiritualism. The facts championed by the spiritualists differ but in their interpretation from those we meet with in psychical research. Basically they are the same, though in spiritualistic experience they steep deeper into the marvelous . . . . Of occultism, theosophy, and mysticism I steered clear. [Dr. Fodor's own definition of occultism in his encyclopedia betrays the fact that he did not steer clear of occultism: "Its practical side connects with psychical phenomena," he says.] The issue of psychical research and spiritualism are purely empirical and merge into orthodox science. The inquirer needs no initiation, no preparation, no mystic disposition, no special faculties.[3]

In other words, spiritism and parapsychology differ in interpretaion and manner of involvement, but not in material studied or data analyzed. He points out that while parapsychology studies mediumistic phenomena, no occult initiation or other trappings are necessary. The researcher can remain separate from required dogma and ceremony. Yet in Dr. Fodor's own life, we see what is a clear hazard for parapsychologists—the impact on their own lives of the phenomena which they study. They often *do* adopt an occult worldview. In another of his books Fodor states that as a result of attending a particularly convincing seance, "I was now convinced of survival after death. From then on I was a spiritualist."[4] (As far as we know, he did not become a medium, but held to many spiritistic beliefs.)

In fact, Fodor's own life as a parapsychologist parallels the history of the movement: birth within occultism and intense excitement, a period of rigorous scientific investigation, then overskepticism of occult phenomena, and finally a return "home" (to occultism) with an integrated occult philosophy. Leslie Shephard quotes a statement by him from the 1943 *Psychic Observer* article:

> My attitude to psychical phenomena has undergone a tremendous change since I left England. Then I was a psychical investigator, following the routine techniques. A free hand for the researcher is none for the medium. Now I am a psychologist and my attitude is exactly the opposite: a free hand for the medium, none for the researcher.

He confessed that he had "no more joy in tying up mediums and exalting instrumental findings," and commented:

> I see now psychical research has tried to be too scientific for years and has gone bankrupt as a result. Mediums do not function well if they are used as guinea pigs. They are human beings with the same virtues and vices as the researchers themselves![5]

Examination of Representative Parapsychology Organizations: History and Phenomena Analyzed

It is a fact that many parapsychological societies were founded by occultists. Even those founded by scientists were started by scientists interested in phenomena traditionally associated with the occult. Three examples are listed:

1. The Parapsychology Foundation, publisher of *Parapsychology Review* (previously the *International Jour-

nal of Parapsychology), was founded by the famous medium, Eileen Garrett.[6]
2. The Spiritual Frontiers Fellowship, whose academic affiliate is the Academy of Religion and Psychical Research, was founded by the famous trance medium Arthur Ford.[7]
3. The British College of Psychic Science was founded by the famous medium J. Hewat McKenzie.[8]

In the history of parapsychology, there appear to be few organizations founded apart from some connection to spiritism. For example, the International Institute for Psychical Research founded in 1934 contained spiritists and nonspiritists on its council. Even today we find that so-called scientific research laboratories of parapsychology have been involved in the study of mediums, often extensively. Scientifically-minded societies, however, may choose not to reveal their research. For example, the medium Douglas Johnson "has worked extensively with parapsychologists in England, the United States, and Israel, but little of this experimental work has been published."[9]

In Edgar Mitchell's *Psychic Exploration: A Challenge for Science* (and elsewhere) we find that the Psychical Research Foundation, the Foundation for Research on the Nature of Man, the Maimonides Dream Laboratory, and the American Society for Psychical Research—comprising a majority of psi laboratories in the U.S.—have all studied mediums, or "sensitives" which is the more preferred term.[10]

In fact, Mitchell's book, often hailed as a standard work in scientific parapsychology, is strongly dependent upon mediumism throughout most of its thirty chapters. The book itself defines parapsychology as covering most major occult topics, e.g., shamanism, thoughtography, psychic surgery and healing, ouija boards, astral projection, levitation, mediumship, hauntings, spirit possession, reincarnation, I Ching, and other forms of divination.[11] Mitchell admits that "it is not easy to draw lines of demarcation between" occultism and parapsychology.[12] Many of its authors are little more than scientific occultists, i.e., those who are involved in spiritism or who have psychic powers but are studying parapsychology scientifically: Robert Masters, Jean Houston, Lawrence LeShan, Henry K. (Andrija) Puharich, Marcel Vogel, Rex Stanford, Alan Vaughan, etc. The book also indicates that there are many researchers one would not necessarily expect to be involved in studying the occult, e.g., Barbara Brown and Stanley Krippner both have studied psychics.[13]

Our own research supports a conclusion that the vast majority of scientific parapsychologists, and even many scientist sympathizers, have personal involvement in the occult, either through the study of occultists or by being personally involved with psychics as an avocation.

Phenomena Analyzed

Dr. Nandor Fodor eventually became an authority on psychic phenomena. In his *Encyclopedia of Psychic Science* he defines psychical research as "a scientific inquiry into the facts and causes of mediumistic phenomena."[14] No better definition has yet been proposed. He also defined psychic science as "a system of facts to demonstrate the existence of spirits independent of the body, and their ability to communicate with humanity."[15] In his encyclopedia he lists the yearly Proceedings of the old American Society for Psychical Research (1885-89), the new ASPR (1907-1927), *et al*. Mediumistic studies are evident throughout.

From 1933 on, the ASPR and SPR continued mediumistic investigations. For example, C. D. Thomas, a SPR council member for 20 years, was primarily interested in survival (after death). By 1950, he had indexed and annotated over 500 seance sittings for the SPR. His interest in mediumism was continuous.[16]

The official journal of the Psychical Research Foundation of Durham, North Carolina, is *Theta*. It deals almost entirely with the survival after death issue, and hence it is heavily involved in reincarnation cases, poltergeists, mediumism, astral projection, automatic writing, and similar topics.

If the occult and parapsychology were really two unrelated disciplines, there would not be so much disagreement within parapsychological ranks as to "how far" into the occult they should go. Certain parapsychology organizations are more honest. For example, the Occult Studies Foundation (for a time an affiliate of the University of Rhode Island Extension) is "dedicated to the pursuit of scientific information in the field of the paranormal and the occult." They openly declare their interest is occultism. The title of their journal is *Journal of Occult Studies: An Interdisciplinary Approach to Paranormal Phenomena,* and in the editorial of Vol. 1, No. 1, they state, "We will go where the research takes us and in an area as deep and rich as the occult, we think the whole gamut of results can be expected and reported."

Hence their topics of study include astrology, UFO's, yoga, mediumism, and related occult matters. Even organizations that limit the extent of occult involvement and vigorously claim they are "scientific" are more involved in the occult than they claim to be. For example, the January and April, 1979, newsletter of the American Society for Psychical Research contained articles endorsing automatic writing, reincarnation research, mediumism, and the spiritistic community at Findhorn, Scotland.[20] The article on automatic writing by well-known reincarnation researcher Ian Stevenson, M.D., noted that automatic writing and mediumism had produced "some of the best evidence we have for psi phenomena," and urged research into these areas. Similarly, the articles of the last several years (1971-1979) of *Parapsychology Review,* the journal of the Parapsychology Foundation, are full of the studies of occult phenomena.

The Spiritistic Theory

The spiritistic (or demonic) theory of psi solves many "problem" areas of psi insofar as it explains at least the origin, if not the method, of psi. However, this view is *apriori* rejected by parapsychologists on biased grounds (especially the idea of *demonic* spirits). They argue that it is too simple an answer, despite its explanatory value (the principle of Occam's razor is denied) or that it is too unscientific. They realize the implications—psi would forever remain outside the realm of science, and they could no longer use the guise of science to make their study of the occult respectable.

Science	Spirits
Tangible	Intangible
Repeatable/Controlled	Uncontrolled
Neutral	Biased (can interpret/affect experimentation)
Inanimate	Animate
"Simple"	Complex (e.g., living entities with volition, cunning)
Amoral	Immoral

In the old days, parapsychologists were *sorcerers*. If they were honest today, they would admit it. (In fact, at the 1979 annual convention of the most scientifically-oriented research group, the Parapsychological Association, Dr. Rex Stanford of the Center for Parapsychological Research in Austin, Texas, seriously questioned whether parapsychologists were more like scientists *or shamans* (i.e., witchdoctors). This is hardly an insignificant observation.[17] The only difference today is possibly that of intent. Parapsychologists are *studying* sorcery rather than *engaging* in it, although this may be changing rapidly. They are apprentices, not adepts. The intent is to *study* psychic powers, rather than to *develop* them personally, although that can happen, and they are more than happy to see others develop psi powers. Hence, there is a situation here that is similar to yogic development. The yogi is to remain undetached in his quest for union with Brahman or Samadhi—the psychi powers (siddhis) which are naturally developed by yoga practice are not to distract him. In actual fact, however, as is true with parapsychology, the venture is too fascinating and the promise of power too consuming. They become trapped.

Fascination and power have always been the drawing ability of the occult. The participant is *unable* to remain the detached, neutral, or scientific observer. As Eliade notes, the occult powers developed by yoga were supposed to be ignored as distractions. Yet "very few indeed [are] those who succeeded in overcoming the second temptation" (i.e., the personal use of occult powers).[18]

Similarly, many psi researchers become personally involved in the occult, testing and experimenting with their own "latent psi."

When a scientist becomes personally involved in the occult, regardless of attempts at scientific objectivity, there no longer remains any assurance that his results, mental states, conclusions, etc., will not be influenced from without. (And there is no way of knowing the extent of personal involvement among researchers because an admission would detract from the scientific image they are trying to convey.) However, we suspect this outside influence occurs more than most people imagine, even when psi scientists do their best to remain unattached and uninvolved.

The decisive factor here does not seem to be scientific objectivity, but openness. Believers in psi, who are open to and sympathetic with the occult, get better results in their experiments (the same ones) than nonbelievers and critical investigators. Even a scientific, objective, uninvolved researcher who is open to psi may also be open to manipulation, especially if the studies of Dr. Koch are any indicator of the impact that even passive, indirect involvement in the occult can have.

Researchers Become Mediums

Thus, when Dr. Puharich becomes a part-time medium, Dr. LeShan becomes a psychic healer, and Dr. Stanley Krippner allows the input of demonic energy into his body via psychic surgery (the ultimate spiritual consequences of which we haven't the slightest idea), objectivity and neutrality go out the door. There is presently no way of knowing whether or not these scientists, by opening themselves to the demonic, have allowed the intrusion of it into their lives *and* experimentation. This would be at the initiative and time of choice of the latter.

Parapsychology *must* sooner or later return more openly to its spiritistic-occult roots. It is clear that scientific/laboratory work has failed and that the real data are out there "in the field" (working with psychics, mediums, etc., in their own environment, rather than in the psi-stifling conditions of the laboratory). In fact, the largest single evidence of a revolution in psychic research comes from the 1979 annual convention of the AAAS affiliated Parapsychological Association. Many of its most influential members admitted that *scientific* parapsychology was bankrupt, and that a totally new approach was needed, including more personal involvement—to "live psi from the inside," as it were. What else could suffice except a much more broad outlook and more openness to the occult? A return to their historic roots?

Dr. John Palmer, President of the Association and convention host, declared what inevitably is the new trend in psi studies. In the words of theoretical parapsychologist, Barbara Honegger:

> Dr. Palmer ended his historic address with a moving call to fellow parapsychologists to preserve the scientific method in their research but to open the field by applying it to a broader range of phenomena, including "some of the synchronistic phenomena now most commonly classified in that category we disparagingly label the occult" particularly astrology and "the so-called magical traditions." That such a liberal call from one of the field's most conservative and highly respected members should be met by a resounding standing ovation gives but some

measure of the historic transformation now reshaping the field.[19]

It is a portent of things to come.

References for Chapter 23

1. Jose Feola "Parapsychology Today"—*Gnostica*, Jan.-Feb., 1979, p. 60.
2. *The Journal of Parapsychology,* December 1978, pp. 329-30.
3. Fodor, *Encyclopedia of Psychic Science,* Introduction.
4. Fodor, *The Unaccountable* (NY: Award Books) 1968, p. 15.
5. Fodor, *Encyclopedia, op. cit.,* p. xv.
6. Parapsychology Review, Oct. 1970, Special Issue "Eileen Garrett Dies"
7. See Introductory brochures.
8. *Parapsychology Review,* Vol. 9, No. 4, p. 9.
9. Alan Vaughan, "Famous Western Sensitives" in Edgar Mitchell *Psychic Exploration: A Challenge for Science* (NY: Putnams) 1976, p. 82.
10. Mitchell, *ibid.,* p. 82-90.
11. *Ibid.,* p. 41-2.
12. *Ibid.,* p. 43.
13. *Ibid.,* p. 84-6.
14. Fodor, *Encyclopedia,* p. 316.
15. *Ibid.,* p. 315.
16. *International Journal of Parapsychology,* Vol. 8, No. 2, (1966), p. 238.
17. B. Honegger, "Quake Hits Parapsychology" *New Realities,* Vol. 3, No. 2, p. 34.
18. Eliade, *Yoga: Immortality and Freedom, op. cit.,* p. 88.
19. B. Honegger "Quake Hits Parapsychology" *New Realities,* Vol. 3, No. 2, p. 35.
20. Ian Stevenson "Some Comments on Automatic Writing"; E. Douglas Dean, "Findhorn Revisited"; Arthur Hastings, "Current Interest in Past Lives."

Chapter 24

Mediumism and the Occult in Standard Para-Psychological Works

An examination of current texts and guidebooks for the study of parapsychology again points to extensive occult interests. Fodor's *Encyclopedia of Psychic Science,* Lewis Spence's *Encyclopedia of the Occult,* and the more recent *Encyclopedia of Occultism and Parapsychology* are full of mediumism and occult phenomena. These are all standard parapsychological works. The definitive *Handbook of Parapsychology,* edited by B. B. Wolman, urges investigation of various forms of occultism, e.g., spirit photography, psychic healing, poltergeist research, mediumism, etc. A review of the book noted that, "Not all parapsychologists have been willing to accept a restriction of their study for the sake of greater acceptance of their writings. The chapters devoted to poltergeists, survival, and reincarnation, show that some (scientific) researchers pursue these topics despite the inevitable uncertainty resulting from the unavailability of experimental control over conditions."[1]

The author of the review, I. L. Child of Yale University, goes on to note that:

> Without attention to spontaneous cases, there

could be no scientific study of these topics.

The article by J. F. Nicol in the *Handbook* notes that credit for the development of experimental methods "is attributable solely to the rise of modern spiritualism."[2] The scientist, rather than simply believing, wants to find out what is *really* happening in these experiences, as if science alone is sufficient to unravel the mysteries of demonism. He also notes that the occultist and parapsychologist tend to have different views of the same phenomena. A medium will believe she is in contact with the dead—a parapsychologist, because he cannot scientifically prove this, may wonder if she is not clairvoyantly receiving impressions from the living. He goes on to state, in other terms, that parapsychology is wise to continue to study what has been historically known as occultism, with scientific procedures, of course.

"Important Figures" Sometimes Mediums

The *Guide Book for the Study of Psychical Research,* another respected sourcebook for parapsychologists, begins by discussing how to find and sit with mediums.[3] Most of the book deals with mediumistic phenomena, and in chapter six, "Important Figures in Psychical Research," 73 of the 85 people mentioned were either involved in spiritistic research or were mediums themselves. The remaining 12 could be suspected of occult involvement, because "only a few of the most significant facts about each person" were given.[4] In the American Society for Psychical Research's *Parapsychology: Sources of Information,* most of the categories listed deal with mediumistic phenomena and the occult. In chapter six, the "Glossary of Terms," over 75% (100 of 130) of the terms defined relate to seance mediumism—apparition, astral projection, automatic writing, billet reading, control, direct voice, ectoplasm, levitation, materialization, mediumism, seance, sensitive, spirit communication, spirit photography, table tipping, trance, xenoglossy, etc.

It is clear from the above that what makes parapsychology parapsychology is not anything that distinguishes it from occult phenomena, but, *rather,* that it is the *scientific, scholarly, technical research* of the occult that makes it parapsychology. The problem of denials by parapsychologists is evident. According to them, to simply believe in mediumism is occult; *however, scientifically proving mediumism (presumably so we can believe in it) is parapsychology and not the occult!*

Psi as a Child of the Occult

What genuine and consistent psi phenomena are produced apart from psychics? What *phenomena* of mediumism (and the occult in general) is not part of parapsychological research? Which parapsychologists, at least indirectly, have not involved themselves in the occult? Which psychics they study do not have occult involvement in their family history (less developed or transferred psychic powers)?

Parapsychologists *do* use the term parapsychology for phenomena which are clearly occult,[5] and many of them are personally involved in the occult. For example, Eric J. Dingwall, a well-known anthropologist and parapsychologist, noted that in the 1930's, "Many of the parapsychologists who were engaged in card guessing and similar experiments were themselves deeply committed to occult and spiritualistic beliefs . . . ."[6] The same is true today. He also notes that "The alliance between parapsychology and occultism, instead of being broken, was being cemented by the parapsychologists themselves." He declares that in Great Britain today, "parapsychology is so closely linked to it [occultism] as to be practically indistinguishable." In many other countries where parapsychology is studied, the "science" is essentially spiritistic, as in Italy and Brazil.[7] Dingwall goes on to declare that today "parapsychology has joined up with occultism."

In fact, it never left. Once *born,* nothing can change its essential nature. Parapsychology was born from occult parents, and it retains its nature even if human observers choose to place varying interpretations upon it. The very nature and data of parapsychology betray its true essence as occultism. Gardner Murphy, in his *Challenge of Psychical Research: A Primer of Parapsychology*, states:

> In general, modern psychical research has taken the position that all of the claims for the paranormal must be investigated whether they made any assumptions about the deceased or not. There must be investigation of telepathy and clairvoyance, precognition, and psychokinesis in their own right; there must also be investigation of those special sensitives who are called mediums, who offer themselves as mediators between incarnate and discarnate personalities; . . . anything paranormal which is reported to have happened must be investigated.[8]

Murphy himself had sittings with the famous medium, L. E. Piper.[9]

Parapsychologists Urge the Development of Occult Powers

Wherever we look we see parapsychology tied to the occult. What will be left to study if they don't urge and support the development of psychic powers? What book on parapsychology exists which is not a discussion of occult phenomena? For example, psychic researchers wrote *Amazing Secrets of the Psychic World*. It begins with, "The process of spirit communication . . . .", and the entire book is about spiritism and its manifestations. This and many other books by parapsychologists urge the development of occult powers. If we examine astronaut Edgar Mitchell's *Psychic Exploration,* we find that he personally supports mediumship and spiritism: "My own research into the mechanism by which mediums operate has convinced me that spirit communication is a genuine possibility." The impact of such research on him was inevitable: "I am now totally comfortable with the idea of OOBE [out of the body experiences—astral projections], psychic surgery, and dematerialization. My observations of several gifted sensitives such as Uri Geller [a medium] and Norbu Chen have been convincing."[10] Today he personally supports an eastern metaphysical and occult outlook on reality, and believes it important that mankind develop its psychic powers to help in its evolution.[11]

Yet parapsychologists tell us that the occult remains the occult, while parapsychology has become scientific enough to be granted AAAS (American Association for the Advancement of Science) recognition. The definition of science thus becomes wholly methodological. It is as if the use of instrumentation, statistical analysis, laboratory equipment, experiments, and philosophical (some call it "scientific") discussions on purported psi mechanisms miraculously transform the essential nature of occult phenomena from the supernatural to the scientific (parapsychology). Gardner Murphy was more astute: "Psychical research, or parapsychology, consists of observations . . . which cannot by any stretch of the imagination be subsumed under the science of today."[12]

Neither will supernaturalism ever be subsumed under true science unless science be converted to magic. Some are not far off from such a view. Dr. Gerald Feinberg, professor of physics at Columbia University states: "I do not think existing data show that psychic phenomena contradict known physical laws."[13] Yet the journals of "scientific" parapsychology use the term "psi" for what are clearly occult supernatural activities—seance activities, poltergeists, divination, etc. The false hope—that all human experiences can one day be found to function in accord with natural law—denies the possibility of another dimension of reality which can strategically interact with ours.

C. S. Lewis and Demonic Ingenuity

C. S. Lewis once remarked on the subtlety of demonic ingenuity in its potential use of the sciences. The elder devil, Screwtape, is advising his nephew, Wormwood:

> My dear Wormwood, I wonder you should ask me whether it is essential to keep the patient in ignorance of your own existence. That question, at least for the present phase of the struggle, has been answered for us by the High Command.

Our policy, for the moment, is to conceal ourselves. Of course this has not always been so. We are really faced with a cruel dilemma. When the humans disbelieve in our existence, we lose all the pleasing results of direct terrorism, and we make no magicians. On the other hand, when they believe in us, we cannot make them materialists and skeptics. At least, not yet. I have great hopes that we shall learn in due time how to emotionalise and mythologise their science to such an extent that what is, in effect, a belief in us (though not under that name) will creep in while the human mind remains closed to belief in the Enemy. The "Life Force," the worship of sex, and some aspects of psychoanalysis may here prove useful. If once we can produce our perfect work—the Materialist Magician, the man, not using, but veritably worshipping, what he vaguely calls "Forces" while denying the existence of "spirits"—then the end of the war will be in sight. But in the meantime we must obey our orders. I do not think you will have much difficulty in keeping the patient in the dark. The fact that "devils" are predominantly comic figures in the modern imagination will help you. If any faint suspicion of your existence begins to arise in his mind, suggest to him a picture of something in red tights, and persuade him that since he cannot believe in that (it is an old textbook method of confusing them) he therefore cannot believe in you.[14]

Soviet and western researchers, facing the charge of dealing in pseudoscience and superstition (i.e., miracles) have attempted to redefine their ideas more in line with this "Life Force" idea, staying as far away from spirits as possible. The declassified Defense Intelligence Agency Report titled *Soviet and Czechoslovakian Parapsychology Research* noted that when faced "with such criticisms, Soviet and Czech scientists engaged in parapsychology research have, more and more, stressed the 'biological energy' concept . . . ."[15] The *Psi Search* team notes that, ironically, the experimentation into ESP and PK "may now be clarifying such theories and concepts as spiritualism, reincarnation, and the spontaneous psychic events that baffled early investigators."[16] In other words, they are claiming that the latent ESP we all have may ultimately explain all the phenomena of mediumism. No spirits—just psi, the "Life Force."

A Representative Sampling

A short section documenting the kinds of material found in parapsychological journals might be instructive for the reader, who, wisely, does not frequent such literature. It appears that even reading about occultism may have negative effects on one's life, not to mention its seducing factor. Dr. Koch states:

> It is dangerous to read occult books. Reading them for some time one becomes mediumistic without knowing it, i.e., unconsciously. Then your spiritual life is harmed and your intellect is dulled.[17]

Parapsychology Review is a respected journal for both scientific parapsychologists and laymen. Few topics of the occult go undiscussed in its pages. As Kurtz states of the literature in general:

> A perusal of the parapsychological literature reveals the following topics: clairvoyance, telepathy, precognition, psychokinesis, levitation, poltergeists, materialization, dematerialization, psychic healing, psychometry, psychic surgery, reincarnation, retrocognition, tape recordings of the voices of the dead, hauntings, apparitions, life after life [see Weldon's *Is There Life After Death?* for an analysis of this phenomena], regression to an earlier age, and so on.[18]

If we examine the last several years of *Parapsychology Review* journals, we find the following reports, discussions, and statements (listed by volume, number, and page):

A report on Brazil's Institute for Psychobiological Research investigation of outstanding mediums (6:4:17).

John Cutton, honorary Secretary for the London Society for Psychical Research stated, "so far I have ignored that most important aspect of parapsychology concerning mediumistic phenomena. Instruments have, of course, been used in the seance room, particularly photographic instruments" (4:4:26).

The Jersey Society of Parapsychology presented "A Seminar in Parapsychology, subtitled Science Takes a Serious Look at the Occult" (9:3:20).

A recent lecture series of the Psychical Research Foundation in Durham, North Carolina (one of the "solely scientific" laboratories), included lectures on "Survival Research: Past, Present, and Future;" "Recent Explorations of Mediums;" "Research on Psychic Healing;" "My Encounters with Four Poltergeists," etc. (9:4:26).

One report at the 1977 Parapsychological Association Convention included an "ingenious experiment to address the old problem of the source of mediumistic communications. [Dr. Gertrude Schmeidler's] scheme requires that the communicator indicate before death how he plans to communicate and the mediums subsequent transmission is then evaluated from this perspective." This implies that this method will produce an assurance of objective results, or "truth" in the matter. Assuming the biblical view of death and the existence of spiritual warfare, it will only produce "proof" of the occult view of survival—i.e., no biblical judgment at death, and a corresponding impact that will reduce the validity of the Scriptures, especially in relation to their conservative, literal interpretation (8:6:19). (The Parapsychological Association, a member of the AAAS, is one association that boasts of its scientific, nonoccultic nature.) Another organization with similar boasts, the London Society for Psychical Research, at its 1977 international conference presented a speaker much of whose lecture "involved ideas usually relegated to the area of the occult" (8:4:26).

Charles Tart in his address at the 1979 American Anthropological Association's yearly symposia on parapsychology stated that "parapsychologists should be seriously studying shamans [primitive mediums] since these individuals seem to have learned how to control their psi abilities" (10:2:21). [The quote is by D. Scott Rogo.]

The above references are fairly representative, and it appears clear that parapsychologists, even "scientific" ones, are continuing to investigate mediums as they always have. They do not find much that is exciting to study when they limit their investigations to ordinary people.

Closet Occultists

It is reasonable to ask, "Should we, as a general rule, trust what parapsychologists say and write?" We believe not, for over and over again, they are biased and are attempting to scientifically prove a certain occult worldview (e.g., the Life Force idea). Common elements of this worldview include a distinctly antibiblical philosophy (e.g., man is united to the cosmos by his divine energy). Considering the source of parapsychology, this is not surprising. Parapsychology tends to support such things as reincarnation, pantheism, universal salvation, a mediumistic view of the afterlife, etc. In general, parapsychologists will believe almost anything as an explanation for psi phenomena, except that of demons [the same is true for scientific ufologists], but they *will* accept ideas that are even far less likely. As Kurtz states:

> An observer of the current scene cannot help but be struck by the emergence of a bizarre new "paranormal" worldview.... Many of those who are attracted to a paranormal universe express an antiscientific, even occult approach ... unfortunately, many parapsychologists appear to be committed to belief in psi on the basis of a metaphysical or spiritualist [read spiritual] worldview that they wish to vindicate.[19]

Whether they will admit it or not, psychic researchers are biased toward the occult. Hence their views and pronouncements should be received with caution. Unfortunately, even some Christians have jumped on the bandwagon and uncritically accepted the "findings" of psi research. Among two consequences are (1) a more amenable attitude to psychic phenomena and the proposition that we all have psi powers, and (2) a tendency to let the Bible be interpreted *in light of* parapsychology, an extremely unfortunate and consequential approach (see next section). Parapsychologists are not simply respected scientists who accidentally stumbled upon psychic phenomena and decided to objectively proceed with scientific investigation. For many, it was their prior interest in the occult, or occult experiences, which caused them to become parapsychologists. The British critic, J. D. West, once wrote:

> It is quite obvious that this is a highly emotion-laden subject, and one that attracts cranks, dupes, and charlatans in embarrassing numbers. And it is from this unsavory crowd that the extrasensory experimenters have emerged. The field of extrasensory research remains a no-man's land between the lunatic fringe on the one hand and the academically unorthodox on the other.[20]

There are parapsychologists who on the surface appear to be entirely reputable, scientific, and wholly uninvolved with the demonic. Yet it is also true that a good deal of psychic events have no direct, i.e., observable or discernable, relation to the demonic. It is the impact, similarity, and nature of the phenomena produced being similar to what spirits have done in mediumism, shamanism, etc., that ties such events to the demonic. Hence all parapsychologists, as such, must be suspect simply because of their associations. If Jesus called even the religious scribes as being "of your father the Devil," what should we say about anyone who actively engages in *psychic* religious research? At the same time, demons do not have to be behind all psi experimentation either. In some of the statistical experimental work (providing it is not done with sensitives), they are probably absent, and the inability to replicate experiments is due to the vast number of unknowns about the human mind.

If psychology by its nature can never be a strict science, how can parapsychology ever be, as it not only has the problems of psychology, but those of an entirely new realm, as well?

References for Chapter 24

1. *Parapsychology Review,* Vol. 9, No. 2, p. 11.
2. Wolman, *op. cit.,* p. 306.
3. Ashby, *Guidebook for the Study of Psychical Research,* (NY: Samuel Weiser), 1972, p. 5-6.
4. *Ibid.,* p. 131.
5. eg. cf., *The International Journal of Parapsychology,* Vol. 8., No. 2, p. 234-6.
6. *Parapsychology Review,* Vol. 3, No. 6, p. 23.
7. *Parapsychology Review,* Vol. 8, No. 5, p. 23; P. McGreggor, *Jesus of the Spirits.*
8. Murphy, *op. cit.,* p. 183-4.
9. *Ibid.,* p. vii.
10. Mitchell, *op. cit.,* p. 40, 673.
11. *Ibid.,* p. 25-53; 670-83.
12. Murphy, *op. cit.,* p. 1.
13. Foreword to Mitchell's *Psychic Exploration, op. cit.,* p. 22.
14. C.S. Lewis, *Screwtape Letters,* p. 32-33.
15. L.F. Maire, J.D. LaMothe, *Soviet and Czheckoslovakian parapsychology Research,* (Defense Intelligence Agency Report, U.S. Army Medical Intelligence and Information Agency, Office of the Surgeon General), Sept., 1975, Code DST-18105-387-75, p. 61.
16. Bowles, Hynds, *op. cit.,* p. 96.
17. Personal letter to the author. Dr. Koch was not certain "dulled" was the correct English term.
18. Kurtz, *op. cit.,* p. 25.
19. Kurtz, *op. cit.,* p. 14, 29.
20. Bowles & Hynds, p. 13 citing his articles in the CIBA Foundation Symposium on Extrasensory Perception (N.Y. Citadel) 1966, p. 20-21.

Chapter 25

Researchers and Psychic Labs: What You See is Not What You Get!

We cannot really be certain of the extent of occult involvement among even the most reputable parapsychologists. Caution is needed here as well. As we have said, many of them can appear to be uninvolved in the occult. Yet of those researchers who fit in this category of parapsychology, our research turned up the fact that many of them were more occultly involved than had been expected.

Experimentation With Mediums

We have seen that J. B. Rhine was a foremost researcher in parapsychology. One hears that he is antioccult, but how many readers know of his early and even continued experimentation with mediums?

We have mentioned Dr. Robert Bradley in passing—he is developer of the Bradley method of natural birth. He seems to be very legitimate until research uncovers the fact that, as he admits in his book *Psychic Phenomena*, he and his wife have been involved in the occult for 27 years: "We have . . . sought out and sat in seances with every 'sensitive' or medium available.'" He is President of the occultly oriented Academy of Parapsychology and Medicine and states:

> I personally think spirit communication is going on constantly, that we are never alone. The talks I give, the ideas I have on natural childbirth came to me either in sleep or from direct spirit communication.[2]

He says, "I am a Christian," but believes that "mediumship can be used for therapy and spirit communication in religious-type treatment, particularly if people have a fear of death or lack of belief in their own religion."[3] He even accepts the unpardonable idea of advocating spiritism for children! Some feel his birthing methods are unwise.

For another example, reading in the *Brain-Mind Bulletin* of March 9, 1978, we find that, "The first *objective* evidence of the existence of auras and chakras may have been obtained in a UCLA study incorporating a number of measurements (emphasis added). The study involved Rosalyn Bruyere who described auras and chakras of subjects who underwent Rolfing, or structural integration, a system of body manipulation that has been known to open one to psi experiences.[4]

The report was scientifically oriented and described the rigorousness of the procedures. It gave no indication that Bruyere was anything other than an ordinary lady. Yet if we turn to a two-part analysis/interview of her in the February and March, 1979, issues of *Human Behavior,* we find that she is a very experienced occultist with numerous spirit guides. If we continue research, we even find that the scientist who studied her, Dr. Valerie Hunt, is also a psychic.[5] It was her psychic experiences which moved her into researching psychic energy. This is *objective* evidence? Can we believe that a scientist who is a psychic—investigating a medium with spirit guides—will *ever* produce *objective* evidence?

Another is Dr. Robert W. Laidlaw, the former secretary and president of the American Association of Marriage Counselors, a member of several scientific societies, a pioneer of modern psychiatry, and active in the Laymen's

Movement for a Christian World—yet he was also a trustee of the American Society for Psychical Research, with a special interest in mediumship.[6]

Carl Jung and Seances

Carl Jung, the famous and extremely influential psychoanalyst, would not admit publicly in his lectures or books anything about his involvement in seances and his spiritist worldview because, "My colleagues would regard me as mentally unbalanced."[7] Jung's ideas have had tremendous impact in support of occultism.

In a recent *Los Angeles Times* article on Dr. Robert Leichtman, M.D., who utilizes clairvoyant diagnosis, there was no mention of anything occult in his method of clairvoyance—it sounded like a very "natural" talent. He received a patient's name or address, and the diagnosis just came to him. Many would read the article and assume that (due to parapsychological indoctrination) this individual had simply taken the time to develop his latent and natural psi ability for the benefit of his patients. Yet when we take the time to research his life, we discover that he is an advanced occultist with spirit guides who *give him* the diagnosis.[8] Because many scientists wish their occult involvement to remain a secret, it can take a great deal of time to prove what is suspected, and often it cannot be proved at all. Who then can be trusted? *Anyone* involved in the "new age" "higher consciousness" eastern psychic world should certainly be avoided when it comes to selecting any kind of treatment.

What we are attempting to show is that the actual facts can be greatly different from how they appear on the surface. We read about few parapsychologists who did *not* become involved in investigating seances. Yet the view parapsychologists are attempting to project is that they are not occultists, they do not attend seances, and they *are* scientific, unbiased, etc. This is hardly objective.

A reading of only the scientific literature on parapsychology does not give one any idea of the extent of occult involvement of parapsychologists. Often you will not discover a parapsychologist is an occultist until you have read nearly everything by him or about him. (How does such occult involvement affect their experimentation and results?) In fact, they have little reason not to become involved in mediumistic studies—orthodox science rejects such studies, but that is where the data is. As even the Psi-Search team admits: "Irrespective of the technique used, strong evidence of psi is frequently best obtained through the testing of sensitives, popularly known as psychics."[9]

The Occult and Humanistic Man's Judgment

There are theological reasons for their involvement, as well. For some, seances provide the hope of a disproof of judgment after death. An occult philosophy is supportive of humanistic man's rebellion against God. It encourages belief in autonomy and independence, denies a personal God, supports the idea of works or evolution to higher levels, has no moral absolutes (often just the opposite), and feeds the ego.

The next logical step for parapsychologists, after determining that psi existed, was to attempt to develop psi powers well enough so that they could be easily observed, measured, evaluated, and then used for man's "evolution." It is also true that some parapsychologists deplore the scientific approach to parapsychology, noting that because of that approach much relevant data from occultism is neglected.

Parapsychology and Out-of-the-Body Experiences

Psychic researchers are not the only ones who can be found to have occult ties. This is true of certain other phenomena, as well, which we are told is natural and beneficial. Parapsychology has become very interested in out-of-the-body experiences, both from research into psychics and the clinical death experiences published by Raymond Moody in his *Life After Life*.

Perhaps no man living or dead knows more about astral projection than Robert Crookall. In his 90's, he recently published his sixth research volume on the topic. Few people know, however, that his interest and data first came from mediumism. D. Scott Rogo states:

> Initially, Crookall had been primarily interested in studying mediumistic communications and what they had to say about the death experience and the posthumous journey of the soul. So in the 1950's he began cataloguing what mediumistic "communicators" [the "dead"] reported about their own deaths. As he expected, most of these communicators described virtually the same set of experiences; i.e., that their souls left their bodies in an apparitional form; that they traveled down a dark tunnel; were greeted by apparitions of the dead, etc. Eventually, Crookall also realized that these mediumistic utterances described experiences absolutely identical to the adventures reported by people who have undergone pseudodeaths or OBE's [out-of-body experiences] while seriously ill. So in 1961 he presented his first book to the public, *The Supreme Adventure,* in which he points out the intricate parallels between the OBE, pseudodeath experiences, and the journey through death as described by the dead, through mediums . . . . After the publication of *The Supreme Adventure,* Crookall turned his attention almost completely to the study of the OBE and near-death encounters and published vast catalogues of these cases in 1960, 1964, and 1972. Crookall's data make it clear that pseudodeath cases are in no way qualitatively different from the OBE's reported by people in good health. He also found that there were specific patterns within the OBE data, and that these same patterns turn up in near-death cases.[10]

Again, those interested in a biblical evaluation of this phenomena should consult Weldon's book, *Is There Life After Death* (Harvest House, 1977).

The Trend

In light of the failures of solely experimental psi, we could expect to see a "return" to the study of direct occultism. What most people are aware of, however, is that most psychic research has never really "left" the occult.

Alan Vaughan is a psychic whose abilities were developed by medium Douglas Johnson at the London College of Psychic Studies, a mediumistic organization. As early as 1973, writing in Mitchell's *Psychic Exploration,* he stated:

> Since the advent of Spiritualism over a century ago in America, certain individuals with unusual psychic abilities have dominated the scene of psychic research. At first these psychic sensitives were mainly mediums . . . . Twentieth-century investigations (finally) shed light on the puzzling nature of their trance personalities. Other types of sensitives include trance diagnosticians, readers of past lives, and even mediums who produce voices directly on recording tape, an electronic equivalent of automatic writing . . . . Recent work in parapsychological laboratories by a number of sensitives is bringing increased interest in parapsychology to scientists and laymen. The latest trend is to develop methods for training sensitives."

Note that psychic research here is dominated by *psychic* individuals, not normal individuals, the latter being the view often presented to the public. Again, this is no doubt intended to support the idea of universal latent psi. Vaughan also notes that "increasingly the scientific establisment is showing interests in the talents of psychic sensitives, giving rise to investigations in laboratories that are not primarily parapsychological."[2]

As evidence of the occult trend, we would cite Hintze and Pratt's *The Psychic Realm! What Can You Believe?* It has received favorable reviews in the parapsychological literature. In each chapter popular author Naomi Hintze first describes various spontaneous psychic phenomena. Next Dr. J. Gaither Pratt analyzes them from the scientific view. Dr. Pratt has been on the research staff of the Duke Parapsychology Laboratory for over one-quarter of a century and was a Past President of the AAAS affiliated Parapsychological Association, so we should "expect" to find a clear avoidance of the occult, if the claims of the PA and scientific psi laboratories are to be trusted.

What do we find? Over one-fourth of the book deals directly with spiritism in various forms, and 60% of it deals with the occult in a favorable light. Chapters discuss poltergeists, psychic healing, ouija boards, and the Mrs. Curran-Patience Worth-automatic writings, possession, mediums, survival, and reincarnation. There is a strong support given to the study of mediums, (in fact, we are told that parapsychologists must not leave them out of their research); there is an irresponsible advocacy of the "safe" use of the ouija board, and positive endorsement of psychic healers like Olga Worrall (whose healing abilities, she admits elsewhere, come from spirits), as well as many mediums.

Dr. Pratt admits that, "A new generation of scientists has come upon the scene, and the recent reports of the successful tests of the Icelandic medium Hafsteinn Bjornsson are perhaps only the first signs of a renewal of scientific interest in mediumship."[3] Dr. Pratt himself investigated the trance mediumship of Eileen Garrett in the 1930's. He notes, "In contrast with the intense interest of previous years, the attention given to mediums during the past half century looks like neglect, but parapsychologists never got completely away from an interest in them. In particular, we needed ways of conducting the mediumistic sittings and checking the records that guarded against the possible effects of suggestibility . . . ."[4] He concludes his chapter on "The Mediums" by declaring of mediumism, "Further research is amply justified."

There is one reason in particular why parapsychologists have little choice but to often use psychics or mediums in their experiments. This is discussed in the *Psi-Search*

book:
> Some psi experiments require highly complex monitoring equipment. However, monitoring large groups of subjects can be immensely costly, and most experimenters suffer from a chronic shortage of research funds. Fortunately for researchers struggling with tight budgets, a series of tests with single subjects may yield results equal in statistical importance to tests with large groups of subjects (depending on the nature of the problem being investigated). It is obviously less expensive to monitor just one person than a large and unwieldy group of subjects. A sensitive is nearly always used in such instances.[15]

Using the results of a psychic's experimentation, they then tell us that *everyone* is psychic!

Concluding Remarks

These chapters have documented the fact that parapsychology, despite vociferous claims to the contrary, is still heavily involved in the occult, principally mediumism and other forms of spiritism. It has remained so for 100 of its 130 years. Even in the 30-year period of scientific study, it never really removed itself from occultism. This is true in other countries, as well. In Russia, for example, it has been noted that its parapsychologists have often studied eastern metaphysics and the occult.[16] Thus, to call parapsychology occultism *is an accurate assessment of its nature* and is amply demonstrated by the facts. Scientific parapsychology is no more than "scientific" occultism. Dr. Koch states:

> Thousands of cases reveal that occultism in any form, even in a scientific form, harms people. This applies even to scientific parapsychologists who attend spiritist seances in order to study the activity of mediums. The Scriptural command to have nothing to do with spiritists applies not only to ordinary people, but also to

parapsychologists who work by scientific methods."[17]

To be involved in demonic supernaturalism is to be an occultist. Parapsychologists are involved in occultism, and the evidence strongly suggests that they should be classified as occultists. Nevertheless, there are those who argue that some parapsychology is "Christian." To that we turn in our next chapter. First, however, a brief look at the occult ties of leading *scientific* psi research laboratories, and then a concluding "shocking" story.

Parapsychological Laboratories and the Occult

Bowles and Hynds, in their book *Psi Search,* attempted to retain a thoroughly scientific approach to psi, although they still attended seances in their research. This approach was facilitated by help from the Parapsychological Association—"The only international professional organization of researchers into psychic phenomena." (One can but wonder what research into the lives and family histories of its 27 founders might uncover!) The book lists six U.S. parapsychological laboratories. These are claimed to be *strictly scientific* laboratories. Having done only a very small amount of research into 5 of them, we find that all of them have direct or indirect occult ties.

1. The Chester E. Carlson Research Laboratory of the ASPR, N.Y., N.Y. The ASPR has a history of mediumistic studies. Its name is more than coincidental. The Carlsons were involved in spiritism. Mrs. Carlson reportedly was a medium. It is also reported that it was her revelations from the spirit world which allowed her husband to complete his invention of the Xerox machine. In return for this favor, he was to give a great deal of money to help establish parapsychology as a science. This money was given to the Duke University and started its Parapsychology Lab (now the Foundation for the Research on the Nature of Man).[18]
2. The Center for Parapsychological Research, Austin, Texas, is really a subdivision of the Association for the Understanding of Man. The AUM is headed by Ray

Stanford, a medium who channels messages from the Space Brothers, ascended masters, etc. An introductory brochure from the organization tells us the primary source of these messages is not a discarnate entity, but this is merely semantics. The source is still spiritistic. The brochure declares, it is "The unconscious and superconscious mind and spiritual being of Stanford" in contact with other minds, living, dead, or in outer space. Dr. Rex Stanford, Ray's brother, who is also a psychic, is the head of the Center for Parapsychological Research.

3. The Institute for Parapsychology of the Foundation for the Research on the Nature of Man, Durham, North Carolina, formerly Duke University Parapsychology Lab. Parapsychology Press, publishers of the *Journal of Parapsychology,* is a subsidiary of the FRNM. It was founded by J. B. Rhine who attempted to prove the survival hypothesis by mediumistic research. It was apparently heavily supported as a result of the spiritistic revelations from Mrs. Carlson. As mentioned, the requirement for obtaining the Xerox information was purportedly a heavy subsidy for the Duke University Department of Parapsychology. Dr. Randall states:

> To this day no other university in the world has sponsored parapsychology so strongly and so continuously as Duke.[19]

It is not surprising to find Dr. Rhine was and has been doing his best to prove to us that we all have natural psychic powers. The common public reaction to this will be to try and develop them, mostly from wrong motives. Nor is it surprising that nearly every scientific parapsychologist today was trained by him to have a similar outlook.[20]

4. The Psychical Research Foundation, Durham, North Carolina, publishers of *Theta,* a journal devoted to the survival question, and dealing heavily with mediumism, poltergeists, apparitions, and reincarnation. The Foundation was created in 1960 by Charles Ozanne specifically for scientific research into survival of the personality after death.[21] Issue No. 1 of *Theta* noted that "The

Foundation has been active in both areas"—i.e., of investigating mediumship and poltergeists, and that "The Foundation will investigate any claim that appears relevant to the survival hypothesis. Each ghost will have its day in court."[22] The Board of Directors included many involved in the psychic world including J. G. Pratt, Chester Carlson, Ian Stevenson, and others.

5. The Mind Science Foundation of San Antonio, Texas. According to the American Psychological Association *Monitor* of April, 1973, the MSF is heavily subsidized by and "now appears to be under the wing of its 'client donor' [Silva mind control]." Silva Mind Control is an occult organization devoted to the development of psychic powers.

Running an Electric Current Through Nitroglycerin!

A talk by Forrest J. Cioppa titled "Medicine and Psi," delivered at the Holiday Inn in Monterey, California, November 25-27, 1977, contained a rather enlightening example of parapsychology research and its suspension of critical judgment. After discovering that both Edgar Cayce and a Tibetan psychic, T. Lobsang Rampa, gave similar instructions for the building of an "aura-scope" (i.e., a machine that could supposedly enable nonpsychics to see auras), Cioppa and an engineer friend decided to pursue an investigation further. A local psychic's spirit guides, it turns out, also gave them similar instructions to those of Cayce and Rampa.

Deciding to suspend rational judgment entirely, for three months, they worked on the "aura-scope," according to the *specific* instructions of the spirit guides. The only catch was that a key part of the process involved running an electric current through nitroglycerin. The engineer was obviously cautious at this point, but they both returned to the psychic's house and stated, in essence, "If you really believe in your spirit guide's integrity and instructions, we will go ahead with the experiment, but we will do it here, in your house." The psychic, fortunately, said she would not permit it.

The lesson is this: had this psychic really trusted her spirit guides, at least three people would probably be dead today. Obviously, that was the intent of her spirit guides. That intelligent men would be so willing to blindly obey, given such circumstances, merely to supposedly see a human aura, speaks volumes, both about human gullibility and psychic "setups." That the spirits would so willingly murder (as the evidence makes abundantly clear) also speaks a great deal about the advisability of not participating in psychic research, given the fact of invisible entities behind the scene.

References for Chapter 25

1. R. Bradley, *Psychic Phenomena* (NY: Paperback Library) 1971, p. 14.
2. Academy of Parapsychology and Medicine, *The Varieties of Healing Experience,* transcript of an Oct. 30, 1971 symposium, p. 101.
3. *Ibid.*, p. 106.
4. *Human Behavior,* Jan. 1979, p. 39-40; *The Christian Parapsychologist,* Vol. 3, No. 2, p. 74 (March 1979).
5. *New West,* Feb. 13, 1978, p. 43-44.
6. *Parapsychology Review,* Vol. 9, No. 5, p. 13.
7. From a private conversation with Jung, reported in Koch, *Satan's Devices, op. cit.,* p. 156. Numerous other sources also document his occult involvement.
8. Robert Leichtman "Clairvoyant Diagnosis" *The Journal of Holistic Health,* 1977, p. 40-41.
9. Bowles and Hynds, *op. cit.,* p. 36.
10. *Parapsychology Review,* Vol. 1, No. 1, P. 25.
11. Alan Vaughan, *op. cit.,* p. 74.
12. *Ibid.*, p. 87.
13. Hintze and Pratt *The Psychic Realm: What Can You Believe?* (NY: Random House) 1975, p. 215.
14. *Ibid.*, p. 215-16.
15. Bowles and Hynds, *op. cit.,* p. 44.
16. Thelma Moss, "Psychic Research in the Soviet Union," in Mitchell, *op. cit.,* p. 476-81.
17. Koch, *Satan's Devices,* p. 159.
18. G. Cerminara *Insights for the Age of Aquarius,* p. 203-4.
19. Randall, *op. cit.,* p. 73, Bowles & Hynds, *op. cit.*
20. Bowles & Hynds, *op. cit.,* p. 34.
21. *Theta,* No. 1, 1963, p. 1.
22. *Ibid.*, p. 3.

Chapter 26

Is There Such a Thing as "Christian Parapsychology?"

Despite the available evidence, a concept of "Christian" parapsychology is growing today within liberal churches. The encouragement and intimidation of Christians to accept psychic research is beginning to have an influence. The Rev. William V. Rauscher states:

> Our theological seminaries face the very obvious and relevant task of including parapsychology in their curriculae.... We are not dealing with demons and witches, but with science, and with the deeper needs of the human soul, of which we still know too little.
>
> A Christian who looks at parapsychology must have a very special fondness for its researches....[1]

H. Richard Neff, pastor of the Christian Community Presbyterian Church in Bowie, Maryland, states:

> I cannot draw the line that consigns everything that people associate with the name of the Holy Spirit to the Kingdom of God, and everything associated with mediums to the realm of the devil. One must look at the results and ask if they are good or evil.[2]

J. C. Crosson states:

> If Christians warn against psi as "a thing of the devil," better informed individuals may eventually question the responsibility of Christianity.[3]

Some have publicly stated that to oppose occult investigations may be to oppose God himself.[4] Unfortunately, in the writings of "Christian parapsychologists" there is little if any awareness of the *subtlety* of the demonic; there is no spiritual (biblical) discernment exercised, and there seems to be a philosophical premise that everything in the psi realm is all, or mostly all goodness and light. The psychic realm is viewed as an exciting and rewarding new area of exploration of the human mind.

We must not view psi as neutral or benign. We must exercise discernment, not curiosity. The degree of awe that can be evoked by psychic demonstrations does not mean such abilities are either ethical or neutral. Satanic powers are innately deceptive—that is, initially such events cannot be seen as either evil or misleading. The fact that an event *occurred* does not validate it ethically—even if there are short-term seemingly good results. The issue of discernment does not deal primarily with how psi works, but with the question: Should one be investigating it in the first place?

Christian Parapsychology?

So we ask, "Is there such a thing as Christian Parapsychology?" No—the terms are mutually exclusive. The study of parapsychology is the study of the occult. We have briefly summarized the argument in our previous chapters.

To be a Christian parapsychologist one would have to be a Christian occultist, and the Bible is absolutely clear in its stand against occult involvement of any kind. No concept is more anti-Christian or diabolical. Yet we do find Christian parapsychologists, and some purported Christians advocate that the Church should be involved in psychical research. A partial list of Christian organizations engaged in and supporting the idea of parapsychology and the occult includes: The Foundation for Christian Psychic Research of Ridgefield, Connecticut, publishers of *Soul Searcher* (the Foundation holds to the Apostles' and Nicene Creeds); The Churches Fellowship for Psychical and Spiritual Studies in London, publishers of *The Christian Parapsychologist;* The Academy of Religion and Psychical Research of Bloomfield, Conn., which publishes the *Journal of the Academy of Religion and Psychical Research;* Spiritual Frontiers Fellowship of Independence, Missouri, which publishes *Spiritual Frontiers;* and the Christians' Institute of Parapsychology in Atlanta, Georgia.

Numerous books by Christians have been published which adopt a highly positive view of parapsychology. These include E. Garth Moore's *Try the Spirits;* Charles E. Cluff's *Parapsychology and the Christian Faith;* H. Richard Neff's *Psychic Phenomena and Religion;* Morton T. Kelsey's *The Christian and the Supernatural;* and there are others. Even though they strongly support the occult, all these books are carried by many Christian bookstores.

It appears that most of these groups and authors are nominally Christian only, although we cannot rule out ignorant or deceived genuine Christians being among them. Dr. Koch states he knows of no genuine Christian who is a parapsychologist, and that, "I cannot believe that a Christian who has really given his life to Christ, would be able to take part in parapsychological experiments involving mediums."[5]

NOT Gifts of the Holy Spirit

The extent to which psychic groups that label themselves "Christian" have influenced the Christian community is neither fully appreciated nor adequately opposed. Rather than having spoken out, Christians have been silent, mostly from ignorance. Many have even viewed parapsychology as something positive, as scientific proof of the existence of the supernatural. This is really stepping into the enemy's camp, however. As with using clinical death research (e.g., Raymond Moody's *Life After Life,* etc.) to "prove" life after death, one really ends up with an occult view of things, not a biblical one, and people are caused to stumble.

Clinical death research supposedly proves the occult view of death, which denies any concept of biblical judgment or salvation. People who trust in it are lulled into a serene and dangerous false security. Similarly, parapsychology views occult powers as latent, natural, and available to all, rather than as demonic powers. Worse still, "Christian" parapsychology views them as the gifts of the Holy Spirit. The things of Satan become the things of God.

The fact is, the worldview promoted by parapsychology is Eastern-occultic, not biblical. In viewing demonic supernaturalism as natural human capacities, certain logical conclusions are drawn about man and his world. We have already seen that the evidence of psi actively supports such concepts as the deity of man, pantheism, reincarnation, universal salvation, and occult evolutionary progression in the after-life, etc. For example, hypnotic regression into past lives certainly tends to make one believe in the preexistence of souls—a nonbiblical concept.[6] It also denies physical resurrection and immortality. Contact with the supposed dead through mediumism both denies biblical judgment (Heb. 9:27, etc.) and supports the idea of continuing dimensions of spiritual evolving, i.e., works' salvation. In both views the atonement of Christ is rendered unnecessary. "Psi" powers give a hint of omniscience and omnipotence, deny validity to time and space, and stongly support the idea of a universal divine essence of which we are all equal partakers. (Since these powers are not viewed as miraculous, but natural, the natural means through which they are done must be a universal divine life force which connects all things in one unity.) Hence, they cause rebellion against the created order and our own status as creatures, teaching that we can become as gods and escape the limits of time and space. No greater deception is being fostered today than the idea that these psychic abilities are natural to, and latent in, man; and that they result from unknown natural laws.

Parapsychologists, Neohumanists, and Occultists Join Hands

It is not surprising that parapsychologists, neohumanists, and occultists join hands in declaring this truth. From this one concept flow several possible conclusions, each of them destructive to the biblical worldview: The powers cannot be demonic, since they are natural; biblical miracles are not supernatural, therefore neither was Jesus—he is no longer unique; impersonal law is the supreme reality that religions have conceived of as God; man can be as God, or inner man is divine; there is a divine, universal essence—monism or pantheism; denial of validity to the created order, thus teaching that time, space, and creaturehood are "illusions;" denial of the Fall of man—man is psychically evolving into divinity; amoralism—being impersonal, the divine essence (Reality) is amoral, etc.

Again, some Christian writers (e.g., Watchman Nee) have advocated the idea that psi powers were originally God-given and are now latent due to the Fall. Other Christians have adopted this view despite the fact that such an idea raises problems. For example, why could not a Christian develop his latent psychic powers and use them to God's glory? Why would God need to give His people spiritual *gifts* (which implies they are not latent), when they could use their own natural (and by implication neutral) powers that God gave man originally? How do we distinguish between gifts of the Spirit and latent psi?

"Christian" parapsychology has several fatal flaws. The central problem of the theologians and laymen who advocate psychicism is that *they do not hold to biblical authority*. To advocate occultism, such authority must be abandoned. The majority of Christian parapsychologists are theologically liberal, hence it has been the liberal pastors, priests, and other professional theologians who have championed and promoted Christian parapsychology. In actuality, they are simply reaping the fruits of their unbelief and becoming indirect instruments of the god of this world (II Cor. 4:4).

Darwinism, Evolution, Rationalism, and Parapsychology

As mentioned earlier, a century ago Darwin's theory of evolution virtually destroyed faith in God and the Bible for a large number of an entire generation, and its fruits remain to this day. It is indeed possible that no other modern idea has been more responsible for denying the truth of God's Word and for denying the very existence of God Himself than evolution. Christian evolutionists and "Christian" parapsychologists are bonded closer (in their approach to scripture) than the former would care to admit. It is evident today that Darwinism indirectly provided an impetus for a turning to occultism. Darwin left man with no transcendence—where could he get it back? In the late 19th century, the very theologians who jumped at psi research as proof of a spiritual dimension were precisely the ones who capitulated to the antibiblical evolutionary materialistic worldview propounded by Darwin, because they rarely held to biblical authority to begin with. Their denial of biblical authority forced them to accept Darwinism, and then the miseries of Darwinism forced them to accept psychic research. This is also true to a great extent today. Darwinistic evolution and rationalism undercut confidence in the Bible. It supposedly became a book of creation myths, superstition, and unbelievable miracles. Yet Darwinism also exacted a heavy cost in its meaningless and materialistic outlook on life. When Darwin removed God, he left *man* dead as well. It is simply a fact that many of our modern ills result directly from a purely materialistic philosophy of life. Today, the very theologians who have abandoned biblical authority jump about in excitement over parapsychological research and the psychic world because it gives "life and meaning" to the dead world of Darwinism and materialism they have helped to produce by their lack of faith in the Bible. Even though they are confusing the Satanic with the Divine, they see psi research as "confirmation" of the Bible they once rejected. Only instead of a *proper* biblical interpretation, the Bible is now interpreted *in the light of* a psychic worldview, e.g., rather than biblical miracles being evidence of God's power or Jesus' Messiahship, they are confirmation that the presuppositions of parapsychology (that all men can develop psychic powers and are divine) are valid after all. These theologians can use the results of psychic research to show others that the Bible *is* "true" after all.

However, there is a faulty premise operating here. It is true that most Christian parapsychologists see psi research as a confirmation of biblical miracles, evidence of survival after death, and evidence of the truth of a genuine spiritual (not necessarily supernatural) reality beyond materialism. The problem is that the Bible's evidence shows that miracles will not convince the unbeliever to begin with. The Pharisees saw many of the most astounding miracles that Jesus did, and their only reaction was to try to murder Him. Jesus said it was an evil generation that sought for a sign. The resurrection is stated to be proof enough for all men (Acts 17). Therefore, Christian parapsychology is flawed at the outset, and even unnecessary according to its own stated purposes and hopes—that of "proving" the Bible, or more accurately, proving that "another dimension" exists. Biblical authority is still not the issue here for the Christian parapsychologist. The primary concern is to escape the consequences of pure materialism and unbelief.

Given the fact that Christian parapsychology is of necessity involved in occultism, it is also dangerous. The true Christian already believes in the miraculous. Parapsychological "proof" that psychic manifestations occur are a useless addition to one who believes in the Bible and the reality of Satan. Again, Christian parapsychologists are excited about psi only because they never fully trusted the Bible to begin with. We will document this in our next section, "The Theology of Christian Parapsychology."

References for Chapter 26

1. "Faith and Science," in *The Signet Handbook of Parapsychology,* p. 168, 163.
2. Neff, *Psychic Phenomena and Religion* (Philadelphia: Westminster Press) 1974, p. 167.
3. *Parapsychology Review,* Vol. 8, No. 5, p. 15.
4. Cluff, *Parapsychology and the Christian Faith* (Valley Forge, PA: Judson Press) 1976, p. 27.
5. Koch, *Satan's Devices,* p. 159.
6. See Augustus Strong, *Systematic Theology,* Vol. 2, Part 5, Chapter 1, Part 4.

Chapter 27

The Theology of "Christian Parapsychology

The first issue of *The Christian Parapsychologist* states that its purpose is to see psi phenomena from a particular perspective: "If these phenomena are being studied from a Christian standpoint, they should be seen by us in the light of Christian revelation .... It is to the Holy Spirit that the Christian will look for guidance in making this correlation."¹

As the Holy Spirit is the Author of Holy Scripture (II Peter 1:21), let us first see whether Christian parapsychologists truly believe what He has spoken, and then we will know whether they in fact look to Him for guidance. Not unexpectedly, Christian parapsychologists are not really distinct from their secular brethren. Their literature reveals they support each other's work, and have the same basic outlook on psi, except that the former covers it with a Christian veneer. However, the effect of psi research on biblical interpretation is only too clear. Time and again biblical passages have been grossly misinterpreted, or simply thrown out, to make the idea of Christian parapsychology "valid."

"Christian" parapsychologists cannot understand the conservative Christian's opposition to parapsychology when theologians from Roman Catholic, Protestant, and Jewish liberalism are so open to the idea. They believe such opposition to be uncalled for, and repressive of a search for "truth." What they seem *not* to understand is that conservative Christians oppose the idea of parapsychology simply because they believe the Bible is fully authoritative. They accept what the Bible claims for itself: divine revelation, and hence authority. In this sense they are more honest and consistent than those who "pick and choose" what parts of Scripture they will believe. A high view of Scripture leads one to reject parapsychology, as it also does evolution. A liberal or low view of Scripture can incorporate anything into Christianity, because if the Bible is not *fully* authoritative, we can choose which parts we wish to accept and which we wish to reject. In place of the parts we reject (because they deny what we wish to believe) we can place our own ideas, e.g., evolution, parapsychology, reincarnation, etc.

Declining "Organized Religion"

Parapsychologist theologians bemoan the fact today that while organized religion declines, interest in Eastern religions, cults, and the occult blossoms. They do not seem aware of the fact that to begin with it is often the rejection of biblical authority—and their liberal, dead, theology—that has driven people from the churches in search of a spiritual reality. Denying the power of God and His Word, and therefore dishonoring God, is what reinforces spiritual impotence in liberal churches. The Holy Spirit does not promote lies; He honors the reverent, honest teaching of the Bible as the Word of God. Even while denying biblical authority, some liberal theologians see in parapsychology the hope of infusing spiritual reality into their congregations. However, when they promote psi research as the means to bring back "life and vitality" into their churches, they complain that the conservative church rejects them. They are unable even to think of the possibility that because of their denial of God's Word they have opened themselves to deception by "principalities and powers" (first to drive people from the church into false religions and secondly to bring false religion [the occult] back into the church).

It is surprising today how even "science" is being manipulated. Two recent attacks by Satan on the authority of Scripture have both appealed to scientific proof. The clinical death research of Dr. Moody and others insulates people against biblical salvation and trust in the Bible because of its "scientific" disproof of judgment and the biblical view of death.[2] Similarly, psi research will lead to an occult interpretation of biblical events which nullifies their biblical meaning. No knowledgeable Christian can permit such dismantling of the Gospel, particularly when it is clearly demonic activity behind both attacks. Another example of the dismantling of the Gospel is seen when R. H. Thouless, former President of the Society for Psycical Research, states in light of the reincarnation research of Dr. Ian Stevenson:

> It may be argued that the possibility of reincarnation is not denied by Christian teaching. If reincarnation ever became an assured fact of parapsychology, I think that it could be incorporated into Christian thinking with no more difficulty than was the idea of organic evolution a century ago. This also was an unexpected fact for Christian thinking, but is now generally accepted without alteration of the essentials of Christian belief.[3]

However, reincarnation is just as destructive to biblical authority as is evolution. Both are "incorporated" only by denial of key Christian doctrines: reincarnation is a works system of salvation denying necessity for a savior. If we work off our own karmic debt by many lifetimes, we essentially save ourselves. If Christ has died for *all* of our sins, what is there left to "work off?" Evolution denies that Adam was the first man and that death entered through one man, and makes Christ a liar because he believed that Adam and Eve had been created "in the beginning"—which leaves out hundreds of millions of years of evolution prior to the first "man" (Matt. 19:4). It also makes God state that hundreds of millions of years of death, decay, and struggle were "very good" (Gen. 1:31). Again, the problem here is a refusal to believe in Scripture.

Geoffrey West provides us with an overall view of the Christian parapsychologist's view of Scripture by stating of the cannon of Scripture that "scholars are still sifting the chaff from the wheat. No Christians draw a major part of their total of common sense beliefs from that cannon and would be suspected of obsessional neurosis if they tried to do so."[4] We can go from the general to the specific here in examining Christian parapsychologists' view of Scripture.

A very positive review of Martin Israel's book, *Smouldering Fire: The Work of the Holy Spirit,* is given in the December, 1978 issue of *The Christian Parapsychologist*. They tell us that the Holy Spirit speaks to mankind in non-Christian religions and cultures. Even atheistic humanism, Spiritism, Christian Science, and Theosophy "have the Spirit coursing through them." The Holy Spirit is described as "that divine discontent that drives all creative persons on to their full stature as sons of God" and as "the power that integrates." We find that Jesus may have been simply an occult adept:

> Again, what we call the miracles of Jesus may be neither more nor less than the works of a man who was so perfectly integrated that he had access to forces about which most of us have little knowledge.[5]

Elsewhere we are told that the real modern prophets of the church are mostly liberals and philosophers—Dostoevsky, Kierkegaard, Bonhoffer, and Simone Weil—"And through the true prophet the Holy Spirit brings all men nearer the great day when they will be like Him and see Him face to face."[6] Similarly, a recent conference of the Academy of Religion and Psychical Research discussed numerous occult topics and one speaker, Dr. Ken Wapnick, noted that the mystical "experience of light and love has a name —Jesus—but that no matter what name we give it, we ought to accept and follow this being that speaks to us from within."[7]

The January, 1979, issue of the Journal of the Academy of Religion and Psychical Research carried an article on "The Importance of Psychical Research for Religion." We again see the lowest common denominator of "Christian" parapsychologists: rejection of the Bible and the hope that psychic studies can offer them the very same thing they reject in the Bible: spiritual reality and truth. Of course, they would not necessarily claim to reject the Bible, but only its conservative, "overly rigid" interpretation. The article states:

> Psychical research is profoundly important for religion, for it builds a case for a meaningful survival of bodily death on scientific, as opposed to dogmatic, grounds. For those of us who can no longer base a faith on the "revelation" of a scripture, such news comes as a gospel of extraordinary hopeful tiding.[8]

One need not think too long before recognizing the consequences of such a position.

In general, several statements taken from the literature of Christian parapsychology can help us to see the overall mindset of religious parapsychologists. In Vol. 1, No. 1, of the Academy of Religion and Psychical Research newsletter, there is an article by M. J. McCleave supporting "Christian Mysticism and Kundalini." She states:

> My approach to religion always remained Christian-oriented, but I soon discovered the value of incorporating insights from other areas . . . . I was dissatisfied with theological explanations of the Bible, but not with the Bible itself . . . . Still, I could not understand the meaning of God, Christ, the Holy Spirit, love, good, evil, heaven, and hell, nor could I accept the infallibility of the scriptures.

Her rejection of scriptural authority and openness to "insights" from other areas eventually led her into reading occult books—which she was surprised to find often contained moral injunctions and thoughts of beauty, truth, and love. "The more I read in forbidden books, the more I understood the Bible." Ultimately she ended up having an occult conversion experience (the rising of the kundalini, or serpent power) and interpreted the Bible accordingly. Her article is a classic example of how a person's life—mental, spiritual, and otherwise—can be completely ruined by occult involvement. After psychiatric hospitalization and years of therapy and unnecessary mental and physical suffering (brought on by her occult kundalini experience), she still holds to an occult interpretation of the Bible, which for her justifies her continuing occult activities despite the fact that she repeatedly distorts and perverts the Scriptures. In fact, to Christians who oppose occult investigations, she says, "I can only repeat Christ's words, 'But woe unto you, scribes and pharisees, hypocrites! for ye shut up the kingdom of heaven against men: for ye neither go in yourselves, neither suffer ye them that are entering to go in' (Matt. 23:13)." For her, entrance to "the kingdom" is through parapsychology and occult experiences, and—in her opinion—if you oppose this, you oppose God.

Liberal View of Scripture

Another example is from the influential Episcopal clergyman Morton Kelsey's book, *The Christian and the Supernatural*. As a Jungian psychologist associated with the Catholic charismatic movement, we find his Jungian outlook and openness to spiritual experiences have influenced him to the point of accepting occult experiences as being godly. Virtually all ESP—whether good or evil—is at least potentially a gift from God. Jesus is seen as the ultimate witchdoctor, "greater than all the shamans . . . ." Theologically, his belief that the stories of Jacob, Joseph, Adam and Eve, etc. were symbolic events, points out his liberal view of Scripture.[9]

As a third example, we cite *Parapsychology and the Christian Faith*. Here, we see personal doubts expressed about the Bible: God *apparently* ordered the extermination of the Caananites; hell *apparently* exists forever, etc.[10] The possibility of reincarnation is presented, as well as the implication of universalism, and that God might be encountered *apart* from Christ:

> I believe that some people, maybe many, can have an encounter (a conscious one) with God through Christ in a sequence (or progression) of awarenesses, as we have just mentioned, that leads them to a life-changing experience with God, without their even being consciously aware of who Jesus Christ is, in terms of a formulated doctrine of faith. Christ is the initiator of all genuine spiritual experience [sic]. Whether one is consciously aware of this or not may not be as critical as many Christians believe. The issue is: "What has happened to the entity that has encountered God?" If there is deep and genuine love for God and other persons (even though God may be conceptualized a bit differently), it would seem to be of God's Spirit with Jesus Christ as the initiator of it. Sometimes we may put too much emphasis on the "head" part (formulated doctrine) often to the exclusion of the life God wants us to live. From the continuance of life concept (reincarnation), genuine persons seeking God, will, in this life or another time, meet, know, and accept the One (Christ) leading them in their spiritual journey.[11]

Finally, spiritist minister Archie Matson writes in *Spiritual Frontiers,* the journal of the occult-oriented Spiritual Frontiers Fellowship, "As long as we take the whole Bible as literally true it will continue to shackle free study of many basic questions."[12] He states that the Bible "is the biggest religious obstacle to the study and understanding of the life beyond death," and that certain false interpretations of it "have largely shackled progress in all forms of psychic research among Christian people." Of course, since he and other in SFF wish to study and/or become mediums, they *must* throw out God's Word as being "an obstacle" to them. This they do, with ease and sometimes relish.

We must end this section by noting that to a large extent it has been the impact of liberal scholarship which has provided Christian parapsychologists with the intellectual and theological justifications for rejecting those passages they wish to reject and retaining and/or reinterpreting those passages they wish to use to justify their occult involvement. For example, E. Garth Moore, in *Try the Spirits,* states that in quoting biblical verses, "It is not to be thought they are all of the same weight. The differing conclusions of a host of biblical scholars are not to be ignored, when it comes to assessing the reliability and relative weight of different passages."[3] Thus, for example, they feel that the spiritistic ban in Deuteronomy is ethnographically and culturally conditioned and is irrelevant today.

To the Bible-believing Christian, however, it is still relevant to accept ALL Scripture as inspired of God (II Tim. 3:16). After all, this is the view of their Lord, Jesus Christ. (See John Wenham, *Christ and the Bible.)*

References for Chapter 27

1. Leslie Price, "The Role of the Christian Parapsychologist" *The Christian Parapsychologist*, Vol. 1, No. 1, p. 11.
2. See Weldon, *Is There Life After Death?* and Johnson and Weldon, *Parapsychology: Scientific Study of the Occult*, (forthcoming)
3. *The Christian Parapsychologist*, June 1977, p. 116.
4. *The Christian Parapsychologist*, December 1978, p. 12.
5. *Ibid.*, p. 16.
6. *The Christian Parapsychologist*, September 1977, p. 139.
7. *The Academy of Religion and Psychical Research Newsletter*, Vol. 1, No. 2, p. 22.
8. L. Stafford Betty, p. 5, *Journal of the Academy of Religion and Psychical Research*, Jan. 1979, p. 5.
9. Kelsey, *The Christian and the Supernatural*, p. 164-5.
10. Cluff, *op. cit.*, p. 89-91.
11. Cluff, *op. cit.*, p. 86.
12. Matson, "The Bible Shackle or Spur," *Spiritual Frontiers*, Spring 1972.
13. E. Moore, *Try the Spirits*, (NY: Oxford Univ. Press) 1977, p. viii.

Chapter 28

The Impact of "Christian" Parapsychology

Basically, Christian parapsychologists are theologically liberal occultists, *not* Christians. Parapsychology is eminently well suited for transforming liberal ministers and laymen into "Christian" occultists. It provides the necessary connecting link between the two worldviews. The problem is that a step has been taken backward, not forward.

Liberal . . . to Occult

Parapsychology does not lead a liberal minister to a conservative view of Scripture, but rather to an occult view. The unbelief remains, but now, in addition, people are "helped" in the name of Christ to be opened up to the occult. On the surface, a liberal theologian who is converted to a psychic theologian may appear to trust in Scripture more, but the issue is *how* he believes in it "more." Let us give two illustrations:

1. Whereas before, his universalism was somewhat vague undefined, he may now hold to a "more concrete" mediumistic view—that the dead progress to various levels and can communicate with us whenever we call on them. Psychic research has lent a great deal of

"credibility" to this view, so this is the framework into which his new interpretation of Scripture is placed. The communion of the saints (actually tradition, not Scripture), is now more real and believable. Since, to a liberal, just about everyone is a saint, just about anyone is acceptable in spirit contact. However, the biblical view of death remains in unbelief, i.e., that it brings eternal judgment.

2. Before the input of Christian parapsychology, the liberal's view of Jesus was also somewhat muddled—a great man, exceptional teacher, possibly semi-"divine," but His miracles were always a problem. However, after assessing Christ in light of the findings of Christian parapsychology, we are now supposed to believe He was only a man Who had great psychic insight into the workings of unknown natural laws and was able to use these laws to perform his "miracles"—and that what He was, each of us can become if we develop the same knowledge (gnosis) of psi that he had—that is, if we study the occult and develop our psychic powers. Yet the biblical view of Christ—the second Person of the God-head Who performed violations of natural law (miracles)—remains in unbelief. We must remember that for the psychic theologian or minister who still has to maintain his respectability, studying the "scientific psychic evidence" is a far cry from "primitive occult involvement." Of course, as "Christians," they would never urge their congregation to study the occult. *Occult study is, we know, entirely different from the scientific findings of parapsychology—or so they would have us believe!*

Discovering New Vistas?

We could go on with other examples—how Satan still remains hidden, despite accomplishing his will; how demonic involvement is *seen as* discovering exciting new vistas of the mind of man and his world; how psychic powers are viewed as gifts of the Holy Spirit; etc. However, the ultimate impact of Christian parapsychology is to keep the person in unbelief while simultaneously achieving two victories: (1) opening them to the occult; and (2) making them think they are now true believers in Scripture with an accurate "scientific" and modern interpretation. Considering the implications for Scripture and people, it would require the devil himself to pull off such a subtle transformation.

It is alleged that the Bible, once held to be worthless to varying degrees, now "comes alive" when viewed with a psychic interpretation; that prayer is meaningful because psi has demonstrated that mind can reach mind (God, as usual, is left in the background, or, if considered, is usually only an impersonal force); that dying no longer leads to nonexistence—that the dying people can be comforted by the glimpse of the beyond provided by psi (occult) research —a glorious universalism.

United Church of Christ minister George W. Fish relates how parapsychology revitalized his Christian life. From a troubled materialist who did not know what to believe, he came to an occult view incorporating a new trust (actually a new interpretation) in Scripture that opened him to the guidance of the dead:

> From almost no belief in heaven, I have come to a deep conviction in the spiritual world that is as close as breathing. I am not only buoyed up by my friends in the beyond . . . . I am convinced that others both in this world and the next can reach us in dreams.

"Higher Powers of the Mind"

In speaking of the higher psi powers of the mind, he states:

> To begin to recognize that we have these higher powers of the mind and to begin to use them for the service of God, is a revelation and will open new doors for the pursuit of our ministry. One of the greatest joys that has now come into my life is to work with others—clergy and lay persons alike—to open up the too-long dormant abilities. To become open as a channel for the

operation of the Holy Spirit . . . .[1]

This is exactly the view endorsed by the Spiritual Frontiers Fellowship. The SFF was founded by the trance medium Arthur Ford. Ironically, it was Paramahansa Yogananda, founder of the Self Realization Fellowship (which reinterprets Christianity into Hinduism) who talked Ford into becoming a medium rather than a minister. The entire purpose of the SFF is to integrate an occult worldview into Christianity—exactly the impact parapsychology is having. Thus, psychic powers are seen as the biblical gifts of the Holy Spirit, which results in people exercising demonic gifts *thinking* they are from God.

Two Christian Parapsychological Societies: The Spiritual Frontiers Fellowship and The Churches Fellowship for Psychical and Spiritual Studies

An examination of these organizations will indicate that spiritual warfare is involved in the workings of Christian Parapsychology. Before discussing SFF and the CFPSS, we wish to make it very clear that these are occult organizations being used by Satan to infiltrate the church with occultism. There can be no compromise with this position. For years, we have watched the destruction brought into lives and churches as a result of these and similar "Christian" psychic organizations. Those who promote or advocate Christian Parapsychology should be counseled, and, if not repentant, they should be removed from the church for the sake of the body.

Unfortunately, since the impact of evolution, clerical involvement in psychic research has been extensive. One discussion giving some idea of the extent of involvement is found in F. Nicol's "Clerical Contributions to Parapsychology."[2] He states: "A history of clerical activity in parapsychology would fill volumes," and notes that the four chief founders of the SPR (Society for Psychical Research)—Sir William Barrett, Edmund Gurney, F. W. H. Myers, and Henry Sidgwick—were all sons of clergymen. His article indicates the fraternization with mediumship among numerous clergy who jumped on the parapsychological bandwagon.

The S.F.F.

The SFF was founded in 1956, and its bimonthly journal is *Spiritual Frontiers*.

Our intent here is to briefly document the occult nature of this organization, so that true Christians will not be misled by its Christian veneer. Their Membership Application form discusses their interests: "Spiritual Healing . . . Prayer and Meditation . . . Psychic Communication and Survival . . . and Psychic Research . . . as a means to Spiritual Development."

The 8,000 member SFF was founded by Rev. Paul L. Higgins; Albin and Margueritte Bro, a psychic healer and spiritist respectively; the famous trance medium, Arthur Ford; and psychic researcher, Alson J. Smith. Although SFF disclaims an interest in mediumship and in creating individual psychics, one could not tell this from researching their organization and history. SFF conferences are full of lectures on occultism, many by mediums and psychics. Mediums such as Ruth Montgomery, as well as other psychics, urge individuals who want to develop their psychic powers to join SFF.[3] A statement by Founder Paul Higgins is used in its introductory brochure, "Spiritual Frontiers Fellowship," as exemplifying a central element of SFF:

> We know in whom we believe, Jesus Christ, our Lord. We know that we live after death. We know that the communion of saints is a reality, for many of us have been in direct contact with the spirits of the departed. We know that Christ retains His power to heal, for we have seen the mentally, spiritually, and physically sick made whole in His name. We know that prayer is the greatest power of all and that we can be linked effectively through prayer with God and all the company of heaven.
>
> We want Spiritual Frontiers Fellowship to

spread this good news as we work within the Church we love. We pray for God's blessing, that our work might abound, knowing that "our labor is not in vain in the Lord" (I Corinthians 15:58).[4]

"Not Everyone Who Says to Me, 'Lord, Lord'!"

In considering SFF's deliberate rejection of the biblical view of occult and spiritistic practices, as well as their profession of Christ, we cannot help but be reminded of Matthew 7:21-23:

> Not everyone who says to me "Lord, Lord," will enter the kingdom of heaven; but he who does the will of my father who is in heaven. Many will say to me on that day, "Lord, Lord, did we not prophesy in your name and in your name cast out demons and in your name perform many miracles?" And then I will declare to them, I never knew you, depart from me, you who practice lawlessness.

In their brochure, "Spiritual Frontiers Fellowship—Its Principles, Purposes, and Program," they declare they are a Christian organization—close to the fundamentals of New Testament Christianity—and that they accept the insights of modern (and destructive) biblical criticism "as gifts of God." They believe God is still speaking today, that "the doors of revelation are never closed." They stress the validity of psychic gifts and that the purpose of SFF "is to bring them back into the life of the church." Finally, they believe SFF has been "called by God for such a time as this."

Interestingly, according to Arthur Ford, the principal founder of SFF, the man most responsible for the idea of SFF was Dr. Sherwood Eddy, internationally famous for his work with the YMCA.[5] His book, *You Will Survive Death,* a result of 13 years research into occultism, according to Ford "had a tremendous impact on Christian laymen and clergymen throughout America."

An examination of the literature of SFF as it relates to

mediumism clearly shows its allegiance, despite claims to the contrary. They have had a history of support of mediumship from the beginning. For example, note a sampling of articles from *Spiritual Frontiers:*

Vol. 1 No. 3 (1969)	"Techniques for the Study of Mediumship"
Vol. 3 No. 1 (1971)	"In Defense of the Witch of Endor"
Vol. 6 No. 3 (1974)	"The Findings of the SFF Survival Research Questionnaire"
Vol. 8 No. 1 (1976)	"Research in Mediumship"
Vol. 12 No. 1 (1980)	"Does the New Testament Teach Communion with Spirits?" (Yes!)

In the last article, J. S. Setzer presents a view that Jesus was an advanced mystic shaman (witchdoctor); angels are (mediumistic) spirit messengers from a higher plane; the Holy Spirit "may well be a spirit guide similar to those given to other mediums, although Jesus' spirit guide is apparently from an extraordinarily high plane of light and power;" the Father, according to Jesus, is "the archangel who is responsible for all life on earth;" Peter, James, and John have spirit counsellors; when Jesus told his disciples to pray for the paraclete, he meant "a holy spirit-guide similar to the one Jesus received at his baptism (John 4:16) who will be sent upon request. And there is no reason in the Gospels themselves to keep us from viewing this as a prayer for the spirit guide acclaimed by spiritualism as so helpful in healing and spirit rescue work." Also, the last supper in the upper room was a seance; refusing to receive a spirit guide is the blasphemy against the holy spirit, which has no forgiveness. He concludes, "In fact, viewed from the largest perspective, communication with the dead is everything that the New Testament is about." For Setzer, the New Testament is grossly misinterpreted as being merely a guidebook for mediumistic phenomena. Dr. Setzer was the author of *What's Left to Believe?* (Abingdon, 1968), and in a letter written the day before his death, he stated, "I am much more spiritistic now, having delved deeply into parapsychology since I wrote the book" (p. 4). Setzer's entire approach is refuted very simply by noting that Jesus Christ was a conservative Jew who, as such, held to the divine inspiration of the entire Old Testament. This is proved by a study of his quotes of it and statements about it. Also he interpreted it in a literal, normal sense (e.g., He believed in a real, directly created physical Adam and Eve who were the parents of all mankind—Matt. 19:4). He said of the entire Old Testament, in a prayer to God, "Thy Word is Truth" (John 17:17). He called the words of Moses Scripture, or to a Jew, the Word of God (Lk. 16:29-31; 24:27, 44, 45). Hence, Jesus had to believe in the condemnations of spiritism in Leviticus, Deuteronomy, etc. (Lev. 19:26, 31; 20:6, 27; Ex. 22:18; Deut. 18:9-12). Setzer, along with the SFF, simply does not want to accept the words of Jesus. In light of all this, SFF's claim that it is *not* spiritistic or mediumistic is incredible. Those who wish to read a converted medium's testimony as to medium's misuse of Scripture should read Gasson's *The Challenging Counterfeit*.

A Defense for Spiritism?

Two of the SFF apologetic papers against the biblical teachings on mediumism are typical of their attempts to justify their occult activities. In "The Biblical Prohibition in Deuteronomy" (publication M-3 of the CFPSS—the Center for Psychic and Spiritual Studies is the sister organization of the SFF), Rev. John Mac Donald presents the "right motive" theory. If spirits seek us out, "we would be doing less than our moral duty if we did not inquire into this. It is *how* we do so that matters" (p.9). "The things of prime interest to the Churches Fellowship (for Psychical and Spiritual studies) are not referred to in Deuteronomy, except possibly for the matter of a consultation with the familiar spirit" (p.9).

He goes on to leave a way out for members who wish to engage in spiritism, while trying to wrestle with what the Scripture plainly states. The Rev. J.D. Pearce-Higgins is more bold in his "The Church and Psychical Research" (publication M-5 of the CFPSS). He states, "But the Deuteronomic writer does not forbid seeking for guidance from a medium . . ." (p.6), and that even if it meant forbidding all contact with the dead "is there any reason why we today should be bound by it anymore than we are bound by other regulations in the Book?" (p. 7).

Yet this same "minister" admits, "We have had distressing cases of people becoming obsessed, and even possessed by pursuing such communication" (p. 7). He ends the article with, "Let us lay aside the sin that doth so easily beset us, and run with patience the race that is set before us, looking unto Jesus, the author and perfector of our faith." Such is the extent of deception possible when human and Satanic rebellion intermingle.

Still NOT a Gift of the Holy Spirit

One example of how SFF has infiltrated even conservative Christian ranks is the book *Rediscovering the Gift of Healing,* by Lawrence Althouse. It can be found in many Christian bookstores. Yet Althouse is a former national president of the SFF. In his book, which seeks to bring his concepts of healing into the Church, he tells us how spiritist Olga Worrall (whose healing ministry he supports) was the one who told him he had the gift of healing, and to start healing services in his church (p.24). (Mediums are often psychically sensitive to others who have psychic potential.) Coming from a position of disbelief in the Bible (p. 19), he did not know what to make of the request. However, through attending this medium's services and accepting her encouragement, he now believes his ministry is to bring the gift of "healing" back to the Church.

Can we in any sense believe that a man who supports mediumistic healing has a gift from the Holy Spirit? He says of those who suspect that Satan may heal through him, or even heal at all, "Well-meaning or not, these people are dangerous to others and to themselves" (p. 90). We personally doubt this man's "gift" being from God, yet churches everywhere have accepted him as a charismatic healer.

It is a sign of the times.

The Churches' Fellowship for Psychical and Spiritual Studies

The CFPSS is the sister organization of the SFF, and its journal is *The Christian Parapsychologist,* published quarterly.

In reading the dozen plus issues of *The Christian Parapsychologist,* we find a strong support of mediumism expressed by several of its writers, Edwin W. Butler, Barrie Colvin, and others, that some are psychics (John Mac Donald), and that, like SFF, there is a consistent attempt to infiltrate churches with the occult, all for its own good, of course. The same approach to Scripture is evident that the cultist uses—improper and biased interpretation through ignorance of cultural factors; a selective use of Scriptures usually taken out of context to support their position, while disregarding the rest; etc.

It is surprising, however, to see those claiming (sincerely) to be Christians giving so much weight to those whose revelations have consistently and venemously attacked Christianity, i.e., the mediums. While Scripture tells us to be separate from the deeds of darkness of unbelievers, the SFF and SFPSS are eagerly uniting with occultists. In separating themselves from true believers and joining themselves to occultists, they have fulfilled the Apostle John's statement to the gnostics:

> They went out from us, but they were not really of us, for if they had been of us, they would have remained with us; but they went out, in order that it might be shown that they all are not of us (I John 2:19).

A Case in Point

Rev. John MacDonald, Professor of Hebrew and Semitic Languages at the University of Glasgow has a three-part analysis, "The Deuteronomic Condemnation of Pagan Occult Practices" published in *The Christian Para-*

psychologist, (1976). In complete disregard of the facts, he concludes:

> Finally, how do we evaluate our eight categories of practitioners (in Deut. 18:10-12) in terms of modern parapsychological studies? There can be no doubt that the practitioners involved in our Deuteronomy passage have no connection, in practice of ideology with the modern psychic —and particularly the Christian psychic. Today's psychic expresses "natural" abilities God made in him . . . we can rule out any connection between the parapsychological activities of today and the sorceries of long ago.

Such a naive and irresponsible statement neglects the fact that the modern occultist, whether he be a psychic, medium, or "sensitive," is essentially the same as his historical and ancient counterpart. The source, phenomena, general methodology, general worldview, impact, and consequences of occultism are the same whether modern or ancient.[6] The only real difference involves cultural variables, e.g., the ancient mediums (shamans) openly admit cavorting with spirits; the modern sensitive may view his activities as his own "higher self." Anyone who denies this very clear fact of the essential historical unity of occultism has either not studied occult history or has a bias to uphold.

Even though God has plainly said that such practices were "an abomination" to Him, the Rev. MacDonald states, "We would not express our warning in these terms . . . . In our darkest action we [all men] are never abominable to Him, because He is love. Love cannot abominate" (See John 8:47).

Demonism . . . and God's Wrath

Such a naive, simplistic, and mushy view of both demonism and God's wrath speaks for itself. The logical consequences are again evident as MacDonald goes on to urge occult studies to the glory of God:

> The last word, at the practical level, is that for

such Christian organizations as the Churches'
Fellowship for Psychical and Spiritual Studies
or Spiritual Frontiers Fellowship, all research in
the parapsychological sphere must be intended
to widen and deepen our experience of God.[7]

In somewhat the same manner, the Love Family (Children of God) teach that fornication widens their love and experience of God; or The Native American Church makes a similar claim for drugs; and sub-Christian cults adopt Eastern meditation and yoga (which may cause temporary insanity) as the path to wide and deepen their experience of God. Spiritual destruction is the eventual result, but it is all in the name of "spiritual growth."

Christians *must* take a firm stand on Christian parapsychology. Biblically, there can be no such entity. It is demonism in a religious cloak. Christian parapsychology journals are full of occultism. Just as there can be no "dialogue" (i.e., openness) to Christian-Marxism, and there *should be* no compromise with the idea of evolution, there *must* be no openness to "Christian" parapsychology. In each case the full authority of Scripture is compromised, and the short and long-term effects have been devastating.

Also, in talking with "Christian" parapsychologists, we need to be careful not to be misunderstood. If Christians who are attempting to be "reasonable" and not "closed minded" in potentially unknown areas (and what of demonism is not at least partially unknown?), leave an open door for what is basically Satanic, the "Christian" parapsychologists can use this to justify the correctness of their position of psychic exploration. In contrast, an uncompromising view leaves them with a clear decision to make and no possibility of walking the fence. Otherwise, in the name of scientific objectivity and human curiosity, they will be reinforced to explore those unknown areas.

While it can be difficult to know at what point one might become unproductive in reaching someone for Christ, that is "becoming all things to all men," as Paul put it, we feel certain issues must not be compromised at all. For example, had Christians done this with evolution, and not made a totally unnecessary capitulation, many people would have retained a belief in the historicity of Genesis 1-3. Likewise, some Christian TV networks do not like to mention by name certain antibiblical groups like Mormons and Jehovah's Witnesses (in a critical light) for fear of alienating members of that group, lest they turn off the Gospel and not be saved. That is a perfectly fine motive, and there is some truth to it, but our responsibility is also to the *believer,* not just to the unbeliever. Knowledgeable cult members reject the Gospel anyway. It would seem more important to sometimes warn the "sheep," rather than to have a fear of offending unbelievers, even deliberate heretics. In the same way, in so-called "Christian" parapsychology, most will continue to engage in it because they want to, and will refuse to believe it could be Satanic. We should not undercut the necessity for an uncompromising presentation of truth. But if a door is "left open" in "unknown areas" by evangelicals, as perhaps being open to exploration, are we potentially either causing the sheep confusion or perhaps even leading them astray?

References for Chapter 28

1. The Journal of the Academy of Religion and Psychical Research, Vol. 2, No. 1 (Jan. 1979), p. 16.
2. *International Journal of Parapsychology,* Spring 1966.
3. Ruth Montgomery, *A World Beyond,* last page.
4. Rev. William V. Rauscher, "Spiritual Frontiers Fellowship," *Psychic* Magazine, Sept.-Oct. 1970.
5. A Ford, *Unknown but Known* (NY: Harper & Row) 1968, p. 78.
6. A book such as Michlove's *The Roots of Consciousness* clearly shows this continuity.
7. John Macdonald "The Deuteronomic Condemnation of Pagan Occult Practices Part 3: Implications and Evaluations" *The Christian Parapsychologist,* Vol. 1, No. 5, Sept. 1976, p. 61-62.

Chapter 29

Discernment is Lacking About "Christian Parapsychology"

Christian discernment in the area of the psychic needs to be strengthened. The books currently published on the topic from a Christian perspective are either outright supporters of the occult or are often too accepting in certain supposedly "borderline" areas.

Some Books About the Christian's Involvement in Parapsychology

One example is well-known Christian writer (Seventh Day Adventist) Rene Noorbergen, who has written two books on occult subjects. His book with Jeane Dixon, the million seller *My Life and Prophecies,* was responsible for informing and deceiving tens of thousands of people about her. She is not a prophetess or woman of God. She is an occultist who uses Christian terminology, but who supports the use of astrology, reincarnation, crystal balls, psychic visions, inner voices, ESP, etc.

In his preface, Noorbergen hints that psychic abilities may be "a restoration of something God endowed mankind with at the time of creation," that is, neutral abilities. According to his note and prologue to the book, he believes in and supports Jeane Dixon as a prophetess of

God for the Church.

His second book, *You Are Psychic: The Incredible Story of David N. Bubar,* is another book in support of the occult. One of its premises is that psychic power is available to anyone who wishes to use it, and that it should be used. Any Christian author who actively supports occultists like Dixon and Bubar should be viewed with caution, for they are not maturing the Church or glorifying God. Unfortunately, Noorbergen is deceiving many. What would Paul's reaction have been? or Jesus'? For the record, both Dixon and Bubar have, biblically, proven themselves false prophets. (Simply stated, according to the Bible, we know they are *true* prophets if their prophecies *come true.*) Dixon's false prophecies are a matter of record.[1] Bubar falsely predicted that by 1977, "A highly developed form of life" would be discovered in outer space: "Within the next sixty months [the book was published in 1971], we will discover that a highly developed form of life exists in outer space and *has* existed there for a long time. I don't know the names of the planets involved, but I have seen this extraterrestrial life and know we will find facts that will verify this" (p. 168).

A Report from the United Presbyterian Church

Another examle of limited discernment is from the United Presbyterian Church's 1976 "Report on Occult and Psychic Activities," prepared by the Advisory Council on Discipleship and Worship. The report is entirely too accepting of psychic research. Parapsychology is not defined as occult and demonic, which it is, but as "an intelligent and concerned study of psychic phenomena as it relates to the well being of the total person" (p.7). Perhaps its acceptance of the occult was due to the fact that they appointed SFF cofounder (and medium), Mrs. Margueritte Harmon Bro as one of the seven to serve on the Task Force.[2] How many of the other Task Force members were open to the psychic is anyone's guess.

The seven guidelines they recommend for pastors and **laymen concerned with questions and problems about the** psychic realm basically leave the door open for Christians to develop an interest in the occult—and even to develop psychic powers. Amazingly, the report also encourages "study of these phenomena within the churches" (p. 3). The appendix to the report on representative literature gives no discernment when reviewing occult books, and even gives favorable reviews of the medium Olga Worrall's book, *The Gift of Healing*. A paper used by the Task Force in its final assessment was *The Psychic and Occult Challenge to the Church,* by Rev. John Foss. In that paper psychic research and parapsychology are labeled as "benign;" ESP self-help programs, meditational groups and demonology are labeled as "neutral," the medium Edgar Cayce is referred to as "a continuing enigma" with no warning given of his clearly demonic contacts; and a favorable review is given to Dechanet's book, *Christian Yoga*. H. L. Cayce's book, *Venture Inward* (which supports mediumism as "a safe doorway to the occult"), is "desperately needed" because of its "positive suggestions for helpful directions that can be taken," etc. When the Presbyterian Church uses such literature rather than Scripture in forming its assessments, it is responsible for bringing occult bondage into the lives of its members.

Four Books Supporting Mediumism

Four of the six standard books seeking to relate Christianity and parapsychology also support mediumism, to one degree or another. A thorough analysis and refutation of their individual argumentation in support of the psychic will have to wait for a future study. However, in documenting their support of spiritism, it will at least be very clear in which camp they place themselves. There is much more in these books which needs refutation; unfortunately space does not permit it here. We can only document their support of mediumism.

Charles Cluff, Director of the Family Counseling service in Merced, California, states in his *Parapsychology and the Christian Faith:*

> If an outside entity comes to you, be open to

> it . . . if the "messages" are good and for the good of all mankind, the entity may be a messenger from God. If messages are selfish and just for personal gain, it may not be (p.66).

This assessment ignores the fact that the vast majority of appearances of demons to people involve moralistic and humanitarian messages, as former mediums turned Christian have testified, e.g., Victor Ernst in his *I Talked With Spirits.* While condemning some mediumship, he leaves the door wide open for the "Christian" spiritist movement: "What if the medium loved God, felt called by God, sought him and obeyed him, and [by contrast, a] prophet followed his own evil intents? Then the medium would possibly be the true prophet of God and the prophet false" (p.67). What such a view overlooks is that *by definition* a medium disobeys God by *being* a medium (Deut. 18:9-12). Further, what of Jonah vs. the medium Saul used? Was Jonah ever a false prophet even though he followed his own evil intents, or was the spiritist of Endor ever a prophetess of God? The issue here is that mediums are *never* to be consulted. Anyone who truly loves God will not become a medium. If they do, it is evidence that, far from loving Him, they disregard and hate Him, by willfully practicing what He has said is an abomination to Him, worthy of death. (See Lev. 19:26, 31; Ex 22:18; Lev. 20:6, 27; Zech. 10:2; Ezek. 13:9; I Sam. 15:23; Jere. 27:9.) This is true regardless of how often they *claim* to love Him.

Cluff's book is dangerous because it gives a qualified acceptance of occultism to Christians. Besides mediumism, he seems to support astrology, palm reading, TM. Edgar Cayce ("a very dedicated Christian"), and advocates reading occult books (pp. 36-7, 42, 56-7, 81-2).

The second book advocating spiritism for Christians is E. Garth Moore's *Try the Spirits: Christianity and Psychical Research*. Moore is President of the Churches' Fellowship for Psychical and Spiritual Studies. His chapter on "Mediumship and Seances" is entirely supportive. "The activities of mediums are, however, also of interest to psychical researchers . . ." (p. 21). "But a God-fearing modern medium is not to be equated to the fraudulent medium condemned in Deuteronomy, Chapter 18 . . . our God-given talents, whatever they be, should be used to the glory of God who has given them" (p. 114). This argument is common to many Christian parapsychologists: They claim that "godly" mediumship is not condemned in Scripture, only fraudulent mediumship. Again, however, they simply refuse to believe what the Bible says and use it to support their own rebellion and sorcery. The Bible makes no such distinctions.

Arthur Ford's Spirit Guide

Our third example involves H. Richard Neff, Pastor of the Christian Community Presbyterian Church of Bowie, Maryland, the author of *Psychic Phenomena and Religion*. He attended seances by Arthur Ford and even received Fletcher's (the spirit-guide) advice on his own ministry (p. 117). Of a personal friend (a medium), he states:

> In my opinion, she is a sincere Christian, devoted to Christ and his church" (p. 167).

He also states, "Occult practices . . . may be beneficial and helpful for many people" (p. 166).

Because he believes in the "limited condemnation" theory (that biblical prohibition against spiritism relates only to fraudulent mediums), he advocates mediumism for others (pp. 166-7, 130-1, etc.). He says, "I cannot personally believe that all or even a major portion of parapsychology is a work of the devil" (p. 165). His view that "Holy Spirit trances" and mediumistic trances are indistinguishable and that the goodness of either must depend on the fruit borne, needs little comment (pp. 166-7). The devil produces a great deal of *seemingly* good fruit to naive people. The fruit of occultism is the support of occultism —by whatever means.

Finally, in our fourth example, Morton T. Kelsey, an Episcopal clergyman and professor at Notre Dame, has written a volume in support of the occult, in *The Christian and the Supernatural*. The book has no discernment and supports a wide variety of occult practices for Christians:

"Another way of coming into contact with the realm which mediums reach is by using a ouija board . . . they often supply amazing insights and even information" (p. 71-2).

The above books should hardly be placed in Christian bookstores. Some of their argumentation will tend to confuse Christians about the occult. We suspect these authors have no idea of the harm they have done, but even so, each is held accountable. Hopefully they will revise their position in accordance with God's Word and will begin to counteract some of the damage they have perpetrated in the Name of Christ. Hard or soft-peddling of the occult is nothing to gloss over. It must be called what it is and condemned.

A Point of Caution

Two basic evangelical assessments of psychic phenomena are by J. Stafford Wright: *Mind, Man, and the Spirits* (1955) and *Christianity and the Occult* (1971). There is no doubt as to Canon Stafford Wright's trust in Scripture. In fact, he provides an excellent refutation of the linguistic arguments of Christian parapsychologists who attempt to circumvent the Deuteronomic prohibitions.[3] However, there are a few aspects of his thought which we feel need to be viewed with caution. One of the consequences of accepting the validity of parapsychological research and its findings is that ideas or concepts may then be based upon it. If the findings are later not confirmed by other experimentation (nearly always true), those ideas and concepts may be found useless or even harmful. For example, J. B. Rhine's research *seemed* to indicate that everyone had latent psi. Although subsequent experiments have failed to confirm this, Rhine's experiments made Wright opt for a universal psi theory (1971, pp. 75-6; 1955, p. 44). Not unexpectedly, this has influenced some of his ideas on parapsychology. It is regrettable that some aspects of his book must be strongly rejected because of the possible impact his borderline stance might have upon Christians, most of whom are very unknowledgeable about the psychic realm. Even with knowledge of it, it can be difficult to discern properly.

Sadly, many Christians are entirely too gullible. Witness the destruction and division wrought by the thousands who were/are deceived by John Todd. (For documentation of his deceptions, see *The Todd Phenomenon: Fact or Phantasy?* by Hicks and Lewis, New Leaf Press, Harrison, Ark.)

With an overly open attitude to spiritual and miraculous events so often seen in the charismatic movement, we feel a stronger stand needs to be taken than Canon Wright has given. The psychic realm has too many unknowns—which are potential traps for Christians—to risk having anything other than an entirely negative attitude toward it. Some areas of concern from Stafford Wright's writings are as follows. Unless indicated otherwise, all references are from his 1971 book.

Wright accepts the idea of an entirely neutral psychic force whereby such events as water-divining (or dowsing), and neutral psychic healing take place (p. 94-5; 101-3; 151): "We postulate, then, a realm and activity of psychic force, whereby, without introducing the intervention of spirit beings, some people can project an invisible influence beyond the reach of their physical senses. It may be that in turn they can receive an inflow from other individuals and also from a force that permeates the universe" (p. 101).

No Entirely Neutral Psychic Force

For reasons given elsewhere, we believe that no entirely neutral psychic force exists. All truly supernatural phenomena come from God or Satan.[4] If it were neutral and universally latent, why cannot everyone dowse or heal? Regarding dowsing, a perusal of the literature indicates it is heavily tied to occultism (e.g., pendulums), and that the ability to dowse come from the *person*—not the *stick*. Even Dr. Koch initially gave warnings in this area, although he recognized there was disagreement among evangelicals.[5] Further research has convinced him it is an occult power.[6] Like him, we have encountered Christians who believe in and use this ability as a natural gift from God. However, Scripture seems to warn against it. This is what we read at Hosea 4:12:

> My people consult their wooden idol, and their diviner's wand informs them; for a spirit of harlotry has led them astray, and they have played the harlot, departing from their God. [NASB—The Hebrew word translated wood or staff in other translations can mean a wandering rod cut from a forked branch.]

Stafford Wright states, on the other hand:

> A gift like water divining has no connection with spirits, and I see no reason why it should not be used for the good of mankind. It is probably an unusual, but natural sensitivity to radiations" (p. 151).

We find similar problems with a concept of neutral psychic healing. Wright uses the example of medium Edgar Cayce's supporter and universalist,[7] Agnes Sanford (a very popular writer among charismatics):

> Moreover there are people who have a natural (i.e., neither of God or Satan) gift of healing. Often they project healing through the laying on of their hands. Some patients who have been helped by such healers as Agnes Sanford have been aware of a feeling of warmth passing into their body from the healer's hands. Like every natural capacity, this gift should be put into the hands of God to use as He prompts; but only too often it becomes linked to spiritualism.[8]

Hands Up and Down the Body

However, Dr. Koch provides a more sobering assessment: while clearly advocating the biblical practice of James 5, he notes that "unhappily, there are many cases, too, which illustrate how dangerous the laying on of hands can be when administered by occultly oppressed Christian workers."[9] Elsewhere he states of healing mesmerism (using hand passes up and down the body): "Although certain Christian workers believe that some types of healing mesmerism are dependent on neutral, rather than mediumistic, powers, I would say that I have personally hardly ever come across a neutral form. Many years of experience in this field have shown me that even in the case of Christian mesmerizers the basic mediumship has always come to surface in the end."[10] While leaving open the possibility of a very few cases of weak natural healing magnetism, he also states:

> There are many people, particularly in the Far East, who are able to cure or to help people suffering from headaches, rheumatism, and arthritis by making stroking movements over them with their hands, but whenever I have come across a person who possesses this gift, I have always found that either his parents, grandparents, or great-grandparents have dabbled in magic or spiritism. For this reason, even in the case of natural magnetism, I am not altogether happy with its use . . . .
>
> There is a terrible error being propagated in the world today whereby demonic healings, because of the Christian facade behind which they take place, are being claimed as charismatic miracles. One minister wrote me a furious letter claiming that his ability to use a pendulum was a gift from God, and as such had to be used for the benefit of mankind. It was unthinkable for him to believe that mediumistic healings are basically occult and not charismatic in character."[11]

Wright states that, "If God wishes to use any man's latent psychic force, He will naturally do so. We only run into trouble when we try to manipulate it for ourselves" (p. 102). But, how is someone to determine just who it is using this psychic force? Can a man distinguish the source behind *invisible* energy? Are warm feelings enough? Many appearance of demons surround a person with intense feelings of love, joy, and peace. If they can induce such emotions, or exude such vibrations, how can we distinguish?

In *Mind, Man, and the Spirits,* Wright says of occult forces:

> The Christian accepts that there are psychic forces that may be unleashed by those who understand the technique. The thing that is uncertain is the legitimacy of unleashing these forces deliberately . . . (p.99).

First, in our minds there is no uncertainty whatsoever. Second, how are evil psychic forces to be distinguished from natural psychic forces? What of the many people like Edgar Cayce who honestly wanted to use their psychic powers for good, but brought such destruction and evil as a result that the toll is uncountable? What of the thousands of people who have a hereditary predisposition to the occult or psychic from the sins of their forebears? How are they to distinguish neutral psi from demonic psi, particularly when most of them have no idea of occult involvement in their family history? To advocate the concept of a neutral psychic force, in a world where Satan is its god and man is fallen, has so many consequential implications that we had best be absolutely certain before even thinking of advocating such a view. To then rely upon the dubious research of parapsychology is insufficient and unwise, as we have earlier indicated.

The Dead CANNOT Return

Wright accepts the idea that the dead can return, although he does not advocate communication with them in seances (pp. 138, 143-5). Tied to this is what we call a "delayed judgment" theory. If the true dead can return, they are not immediately judged. Here he appears to have taken the weight of psychic research into apparitions too seriously. He is too accepting of stories which can initially appear nondemonic, but, as we have often found, ultimately are shown to be demonic. One problem with the delayed-judgment apparitions theory is that it tends to confirm the mediumistic view that spirits are floating around and can freely interact with our dimension.

Wright implies that if no medium is present and a dead

person appears, it may really be that dead person. This ignores the fact that demons commonly impersonate the dead via apparitions, with no connection at all to seances or mediums. If demons impersonate the dead in seances, why should they not do so outside of seances? Psychic literature is full of such examples, and the result to the contacted person is usually to confirm the mediumistic view of life after death, rather than the biblical view. We have given Scriptural reasons elsewhere why we believe the dead cannot return: that unbelievers are confined and under punishment, while believers are with Christ (e.g., Luke 16; II Peter 2:9, etc.). Readers should pursue the issue further there.[12]

Also, considering their circumstances, the three exceptions in Scripture (which always involved believers—Mt. 17:3; II Ki. 2:11; Mt. 27:52-53), are hardly normative. It is one thing to recognize that if God wants to, He can sovereignly choose to allow the saved dead to visit the earth. It is another matter to make the apparitions research of parapsychology normative, and believe even the unsaved dead can return. The first is a *very* rare event; the other is *believed* to be fairly common. One is godly, the other is demonic.

Apparitions of the Dead

This area of apparitions research is a good example of what is a frequent occurrence in psychic research: the subtlety of the demonic. From a Christian's viewpoint, the less demons tie themselves to an event, the more neutral and natural it will appear to be. If a Christian cannot see the immediately demonic, he may assume there is none; which can be a fatal assumption. Many psychic events have no immediate, direct, discernible tie-in to demons. It is their similarity to what we know demons do which provides the tie-in. However, it may take a great deal of research into a particular event before demonic ties are uncovered.

This is true of apparitions research. In 1886, three famous SPR psychic researchers published *Phantasms of the Living.* This presented a large number of cases of spontaneous apparitions of the dead to the living, within 12 hours after their death. The evidence suggested that the dead may appear to the living before "going on." The survey canvassed 5,705 people at random, of whom 702 (12%) reported phantoms of the dead. A subsequent study in 1889, the *Census of Hallucinations,* involved 32,000 reports. Of these 17,000 were in English and of them 1,684 (10%) were recipients of apparitions.[13] The results were felt to give evidence that everyone has the potential for psychic experiences.

These spontaneous cases appear to have no occult or demonic origin. There is no way we can say they are demonic unless we can investigate the lives of each individual recipient to discover common elements indicative of demonic activity—such as personal occult involvement, or a hereditary or occultly transferred predisposition to the psychic realm and/or psychic powers, etc. However, we would expect this to prove to be the case, especially since the phenomena were confined to 10% of the population, i.e., they were far from normal experiences. We would also expect that such apparitions, like poltergeist events, were techniques of spiritual warfare to discount the biblical view of death and support the mediumistic one. However, accepting this research at face value leads to a natural/neutral hypothesis: the dead may appear spontaneously to the living.

It is only further investigation which tends to support a demonic hypothesis. First, the researchers were not unbiased—e.g., F.W.H. Myers admitted his debt to the mediums, even though he interpreted the phenomena differently:

> How much I owe to certain observations made by members of this group—how often my own conclusions concur with conclusions at which they have previously arrived.[14]

A Mediumistic Element in Apparition Appearances

Second, Dr. Fodor has noted the necessity of a mediumistic element in apparition appearances.

> In the majority of cases there is some mediumistic intervention or some sufficiently potent driving motive to achieve the manifestation to nonsensitive [i.e., nonmediumistic] people provided they happen to be in a receptive state.[15]

Thirdly, apparitions are often found in psychic and occult literature, not only to be associated with those occultly involved, but also to bear occult fruits. Biblically, the important question appears to be one of duration. Is there a several hours' or several days' (or even weeks'?) "waiting period" to go to be with Christ, or into judgment? The biblical language seems to rule out this idea. "To be absent from the body, *is* to be present with the Lord" (I Cor. 5:3). It is given for every man to die once, *then* comes judgment (Heb. 9:27).

If there is a delay in time, then a nondemonic hypothesis is permitted, even though it can be held to support a mediumistic view of death. It can be stated that if angels can come and go freely from God's presence to man's, perhaps God may permit this with believers. But to argue from Scriptural silence to spiritual fact is not a sound practice, and we believe the best conclusion is that apparitions of the dead (both saved and unsaved dead) are to be viewed with caution.

Our final concern with Wright's books involves what we feel is poor advice. For example, he urges Christians to record precognitive dreams and send them to the Society for Psychical Research "to provide positive proof when the dreams come true" *(Mind, Man, and the Spirits,* p. 53). It is unwise for Christians to have any involvement with occult societies, whether for research purposes or not. How can the follower of Christ support the camp of the enemy? He also seems to advocate the acceptance of parapsychological research with mediums (*Ibid.,* p. 85). That should be opposed in the strongest terms possible, not only for the damage it does to individuals, but also to a culture, and for its promotion of occultism in general. We would think that Wright would be loath to advocate that occultism can have a "good" side to it. However, he states: "Occultism has the hidden areas (of the mind) well mapped, and knows how the secret powers can be mobilized for good or evil *(Mind, Man, and the Spirits,* p. 88).

Not Latent or Neutral, But Demonic

In conclusion, our concern about these two books boils down to one central divergent opinion: what Wright often sees as actually or potentially latent and neutral, our research leads us to conclude is demonic. The implications of confusing the source of such phenomena are not small. We believe he has accepted the premises and fruits of psychic research too readily. As a result, a soft stand is taken in areas where a hard stand should be taken. In his concluding sections, where he discusses a variety of psychic phenomena, he rarely indicates the phenomena are demonic. He appears reluctant to assign to demonism what we believe the evidence amply justifies *is* demonism, e.g., in the case of psychometry (discerning clairvoyant information about people and their past, present, and future by handling objects they owned).

In a 1977 article his views appear in part to be more acceptable:

> The consistent attitude of the Bible is that, while there are nonmaterial and spiritual levels, it is for God to use them as He sees fit. It is not for man to intrude in their domain.

And he says, "I am against these things." However, he qualifies this at the end of the article:

> Any communication from the unseen [world] must be initiated by God and not manipulated by men and women.[16]

Again, the problem is that when demons appear to people as "the dead," "ascended masters," "angels," UFO entities, or in a hundred other guises, they often claim to be from God and to carry a message from Him. Even if they do not, most people assume an "angel of light" is from God anyway.

Using Psychic Powers is Sin

Wright also states:

> I personally would include natural psychic capacities as part of the make-up of some men and women and children. These gifts should be handed over to God, like every gift, and He will either use them or suppress them as He sees fit.[17]

Such an attitude as Wright states in the above paragraph is hazardous, to say the least. It disguises hereditary occult powers, and far too many nominal Christians today believe their demonic powers are God's gifts. We prefer the view of Dr. Koch whose vast experience and authority in this area should not be lightly dismissed:

> The question of whether there is such a thing as psychic powers which are neutral has often been discussed. If a Christian discovers he has a psychic disposition, he should ask God to take it away. The idea of some theologians that psychic powers can be purified and then used in the service of God's kingdom is unscriptural. This is shown by the story of the fortune teller of Philippi in Acts 16:16-18. If a Christian uses psychic powers, he is committing sin and is in need of forgiveness.[18]

References for Chapter 29

1. Bjornstad and Johnson, *20th Century Prophecy-Jeane Dixon and Edgar Cayce* (Minneapolis, MN: Bethany Books) 1977, Bringle, *Jean Dixon: Prophet or Fraud* (NY: Tower) 1970.
2. Spiritual Frontiers, Fall 1977, p. 5.
3. *Faith and Thought,* Journal of the Philosophical Society of Great Britain (Victoria Institute), Vol. 104, No. 2, p. 147-155.
4. See the forthcoming *The Holistic Healers: A Candid Look at the Old Occultism in the "New Medicine"* (1982), by Reisser & Weldon and *Parapsychology: Scientific Study of the Occult* by Johnson and Weldon.
5. Koch, *Christian Counseling and Occultism,* section on hypnosis.
6. Koch, *Satan's Devices,* Chapter 51, p. 185-91.
7. See *The Healing Power of the Bible,* p. 220-23; *The Healing Gifts of the Spirits,* p. 170-71, *New Thought Journal,* Spring 1979, p. 5.
8. J. Stafford Wright *Christianity and the Occult,* p. 94.
9. Koch, *Demonology Past and Present* (Grand Rapids, MI: Kregel) 1973, p. 110.
10. Koch, *Occult Bondage & Deliverance* (Grand Rapids, MI: Kregel) 1970, p. 40.
11. Koch, *Demonology Past and Present,* p. 116-17.
12. Weldon, *Is There Life After Death,* Ch. 8.
13. Rogo *Parapsychology: A Century of Inquiry, op. cit.,* p. 66-67; Fodor, *Encyclopedia of Psychic Science,* p. 8.
14. F. Myers *Human Personality and its Survival of Bodily Death* (NY: Longmans, Green Co.) 1935, p. 7.
15. Fodor, *Encyclopedia, op. cit.,* p. 5.
16. J.S. Wright, "The Biblical Assessment of Superstition and the Occult" *Faith and Thought, op. cit.,* Vol. 104,

No. 2, p. 147.
17. *Ibid.*, p. 156.
18. Koch, *Satan's Devices,* p. 188.

Chapter 30

Parapsychology and "Psychic Development"

Clearly, parapsychology has psychic and occult overtones and there are many ways that it can be shown to lead to dangerous practices. The realm of "psychic development" is typical of the subtle deceptions associated with this area of spirit activity.

Psychic Development

Psychic development is now a common term. Classes all over the country are offered by occultists of all stripes on how to develop your psychic abilities, untap your "inner potential," or release your hidden powers. This, too, is not new. In 1920 the distinguished psychic investigator, Dr. Hereward Carrington, wrote *Your Psychic Powers and How to Develop Them* (recently reprinted). He notes that the basic method is through the various forms of mediumship, and that this is always the path one must take.

If there is no hereditary transmission (or susceptibility), then psychic powers will not come too easily. They may take years to develop. Again, contrary to much common thinking, they are not innate or natural, or part of a realm which science simply needs to investigate further in order to understand its laws, etc. They are supernatural powers that are *given* to those who open themselves to the influence of the spirit world. This can happen directly or indirectly, overtly or covertly.

The psychics of the world see themselves as channels of higher power, whether they are Indian Sadhus, all of whom admit their powers come from spirits, modern mediums, astrologers, or psychics. Note the following assessments: We repeat well-known scholar Idries Shah:

> It is true that the Sadhus (India's miracle workers) claim that their power comes exclusively from spirits; that they within themselves possess no special abilities except that of concentration.[1]

Colin Wilson notes in his authoritative *The Occult: A History,* that:

> Astrology, then, is based upon the same system of "lunar knowledge" as the I Ching, the tree alphabet, and the Kabbalah, and it is no more an "exact science" than palmistry. Like palmistry, it depends upon an almost mediumistic faculty.[2]

Not Innate Powers, But Channels for Outside Powers

Psychics may view their powers as innate in the sense that anyone can develop them, but they all recognize that the power is something they *cannot control* at will, and that they are "channels" for this ability. The claim that these powers are innate and natural is not supported by the data. *Without specific occult instruction and technique, these powers are not developed.* The only exception is when they are hereditary, in which case they may develop at childhood or appear spontaneously at some point in a person's life. (In the latter, it is usually at the time of some "accident," which makes the person believe some natural power was "jarred loose.")

We may ask ourselves, what, if any, powers exist, which are claimed to be natural, that mediums do not demonstrate as coming from their spirit guides? What branch of parapsychology or psychic research exists apart from mediumistic association and involvement? The answer to both questions is: None. Dr. Nandor Fodor's authoritative *Encyclopedia of Psychic Science* defines psychical research as "a scientific inquiry into the facts and causes of mediumistic phenomena."[3]

Our concern here is to sound a warning again. Granted that most parapsychologists do not take their own advice, we still have quoted them, because if anyone should know, they should. Many of them do not abandon the occult, even when aware of the dangers, because *they cannot*—they are held by a power greater than themselves. Many have found out how difficult it is to leave the occult, only when their foot is inside the door. Some have suffered severely—and even died—attempting to back out. The world they have contacted does not easily let go of its victims (which they sooner or later become). There is a bondage which results from psychic involvement.

Ex-Satanist high priest Mike Warnke was one who paid the price. In *The Satan Seller* (Logos, p. 120), he states:

> With Satan, everything is on a cash-and-carry basis. As long as you do for him, he will do for you. He will answer your "prayers"—if you are useful to him. He will give you what you desire. But the moment you quit giving him what he wants, the moment he decides you are no longer useful to him or someone else does it better—then you have had it. With Satan, there is always a payback—not just when you die, but right here on earth!

Psychic Dr. H. H. Bro states:

> Psychic development is like playing psychological Russian roulette—like being hypnotized by a stranger of unknown training and intent.

Yet he still urges it. He says that some people can benefit from it, "but far more persons" who try to develop them from wrong motives "embark on a course of increasingly distraught behavior, compulsive actions, alienation from friends and relatives, and finally multiple-personality symptoms [possession] or suicide."[4]

Many Mental and Physical Casualties

Dr. Bro say the proportion of casualties "is probably quite large," and that they suffer from mental and physical illness, divorce, vocational calamity, drug addiction, and sexual deviation.[5] Dr. Carrington comments on the standard symptomatology of psi development, noting its parallels to insanity. (The eastern path [kundalini yoga; meditation] also has insanity as standard symptomatology. So does the path of mysticism. An interesting study could be done on abberational spirituality in this regard.)

> A careful student of the occult might point out that the symptoms mentioned above and in the first chapter, are alarmingly similar to those in the early stages of some types of insanity. This is true! I described them earlier in this book, be it understood, not as desirable symptoms, but as those which are likely to appear, and for which the student should be on the lookout . . . in the cultivation of mediumship.[6]

Dr. John Raupert warns:

> As the "psycic development" advances, the entire mental and moral nature of the experimenter becomes disordered; and he discovers to his cost that, while it was an easy thing for him to open the mental door by which the mind could be invaded, it is a difficult, if not an impossible thing, to shut that door and to expel the invader. For the impulse to communicate or to write now asserts itself imperatively and incessantly, at all hours of the day and in the midst of every kind of occupation and, in the end, even at night, either suddenly awakening the victim or preventing him from securing any refreshing sleep. A pitiable condition of mental and moral collapse, often terminating in suicide or insanity, is frequently the ultimate result.[7]

Robert Ashby, Director of Research and Education for the Spiritual Frontiers Fellowship, warns about the dangers of courses attempting to develop psi powers:

> It is precisely because so many people have been psychologically harmed by this type of instruction that a large number of psychologists, parapsychologists, and psychiatrists are vehemently opposed to them altogether.[8]

Margaret Gaddis notes that no one who opens himself or herself to the psychic world can open himself only to the "good" entities—the evil ones come along as part of the package. In the occult realm, however, those thought to be good entities are, in fact, evil entities masquerading as good ones to cultivate bondange and to prepare the person for long-term "service" and often ultimate destruction.

We are amazed at the large number of naive people who have such a blind faith in the goodness of the entities with which they communicate. It is a totally irrational trust. Such people will only see the true nature of these beings if they truly give their lives to Christ, but unfortunately this can be very difficult for them. Gaddis states, "My personal feeling is that sweetness and light are overstressed and too little emphasis is given to the dangers . . . [these people] should hear also of the sometimes horrifying cases of poltergeists and hauntings, and of the disasters that have followed dabbling in black magic, hypnotism, and 'mind-control' classes."[9]

She also speaks of "the darker side of psychic phenomena and the danger of accidental contact with dangerous, evil forces. Even objects may become malevolent. She wonders, in light of this, "if having witches, Satanists, and [scientologist] 'clears' addressing school-sponsored groups is really harmless entertainment." She notes there are "far more stories than space permits to prove these dangers real."

Warnings Are Few

It is not too common that either occult books or those who so naively urge occult involvement openly warn of the dangers, hence it is refreshing to find an exception, although again, the warnings are rarely heeded. J. H Brennan, active occultist for 15 years, has the following opposite Chapter 1, page 1, of his book, *Astral Doorways:*

WARNING

> Several techniques outlined in this book are dangerous. Readers are advised to take this fact into consideration before attempting to experiment with *any* of the doorways.

He warns of the practitioner who may be taking a "short road to insanity" if he is not careful (p. 110).

Dr. L. E. Bartlett, visiting sociologist at U.C. Berkeley, refers to California clinical psychologist Alan Y. Cohen, who has stated:

> There are at least 2,000 documented cases of individuals needing psychological help, because of symptoms caused by prematurely and forcibly trying to develop psychic powers.[10]

Ernest Pecci is one psychiatrist whose specialty is "salvaging psychic casualties."[11]

Poltergeists

For demonologists of the 16th Century (Guazzo, Remy), the phenomena was diabolic. For "more enlightened" people today, poltergeists are harmless "ghosts" that haunt houses. In fact, this is a naive assessment. Poltergeist incidents tend to have two distinct consequences.

First, they tend to involve people in the occult. A parapsychologist may be called in to "investigate" and usually a medium is brought in to "exorcise" or "help" the troublesome troubled spirit.

The phenomena are so startling that participants become converted to the supernatural and often end up involved in psychic investigation. Second, they tend to discredit the biblical view of judgment at death (Heb. 9:27), because people think of them as spirits of the human dead, rather than cunning demon spirits. If all these "spirits of the dead" are roaming around, no God has judged them. Thus poltergeists are one more of the disguises of demons, and their actions clearly indicate this (cf. Dr. Unger's *The Mystery of Bishop Pike)*. It is also possible that the nearly one hundred recorded instances of spontaneous human combustion (people literally bursting into flames) are either kundalini yoga or poltergeist events. Only a few charred bones are left of what was a person, while the surrounding environment always remains nearly untouched.

Dr. G. H. Playfair, a member of the parapsychological Brazilia Institute for Psycho-Biophysical Research (a spiritist organization), describes poltergeist actions in his *The Unknown Power:*

> They throw rocks around, overturn furniture, wreck kitchens, set clothing on fire, soak rooms with water, rearrange people's personal belongings and often steal them, transport anything from babies to two-ton trucks, and generally drive a lot of peace-loving citizens out of their minds. There is also evidence that they do far worse things, seriously wounding and even killing people.[12]

He refers to the fact that poltergeist cases can continue for many years and can drive a family to desperation, even suicide. The controversial book, *The Amityville Horror*, whether or not the incidents in this particular case are true, is one representative example. He mentions one incident which is more indicative of their true nature, "For in this case not only was a house totally wrecked, but several attempts were made on the life of a baby. After narrowly escaping death by burning more than once, the baby simply disappeared after a particular violent outburst of poltergeist activity. Hearing stifled cries coming from a basket of dirty clothing the desperate father rushed over to find his baby entirely buried under the clothes in the process of suffocating to death. The family had to abandon the house after all the furniture had been damaged by fire and even the roof had been pounded to pieces by the furious spirit. The place looked as if a bomb had gone off inside it, and their baby, which had not yet learned even to crawl, was lucky to be alive."[13]

Psychic Attacks

Psychical attacks from the spirit world are not as uncommon as one would hope. Coauthor Weldon has personally talked with an individual who was beaten by astral entities. He was astral projecting (an out-of-the-body experience) and had his "spirit" purportedly thrown back into his body by other entities with such force that he was seriously dazed for days afterwards. A similar event happened to his roommate, with resultant insanity. Both experiences were induced by Transcendental Meditation. (For a look at the real purpose and dangers of TM and the serious implications for our culture of the eastern worldview, see Weldon's *The Transcendental Explosion.)*

John Keel refers to various occult practices when he says:

> Both the literature of the secret societies and the more readily available general occult literature warn about the hazards of these practices. Poorly informed, emotionally unstable practitioners can be overwhelmed by the forces they unleash. The blundering amateur wizard can become possessed or driven insane or experience elaborate hallucinations for extended periods. All kinds of weird manifestations can descend on him, ranging from poltergeists to violent physical attacks by invisible hands. These classic psychic attacks are very similar to the problems suffered by some innocent UFO witnesses and contactees after their sightings begin. The two phenomena seem to be inexorably linked.[14]

Psychic attacks often occur in poltergeist manifestations. Dr. Fodor lists a case with fairly common elements, which also involved an attempted murder by the poltergeist:

> The next night Esther Cox had a frightful experience. Her body began to swell and puffed out to an abnormal size. Soon after a terrific noise, "like a peal of thunder," woke everyone

in the house. The bedclothes flew off Esther's bed night after night, as invisible hands cut words into the plaster of the wall, while everyone heard the noise of writing, "Esther Cox, you are mine to kill"; cold water placed on the middle of the kitchen table bubbled and hissed like boiling water, yet its temperature remained unaffected; a voice announced that the house would be set on fire and for many days lighted matches were seen to fall from the ceiling on the bed; the ghost communicated by raps, said that he was an evil spirit bent on mischief and would torment Esther until she died; and things generally became so bad that Esther was compelled to leave. In the house of a friend, Mr. White, for a month everything was quiet. One day, while she was scrubbing the hall floor, the brush suddenly disappeared from under her hand. A few moments later it fell from the ceiling, narrowly escaping her head. The ghost was heard to walk about the house, he banged the doors, made attempts to fire the house, stabbed Esther in the back with a knife, piled up seven chairs in the parlour on top of each other and pulling out one near the bottom allowed them to fall with a terrific crash. The terrible persecution lasted for nearly a year. Walter Hubbell, the actor, was a personal witness. In 1907, Hereward Carrington interviewed some of the surviving witnesses at Amherst. The testimonies he gathered confirm Hubbell's narrative.[15]

He notes that "the most alarming poltergeist manifestation is the lighting of fires as they often result in serious material damage and in bodily burns." Related occurrences are stone-throwing poltergeist phenomena. In one case a girl who had hysterical fits and vomited pins "was tormented by stones continually flung at her. The stones vanished as soon as they fell to the ground."[16] In another case, pins and needles were stuck into a girl by "ghosts."[17]

Poltergeist Intelligence

Playfair states:

> It also seems fairly obvious that there is some sort of intelligence behind poltergeist activity; over and over again they have been able to outsmart even such experienced investigators as Roll and Barrett, and they have rarely if ever been caught red-handed. Their sense of timing is thoroughly uncanny, and they seem as determined to confuse researchers as they are to drive victims out of their minds.[18]

Dr. Fodor concludes his earlier discussion with:

> The deadly aim of the missiles admits the speculation that it may not be the laws of physics alone which prescribe their course. The impression is of something like temporary consciousness associated with the flight of every single missile as if they were intelligent blows, or as if a strong will power were setting an unalterable course from the point of departure.

Needless to say, the research of the authors points very clearly to a demonic origin of poltergeist activity. Dr. Koch lists one particularly brutal case and notes that in every poltergeist incident he investigated, "Occult practices lay at the root of the phenomena."[19] In this instance, a pastor had come to preach at a church containing a good number of occultists, and strange happenings took place. Koch tells us:

> This thoroughly sober, intelligent man of sharp judgment gave no further attention to the happenings in the parsonage. But one night he was compelled by a remarkable incident to take note of the unusual occurrences. Their baby, which slept in the adjoining room to its parents, suddenly set up a most horrible cry. The young wife hurried through the open door into the adjoining chamber to comfort the child. But she started back in astonishment, and called her hus-

band. Both parents saw how the child had been drawn out of its bedclothes and had been turned around in its cot. On its body there were blood-smeared fingerprints. The man first thought it must be some brazen trick. He carefully checked the window catches and the doors into the corridor, and then searched the whole room with a torch. The child's clothes and nappy were then carefully checked for a cause of the injuries to the child. But the parents could not find the slightest clue to explain this painful occurrence.

The mother settled the child again in its cot and quieted it. They then went back to bed. But almost immediately the terrible cries and moans broke out again. The parents together hurried into the room. The baby was again unwrapped, drawn out of the clothes and turned around in the cot. The little body showed new traces of having been violently seized, with the typical marks of a human hand. The couple now had a distinctly uncanny feeling. They took the baby into their bed, and the husband said to his wife, "Something mysterious seems to be going on after all. Come, let us pray." The couple earnestly prayed for God's protection and in faith committed themselves consciously to His care. Then they lay down quietly to rest, and were troubled no more in their sleep.[20]

Cuts appear on a Mans Legs

In *Phenomena: A Book of Wonders,* Mitchell and Rickard list several poltergeist-related psychic attacks.[21] In South Africa in 1962, twenty-year-old Jim deBruin was being questioned about the disturbances when "the Police Chief, John Wessels, and three constables heard twenty-year-old Jimmy scream with pain. He was wearing shorts and they could see cuts appearing on his legs even as they watched. The next day, in the presence of two officers, a deep gash appeared on his chest, although nothing had penetrated his shirt. These cuts continued for several days. They were clean, as though made with a razor or scalpel—and all who saw them agreed that the young man could not have inflicted them on himself."

In another case, "the poltergeist connection was more clearly established in the celebrated Phelps case in Stratford, Connecticut, in 1850. The disturbances centered on Dr. Phelp's twelve-year-old son, Harry. In *Ghosts and Poltergeists,* Father Thurston's summaries of some events read like attacks on the boy—stones would be pitched at him and a violent force would lift him off the ground to strike his head on the ceiling. Once he was thrown into a water tank; and before the eyes of shocked visitors he was caught up and suspended in the branches of a tree while his clothes were methodically torn to ribbons by something invisible. In a pamphlet published in 1800, *A Narrative of Some Extraordinary Things That Happened to Mr. Richard Giles' Children,* by a Mr. Durbin, extensive attacks by invisibles on the children are detailed—only these left teethmarks in young flesh, like the case of Eleonore Zugun. The witnesses describe the horrific sight of the little girl throttled by an invisible hand, seeing the sides of her throat pushed in, but without any obvious contraction of her neck muscles. Later the children were pushed and pulled, slapped and spat upon. On one occasion, five witnesses saw 'their arms bitten about twenty times that evening . . . they could not do it themselves as we were looking at them the whole time. We examined the bites and found on them the impression of eighteen or twenty teeth, with saliva or spittle all over them, in the shape of a mouth . . . very wet and clammy like spittle, and it smelt rank.' Attacks by poltergeists, or whatever they are, do happen, and more often than you might think."

Dead . . . and Clothes Torn into Fine Shreds

Mitchell and Rickard's final case is a gruesome one, reminiscent of the J. Prestes Filho UFO incident which these authors reported in an earlier book.[22]

In 1761, five women were returning from collecting sticks near Ventimiglia, in northern Italy. Suddenly one of them cried out and dropped dead. Her companions were shocked by what they saw. Her clothes and shoes were torn into fine shreds and scattered up to six feet around her. There were wounds on her head that exposed the skull; the muscles on her right side had given way exposing her intestines; her sacrum was broken and most internal organs were ruptured or livid; her abdominal region bore many deep and parallel incisions, and the flesh on one hip and thigh was almost carried away, exposing the pubic bone and the broken head of the femur which had been forced from its socket. This horrific event was reported to the French Academy of Sciences by M. Morand, and the Annual Register for that year quotes him as noting that these grievous effects took place with no sign of penetration of the woman's clothes, nor was there any blood on the scene, nor any sign of her missing flesh. It was as though she had been the focal point for an instantaneous, silent, and deadly explosion.

In conclusion to this section, we ask ourselves the question, "Where does it all lead?"

References for Chapter 30

1. Shah, *Oriental Magic, op. cit.,* p. 123.
2. Wilson, *The Occult, op. cit.,* p. 250.
3. Fodor, *The Encyclopedia of Psychic Science,* p. 316.
4. Los Angeles Times, Feb. 17, 1974; *Fate,* Feb. 1971, p. 102-3.
5. *Ibid.*
6. Carrington, *Your Psychic Powers and How to Develop Them, op. cit.,* p. 206.
7. Ed Gruss, *Ouija Board, Doorway to the Occult* (Chicago: Moody) 1976, P. 64.
8. Ebon (Ed.) *The Satan Trap: Dangers of the Occult,* (Garden City, NY: Doubleday) 1976, p. 38.
9. *Ibid.,* p. 54.
10. *Readers Digest,* August 1977, p. 86.
11. *Ebon, op. cit.,* p. 58.
12. Playfair, *The Unknown Power* (NY: Pocket) 1975, p. 240, 253-54.
13. *Ibid.,* p. 265.
14. Keel, *Our Haunted Planet* (Greenwich, CT: Fawcett Gold Medal) 1971, p. 162.
15. Fodor, *Encyclopedia, op. cit.,* p. 292.
16. *Ibid.*
17. *Ibid.*
18. Playfair, *op. cit.,* p. 266.
19. Koch, *Christian Counseling and Occultism,* p. 181.
20. *Ibid.,* p. 175.
21. *Phenomena,* p. 56.
22. *Close Encounters: A Better Explanation,* p. 128-30.

Conclusion to Part III

Where Does It all Lead?

Today even the secular world is beginning to realize that psychic/occult involvement is dangerous. Editor Martin Ebon's books, *Demon Children* and *The Satan Trap: Dangers of the Occult,* as well as the March, 1978, special issue of *The New Age Journal,* "Perils of the Path," are representative. The difficulty is that those sounding the warnings are usually the ones most heavily involved in the occult—psychics, parapsychologists, occult researchers, "new consciousness" promoters, etc. They believe the occult is good and even beneficial for society, if handled properly. They make a distinction between "safe" occultism and dangerous occultism, the latter occurring primarily from lack of knowledge or instruction on the part of the practitioner. (The ancient gnostic view of salvation by the *proper* knowledge is rampant in these circles.)

They proclaim that the occult is safe so long as we have good motives, are cautious, and use the powers wisely. With this attitude we can usher in a "new age" of advancing evolutionary consciousness that will help the world unite into one planetary body, at last free from its historical bondage.

But what if such arbitrary dividing of the occult into "good" and "bad" is false? The truth is, all occultism should be avoided. Contrary to popular opinion, we are not dealing with a neutral area of human potential. We are not dealing with that which is *human* at all, unless it be manipulation of humans. Too many humans are naively entering the domain of "principalities and powers" of another dimension—call it the spirit realm, "next world," or what you will. Here there exist created beings of impressive cunning and great malevolence. The biblical warnings are particularly applicable. To align oneself with these powers is to openly oppose God.

It can be demonstrated that whether it is the individual or the culture that becomes involved in the occult, the end result is tragedy. Moral collapse, economic breakdown, emotional ruin, and spiritual destruction are the consequences of personal or cultural involvement in this area. The wise will heed this warning and turn to true spirituality and enlightenment, as represented by the teachings of Christ. The rest will continue their perilous path and if their numbers and influence keep increasing, they will drag many down with them in the judgment that must follow. Only the pillars of near infinite human suffering will one day measure the cost of abandoning God. To substitute Satan in God's place can only mean eternal torment.

Appendix: Part I
Help and Counsel for Occult Involvement

How Involvement With the Occult Takes Place

There are two basic reasons why people become introduced to the occult. The first is when the involvement starts as a result of one's parents, grandparents, or great-grandparents, having been personally involved. We shall see that there is clearly a hereditary coherence to four generations which can predispose, and can even ensure, that a person will be subjected to demonic forces. The individual may have no personal interest until certain psychic things start happening in his life, which he may mistake for "God's leadings" or as a sign of spirituality. Thus, in the case of spontaneous psychic development or abilities (in children or adults), there is usually occult involvement somewhere in the past history of the family.

The second cause of occult bondage is personal choice. This can occur in various ways: (1) Deliberate involvement (in automatic writing, witchcraft, white magic, etc.); (2) It may result from what is thought to be a "harmless pasttime (ouija boards, tarot cards, levitation games, etc.); (3) By an attempt to "better" oneself via being healed psychically, using self-hypnosis, or one of the many mind-control techniques (e.g., Silva mind control); (4) By drugs, particularly the consciousness expansion types—LSD, peyote, mescalin, and, to some extent, marijuana; (5) By following virtually any eastern path or guru. In general, any spiritual movement, discipline, or technique which cultivates continued altered states of consciousness is a tacit opening of the door of your mind to the potential influence of supernatural forces.

There actually are literally hundreds of specific methods of involving oneself in the occult. If there is an umbrella definition, it is through cultivating altered states of consciousness. This can be done through yoga, meditation, hypnosis, seances, astrology, astral projection, drugs, etc., all of which can develop psychic powers.

Many "modern" techniques for expanding consciousness are really ancient devices used for establishing spirit contact. Ouija boards date to seances held by Pythagorus in 540 B.C.[1] The ASCID (altered states of consciousness induction device is really the old time "witch's cradle" and shaman's (an animist witch doctor) trance inducer. On the other hand, because of technological advances, there are new modern devices available for cultivating altered states, e.g., biofeedback and other forms of autogenic training. The use of biofeedback for occult purposes is seen in Dr. Elmer Green's *Beyond Biofeedback*. In fact, we are now close to using technology to produce mediumship.

Even many of the new experiential psychotherapies can cause psychic experiences. This includes structural integration (rolfing), the Neo-Reichian approaches (e.g., Bioenergetics), Gestalt practice, primal therapy, guided imagery with music, sensory isolation and overload, sleep deprivation, the various forms of re-birthing and use of kinesthetic methods (kinesthesia involves the sensation of bodily position, presence, or movement, e.g., the Feldenkrais method, Alexander technique, etc.) (*Human Behavior,* Jan., 1977, p. 39-40; *The Brain-Mind Bulletin,* March 9, 1978; *The Christian Parapsychologist,* Vol. 3, No. 2, p. 74; Brochure on the 5th International conference of Transpersonal Psychology held in Boston, Nov. 9-

14, 1979, sponsored by Esalen, the Association for Transpersonal Psychology and other organizations.)

Hereditary Coherence

Occult involvement carries a ban on it, with the curse lasting to four generations. Dr. Kurt Koch, the author of some 60 books and considered a top authority on occult subjection, has documented this from his 40 years of counseling over 20,000 people (up to 1970). He states:

> In the field of heredity, a coherence persisting into the third and fourth generations is seen in the case of active occultists. These effects are thus no less persistent in their hold on succeeding generations than those of alcoholism, syphilis, and psychoses. In our study we have already shown in Examples 24 and 60-66 how psychological disturbances and mediumistic gifts developed through occult practices extend as far as the third and fourth generations.

He next discusses the ease with which what many would call "minor" or "harmless" occult involvement leaves its effect. In the following case being "charmed" magically (e.g., having spells cast over oneself for protection against illness, for power, etc.):

> In our discussion of the many cases of magic charming, we made the startling discovery that in the second to fourth generations, clairvoyance developed as a secondary effect, after one or more conjurations. This is evident from [he lists 14 examples numerically]. The development of clairvoyance also tends to appear, especially in the form of spirit-visions, in the case of blood pacts and amulet pacts.
>
> Besides the development of clairvoyance, there appears in connection with occult practice also an increase of mediumistic sensitivity. We have already mentioned that mediumistic gifts will appear in the next generation, where rejected, in a recessive form, but where there is further occult

practice will appear as dominant. Mediumship is susceptible of both decline and development. If four generations all actively practice occult arts, then very strong mediums will develop. In the case of a person with a mediumistic predisposition who turns to Christ, the sensitivity may either be retained or vanish.[2]

It is important to realize here that occult involvement is active rebellion against God.

Dr. Koch states, referring to the laws of God against occult involvement, "The aim of proclaiming the Law is to point out to the occult practitioner that whether he be actively or passively involved, he is standing under the judgment of God, because he has by transgressing the first, second, and third commandments entered into a pact with powers alien to God."[3]

The Bible implies that occult involvement is, in effect, declaring one's hatred toward God and obviously this carries severe consequences. In the Old Testament God Himself prescribed the death penalty for occult involvement. "As for a man or a woman, if there is a medium or a spiritist among them (that is, one in whom there is a divining demon), they shall surely be put to death. Their bloodguiltiness is upon them" (Lev. 20:27). Virtually the entire range of occult practices is summed up in Deut. 18:9-12 as being detestable to God. Those who practice occultism do not realize what they may be doing to their children. When it is a matter of purposeful rebellion, God may deal with people as they deal with Him.

These are some of the ways in which involvement with the occult can take place. What about exorcism? Do we believe in it? We turn to that now. This is adapted from Apendix III of *The Occult Explosion* and is used by permission of the publishers.

How Can Exorcism Be Effective Today?

We have given evidence that demons must be recognized as really existing. One consequent question is, "Can exorcism be effective?"

The evidence around the world indicates that at times exorcism can be effective, but it is also true that some activities whereby demons are supposedly cast out are, unfortunately, little more than exhibitionism. Shouting at the top of one's voice at a "demon" might be very effective in stirring up the emotions of those who are watching the ceremony, but it is hardly in the Spirit of Him of Whom it was said, "He shall not strive, nor cry; neither shall any man hear His voice in the street."

Similarly, many people seem to think that the greatest effect is ensured by shouting prayers loudly at God, almost implying that He is deaf. The Christian teaching is that it is not even necessary to express oneself audibly for God to hear. Spoken prayer is desirable and necessary in public, but loud shouting and virtually commanding God to act is not really convincing, though it might satisfy some observers that they have been present at a really good show.

What Actually is "Exorcism"?

It is relevant to explain a little about exorcism itself. The word has come to mean the driving out of demons, whether it be from individual people, places, or things that are possessed by these invading forces. In the Christian concept, a prayer is made to God in the name of Jesus Christ. We shall see that with some churches there is also a ritual that involves a crucifix and/or other religious symbols.

The Christian teaching is that the demons involved are fallen spiritual beings who have been shut off from fellowship with God and have an implacable enmity against man. They regard man as a being created for special fellowship with God, beings who, in a sense, have replaced Satan, who previously had enjoyed the special place of privilege next to the Godhead.

Christians believe that if a person is demon possessed, (strictly, it is "demonized"), that demon can be exorcised only through the power of Jesus Christ. Jesus Himself taught that if Satan cast out Satan, then his kingdom would not stand. Hence, according to Christian theology, it is not possible permanently to cast out demons by using the power of a greater demon, as with non-Christian "exorcism."

Some would object to this and point to practices such as an Australian Aboriginal tradition where a witchdoctor can "point the bone" at another Aborigine, and that man will, before very long, become seriously ill and die. However, many who have studied these practices believe that this is not really a case of demon possession, but rather of an induced illness with serious psychological overtones. The man ceases to eat, believes he is going to die, and virtually wills himself to death.

According to those traditions, the only way in which such a man can live is to find a witchdoctor with greater spiritual powers who will cast out the evil spirit. If the individual does believe that the second witchdoctor has greater powers than the one who "pointed the bone," then recovery is likely to be complete.

What we have just referred to is not necessarily demon possession or exorcism, but is a demonstration of the power of human belief, e.g., as demonstrated in placebo research.

Some psychologists argue in a similar way that success with exorcism merely means that there has been a psychic penetration, so that a "possessed" person has a degree of deliverance from torturing processes within his own subconscious. Undoubtedly such a form of deliverance is true at times, but it is not always the answer.

In passing, an interesting point sometimes made by those who specialize in exorcism in this "primitive" sense is that there is a law of rebound. They claim that when evil curses are pronounced against people, and those curses do not work, the effect must rebound on those who pronounced the curses.

Forms Used by Christians in Casting Out Evil Spirits

Roman Catholics, Protestants, and other churches and religious groups practice exorcism. Various rites of exorcism are used by declared Christians; some use various religious symbols which are themselves supposed to contain latent power, or they celebrate the communion, believing that same latent power is in the symbols of bread and wine that speak of Christ's broken body and shed blood. Other Christians simply pray earnestly in the Name of the Lord Jesus Christ and command the demon to depart. We accept the "simple" approach, claiming that the power of Christ should be sufficient, apart from ritual. He shed His blood to make possible our constant communion with God. *Christ's* power is available to *us!*

At Times There is Over-stress on Ritual

Various rituals are given in exorcism manuals, such as for the blessing of holy water, and even for the exorcism of evil from the salt that is to be used. The blessing of God is then invoked on the water. One wonders at the necessity for such form and ritualism, for we certainly do not read of Jesus looking for salt and holy water and conducting a ritual before He commanded demons to depart, as He did so often.

The same can be said for the blessing of the oil for the anointing of the sick, as is sometimes prescribed. Many Bible believers would agree that the sick person who is to be anointed should first undergo careful teaching about faith, repentance, and prayer; but they would not necessarily endorse ritualistic aspects which go beyond the simplicity of the New Testament.

An "amusing" example of the uselessness of ritual is the story related by spiritist Dr. Elizabeth Kubler-Ross (referred to earlier in the book). It appears that a Catholic priest was certain her spirit guides were demons and requested she sprinkle "holy water" on one of them to prove it. She agreed. When "Salem" appeared before her (in a fully physical materialized form), he agreed immediately, telling her that Catholic priests take such things very seriously. He even bowed before her, and in a kneeling position let her sprinkle the holy water on him. He demanded the entire conversation and process be recorded on tape for the priest's sake. Obviously, the water did not force the demon to disappear. Kubler-Ross soaked him with it, and they both waited for it to "prove" he was a demon. Finally, Salem said, "Don't you think we waited long enough and I didn't disappear?" Both he and Kubler-Ross got a great laugh out of it all, at the expense of the priest, who, still clinging to his holy water concept, maintained the demon de-materialized the holy water and replaced it with ordinary water. *(Human Behavior,* September, 1977, p. 26-7). Such an incident would indeed be funny if it were not so tragic.

Although there is no actual formula given in the New Testament, some who practice exorcism first pray that others present will be protected. Then the demon is commanded to identify itself, and some surprising answers are given at times. Sometimes, the names seem odd, and there are those (ourselves included) who have real reservations about some reports; yet the voices used are not those of the person so invaded. Even their electrocardiograms are temporarily different. Such cases as reported in Basham's *Can A Christian Have A Demon*—e.g., demons of post nasal drip, fingernail biting, arthritis of the knees, and eternal security, and much in the so-called "deliverance ministry" is simply placing Christians under a fear of demons and a bondage that the New Testament delivers them from. To believe, as some do, that most Christians have demons denies the clear teaching of Scripture which indicates the believer's authority over Satan, e.g., "Resist the Devil and he will flee from you."

Jesus Himself did not use a set formula or ritual, nor did He have lengthy conversations with demons. He simply exercised the power He claimed as His right, a power He communicated also to His followers. Only a true believer in Christ should dare attempt the exorcism of evil spirits; but such a person can become a spiritual "superman," for the weakest Christian is potentially stronger than the most demonic of all the powers of hell. New spiritual power is available for even the weakest child of God. There are many stories in missionary literature where a demon complained that it could do nothing, simply because a Christian was present.

Exorcism can be effective, not because of prescribed rituals, but because of the victorious Person in Whom the Christian can still place personal trust. Nevertheless, it should be stressed that the casting out of demons is not a field for immature Christians. In I Corinthians 12:10 we read that "discerning of spirits" is a gift of the Holy Spirit—it is not something to be lightly tackled by enthusiastic babes in Christ.

In any case, the Bible does not "major" on demons. The Christian should concentrate on Jesus, not on forces of evil. We need not fear such beings, and as we follow Christ we are safe in His hands and in His Father's hand; so Jesus Himself said in John, Chapter 10.

References for the Appendix

1. Fodor *Encyclopedia, op. cit.,* p. 270.
2. Kurt Koch, *Christian Counseling and Occultism,* p. 186-7.
3. *Ibid.,* p. 335.
4. Koch, *Occult Bondage and Deliverance,* p. 26-7.

Appendix: Part II

Counseling: A Brief Look at Some Means of Helping Those Involved With the Psychic World

The devil is real, and demons are equally real. They are timeless as humans think of time, yet their days are numbered. They know this, for "the demons believe and tremble" (James 2:19). They fear the judgment of God, but in their continuing rebellion have accelerated their activities in these "last days."

The Lord Jesus Christ tells His Church that we have nothing to fear. Calvary was the death blow to the Satanic forces, and it is our privilege to serve Him for a brief time and then to know eternity in His presence, with no sin, sorrow, or sadness. To Him be the glory!

Help on Occult Counseling

The following are only intended as a brief and general guide to help those whom you contact who are suffering from occult involvement. We ourselves have had comparatively little personal counseling experience with the occultly oppressed. Most of our research has been from literature. However, Dr. Kurt Koch's book, *Occult Bondage and Deliverance* (Kregel Publishers, Grand Rapids, Michigan), is highly useful, and he has had extensive counseling experience. The following material is adapted from pp. 85-131. For a complete treatment, the reader should consult the full text. **Note:** We are primarily dealing with occult oppression; we are *not* listing rules to be followed; we have only numbered some of his comments for easy reference.

1. We must recognize the battle that is going on. We have a very real and dangerous enemy, and we must realize that Christ has obtained victory for us. Remember there are

many things we do not understand in the spiritual realm. Do not rush into occult counseling. Seriously look to God for a leading in this area. Spiritual maturity and insight are vital. Do not go searching out occultists. "Without a commission from God, a Christian should not venture too far into the area of the demonic and the occult. There are certain rules that have to be obeyed .... People with a sensitive nervous system or maybe with an occult oppression of their own should never attempt to do any work in this field. Recent converts and young women should also refrain from this type of work" (p. 87-8).

As Christians, we should always warn others of the dangers involved and help when we can, according to the leading of the Spirit, our maturity, and experience, etc. But we should not become heavily involved in an occult ministry unless God is so leading us and we are aware of what is involved. Medical and/or psychological training, if possible, is helpful.

2. Let God be sovereign. He can do things His way—through you or around you. No pattern or singular method need always be involved. God does not need our "often complicated counseling procedures," however, deliverance without counseling is rare. Complete deliverance may take weeks, months, or sometimes years; or it may take just a few hours. Christ and Christ alone is the source of deliverance. Any form of psychology, hypnosis, meditation, or religion alone is useless. Also, we must be sure of correct diagnosis. Do not mistake mental illness for occult bondage. (Part II of *Occult Bondage and Deliverance* discusses this.)

3. Every object of occultism must be destroyed (Acts 19: 19). "Magical books and occult objects carry with them a hidden ban. Anyone not prepared to rid himself of this ban will be unable to free himself from the influence of the powers of darkness" (p. 90). "Yet even the little figures made out of precious stones which often originate from heathen temples have to be destroyed if the owner finds he cannot free himself from his occult oppression" (p. 92). Gifts from occultists should never be accepted.

Occult contacts and friendships must be broken. In the case of a person saved whose parents are occultists—what might seem strange counsel at first—it may be advisable for them to move out, or not to pray for their parents, if, because they are praying, they are attacked by demons and/or their spiritual life declines. Prayer could resume after their Christian life has been built up more. Apparently, this is sometimes the only way. The powers of darkness often try to strike back.

Our first responsibility is to Christ and our relationship to Him. We cannot help others at all until we ourselves are securely grounded as Christians. Thus, Dr. Koch advises "the children of spiritistic families not to pray for their parents at all if they are still engaged in occult practices" (p. 93). "Inexperienced counselors, however, will be unable to appreciate decisions of this nature, for they will have little knowledge of the terrible attacks which can be leveled by the powers of darkness" (p. 94).

"Every person who really wants to be delivered must be prepared to commit his life completely to Christ." There can be no half-hearted decisions. (Koch, *Between Christ and Satan,* pp. 125-30.)

4. Confession must be voluntary, or it is worthless. The idea is to bring into the light that which is occult (hidden, secret). Dr. Koch advises that confession be made in the presence of a mature Christian counselor. "Occultly oppressed people should, in fact, make an open confession of every single hidden thing in their lives in order to remove the very last foothold of the enemy" (p. 98). "The confession of a subjected person should not only cover the occult, but also every other department of his life" (p. 99). Nothing should be allowed to build up or develop which may give the devil an opportunity. (We repeat—*this should only be in the presence of a mature Christian counselor.)*

5. *The prayer of renunciation.* "In the normal way the thing that follows confession is absolution—the promise of the forgiveness of sins. In my counseling work among the occultly oppressed, however, I have found that I have had to abandon this sequence since the subjected person usually

finds it impossible to grasp the fact that his sins have been forgiven. He is simply unable to believe. A barrier seems to lie in his way. I, therefore, always encourage the victim of occultism to pray a prayer of renunciation first of all" (p. 99).

"In counseling the occultly oppressed, a prayer of renunciation is, however, of great significance. The question is 'why?' Every sin connected with sorcery is basically a contract with the powers of darkness. By means of sorcery, the archenemy of mankind gains the right of ownership over a person's life. The same is true even if it is only the sins of a person's parents or grandparents that are involved. The devil is well acquainted with the second commandment which ends, 'for I the Lord your God am a jealous God, visiting the iniquity of the fathers upon the children to the third and the fourth generation of those who hate me.' The powers of darkness continue to claim their right of ownership although quite often the descendants remain completely unaware of the fact, perhaps since they have had no contact with sorcery themselves. Nevertheless, immediately after a person in this situation is converted, Satan very soon makes his claim felt.

"In praying a prayer of renunciation, a person cancels Satan's right both officially and judicially. The counselor and any other Christian brothers present act as witnesses to this annulment of ownership. Although many modern theologians ridicule the whole idea, the devil is in earnest. Hundreds of examples could be quoted to show just how seriously he takes the matter. When the occult oppression is minimal, the person who has made his confession will have little difficulty in repeating a prayer of renunciation after the counselor. The prayer can take the form 'In the name of Jesus I renounce all the works of the devil together with the occult practices of my forefathers, and I subscribe myself to the Lord Jesus Christ, my Lord and Savior, both now and forever. In the name of the Father, and of the Son, and of the Holy Spirit. Amen'

"The prayer is not a formula. Every time it is prayed it can take a different form. In severe cases of oppression, on the other hand, a number of complications can arise when it comes to praying a prayer of renunciation" (p. 100-101). The person may be unable to bring his hands together to pray, or his lips or vocal chords my be unusable. He may fall into a trance when it comes to renouncing the devil. "What can we do in circumstances like this? One can either command the evil powers in the name of Jesus, or else call some other Christian brothers to join in praying for the subjected person" (p. 101). Renunciation may be followed by a remarkable change for the better.

Note: "Not everyone experiences such elated feeling after deliverance but the change of ownership is still valid no matter how one feels . . . . Renunciation is particularly important in cases where natives are converted out of a heathen background" (p. 102).

6. Let the person know that in Christ his sins have been forgiven. No matter how bad they are, they have been forgiven. Appropriate Scripture passages may be read to him —Rom. 5:20; Gal. 1:4; Eph. 1:7; Col. 1:14; I Pet. 1:19; Heb. 1:3; Isa. 53:4-7; I Pet. 2:24; I John 1:7-9; etc. Explain that the work of salvation is complete—Eph. 1:13-14; John 19:30; etc.

Note: "Occultly subjected people . . . often suffer their first attacks when they seek to follow Christ or serve Him in some way" (p. 104). "There is a possibility that if a person puts too much of his own effort into trying to help the demonically oppressed that a transference will take place" (p. 105).

7. *The Prayer Group.* "Counseling the occultly oppressed is really a matter of teamwork. The individual counselor is far too weak to take upon his own shoulders all the problems he meets" (p. 105). "Occultly oppressed people are still very vulnerable even after their actual deliverance. For this reason, a small group of Christians should take it upon themselves to continue to care and to pray for them even after their conversion. If necessary the group need only consist of two Christians. They should meet together at least twice or three times a week for perhaps a quarter of an hour at a time in order to pray for the oppressed person.

The best thing is for the subjected person to be present as well, yet this is not absolutely necessary. Neither is it essential for the oppressed person to have made an open confession before *all* the members of the group. This need only have been made before the counselor at the very start" (p. 106).

Prayer and Fasting (Mt. 17:14-21). For a good book on fasting see *God's Chosen Fast* by Arthur Wallis. Some can be delivered only through these means.

Note: "When a person is delivered and liberated from his occult oppression, he must really lay hold of the four spiritual elements which go to make up our Christian discipleship. These are: the Word of God, fellowship with the children of God, the breaking of bread, and continuous prayer" (p. 114).

8. *The Return of Evil Spirits* (Luke 11). We must distinguish between the apparent return and actual return. Note: Often when a person who has been healed occultly turns to Christ, that sickness from which he was occultly healed then returns. The reappearance of the illness is an indication that the occult ban was broken, not that evil spirits had returned. One may then pray and humbly ask the Lord to heal the person. When the demons do return, "The battle is always fiercer than before. Very often one finds that the powers of darkness return when a person is *liberated* in a *Christian atmosphere,* and then has to return and *live* in an *atmosphere of occultism and sorcery.* This is frequently what happens in the case of young people from spiritistic families who are converted when away from home and later have to return and live in the demonically affected house of their parents" (p. 119).

"People who have been delivered from occult oppression and yet have to return again and live in an occult or spiritistic atmosphere never find real and lasting peace. I usually find that I have to advise young people stemming from such environments, 'Stay away from your parents—or from your uncle, aunt, or relation—if they are not prepared to forsake their occult practices and interests.' This advice is not always appreciated, however. In fact, on occasions I have been actually rebuked for having given a person advise of this nature. Finally, repeating what we have just been saying, anyone who fails to act on all that the Bible says for our protection will live in continuous danger of falling victim once more to the influence of the exorcised spirits" (p. 120).

9. "No matter how difficult or how wearying the counseling of occultly subjected or even possessed people may be, the fact remains that the victory is ours through what Christ has done" (p. 124). Believe God's promise and act in faith in what seem to be hopeless situations.

Complete Surrender to Christ—This includes counselor and counselee. "When a person is delivered from a state of occult subjection, he must withhold nothing in his life from the Lord. Those areas which are not surrendered to his Lord will soon be occupied again by the enemy" (p. 126). "Only when Jesus is our Lord will he protect us from the lordship of others."

10. "One must never imagine, however, that we have somehow arrived at a set method for dealing with such people. What we have been saying is not a recipe. The Lord in his sovereignty can at any time bypass each and every one of these steps, as we saw. We have merely been considering these things to ensure that we are fully equipped for the conflict, for these weapons of counseling have proved effective now over a number of years" (p. 127).

"It is also very important to remember when counseling and caring for the occultly oppressed that this kind of counsel will only thrive in the right spiritual atmosphere. One must never look upon a person and his needs as just another 'case,' or as some new 'sensation' or 'object of investigation.' True deliverance will never be forthcoming in an unscriptural atmosphere—even if the battle for the oppressed person appears to be very dramatic. We must be on our guard against every kind of excess, and above all against exhibitionism. Let us therefore be: Sound in our faith, Sober in our thoughts, Honest and scriptural in our attitude" (p. 128).

Index

A

Acupressure, 159
  occult origins, 260
Acupuncture, 193-197
  and kundalini symptomology, 192
Alexander Method, 229
American Research Team
  astral sound tape, 188, 189
Animal Magnetism (Mesmerism)
  and Christian Science, 255
  and hypnosis, 255, 256
  and Orgonomy, 220, 221
  and Phineas Quimby, 255
  and spiritism, 253-255
  and von Reichenbach, 256
  Mesmer's interest in occultism, 253
  occult energy, 253-256
  same as prana, mana, od, 253, 254, 256
Applied kinesiology, 189-194
Apparitions research
  and Christian theology, 432-436
Astral projection (see Out of the body experiences)
Astrologic medicine, 199-204
  problems, 203, 204
  theory, 201, 202
Astrology
  and Christianity, 116, 118, 122, 123, 127
  and universal energy, 201
  beliefs, 112-114, 123, 124
  foundation of occult, 199, 200
  harm, 203
  history, 112, 113, 121, 123-125
  mediumistic aspect, 442
  problems, 114-127
Autogenics, 188, 189, 221-226

B

Basham, Don, 464
Bioenergetics, 217-221
Biofeedback, 221-226
  need for caution, 222-224
  nonoccult use, 222, 226
  occult aspects, 222-226
  theory, 221, 222
Blavatsky, Helena, 255
Body therapies, 228-231
  Alexander Method, 229
  Do'in, 230
  functional integration (Feldenkrais Method), 229
  massage, psychic aspects, 229, 239, 240
  polarity therapy 230, 231
  psychic experiences reported in, 229-231
  Rolfing, 229
  Shiatsu, 230
Books commented upon or reviewed
  Chariots of the Gods, 129-139
  Christian and the Supernatural (The), 404, 427, 428
  Christianity and the Occult, 428-437
  Jeane Dixon: My Life and Prophecies, 423, 424
  Latent Power of the Soul (The), 273-278
  Lord of the Air (The), 29
  Mind, Man, and the Spirits, 428-437
  Occult Bondage and Deliverance, 467, 468
  Parapsychology and the Christian Faith, 404, 405, 425, 426
  Psychic Phenomena and Religion, 427
  Rediscovering the Gift of Healing, 417, 418
  Report on Occult and Psychic Activities (United Presbyterian Church), 424, 425
  Return From Tomorrow, 95, 96
  Smouldering Fire: The Work of the Holy Spirit, 402
  Try the Spirits: Christianity and Psychical Research, 406, 426, 427
  You Are Psychic: The Incredible Story of David Bubar, 424
Bradley, Robert
natural childbirth and spiritism, 166
Bro, H. H. and M., 424
Bruyere, Rosalyn Lee
and spirit guides, 195
Buddhism, Zen
  and Christianity, 63-67
  bibliography, 70
  monistic worldview and practices, 62, 63, 65

C

Cayce, Edgar, 53, 155, 230, 251, 258
Center for Parapsychological Research, 385, 386
Chariots of the Gods, 129-139

Chester Carlson Research Laboratory, 385
Ch'i, 267
Chinmoy, Sri, 22-24
Chiropractic, 190, 204-217
  occult theory the basis for students' involvement in psychicism, 208-217
  theory, 205
Christian and the Supernatural (The), 404, 427, 428
Christianity and the Occult, 428-437
Christianity, compared with
  astrology, 116, 118, 122, 123, 127
  est, 310-313
  Hinduism, 29-32
  parapsychology, 391-437
  reincarnation, 79-81, 84-87
  Transcendental Meditation, 37, 45-47
  zen Buddhism, 64-66
Christian Parapsychologist (The), 418, 419
Christian parapsychology (see also Parapsychology), 391-437
  and biblical interpretation, 396, 397, 399-406, 418, 419
  consequences, implications, 393-397, 403, 409-421, 428
  historic impetus in Darwinism, 396
  liberal theology, 395-406, 409, 410
  research societies, 413-421
  united with secular parapsychology, 399, 400

Chromotherapy, 181-184
CFPSS - Churches Fellowship for Psychical and Spiritual Studies, 418-421
Counseling
  for psychic involvement, 457-473

D

Dead
  communication with, 98-100
Death
  biblical contrast, 93
  bibliography on biblical view, 102
  caution on Christian experiences, 95, 96
  clinical death research, 91-96
  description, 92
  est view, 299
  hex death, 2, 5
  occult aspects, 94, 95
  seance necromancy, 98-100
Deliverance ministry
  for Christians, 464
Demons
  can Christians have them? 464
  explanatory value, 320, 321
  ingenuity, 369-371
Denver, John, 290
Deuteronomic prohibitions vs. mediumism, 418-420
Dixon, Jeane, 423, 424
Do'in, 230
Dowsing (divining rods), 429, 430

E

Energy (mystical)
  active and passive uses, 159, 160
  analysis of five examples, 249-260
  analysis of mystical energy concepts, 150-154, 158, 159, 247-261, 259, 260, 266-269, 273-284
  ancient, 247-261
  and holistic health techniques, 172
  and modern physics, 152, 153
  and parapsychology, 370, 371, 373
  and spiritism (see analysis), 268-271
  animal magnetism, 253-256
  basis for deifying man, 156
  characteristics, 269-271
  conclusion, 269
  higher sense perception, 257, 258
  implications, 161, 162
  key issue, 153
  mana, 251-253
  manipulation of supposed body energy, 189-198
  misinterpreted, 152
  no neutral science of life energy, 195
  occult aspects, 258-260
  occultly originated, 259, 260, 266
  od, 256
  "personal" aspects, 158, 159
  prana, 249-251
  use in holistic health, 154-157
  various historic designations, 248, 266-268
  yin-yang, 260
Erhard Seminars Training (est), 289-315
  and Christianity, 310-313
  hazards, 307-310
  Hunger Project, 303, 304
  impact/history, 289-291
  morality, 298-304, 314
  theory, 291-297
Erhard, Werner, 289-291
Evolution
  impact on Christianity, 341
  impetus for psychic research, 341, 396
  unbiblical, 401, 402
Exorcism, 460-465

F

Functional integration (Feldenkrais Method), 229
  and psi, 458

H

Hand passes, 194, 430, 431
Hare Krishnas, 26-28
Healing
  mediumistic as Christian, 417, 418
Hex death, 2, 5, 462
Higher self spiritism, 252, 269
Higher sense perception, 257, 258
Hinduism, 21-60
  compared with Christianity, 29-32, 45-47

Hare Krishna, 26-28
Maharaj Ji, 28, 29
Ram Dass, 24-26
Sai Baba, 29
Sri Chinmoy, 22-24
Transcendental Meditation, 33-56
Holistic health
acupressure, 193
acupuncture, 193-197
applied kinesiology, 189-194
astrologic medicine 199-204
basic presuppositions, 147, 153, 154, 157, 165
biofeedback, meditation, autogenics, 221-226
body therapies, 228-231
chiropractic, 204-217
Christian? 166, 167, 240
chromotherapy, 181-184
deifies man, 153, 154
evaluative guidelines, 172, 173, 195-197, 237-242
homeopathy, 231-237
hypnotic regression, 227, 228
iridology, 174-181
occult nature, 149-167, 268, 269
orgonomy-bioenergetics, 217-221
radionics, 198, 199
sonopuncture, 197, 198
sound therapy, 185-189
techniques, 171, 172, 174-242
witchcraft, 184, 185
Homeopathy, 231-237
Hahnemann and animal magnetism, 254
Hypnosis
and mesmerism, 255, 256
and occultism, 227, 228
problems, 227, 228

I

Institute for Parapsychology of the Foundation for the Research on the Nature of Man, 386
Iridology, 174-181
basis, 174-176
first U.S. study, 179-181
occult aspects, 178, 179
unreliable, 177-180
Israel, Martin, 402

K

kahunas, 251-253
Karagulla, Shafica, 257, 258
Kelsey, Morton, 404, 427-428
Kubler-Ross, Elizabeth, 91
spirit guides, 95, 463, 464
Koch, Kurt, 335, 384, 385, 467
Kundalini yoga
and acupuncture, massage, 192
dangers, 74-76, 192, 403, 404
theory, 74

L

Latent Power of the Soul, 273-278
Latent psi
false theory, 273-286, 346, 428

M

Maharaj Ji (Divine Light Mission), 28, 29

INDEX

Maharishi Mahesh Yogi, 33
Man, nature of
  not supernatural, 273-284
  scriptural data, 278-281
Mana
  same as prana, 253
  shaman's occult power, 251, 253
Massage, psychic aspects, 192, 229, 239, 240
Meditation
  psychic, 226
  technological, 221-226
  Transcendental, 34-56
Mesmer, Anton, 253-255
Mind, Man, and the Spirits, 428-437
Mind Science Foundation, 387
Miracles
  biblical vs. psychic, 281, 282
  from God or Satan, 278-281
Monroe, Robert, 188
Motoyama, Hiroshi, 267, 268

N

Nazi Germany
  and occultism, eastern gurus, 54, 55, 106
Nee, Watchman, 273-278, 395
Neo-Reichian therapies, 217-221
Noorbergen, Rene, 423, 424

O

Occult Bondage and Deliverance, 467, 468
Occultism
  arbitrary division, 455, 456
  hereditary coherence, 459, 460
  revival evidence, 104, 319, 320
  social costs, 106, 107, 456
  varieties, 323, 324
Od, 256
Orgonomy, 217-221
  and animal magnetism, 220, 221
  and UFO's, 219
  impact on other psychotherapies, 219
  psychometric nature, 218
  sexual, occult nature, 217-219
Oriental massage
  and kundalini symptomology, 192
Out of the body experiences
  and mediumism, 380, 381
  in clinical death experiences, 92-94
  induced by sound, 187-189

P

Palmer, D.D. and B.J. 204, 212, 215
Parapsychology (see also Christian parapsychology)
  and Christianity, 391-437
  and evolution, 341
  and "Life Force", 370, 371
  and military, 370
  and out of the body experiences, 380, 381
  and primitive shamanism, 251, 360
  and science, 352, 360, 362,

366-371, 375
and sorcery, 360
and spiritism, 341-363
bias, 334-336, 374, 369, 386, 410
claims vs. data, 332-334
difference from occultism, 337
foundation of experimental psi, 345
impact of unjustified acceptance by Christians, 274, 374, 428, 436
issue of experimenter involvement, 353, 354
laboratories, 385-387 (cf. 375-387)
lack of repeatable experiments, 352
latent psi theory false, ch. 18, also 346, 428
need for psychics, 383, 384
new spiritistic trends, 362, 363, 382-385
occult history, 341-349
occult nature, 351-363, 365-388
problems and bias of latent psi theory, 382, 386, 394-397, 442
psychic societies, 343-346
scientific claims, 336
spiritistic involvement often undetected, 357, 377-388
spiritistic theory, 359, 360
three periods, 349
Parapsychology and the Christian Faith, 404, 405, 425, 426
Polarity therapy, 230, 231

Poltergeists, 446-453
attempted murders, 447, 449, 452, 453
intelligence of, 450
occult cause, 450
purposes of, 446, 447
Prana
occult energy, 249-251
same as chi, 267, 268
Presbyterian Church and support of occultism (Report on Occult Activities), 424, 425
Psychic abilities (see also Parapsychology)
and insanity, 444
counsel for involvement, 457-473
divine or demonic, 342-388
fact vs. fiction, 332-334
hazards of developing, 442-446, 321, 322, 384, 385
latent or supernatural? 273-284
problems of latent theory for Christian theology, 273-278
Psychic anatomies (meridians, nadirs, chakras, etc.)
revealed clairvoyantly, 260, 266
problems, 285, 286
Psychic development, 441-448
modern methods, 458
not conducted apart from occultism, 442
Psychic Phenomena and Religion, 427
Psychic societies, 343-346

Psychical Research Foundation, 386, 387
Psychosynthesis (Robert Assagioli), 252
Psychotherapies, experiential psi events in, 458

R

Radionics, radiaesthesia, 153, 198, 199
   form of psychometry, 198
Ram Dass (Richard Alpert), 24-26
Rediscovering the Gift of Healing, 417, 418
   mediumistic healing seen as Christian healing, 417, 418
Reflexology, 228
Reich, Wilhelm, 217-220
Reichian therapy (Orgonomy), 217-221
   and UFO's, 219
   influence upon other psychotherapies, 219
   psychometric nature? 218
   sexual, occult aspects, 217-219
Reincarnation, 79-88, 227, 228
   and Christianity, 79-81, 84-87
   and occultism, 81, 82
   birthmarks, 81
   experiences, 81, 82
   morality, 87, 88
   possession hypothesis, 81
   problems, 82, 83
Report on Occult and Psychic Activities (United Presbyterian Church), 424, 425
Return From Tomorrow, 95, 96

Rhine, J.B.
   father of modern parapsychology, 331
   psi experimentation unrepeatable, 346
Ritchie, George, 95, 96
Rolfing, 229
   psi events in, 378

S

Salvation
   Hindu vs. Christian, 29, 30
Satanism, 7-10, 16-20
Semantics
   as cover for occultism, 257, 282, 283, 321, 324-327
Shiatsu, 230
Smouldering Fire: The Work of the Holy Spirit, 402
Sonopuncture, 197, 198
Sound
   and out of the body experience, 188, 189
   occult use, 186-189
   therapy, 185, 186
Spiritism
   and Christian parapsychology, 425-428
   and clinical death research, 93-96
   and mesmerism, 254, 255
   and parapsychology, 341-363
   and philosophy/literature, 346, 347
   and P.P. Quimby, 255
   and Transcendental Meditation, 46-53
   and yoga, 74-76
   biblical defense by Christian

parapsychology, 416-419
  biblical view, 426
  higher self, 252
  necromantic, 98-100
Spiritual Frontiers Fellowship (SFF)
  spiritistic nature, 413-418
Sun, Patricia, 189
  and Seth, 165

T

Television, impact, 126
Theosophy, 255
Tiller, William, 154, 156, 157
Todd, John, 429
Transcendental Meditation, 34-56
  and Christianity, 37, 45-47
  and magic, 47-49
  and possession, 51-53
  and psychic powers, 52-54
  and spiritism, 49-51
  and teachers' pledge, 55, 56
  court cases, 35-37
  hazards, 35, 38-42, 47-55
  Hinduism, 35-38, 56
  intent, 38
  mantras, 34, 35
Try the Spirits: Christianity and Psychical Research, 406, 426, 427

U

Unidentified Flying Objects (UFO's), 143-146
  bibliography, 147
  close encounter UFO abduction experience, 143
  demonic nature, 146
  similar characteristics of close encounters and occultism, 145
  six facts of UFO phenomena, 144, 145

V

Vivekananda, 249, 250
Von Daniken, Eric
  ancient astronaut theories, factual inaccuracies, 130-139
  impact, 129
  literary style, 139-143
  reasons for success, 142
Von Reichenbach, Baron, 256

W

White Magic, 326, 327
Witchcraft, 2-6, 10-20, 184-186, 319, 320
Worrall, Olga, 425

Y

Yoga
  hazards, 72-76
  kundalini, 74-76
  occult nature, 72, 73
  purpose, 71
  theory and practice inseparable, 71, 73
You Are Psychic: The Incredible Story of David Bubar, 424

Z

Zen, see Buddhism
Zone therapy, 228, 229
  reflexology, 228